THOMAS MANN

The World as Will and Representation

Fritz Kaufmann

Beacon Press   Beacon Hill   Boston

A first version of Chapters 3 to 5 appeared in *Philosophy and Phenomenological Research*, Vol. IV, Nos. 1 and 3.

To Alice

Fritz Kaufmann, Associate Professor of Philosophy at the University of Buffalo, is the author of three books of philosophy published in German, including *Sprache als Schöpfung (Language as Creation)*. He also serves as an editor of the periodicals *Philosophy and Phenomenological Research, Judaism, Archiv für Philosophie,* and *Kantstudien,* and as a member of the Advisory Board of the Library of Living Philosophers. In 1953 Dr. Kaufmann gave the Orde Wingate Memorial Lectures at Hebrew University, Jerusalem, under the title "Artistic Communication." He is the author of many literary and philosophic essays, including two in the Cassirer and Jaspers volumes in the *Library of Living Philosophers.*

CONTENTS

NOTES

The notes are separated into two groups, referential and textual. The referential notes are primarily citations of book titles and page numbers. The textual notes are comments and discussions which expand and add to the materials in the text.

The referential notes are indicated by numbers. The textual notes are indicated by letters of the alphabet.

TRANSLATIONS

Except where the contrary is indicated, all quotations from works in foreign languages, including those from the works of Thomas Mann, have been translated by the author.

PREFACE

The somewhat whimsical allusion to Schopenhauer in the subtitle of the present book is an indication of its main concern. This concern is with the convergence between artistic vision and truth, on the one hand, and metaphysical vision and truth, on the other. The dialectical art of Thomas Mann is the realization, in the medium of epic, of a great and precarious philosophical tradition. It is the latest phase of *voluntarism* as the substance and upshot of modern thought.* Hence its ultimate human significance lies in that depth of thinking life in which the conceptions of art and the art of concepts are undivided and stir and vibrate in the same rhythms.

In my opinion the analysis of Thomas Mann's leitmotifs in their origin and growth must have as its counterpart a creative reconstruction of their symphonic context, the tensions which they represent, and the mood which their concord and discord bring into being. My chief end has not been that of writing an elementary introduction to Mann's works. Neither have I sought to write a piece of literary criticism which glories in its semantic remoteness from its object. I have simply tried to serve the better understanding of Thomas Mann's thought. My main emphasis has been on active participation in the most passionate intellectual struggle of our age, and on living communion with the reader in terms which reproduce as well as dissect the dynamic structure of the artist's work. There is an element of the evocative and of *mimesis* throughout the following pages, and particularly in the fugue of the concluding chapter on *Doctor Faustus*. This tenor seems appropriate to the *oeuvre* of a life that sees itself under the category of *imitatio* and derives its strength and right from the creative fidelity with which it renders the voices of the living past and sounds the intimations of aboriginal depths.

The work of an artist is neither a mere subjective expression nor the discovery of a strictly objective truth. Its truthfulness consists in its power of bearing witness to a meeting between life and world and of conjuring up the mood in which this intercourse

*As to this assessment of the life of modern thought cf. Martin Heidegger, *Vorträge und Aufsätze* (1954), pp. 113f, where exactly the same line of metaphysical history is drawn as in the present book.

took place. The artistic revelation which is conveyed by one work does not exclude other possibilities even within the life-work of the same master. They do not cancel each other. It is no weakness in Thomas Mann's works that they do not always proclaim identically the same truth. Even though the unity of the initial conception and a remarkable sameness of personal style and intellectual problems allowed Mann to round off the quartet of the *Joseph* stories more than ten years after the first volume and to put his pen to *Felix Krull* at exactly the point where he had stopped more than forty years before, still the coherence is a plastic one. The unity of a personal account is not that of a scientific system. The works are ethical documents of onflowing, self-searching life, symbols of different ways of approaching things and being affected by them. This is why the more systematic account of Thomas Mann's thought in the first two chapters of the present book is complemented by an analysis of his writings in the different phases of his development, of the complementary aspects of the truth which was entrusted to this one dialectically productive life.

It may be easier for the reader to follow, first, in Part II, the flux of this development than to begin with a survey from above in Part I. To do so is his privilege. From the viewpoint of the philosopher, however, it seemed preferable to work out a theory of Thomas Mann's thought and then to proceed to an analysis of its application in Mann's works.

In thus relating art and philosophy to each other we do not intend to reduce one to the other. We are trying, rather, to reach a depth of experience which underlies both of them and the different ways they compute a sum total of life. This sort of reflection should prove a contribution to a philosophy of philosophy as well as to a philosophy of art. It is the philosopher's way (or one way he can take) of doing justice to the work of the artist. To be sure, the philosopher may be suspected of undoing what the artist has done. He may seem to destroy the airiness of the work which is the triumph of the author and the joy of the spectator. But this is just his task—to show in the lightness of the artistic appearance, in an image without assertive gravity, the weight of the living motifs that have been transformed into a play of ethereal forms and imaginative forces. In a paradoxical manner, by making slightly difficult what seems so easy, the philosopher helps us comprehend the significance of the artistic achievement. And just as art is translated into the language of philosophy, philosophy learns to understand and profit from the language of art and its revelation.

Thomas Mann died the day that I concluded the final version of this book. He had read the manuscript of the first one and helped and encouraged me year after year while my work grew, often more slowly than his. I did not want to turn into the tense of the past and into the form of a retrospect what, in one of its aspects, was conceived as a homage to the living thinker and artist. Hence I have refrained from changing my text since the master's death. There is mourning in my gratitude for him and deep grief in my thank-offering to the beloved to whom this book remains dedicated.

This treatise has so long a history that I am unable to list the names of all those to whom I feel greatly indebted for their help. May I be forgiven for singling out as the recipients of my special thanks three of many helpful friends from my years at Northwestern University—Robert Bretall, Walter Cerf, and, last but not least, Marvin Fox. Without their assistance the book would appear in an even more questionable shape than it does now.

INTRODUCTION

The story of Thomas Mann is a story of stress and striving in the teeth of death, devil, and temptation. It shows not only the divine gift of the artist to lend a golden voice to human woe. It is the story of a man's struggle to overcome the demonic forces within him and without, of his effort to transform his dark yearning for "holy mother Night" into the conviction that all our days on earth are to be hallowed, to ennoble fate and put it into the service of life. Knowing the torturous lure of black magic, the wallowing in the shadows of *décadence*, the sirens' song of a metaphysic which sacrifices either life to spirit or else spirit to life, he presses on toward freedom, universality, and the integration of all human powers. Slowly and painfully, not without paying tribute to the powers of darkness, not without bitter scolding and with much humorous praise of human folly, he gropes his way from the typically German ethos of self-realization out into the air of dedication to mankind.

Thus a son of the nineteenth century advances far into the twentieth, the melancholy romanticism, the somber naturalism of his youth illumined by rays from eighteenth-century Enlightenment, i.e., by ideas of world-wide humanity, tried by suffering and deepened by a new, bitter knowledge of man. The tendencies of three centuries are fused in a spirit of anxious concern for the future, but also of strenuous faith in the idea of humanity. While creating a Serenus Zeitblom out of his own loins, Thomas Mann cannot, in the end, find satisfaction in the politically frustrated or quietistic humanism of the age of Schiller and Goethe, with its retreat into precarious individual perfection, nor can he acquiesce in the elegant scepticism of humanists like Erasmus and Montaigne. His is a militant, open-eyed humanism deeply aware of the intrinsic wretchedness of human existence, yet firmly resolved neither to accept the *status quo* of man-made ignoble pains nor to be daunted by ghostly fears.

A "keeper of holy legacy" like Goethe's Parsee,[1] he sees in the dubious present the challenge of the ideal, and in the amorphous masses the dim form of a new, classless community. He can thus utter in one breath the names of Marx, the materialist, and Hölderlin, the German Hyperion. He stands for a new democracy such as Bergson envisioned, a democracy "which is of an evangelic nature and impelled by love." [2] His is the evangel of one escaped from the ruin of the old world to enlist in the cause of a new one, doing his bit to heal some wounds and keep alive a dream which, often thwarted and betrayed, has never ceased to be the dream of man.

To overcome the antagonisms of our time, which has been Thomas Mann's aim throughout the last three decades, implies a merging of the Stoic-Christian impulses behind the Enlightenment with the dark mysticism of the romantic counter-revolution. Only by some such union of consent and dissent, of friendliness to life tinged by reverence for death can we bridge knowingly the chasm of pessimism to which the nineteenth century succumbed, a pessimism both drunk with death and fanatically, even religiously, insistent on sober, unvarnished truth. This new synthesis, however, is not to be conceived as issuing automatically from a dialectical turning of opposites into one another. It is the possible achievement of man if he lives up to his calling.

The union of opposites, if not a contradiction in terms, is in reality an unending task. Its anticipation in art, appearing to the artist himself as nothing short of a miracle, gives us a presentiment of absolute perfection and bodies forth the ideal humanity toward which the best of us are ever striving.

Thomas Mann's novels show this struggle of divergent powers not only directly in the sphere of real action, by conflicts within individuals and between them, but also in its reflex, by the clash of ideas and doctrines in dialogues of unsurpassed spiritual intensity. Out of this discord, however, and echoing the artist's comprehensive sympathy, the unity of mankind emerges as a symphonic whole of many voices. The full, rich score of his work resounds with our living past, and can be adequately explained only by what would come close to a history of our intellectual world.

Mann has always paid tribute to the century in which he was born. In his peculiar humoristic vein, he is related and often indebted to those modern poets and novelists* whose eyes are full of

---

* The distinction between the novelist and the poet being indicted by Thomas Mann as either superficial or malicious, the terms "poet" and "poetry" will, in the following, be extended to writers and writings in artistic prose.

the unfathomed grief of their times and of all time—Baudelaire and Flaubert, Jacobsen and Bang, Ibsen, Strindberg and Hamsun, Gogol and Dostoievsky, Fontane and Thomas Hardy. And for a long time his metaphysical locus was in the German orbit of Schopenhauer, Wagner, and Nietzsche, the three stars that more than any others illumine the *problems* of his work, if not its final outcome: Schopenhauer, who expressed with classical clarity the somber, romantic view of the world; Wagner, who gave Nirvana the lure of voluptuousness; and Nietzsche, who tried to close the pit of nihilism by throwing himself into the abyss.

But there are others. In no way is Thomas Mann's greatness more clearly revealed than by his unswerving and productive devotion to the great minds of the past.[3] Even what might appear at first sight a purely incidental contact is actually endowed with all the urgency of a personal summons. He has been given, as it were, a divining rod to discover the true sources of his life and work. His spiritual ancestors embody the problems around which his thoughts have circled and his novels crystallized. These are the living motifs which have constantly transformed him and been transformed by him, taking on a new meaning and finding a different interpretation at each stage of his growth.

All of these motifs undergo a process of productive repetition. They play a part in the whole experience of repetition, both natural and moral, which serves Thomas Mann to interpret his own life as well as the lives of his heroes. They are ideas for which no adequate concept can ever be found, though reason cannot help delving into and pondering over them.

Later in Mann's work the fabric of the early motifs is enriched, above all, by the rise of the Goethe theme, which shines forth more and more radiantly in the period between the First and Second World Wars. Under the sign of a very personal and personally qualified *imitatio Goethe* the melancholy metaphysical mood and sceptical irony of the youth brightens and is turned into a manly and serene composure, equally far away from the fascination by the abyss of nothingness and the deceptive "naïvety regained" of a Gustav Aschenbach in *Death in Venice*. The pessimistic humor, which originates in the bitter recognition that "all that is transitory is *but* a symbol," not worthy of any ultimately serious concern, passes into the mellow knowledge that all transitory things are *truly* symbols—symbols of each other and of the eternal which lives within them. Thus it issues in the both festive and roguish mood of recognizing and managing in the changing appearances on life's stage the repetitions of life's ever new problem play. We shall see how the irony of this recognition does not spare the artist's own work. In its continuity with historical life, his work is (and finds itself to be) a perfect and perfectly reverent mockery of the old story of man.

Yet, while in the performance of this play the artist may just appear as God's jester, he fulfills at the same time a twofold mission toward man. He knows of the secrets, the possibilities, and the dangers of the human soul. Thus he raises before man, in his passing hour, his eternal image—an image which is at once a critique of man's actual status and a vision of his future. As such a Pro-vider* of growing life, he is one of the emissaries of the *creator spiritus*— not an idle dreamer but, like Joseph, a benefactor of humankind. On the other hand, his unique contribution to our understanding of life consists in his showing man, not in the remoteness of an abstract ideal, but in a concrete and moving symbol of human truth. This is a truth that shines even through its most wretched and distorted appearance. In man's actual misery and perversion, through a veil of tears, we learn to see and honor the idea of man which both lives and falters in all of us. This is the cathartic experience which, in a union of love and knowledge, fear and pity, an author like Thomas Mann communicates to his readers. To make the most heart-rending catastrophe of our age into a monument to mankind is the final exalted achievement of *Doctor Faustus*.

* The occasional use of hyphens in words such as "existence," "repre-sentation," "atonement," etc., is intended to draw the attention of the reader to implications in the meaning both of those terms and of the phenomena which they express. This seems appropriate in dealing with a German author. While the English philosophical temper tends toward scepticism (also) as regards language, and is wary of the "idols of the market-place," German writing and in particular German philosophy today make the utmost of the potential wisdom which the genius of a language and the experience of the generations have deposited in the depth wherein words are rooted.

Part 1 THOMAS MANN'S PHILOSOPHY

Chapter 1 SPIRITUAL BACKGROUND

Modern Solitude

A man's life normally takes form by crystallizing around the central problem of his youth. A creative life such as Thomas Mann's will be found to have not one but several periods of puberty, hence several different stages of formation and re-formation; but the decisive problem of his life proclaims itself from the very beginning. It appears first in the somewhat conventional guise of the artist's loneliness, one of the leitmotifs of nineteenth-century romanticism, springing out of the alienation of the artistic mind from bourgeois life with its mounting technicalities.

The solitude of the artist is not simply a result of his (half-) exotic nature, though this motif, literally suggested by Thomas Mann's family history, does play a considerable part in his early writings. The problem of the "dark origins" of the artist was never without a symbolic meaning over and above the purely factual one. First discovered as a curse of the *artist's* existence, the isolation motif, the estrangement of man from his world, is nevertheless at bottom a *human* problem—a problem of life, conditioned by modern times yet universal in its scope.

It is as characteristic of man to break away from the patterned life of society as it is for him to establish institutions. Self-liberation and self-enslavement are countercurrents of the same process. Dissatisfaction with the *status quo* is the spur of that self-transcendence which defines human existence. Formation and transformation, besides being natural facts, become historical tasks and personal achievements in the life of mankind. And the artist is man's true representative by virtue of his productive sympathy with the formative powers that account for the past and determine the future. This original sympathy makes him, at the same time, the born foe of the stale conventions which dominate the day and in which life has become stagnant. He is both a conservative in enhancing the living past and a revolutionary in shaking off a *passé défini* whose dead weight menaces the future of life's young and tender shoots. In an often precarious personal union he is a maker and keeper of myths and a critic and analyst at once, a guardian angel with the flaming sword of the judge.

3

The disparity between the dynamic principles of historical existence and the inertia of a static order is inherent in human life as such. So is the contrast between those elected to bear the labor pains of history and the 'nice people,' who are privileged to enjoy the heritage of their forebears. As a concrete experience, however, this contrariety undergoes historical changes and appears in variant attire. In Thomas Mann's youth it adopts the form of the contrast between genius and nineteenth-century bourgeoisie, set against an older background of religious coloring, while in *Tonio Kröger*, for instance, it is interpreted in terms deriving from Schiller's typological contrast between the naïve and the sentimental, the sons of the earth and the aspirants of heaven. For Mann the idea of the solitary genius is not merely a literary fashion or the reflex of a sociological constellation, not merely the homelessness of the artist in a technical age. Substantially, it has its origin in the blending of features of the Renaissance and the Reformation in the life of Northern Germany. It is a late offspring both of the Protestant concept of man in his frightful solitude before God and of the Renaissance individual in his emancipation from the medieval community.

To break the chains of the medieval order meant also to unfasten the hold of human ties. In the political and economic realms the dissolution of original unity resulted in the self-assertion and competition of particular units and in a *bellum omnium contra omnes* with short intervals of an unstable balance of power. In the cultural sphere the inner universality of the great individuals had to comfort them for being strangers in a world of particularities. "The power of the subjective element," "the full development of the individual being," the specious triumph of the *uomo singolare*— to recall some famous phrases of Jacob Burckhardt—have their counterbalance in an "unheard of inner isolation of the single person" [1] and lead to repercussions such as Schopenhauer's, Wagner's, and Thomas Mann's revolt against the "principle of individuation."

Protestant Inwardness

From the religious viewpoint this decay of life's unity appears as the effect of two seemingly antagonistic factors. There was, from the Middle Ages on, a growing privacy of religious feeling, an expression of the want as well as the power of the individual soul. It led to the humanization of the divine figures: Jesus, the man of sorrows, and his mother, rather than Christ and the mother of God, appear, for instance, in the Pietàs of the fourteenth century. The individual seeks in Deity his individual and familiar Thou rather than the universal power and majesty of the Lord. This tendency, however, was to be outdone by a farther and farther withdrawal of the Almighty from the world of the poor and sinful individual, a nonentity in face of an unknown, transcendent God. Protestant inwardness meant, at first, the desperate, more or less exclusive, concern of the individual for his own salvation, a concern to make up, through this unworldly relation, for the unholy life of growing intimacy with the unholy world. It all ended up in an extreme "individualism with a pessimistic tinge, free from illusions." [2] One effect of such an attitude was to accentuate the reticence inherent in the North German temperament to the point of demoniac incommunicado in natures such as Leverkühn in Thomas Mann's *Doctor Faustus*. Such was the intellectual climate that bred Thomas Mann himself. His Thomas Buddenbrook, "threefold akin to him in a mystical way," may sometimes have "toyed with a slight inclination toward Catholicism: at bottom, however, he was imbued with the ardent Protestant's sense of responsibility—a sense earnest, profound and relentless to the point of self-torture." This statement is immediately followed by a reference to the Protestant's ultimate solitude: "In the face of the highest and the ultimate there was no assistance from outside, no mediation, no absolution, no opiate, no soothing syrup. Quite alone, unaided, left to his own strength, one had to solve the riddle, by way of hard, assiduous laboring before it was too late. . . ." [3]

The great epochal events in history are, in Thomas Mann's eyes, beyond praise or blame. They have not only a dramatic and, perhaps, tragic grandeur which disarms the moralist and makes happiness a trifle. Rising as they do from elementary depths beyond the scope of human wishes, they have also a kind of metaphysical dignity. Through them we are what we are: without their functioning as a historical *a priori* we would lose our historical identity—that very self whose appropriation is the central issue with Thomas Mann.

What, in the beginning of the Joseph novels, Thomas Mann

says of Abraham and his like—that they were big with destiny rather than a pure blessing—applies also to his Luther. Neither the greatness nor the faults of the German people, and of Thomas Mann himself, can be separated from the effects of Luther's work—that "great, wild, revolutionary" event which was "fateful in an imposing way that defies critical appraisal, rather than beneficial to Germany and the world." Had Luther not hated the social revolution of the Peasants' League in an asocial religious obsession which still reverberates in the exclusively metaphysical concern of Thomas Mann's own *Reflections of an Unpolitical Man,* "the German Empire might have been reformed on new social grounds and the whole of German history might have taken a happier turn or track." [4]

Holiness of Work

While Luther's outlook on social matters (and on others as well) was still largely medieval, the Reformation in its Calvinistic and Puritan forms became closely allied with the movement of modern capitalism. In Thomas Mann's early uncovering of these relationships we have a first proof of his sense for history, his intuitive power of digging up the hidden sources of life and giving to the historical and sociological theories of his time an independent artistic embodiment.

It is interesting to note how the religious scene changes slightly from one work to the other, and how the accents are placed more and more precisely. In *Buddenbrooks* the atmosphere is still (though somewhat vaguely) that of Lutheran Protestantism. The curtain rises on the amusing scene of little Antoinette rattling off, from Luther's Shorter Catechism, the thanksgiving "for house and home, wife and children, land and cattle." But as early as *Tonio Kröger* (1903) a new note is sounded in the reference to the Puritan Protestantism of Tonio Kröger's father.[5] And in *The Magic Mountain* the young hero's family background is definitely Calvinistic.[6]

In showing up the decrepit religious basis of an apparently secular, mercantilistic civilization, Thomas Mann analyzes the last phases of a process in which God vanishes from human comprehension. *Finitum non est capax infiniti:* that which is finite cannot grasp the infinite. Man's relation to God, precarious by nature, has grown more and more so ever since the days of William of Ockham, the fourteenth-century voluntarist whose doctrine of the absolute inscrutability of the divine will had such influence on Luther's growth and Protestantism as a whole.

In an indirect and rather paradoxical way, however, the Puritan-Calvinistic ethics served temporarily to bridge the gulf between the decrees of heaven and man's understanding of his own life. The *civil* vocation took on a peculiar value in so far as success in one's business could be interpreted as a sign of divine grace and the mark of a hidden *religious* calling. Such success being the only evidence that one was among the elect of God, secular work was hallowed and professional tasks carried out in a spirit of absolute seriousness. Be it noted, however, that the economic sphere was sanctified for the industry put into it rather than for the property acquired as a result. "One should not possess. Longing is gigantic power, owning unmans," says Lorenzo Medici in *Fiorenza* (1904).[7] That he who is saturated is doomed to be unproductive is a motif that springs up over and over again in Thomas Mann's work: it is one of the sociological factors in such an early story as "The Blood of the Walsungs" (1905), and it supplies a partial explanation for the failure of the experiment in *The Transposed Heads* (1940) of uniting definitely the perfection of the body with that of the spirit.

The praise of the aspirational and acquisitive life as against the sterility of mere possession is a symptom of modern dynamism, as is Puritanism itself, in one of its aspects. Words such as Lorenzo's may be found in Richard Baxter's *The Saint's Everlasting Rest* and elsewhere in the literature analyzed by Max Weber in his famous study of "The Protestant Ethic and the Spirit of Capitalism," which appeared in 1904, the very year in which *Fiorenza* came out. As a matter of fact Thomas Mann could justly lay claim, as he did in the *Reflections* to having anticipated in *Buddenbrooks* the theory of Weber, Troeltsch, and Sombart—viz., "that the modern industrialist and capitalist, the burgher with his *ascetic* idea of professional duty, is actually an outgrowth of Protestant ethics." [8]

In our time, ordinary work having ceased to figure as the gateway to salvation, any such absolute devotion to it has become, at best, the token of "a moral self-containedness and independence which is a rare phenomenon and shows something of heroic mold." [9]

Such heroism is not the forte of the modern man like Hans Castorp, the unassuming 'hero' of *The Magic Mountain*. To be sure, work still commands absolute respect with the Hanseatic burghers who are the forebears of Thomas Mann as well as Thomas Buddenbrook and Hans Castorp. "Work was actually the only thing worthy of true respect, it was the principle by which one stood or fell, the Absolutum within time." [10] This conventional esteem, however, was no longer rooted in a living experience. At the bottom of his heart man cannot rest content with a "calling" which no longer presses on toward any ultimate goal, but ensnares him in a network of means. He may seek refuge from the dull pursuits in the "flat-lands" and escape to the heights where we meet Hans Castorp; but even life on the magic mountain, which first seems an absolute contrast to the workaday world, may turn out in the end to be nothing but a symbol and parody of the "whole show" of human decay. "The demon Humdrum" that likes to creep into all of man's affairs will follow him even here and wield its sceptre in a life without care or hope, a life that is sick unto death and whose pseudo-activities are only a feverish race toward the abyss. The tedium of fake activity brings forth the busybodies, and with them "a rising temper, a nameless rancor, an irritability which drew to a crisis," at the Berghof as well as in the world at large. Life had become unbearable in its "assiduous stagnation"—and the "thunderbolt" of the First World War could be welcomed as a kind of release, a purification of the stale and stuffy air.[11]

Imitatio Dei

After its eclipse in the mechanization of industrial life, the concept of work as a test of man's higher vocation had, as it were, its last refuge in the experience of the artist and his productivity. The phenomenon of the artist who is thrown back upon himself and his resources and discovers, in this very 'reflection,' his part in an absolute process—this phenomenon acquires a particular significance in the Protestant world. However, it is bound up with the growth of bourgeois society in general and is, thus, of European scope. Since the days of Michelangelo, artistic absolutism has grown in strength, adopting various forms in Goethe and the romanticists, in Flaubert and Cézanne, the symbolists and the great poets of Thomas

Mann's own generation such as George and Rilke, Yeats and Valéry. While the world around him is lost in a maze of means and conventions, the artist cannot give up his search for a genuine vision of the whole and its original powers. Just (and, perhaps, only) in his productive ecstasy, in the act of unifying and animating his materials, he may still be able to feel a breath of the creative spirit which animates the universe. Yet, behind this godlikeness looms, as in Leverkühn's case, the ghost of nihilism and sterility; when the faith in a universe of divine creation is lost, artistic creativeness will become utopian, and inspiration will die away.

Inspiration means being in touch with and responding to the *formae formantes*, the formal impulsions that shape the face of the world. The world, the whole course of temporal being, can never be known by way of fantastic anticipation of its totality. We can enter into its spirit by taking a responsible risk. Like his Joseph, Thomas Mann tries to feel the pulse of the time and participate in the creative effort that engenders and sustains the movement of the universe as it passes through that one phase which, in part, is entrusted to our care. A work whose form proves congenial to the spirit of the world-hour partakes, in a way, in the creation of the world. The artist may feel it to be an *imitatio Dei* and, *vice versa*, may tend to explain the act of divine creation by analogy to his own experience.

In the mythical-poetic conception of reality the form and forms of being are taken as products of poiesis. The poet finds in the innermost principle of his own being, i.e., in his formative power, the clue to the cosmos. What more natural than for him defiantly to embrace an explanation which writes himself large in the universe and assures him, the outcast of society, of communion with the genius of the whole? At bottom, however, he is but the true man— the productive verification of a claim in which we seek and find with Goethe "the core of nature within the heart of man." "What inspires and justifies the human spirit in its effort to do this is the necessary assumption that what is deepest and most elemental in our own being must have grown up out of the creative depths of the universe and have its roots therein. Hence, we may gain from ourselves hints as to how the world of appearances is related to the true nature of things." [12]

In a solitude comparable to that of the First Maker, Thomas

Mann's Moses, the hero of the Biblical story *The Tables of the Law*, a prophet and artist at once, works on the image of man with a creative fury that repeats the divine joy in the creation of the world. With his mighty fists, the fists of a demiurge, he is conceived after the model of Michelangelo's Moses and after Michelangelo himself, the giant who in the ceiling pieces of the Sistine Chapel deified as it were the *terribilità* of his own artistic temper. Thomas Mann's Moses takes after him even in details: the author tells how Moses' nose was crushed and flattened in the fight with the Egyption, the very thing that happened to Michelangelo in his quarrel with Torrigiano in the Giardini Medici.[a]

The passionate and painful story of Michelangelo's life tells also about the dangerous proximity of religiousness and hubris in this *imitatio Dei*, the work of the artist. Representing as it does a truly Titanic task, "it might be better forbidden" to man (so we read in *Doctor Faustus*). Even so it is only under one condition that art ceases to be a mandate as well as a temptation and, indeed, to have any meaning at all: in the extremity of the faithless life of those who do not see themselves any longer in the succession of men that conspire with and for the Highest.

Religious Concern

To Thomas Mann as an heir of the Christian mystic and Protestant tradition, however, work is still holy, though not as an objective entity, as an *ergon*, a perfect crystal as it was to Flaubert, but rather as *energy*, action, a document of a productive life in search of itself and its truth. Carried through a sea of bleak nihilism, the idea of work marks a task both religious and moral. Thomas Mann feels it as an ex-pression of man's need and guilt and a struggle to justify his life,[13] and as a means, perhaps *the* means, of personal relf-realization, a religious egomania in acceptance of his calling. These two functions account for Mann's restless productivity just as much as does the self-fascination of a born narrator driven to tell his stories. His imposing output is by no means a sign of hasty or facile writing. He certainly made sport of himself when in *Tristan* he proposed a definition of the writer as "one to whom writing comes harder than to anybody else." [14] His work has Flaubert's precision of thematic detail; its language in its symbolic pregnancy is elabo-

rate yet not labored; it is bold and light-winged. Wrested from a
life "on the verge of exhaustion," like that of Wagner and his own
Gustav Aschenbach, it has been "heaped up to a greatness layer
upon layer." "Out of hundreds and hundreds of single inspirations,"
"in short daily shifts of two or three early morning hours full of
fervent, conscientious devotion," [15] it has risen to its full height, a
monumental fabric of minute observations like the richly patterned
tapestry in a painting by Van Eyck, or like some pointillistic scene
of Seurat.

The attitude of the Protestant burgher is thus reflected in the
masterly, careful workmanship of Thomas Mann's novels, a quality
he esteems so highly in the Swiss lyric and epic poet C. F. Meyer.[b]
It persists also in the heart-searching honesty of his analyses. He
finds the same conscientiousness in his venerated Schopenhauer (as
did Goethe and Nietzsche before him). Throughout this spiritual
tradition (contrary to Flaubert's self-mortification for the sake of
art)[c] work is considered an "ethical symbol of life," life realizing its
own potencies, baring its own inmost depths, and opening thus, even
unwillingly and unwittingly, the tongue of the multitude.[16] The
very process of this working out and getting hold of itself appears
as life's ultimate aim. To quote Meister Eckhart: "If you ask life
for a thousand years, 'why dost thou live?', and it should answer,
it might well say, 'I live in order to live.' That is because life lives
out of its own ground and wells up from its own depths; therefore
it lives without wherefore, since it lives for itself alone. Now if
you ask a truthful man, who works from the very depth of his
being, 'Why doest thou work?', he might justly answer, 'I work in
order to work.'" Whoever so lives and works will find this depth
of his inner world truly living and working itself out in him—
which is all that matters in the end. "For here is God's depth my
depth and my depth God's depth."[d]

Thomas Mann's ethos of artistic self-realization and that passionate autobiographical interest in which he wrote stories about his
novels have one of their roots in Christian self-concern; and it is not
difficult to hear this holy egoism in its most intense and most vex-
atious form (i.e., the Augustinian-Calvinistic dogma of predestination) echoing through his account of that fateful distinction which
the artist of his type endures rather than enjoys. For in the eyes of
Tonio Kröger, Gustav Aschenbach, and Adrian Leverkühn, this

artistic calling is ambivalent and is as much a stigma as a sign of grace. The poet bears the yoke of the kingdom.

Lacking a religious basis, self-concern may either become sterile and degenerate into a vain narcissism or serve to reduce everything and everybody to mere materials for one's inner enrichment—a temptation for the artist and, above all, a German danger which Mme. Chauchat holds up to Hans Castorp[17] and which is well known to Thomas Mann himself. At its best, however, this German trend coalesces with the religious experience. It is both elicited and sublimated by Christianity in general, the Protestant tradition and the Pietistic movement in particular (whose half-ludicrous, half-pathetic offshoots still crop up in Consul Buddenbrook's house in the Mengstrasse). This richly cultivated life with its tendency toward painful and "pitiless introspection, self-observation and self-analysis" is Thomas Mann's spiritual homeland, though he has left its localism much farther behind than did, for instance, Goethe's Werther, to whom he himself assigns this Pietistic heritage.* [18] In the *Reflections* he makes his confession of faith by adopting a critical remark of Nietzsche's to the effect that "the religious man's only concern is himself." This position he has never abandoned. He rather supplemented and complemented it, e.g., in the concluding words of the Preface to *Order of the Day:* "Religion is man's ultimate concern; and the moving principle of all thinking and writing is that which in the 'Joseph' series I have called 'concern with God.' "

Man's concern for himself is vindicated by issuing in concern with God, which is the human response to God's concern for man. Man's proud and restless soul reaches out for the Highest; only in the Highest can it find rest, and in its service live. Just as in Leibniz, the individual monad has its true significance only as an organ, an idiomatic expression of the universal. It comes to recognize itself in the whole and the whole in itself. A preestablished harmony connects the artist despite his social loneliness, and even in the disdainful seclusion of a Leverkühn, with the spirit of the whole (which, in Thomas Mann's mind, is never far apart from the Holy Spirit).

---

* Neither all of Thomas Mann's direct or indirect confessions nor his abjurations of faith can be taken literally. The latter are ironical reservations of the mind. The former may testify to his art of *imitatio*, that pious travesty which, in this case, expresses a genuine experience through a mythical prototype, in the guise and disguise of the language of the past.

Luther and Schopenhauer, Protestant *individualism* and that *universalism* which transcends the anguish of individuation—these are the complementary forces that come together in Thomas Mann's work.

The crowning evidence appears in a passage from *Joseph the Provider*, which may be quoted *in extenso* because one of the aims of the present book will be to show how the underlying truth of this declaration has been brought out in the medium of art.

> Religiousness is an internalization of the outer world such that its history becomes a part of the history of the self and its salvation. There is no religion apart from the conviction, enhanced to the point of offensiveness, of God's special, yea exclusive concern for the self, apart from placing this self and its salvation at the very center of all things. To do so is the paramount work of this powerful virtue. Its opposite is found in unconcern with one's own self, relegating it to the periphery of life, to the domain of the irrelevant and unimportant—an attitude which spells nothing good for the world either. He who is not convinced of his own importance is soon lost; but he who thinks highly of himself, as Abraham did in resolving that in him man should come to serve only the Highest—such a man, while he may appear presumptuous, will by virtue of this very presumption become a blessing for many. Thus is shown the interrelation between the dignity of the Ego and the dignity of mankind. . . . Concentration [*Verinnigung*] does not mean contraction [*Verengung*] of human life; and the self-esteem of the Ego by no means implies egoistic separation or callous alienation from the universal, from the non-individual and the supra-individual— in short, from all that reaches out beyond the self. On the contrary, it solemnly recognizes itself therein. In other words, if religiousness is being full of the value and import of the self, solemnity is the mark of the self's expansion and its merging in the eternity of being, which recurs in it and wherein it recognizes itself. Here we have a loss of self-containedness and singularity, which, far from detracting from the dignity of the self, is not only compatible with it, but actually enhances it to the point of solemn consecration.[19]

The Vocation of Man

A truly Platonic concern with the whole, which is never pedantic, but engages in both serene and serious play, makes the writer's conscientiousness an enactment of historical, moral, and religious conscience. This connection was first brought out in the *Reflections*, whose ultimate problem is a religious, not a political one, and it has been repeatedly emphasized ever since. Conscientiousness is a "moral-artistic quality" which "is so substantial a part of my being as an artist, that one might briefly say, the latter is nothing else." [20] To the catechizing question "How do you feel about religion?" Mann usually replies with some reserve. Like Chekhov, to whom one of his last essays is devoted, he has no answer to the last questions. But he has always been haunted by problems which are, at the bottom, variations of *the* fundamental religious problem. Just as, in one of his Diary notes (of 1848), Kierkegaard seeks the ascertainment of his faith in the existential passionateness of an impelling doubt, Thomas Mann appropriates moving words from one of the sketches to *Jaakob's Dream* by Richard Beer-Hofmann:

> *Gläubigem Bejahen*
> *Bleiben wir versagt,*
> *Wollen dem nur nahen,*
> *Der in Sehnsucht fragt!*
>
> *Zweifle, träume weiter—*
> *Zweifel, Traum und Qual*
> *Baun die Himmelsleiter*
> *Auf—zu Gottes Saal.* [21]

("To pious consent we remain opposed. We want to draw close to him only who asks as he longs. Go on doubting and dreaming! Doubt, dream and pain build the heavenly ladder upward—to God's hall.")

The Infinite is present in the infinitude of human longing and this longing experienced as the attraction by the Infinite itself. "The vision of God—that means actually never to be satiated in one's longing" (Gregory of Nyssa).

In Thomas Mann as well as in Master Eckhart and Böhme, Schelling and Scheler, God is not exclusively, but predominantly, the Deity in God, spirit in the sense of the Holy Spirit. Like Schiller, therefore, Mann feels the tension between God and man in the form of dualism between spirit and nature; like Eckhart and Schopenhauer, he sees it in the form of the gulf between the individual being and universal life. Treading in their footsteps, however, and later on under the auspices of Goethe, he has steadily worked his way toward at-onement, a position over and above the conflicts and contradictions of human life.

He has learned to realize that these antagonisms are the expression of man's dialectical function in the progression of being. They exclude neither the definiteness of his destination nor the unity of the movement which goes through him as the mediator between two spheres. The tension inherent both in Aristotle's classical definition of man and in the medieval conception which makes him the highest of the animals and the lowest of the spirits reoccurs in Thomas Mann's anthopology to the effect that in man nature is said to transcend itself and pass into spirit.

In the process of this self-transcendence man functions as the vanguard of life and is responsible for its future. He is at once bound to nature and betrothed to the spirit; herein is his life task, his religious calling. "Were I to determine what I, personally, mean by religiousness, I should say it is *attentiveness* and *obedience*—attentiveness to the inner change of the world, the mutations in the aspects of truth and right; obedience which loses no time in adjusting life and reality to these changes, to this mutation, and thus in doing justice to the spirit. To live in sin is to live against the spirit. . . . 'Concern with God' is not alone the creating of God in one's thoughts, our apprehending and expounding Him, but principally the concern with His will with which ours must coincide; with the demands of the present, the postulate of the aeon, the world hour." [22]

It is with true religious zeal, therefore, that Thomas Mann turned implacably against a movement in which nature, far from laying herself open to the spirit and being sanctified through its ministrations, was idolized by the anti-spirit. Obdurate and without proper outlet into a higher realm, nature herself is doomed to corruption and final decay. But the same holds true of a spirit which scorns incarnation. As *Doctor Faustus* shows, these are complementary dangers. It is no accident that Thomas Mann's religious convictions and his ideas about the dialectical relation of spirit and nature are closely in line with those of Ernst Troeltsch, the great German democrat and distinguished philosopher of religion.[e] Like Mann Troeltsch also sees in humanity "primarily a struggle between the life of nature and the life of the spirit that rises above nature and yet remains bound to nature, even whilst it turns against it." [23] These words were spoken in 1924, the same year in which *The Magic Mountain* was published.

In anticipation of the main thesis of our own book it is instructive to note how, in developing his religious ideas, Troeltsch makes use of Leibniz's theory of representation. "The individual, partaking as he does in the life of the whole, will always represent and realize the common life according to his individual situation, his peculiar environment and the influences under which he is placed." [24] This is also the framework of Thomas Mann's religion: the certitude that he counts as an individual, that he is counted upon in the whole, that he has to account for himself before the Highest. The artistic account is but a version of the existential one.

The Vocation of the Artist

To further the whole by subserving the spirit—this is the essence of religion.* Spirit as nature's youngest child is entrusted to man's chivalrous care. To empower the spirit from the resources of vital energy means to give reality to the Deity in God (to speak with Jakob Böhme and with Max Scheler, who may have been the connecting link between Thomas Mann and phenomenology).[25] Thomas Mann himself feels such responsible care to be the form of religion which, above all, the artist cannot fail to profess. If the word "religion" derives from *relegere* or *religere* and means "originally, in its profane sense, to take care, to heed, to bethink oneself— then every artist, simply by virtue of being an artist, may venture to call himself a religious man. For what is more strikingly characteristic of his moral standards, what is more inherent in his very

* The ethical dialectics involved in Thomas Mann's conception of the whole will be dealt with in Part II, Chapter 7.

being, than carefulness, attentiveness, conscientiousness, caution, profound caution—in short, than *care* in both the deepest and widest sense? The artist, the workman, is of course the careful human being *par excellence*. . . ." [26]

The absolute devotion that lives in this care springs from the feeling that something absolute and, indeed, the whole of life is at stake in the artist's enterprise. The work of art is a whole in itself because in its structure and dynamics it gives the sum total of a human experience in all its dimensions. Each of Thomas Mann's works has deep roots in his life. While he writes, problems not deliberately invoked, various types of solution, reminiscences from time immemorial, the sufferings of the present, dark presentiments and warning voices all "rise from mist and murk around him" (to use the words of Goethe's "Dedication"). They press in upon him and find an expression which is deeper than abstract thought and more effective than explicit teaching, and wherein poet, judge, and prophet are one. Thomas Mann indeed sees himself marching, at some distance, in a procession led by the prophets of old: "The Hebrew prophets, wrathfully warning and admonishing their people, were poets as well, and mighty ones, even though their poetry took a critical form; and prophecy, on the other hand—prophecy as sensitive anticipation, suffering and clairvoyant perception of the time and the future—is an essential part of all higher employment of language, of all creative writing." [27]

Even as a summing up of the past, creative writing advances a new understanding and thus preludes a new phase of life. In this sense one may say that to tell a story means to open and foretell a new chapter of history. By his very nature the artist summons the forces of life for their thrust into the tomorrow. Hence, Thomas Mann's concern for the whole, which the self-portrait of the *Reflections*[28] evinces in the wrinkled forehead of the man of forty, has grown into a more and more anxious concern for the future. Proclaimed first in *The Magic Mountain*, it was instrumental in the choice of the Joseph theme. For the God of the patriarchs as well as the prophets is a God of the future, and the careworn, fatherly eyes of Jacob, "brown and bright, with pouches of soft skin" are not only the eyes of old Jews in Rembrandt's paintings; they are also the anxious eyes of a God-father whose life is bound up with the destiny of his children.[29]

Religious Correlation

The idea of this correlation and mutual dependence between God and man may be familiar to English and American readers through Idealistic thinkers such as F. H. Bradley and Josiah Royce or the Neo-Idealism of Whitehead. It represents, however, an older, mystic heritage, handed down from Eckhart to Hegel. In Thomas Mann it is a very personal appropriation of the wisdom of Angelus Silesius, a seventeenth-century mystic whose teachings (together with Eckhart's) had been absorbed into Schopenhauer's metaphysics. In his essay "Freud and the Future," Mann quotes a famous couplet from the *Cherubic Wayfarer* (I, 8):

> *Ich weiss, dass ohne mich Gott nicht ein Nu kann leben.*
> *Werd' ich zunicht, er muss von Not den Geist aufgeben.*

> ("I know that without me God instantly is lost.
> When I expire He too must needs give up the ghost.")

We may add that its bold religious intensity is equaled if not surpassed by sayings such as this (II, 178):

> *Nichts ist, als Ich und Du; und wenn wir zwei nicht sein,*
> *So ist Gott nicht mehr Gott, und fällt der Himmel ein.*

> ("Nought is, but I and Thou; and when our being ceases,
> Then God is no more God, and heaven falls to pieces.")

Thomas Mann gave this thought a metaphysical turn and enhanced it as a challenge to the artist. In a mythical symbol it appears in his later works as the rotation of the sphere of heaven and earth; and in abstract terms it boils down to the recognition that the ideal needs the real for its embodiment just as the real, i.e., mere nature, needs the ideal, the spirit, for its direction. The Absolute has its life only in this whole and its dynamics, in what we called nature's self-transcendence into the spirit. And in so far as this movement issues in man, who thus has become the trustee of the spirit on earth, everything depends on him. He is, as it were, the executive organ charged with carrying out the meaning of the universal process.

Retranslated into the language of the Bible: "The earnest ex-

pectation of the creature waiteth for the manifestation of the sons
of God." [30] This applies to the creature in man as well as to the
whole creation. Its place at the turning point from nature to spirit
gives to Christianity, in Thomas Mann's eyes, part of its eminence
and almost its definition. "To be a Christian," formulates his Dr.
Riemer as it were on behalf of the author, "is to long for release
out of the bonds of nature into the purity of the spirit." [31] And it
is in this manifestation that God is properly enthroned. To the injunction: "Be ye holy," the Bible replies with: "Ye shall make me
holy." [32] God is entertained in man as nowhere else, so that in this
sense he may be called man's child just as man is essentially the
child of God.[f]

Man being defined by his relation to the Highest, he will see
the Highest in this relationship. God as the God of man grows,
therefore, as man's idea of God grows. There is no sharp dividing
line between idea and reality in this singular case. The absolute,
creative power is all it is experienced to be throughout the phases
of our own development. It is not merely a token of Greek objectivism, a projection of our own mental growth upon the divine
stage, that the Aeschylean Zeus seems to mature from the tyrant
of *Prometheus Bound* to the just and mellow ruler of the universe
in the later parts of the trilogy. Thomas Mann challenges the Aristotelian-Scholastic tradition of God's immutability as well as that
modernistic primitivism *à la* Goldberg-Breisacher (in *Doctor Faustus*) which reduces religious reality to magic technique. "God too
is subject to development; He too changes and advances from the
desert-like and demoniacal to the spiritual and holy; and He can
no more do so without the help of the human spirit than the human
spirit can do without Him." [g]

"No one," so we read in *The Tables of the Law*, "no one can
break the covenant between God and man; for it is unbreakable by
nature." [33] But it is not immune from violation, perversion, and
circumvention. And even were it not jeopardized by callousness
and inertia, man's relation to the Highest needs to be redefined and
reenacted over and over again, according to the order of the historical hour.

The sometimes puzzling ambiguity in Thomas Mann's speaking
of God as the Whole as well as the Holy and the Highest finds its
explanation in the dynamic character, both of the Whole as the

universal movement, and of the Highest as a way—as *the* way—of life.

Being, on the one hand, the inmost secret, the ultimate aim within man's life, God enjoys, on the other hand, an objective status over against man: He 'objects' to man's being as well as to any image in which we, made in His image and to imitate Him, try to fix rather than enhance His appearance. "Since we cannot love that which is outside of us," says Pascal, "we must love a Being which is within us, but is not ourselves. The Kingdom of God is within us; the universal good is within us, is one with us—and is not ourselves." [34] Just so Thomas Mann's God is an offspring of man's thought only because man's being relates to the Divine in a particular, yet distinctive, way.[35] To speak with Rilke, "We are granted to hear the coming of Him who will finally hear us." [36]

The Word

This relation has its explicit expression by way of language, the specific difference of the human race. As recorded in the Bible (Gen. 2:19f), it "is man's prerogative on earth . . . to call things by name and put them in a system. They cast down their eyes before him, so to speak, when he calls them by name. Language is power." [h] Through language we "give an account" of our own being, of our world and the universal power of creation which moves ourselves just as it moves *"il sole e l'altre stelle."*

Logos and cosmos are correlative. The world of man—and we speak here in human, not in physical, terms—the human world is ordered and articulated and is thus a true cosmos only in the world of language. The elements of appearance are crystallized according to the magic formula of the word. In language, being comes to "pronounced" existence. "Whatever sort of existence a thing may have had in itself, it was not truly present until man realized it by language and called it by name." [37] The meaning of the word communicates in a common world the meaning of things, which, thus, obtain the mode of quasi-public representation. The concept of this ontological movement from silent subsistence to express exsistence, and again from indefinite sensory agitation to the definiteness of the logos, is a most valuable guide through the labyrinth of classical metaphysics. The same idea appears in Thomas Mann's

writings together with the complementary Biblical doctrine that
the Word was before the world, and that the divine voice summons
things to assume the being to which they are called.[38]

By "having the word" man participates in the creative life and
the sovereignty of the spirit. In man the universal process attains
to a consciousness of itself and strives for an account of its meaning. Thomas Mann gives this idea a theological turn by speaking
of "the human creature as an instrument for God to recognize
Himself." [39] Though these words breathe, first of all, the spirit of
the Joseph legends, they are also an echo of Mann's German tradition, best exemplified by Angelus Silesius' verses:

> Ich trage Gottes Bild; wenn er sich will besehn,
> So kann es nur in mir, und wer mir gleicht, geschehn.

> ("I bear God's image; hence, / if He himself will see
> He has to look into / my soul and souls like me.") [40]

The motif was given its philosophical rendering in Hegel's *Phenomenology of the Mind*, the sonorous finale out of Schiller's
"Friendship": "From the chalice of the world of spirits sparkles
back infinitude to Him," to the great Maker, who created all these
spirits so that they might serve as "blissful mirrors of His blessed-
ness."

God's self-recognition in the mirror of mankind presupposes,
however, man's recognition of God. It is only in the medium of
the spirit, through man's free devotion to the ideal, that the spirit
can recognize itself and that its recognition can grow. It is through
man that God "makes Himself a name." [41] "God is enthroned upon
the praises of Israel." [42] Man gives honor to God's name and glorifies it by advancing the cause of the Whole and the Holy in prepa-
ration for "the day when the Lord shall be one and his name one." [43]
The unity of the spirit can be realized only in a spirit of unity; and
the unity of God's name implies the unity of approach to the principle of being. To speak the same language means to be one in the
spirit.

The power of language—to conjure up things into a presence
"more intense than even the things ever meant to be" (Rilke)—
this is, above all, the poet's power. If language is distinctive of mankind, the poet is man's representative. It is through him that the
things have their all but final and lasting transformation in the in-

wardness of the spirit and are—*in effigie*, at least—redeemed from the endless course of generation and corruption. The sense of the work of art as a sublime metamorphosis and of the ensuing responsibility of the master is strong among modern artists. It actually applies to each mode of expression. Cézanne liked to speak of the painter as the redeemer of the wavering universe.[44] But does this attribution not fit poetry even better than fine art? Having the organ of language, man is, according to Schelling, "the redeemer of nature, the one toward whom all her prefigurements point. The word which has its fulfillment in man, is a dark, prophetic, (not yet fully articulate) word in nature." [45]

"The secret of language is mighty, the responsibility for it and its purity is of a symbolical and spiritual character—not merely artistic, but concrete and moral responsibility [*Verantwortlichkeit*], human responsibility in its true and literal sense." [46] In his work the writer answers for himself before his nation, just as through him the nation gives an account of itself before humanity, and mankind before God, showing whether they have succeeded or failed in making language an instrument of creation, of a common world. Universal literature thus becomes a religious task.

Thomas Mann's feeling of this artistic mission tends to take the place of the cynicism in which the *littérateur* in *Tonio Kröger* boasts that by "expressing the whole wide world" it has thereby been "finished, redeemed, and done with" once for all.[47] It is rather redeemed to a new state of being present—that can be likened to that "manifest state which," according to the apostle, "is worked out by the sons of God."

But this presence is the perennial one of the artistic form rather than the eternal one of the pure mind or the timelessness of the ideas. It is the lasting and living presence in actual life of things, not in their crude reality but in a showing of their affective nature, in the abiding mood of an experience which summarizes the meaning of our life, and which we can share and communicate "since we have been a colloquy and able to hear from one another" (Hölderlin).

Art creates the most enchanting form of a "common sense"— communion through the senses. It unites men in the sensitivity which it evinces and engenders—though not in the intercourse of human action; hence the artist is always tempted to delight in the niceties of "the well turned phrase without regard to its practical implications." [48] [i]

Thanks to the perfection it gives to sensitivity, art's sense is anchored in the senses. While being not merely the work of the virtuoso[49] or an exuberant growth of vitality (as in the merry crowd of artists at Lorenzo Medici's court), art cannot be a mere sedative of the will either. It is, as Nietzsche[50] has it, "the great stimulant of life" even where it does not indulge in the sensuality branded in "*Gladius Dei*" (1902) and *Fiorenza* (1904). This is the predicament of Leverkühn (in *Doctor Faustus*) [51] who hates the flesh—just as Thomas Mann's Amenophis loves only the light, not also the darkness of the maternal earth.[52] They both would like to create in the ether of pure spirit, without the intercourse of the senses; but there is only tragedy in this way.

Finding a lovely rhyme for whatever there is, art cannot help compromising the stern demands of the spirit. That is why in his swan song the Gustav Aschenbach of *Death in Venice* cautions his young friend against the artist, whose "way to the spirit goes through the senses"; [53] why his Goethe feels himself the paradigm of all temptation, suffered as well as inflicted; [54] and why the rank of a "spiritual prince" is denied to Joseph, the dreamer and storyteller and the mediator between God's people and the worldliness of Egypt.[55] Art, like man, is always the rallying point of spiritualization and sensualization. Even "heavenly revelation" (*Himmelslehr'*), to speak with Goethe, employs in the artist's work the "earthly tongue."

> *Die Dichter müssen, auch*
> *Die geistigen, weltlich sein.*
>
> ("The poets, even the
> Spiritual ones, must needs be worldly.")
> —HÖLDERLIN, *Der Einzige*

But this needs further elucidation of the principles involved, the ideas of spirit, matter, and their relation.

Spirit and Nature

The concept of the spirit is not unambiguously defined by Thomas Mann. It has to be understood within changing contexts.

At first there is, in the Schopenhauer tradition, the idea of the absolute spirit, the intellect in the phase in which it grows beyond its former instrumental functions, defies its former master, the will, and becomes the grave-digger of life.[56] Thomas Mann's not altogether ironical sympathy is with the young fanatic visionary of *"Gladius Dei"* who sees art not as an "unscrupulous fraud," the lure to fleshly life, but as critical analysis, as the "divine fire," the sword of the spirit which is merciful in bringing redemption from a world of shame, grief, and torment. Soon, however, the negative implications of such nihilism are discovered. The unworldly spirit might be loveless and cynical rather than merciful. Compassion ought to mean a redemption *of* the world rather than *from* it. But the absolute spirit knows only of sinful intercourse, not of loving union with the flesh. As the apostate from life, the spirit resides in a "sphere of ice, purity and nothingness" where "defiance reigns and a pitiless logic, the haughty and desperate Ego, liberty, madness and death." Such is the "thin and chaste air" not only in "At the Prophet's," a short story of 1904,[57] but also in the region of that spiritual nihilism to which in the *Faustus* story of 1947 Leverkühn is confined.

Hence the idea of spirit and nature as "the contrast of all contrasts" is soon drawn into the dialectical whirl of Thomas Mann's thinking. In the *Reflections of an Unpolitical Man,* however, this intermezzo of a fervent reaction against a shallow revolutionary pathos, an enlightenment without respect for historical values, without the sense of human transcendence, the spirit of *this* world has the color of the superficial, the mere brilliance of the Western *esprit,* and speaks the windy language of the *littérateur,* of the so-called liberal intelligentsia.

The next step, taken in *The Magic Mountain,* is the search for a position beyond the abstractness of either opposite, beyond the remoteness of the unworldly spirit and the phraseology of the worldly one. Elated at his dream-vision of man's true state, Hans Castorp is inclined to deny any "contradiction" in what otherwise is taken to be "the contrast of all contrasts," the relation between spirit and nature.[58] The meaning is that the two principles ought to penetrate rather than exclude one another. And the "yes" of human compassion should prevail (without suspending it) over the "no" of metaphysical knowledge and piety for death. Thus grows

what *Joseph the Provider* praises as the temperate warmth of active
and, none the less, not deluded human sympathy,[59] a sympathy *for*
this world, which is not altogether *of* this world. In *The Magic
Mountain* the badly shaken worldly intellect, impersonated by
Settembrini, survives the sophisticated and, indeed, infatuating fundamentalism, the suicidal hatred of this world, the spirit of Naphta.

This leads to the loving descent of the spirit into the realm of
the soul, of which we read in the Prelude to the Joseph novels. It
is Joseph's own case. It is the break-through for which Leverkühn
pants in *Doctor Faustus*. The contrast remains, but it is not hopeless, as long as there is time. As long as there is time, there is time
to work. The spirit need not remain the "adversary of the soul"
(as the Bachofen circle has it) even though their final union may
be left "the secret and the silent hope of God." [60] The contrast is
lasting, but in an ultimate sense it may not be radical. The incarnation of the spirit, the realization of the Deity in God is the inmost
meaning of the world process according to the romantic tradition
in whose wake Thomas Mann has to be seen, i.e., the intellectual
movement from Böhme through Baader and Schelling to Scheler.
What differs now may be one in its roots. In his lectures of 1804-
06 Friedrich Schlegel had proclaimed that spirit and matter derive
from a common principle, that of love. And Thomas Mann's Riemer speaks of the personal union in the great man of nature and
spirit; they are one because nature trusts here a spirit somehow at
one with the *Creator Spiritus* himself.[61]

In art, there dwells what Schelling called a *Mitwissen mit der
Schöpfung*, a privy knowledge *(con-scientia)* of the "Once" of
creation, a divination of the original once as well as the ultimate
one. As an echo and a promise of the primitive and final union of
matter and spirit, art cannot be exclusively devoted to the Highest,
the spirit. The whole and the holy are not, or not yet, altogether
one. The poet's heart belongs to the whole; he has roots in both
realms. The unconscious urge, the restless power of formation,
combines with the clarity of planning and the unity of direction.
"The most sensuous functions," says Nietzsche, "will ultimately
be transfigured into a joyous symbol of what is most exalted and
spiritual." [62] Art is "the synthesis *in persona*." [63] At once spiritual
and sensual, it is like Proserpina[64] or her airier counterpart Hermes[65]
equally at home in the realm of the dark chthonic powers and in the

kingdom of light. "Art is no mere objectification of spirit, but the fruitful union and interpretation of the two spheres, immensely heightening to life and more fascinating than either one by itself. . . . The essence of creative art is nothing other . . . than sensuality spiritualized, than spirit informed and made creative by sex." [66]

From its vantage point on *this* side of the struggle, as pure creativeness, art stands for the unity behind the dialectical movement in which nature transcends itself in the direction of the spirit. "Art emerges from those innermost depths where nature and spirit are not yet divided." [67] It thus symbolizes the absolute almost in the way Schelling saw it in his apotheosis of art, "opening up, as it were, the Holy of Holies where burns in a single flame, in an everlasting, primeval unity that which is sundered in nature and history—elements which for all time are condemned to flee one another in active life as well as reflection." [68]

They flee, but they also seek one another; they are not one, except in art. Art represents, of course, but does not present in itself the central problem of human existence; and art becomes an existential problem in view of this very privilege, the privilege not to share the predicament of man. It enjoys the twofold blessing of both spirit and nature. The artist is an intermediary between both worlds. In its gracefulness (as it "clicks") his work is a stroke of genius; that talent "through which *nature makes* art lawful" (Kant); as an *oeuvre* it is at the same time a historical and personal document, the product of his industry, his mental discipline, the productive forces of his age.

Yet, this "charming blessing" of mediation between nature and spirit is not "the highest and sternest." [69] Lovely as he is in his twilight existence, Hermes, the cunning go-between and in that sense the artist's god, is not Zeus, the Lord on high. The ambiguity of mediation, the love of ironical suspense, the equal susceptibility to sensory and spiritual beauty—in a word: "poetical justice" lacks that resoluteness of direction toward actual unity in this world which only spirit can give. The twofold blessing may appear as dual loyalty, if not as double betrayal.

Even so, Thomas Mann has sometimes disclaimed, yet never abandoned, faith in art as a "guiding power of mankind." [70] With some ups and downs, he shares his Amenhotep's trust that "created

in the right spirit, the artist's work may contribute a little to all becoming one in Him." "It may prepare the world for a better, fairer
life, more in tune with the spirit." [71] Art is not only by its very
nature both a reminiscence and a prognosis of primeval and ultimate
unity; it is also, as a *document humain*, the expression of the ardent
effort of the responsible writer to cooperate in the growth of the
whole. Mann distinguishes between the "writer" in this sense and
the "mere artist" as a favorite of nature.[72] The writer is not only
a representative of this whole; he stands to it as a witness to and,
perhaps, really a martyr for it. Mann considered his own exile
from Germany a living testimony to the cause of the "unification
of the world." [73]

As a human being, the artist sides with the whole, which, as an
individual, he represents in but a particular way, or rather in his
personification of a particular type. In betraying this type, however, in trying to transcend it, he will prove faithful to the whole.
In this way, the artist will have his place in the dialectic of human
types; and it is to this typology that we have to turn next.

Dialectical Typology

Thomas Mann's typology developed originally from Schiller's
classical, i.e., history-making, antithesis between the naïve and the
sentimental. This explains the typological contrast which determines Mann's anthropology since the nineties, in his narrative writings as well as in his literary criticism; the rending contrast between
favorites of nature, such as the "blond Hanses" and geniuses like
Goethe and Tolstoy on the one hand, and the children and martyrs
of the divine spirit such as Schiller and Dostoievsky on the other.[j]
The contrast was mediated, however, in a dialectical way which
corresponds to Thomas Mann's own intellectual temperament and
follows out suggestions by Ibsen—Ibsen's concept of a "third kingdom"—and, above all, Nietzsche and Merezhkovsky—Nietzsche's
wedding of the Apollonian and Dionysian trends and Merezhkovsky's advocacy of a union between the pagan and the Christian,
between the beast-god and the god-man.[74] *

* Being somewhat technical in character, a detailed discussion of
Thomas Mann's dialectic and his typology has been relegated to Appendix I.

The stronger dialectical emphasis in Thomas Mann shows in a new feature which he introduces into Schiller's picture of the two types: the idea of a mutual longing between them. While free from the spirit's problems, nature is not sheer happiness, but yearns for spiritual light and guidance. This Christian motive, elaborated by Schelling (e.g., *Sämtliche Werke* I, VII, 359ff), Creuzer, Lasaulx, and others, makes its appearance in Thomas Mann's stories after *Tonio Kröger* (1903). In "Ein Glück" ("A Gleam") seemingly buoyant life goes beyond Hans Hansen's respectful unconcern with the outsider, the exotic Tonio. It now bows reverently before the highness of the spirit, and "two worlds between which longing revolves touch one another for the one fleeting moment" of a kiss.[75]

The representatives of either type act as traitors to it. But their sin is an outgrowth of love. The Judas theme, which is as salient a factor in Thomas Mann's writings as it was in Nietzsche's life and thought, establishes in Mann's eyes a drama of tragic and noble guilt. This drama, enriched by the mixture of loving envy and slight disdain which lives in both partners, is enacted from *Fiorenza* to *The Transposed Heads*[76] and even in *Doctor Faustus*. While personally Thomas Mann definitely sides with the spirit (though more and more with a spirit that is life's very life), and has recently renewed the tribute of kinship and loving gratitude he paid Schiller fifty years ago, the dialectical law of longing for the counter-type accounts for the growing attraction through which his heart was to be drawn into the luminous circle of creative vitality.

It is a long way from the Schiller nocturne of "A Weary Hour" (1905)* to Goethe's morning visions in *Lotte in Weimar* (1939). Schiller and Goethe are to Thomas Mann the protagonists on the human stage of that universal play that takes place between spirit and nature as such, and is condensed in the acting between human spirit and human nature, not only in interpersonal life but within every single soul. Just as in Goethe life disciplines itself and honors the spirit, spirit learns in Thomas Mann to serve life on earth and to thrive on its strength.

The typological contrast thus loses its exclusiveness, especially

---

* This short story is the epical *mise-en-scène* of the dialectical thoughts in Schiller's lyrical poem, "Das Glück" ("Bliss"). Cf. *Versuch über Schiller* (1955), 83f.

within the sphere of art itself. Art is never a mere effluence of naïve feeling; it always has the mediacy of balanced composition, of eventual composure. It is a victory over need, passion, and chaos. In this regard Mann accepts Schelling's and Nietzsche's dialectical amendment of Schiller; the conceptions of the Apollonian and the naïve do not coincide any more than do those of the Dionysian and the sentimental. "Wherever we meet with the naïve in art," says Nietzsche, "it behooves us to recognize the supreme achievement of the Apollonian culture whose first task is always to overthrow some dominion of the titans . . . and which must have triumphed over an appalling depth of insight into the world and the keenest sense of suffering." [77] Both trends, however, have the eternal presence of mythical powers. Hence the precarious character of this triumph; the exacting formative will is never secure against the nostalgia for voluptuous dissolution, and the most rigid discipline of form is the more endangered by the abyss, the more proudly the artist spurns the recognition of this allurement.

Dionysus is the strange, wild fertility god who in *Death in Venice* breaks into the Apollonian world of Aschenbach's artistic discipline (just as he invaded Greece in ancient times) and makes him taste "the wanton frenzy of decline." [78] For as Heraclitus said, are not Dionysus and Hades one and the same? Decades later, in *Joseph in Egypt*, the same motif recurs when the stiff and brittle order of Egyptian life is challenged, and broken, by the tempests of Mut-em-enet's love. "It is the idea of affliction, the sudden invasion of wanton, destructive, annihilating forces into the ordered scheme of a life that is composed, and sworn to discipline and composure—a life bent upon honor, dignity, and happiness in restraint. The saga of peace hard won from conflict and seemingly secure, and again of life laughingly sweeping away the citadel of art and artifice so carefully built and faithfully guarded; the story of mastery overmastered, and of the coming of the stranger god— all this was here in the beginning, just as it was in the mid-course of our life. And at eventide, when we dwell with fondness on the matutinal state of humankind, the unity of our existence comes to the fore in that we are gripped once more by that early concern."[79]

Rigid formalism grows stale, unbridled formlessness grows rotten; both are extremes which touch one another at one point— death. The ghost of sterility appears in the symbol of castration

(*Tonio Kröger, Joseph in Egypt*) and in the trend toward homosexual love (as in *Death in Venice* and *Doctor Faustus*). Cosmos
and chaos are interdependent. This is Schiller's brave insight in "A
Weary Hour"; and it is, in *Death in Venice*, Gustav Aschenbach's
fatal experience. It is not without piquancy that in *The Magic
Mountain* the author leads Mme. Chauchat, that apostle of holy
perdition, to Spain and, to her utter dislike, to the Escorial, the
castle of stiff-ruffed King Philip II, an old favorite of Thomas Mann.
In between is the place of formation and transformation, the true
place of man's life and the artist's work.

A fruitful cooperation of the constructive urge and the depth
of analytical, even subversive insight is the very condition of productivity; and the artist can do as little with finished and frozen
forms as with entirely unmanageable, hopelessly chaotic materials.
While in his personal endowment he may be either more a child
of nature, with her bent toward perpetual forms and laws, or more
a son of the revolutionary spirit, he will be the true representative
of man by always veering toward that absolute totality which, in a
process of conservative revolution, maintains its sovereignty over
the opposites.

In the feeling of our individual and typical restrictions, of a
thirst never finally quenched, we may be aware of the absolute,
just as in the incomplete disc of the moon we see the full moon.
This whole is not merely a pious desideratum: it is the dynamic
whole of a movement whose currents meet in each of us; a whole
without which we would not be what we are and the miracle of
art could not occur. Still, every one of us expresses it only in part
and, weary of his particularity, reaches out for such representation
as may complement his. Behind all partition abides that unity
which Goethe intimates as an ultimate mystery: "Even though one
man may incline more toward the natural, the other more toward
the ideal, one should consider that Nature and the Ideal are not at
war with one another but, on the contrary, intimately connected
in that great living unity which is the goal and miracle of our striving, whilst we may possess it already." [80] It is in this supreme
confidence that Goethe undertook to weld the titanic forces of his
inner nature into a whole, a microcosm within the macrocosm.
"Such a spirit," says Nietzsche in an encomium on Goethe, "having
gained his freedom, stands in the midst of the universe, with a feel-

ing of joyful, confident fatalism, in the *firm faith* that only the isolated and particular is to be rejected, that in the whole all things are redeemed and justified. This is the spirit that no longer denies. . . . Such faith is the highest of all possible faiths." [81]

For Thomas Mann to maintain this belief, in spite of all the doubts of a disillusioned mind on the verge of nihilism and in the face of the reign of terror which sways our earth, is a heroic action indeed. It is no mere indulgence in a paradox of faith or in the platitudes of political moralism. It is a *fighting* creed that is sustained by the wisdom of the heart. To be sure, the promise of a primordial and final unity of life and spirit which art seems to bespeak is belied by the knowledge of the desperate condition of productivity in connection with a hopeless metaphysics which is ever present to Thomas Mann's mind. For its own part, however, this pitiless knowledge is challenged by life's formative will which still impels the artist, and by the spirit of charity, active and loving compassion, which attends to suffering mankind, and which likes to embrace even the foolishness of men with the warm smile of brotherly humor instead of exposing it to the cold laughter of biting irony.

Whether or not this will and this love build up and foster but illusions, their "yes" to life is, at least, not blind, cheap, and complacent. They rise above a never silenced "no." And, after all, their attachment to life may prove metaphysically more profound and humanly more valiant and valid than the detached, stern, perhaps cynical will to truth.[k] Should this creative love have a key to depths of truth which no metaphysics of the woeful will and no depth-psychology can unlock? And will it be instrumental in restoring life to a solidarity of the spirit? Can it bring spirit to a position within life, not aloof from it in the desperate solitude of a Lucifer whose light is murderous rather than beneficial? Will it help to usher us into a new collectivistic age? Will it bring about a totality of social life equally far from the totalitarianism of the party, *any* party, and from man's self-alienation in our individualistic past? "Another love is needed, another love" . . . this is the end of the soliloquy in "The Hungry," as early as 1902.

Chapter 2 THE METAPHYSICAL PATTERN (THE WORLD AS WILL AND REPRESENTATION)

Leibniz's Scale of Representation

In the evolution of Thomas Mann's *Weltanschauung*, individualism and universalism are eventually joined together in a synthesis which has its closest philosophical counterpart in Leibniz's monadology.

Thomas Mann's work exhibits series of representations, lower and higher, ordered in partly the same fashion as the monads in Leibniz's system.* These monads, it will be recalled, are arranged in a hierarchy according to the degree of clarity and distinctness with which they represent the universe from their individual points of view. We pass from those which "mirror" reality unconsciously or subconsciously up to those which reflect the world consciously and even reflect themselves by way of apperception, until we reach finally the level of the creative representation of the cosmos. Even the lowest being involves the whole by the very fact of being a part, and therefore participating in the nature of things. This *objective representation* is greatly intensified in the form of organic assimilation, the *morphological representation* of the little "flower in the crannied wall," and reaches its climax in what may be termed formal or *sovereign representation*, the essence of the whole of being concentrated in a central monad. On this level, however, objective representation takes on some subjective coloring in the more or less clear and distinct awareness of the monad of the sphere of its life, i.e., in *conscious representation*, applying first to the objects of the outer world, then to its own mental operations. Self-consciousness of this sort is one of the prerogatives of man. Moreover, knowing himself as a source of activity and a unifying power, how-

* Within the metaphysical tradition the Leibnizian concept of universal representation seems to me still the most subtle key to the secret of being, even though recently I have tried to introduce "universal communication" in its stead, in order to modify Leibniz's monadism and to make allowance for a greater intimacy of coexistence. Cf. "Karl Jaspers and a Philosophy of Communication" in the Jaspers volume of the *Library of Living Philosophers*.

ever limited, he cannot help looking for a supreme and ultimate cause, the origin of universal order. Thus he becomes a mirror not only of the universe but also of God, attaining to a *religious representation of the Highest*, the unifying principle of the whole. This internal relationship to God is constitutive of and essential to man. Finally, created as he is in the image of the Highest, he too is capable of some sort of *creative representation*. A second maker, he gives his ideas an objective status by framing them into little worlds of his own—a political order, a work of art, etc.

The Artist's Relation to the Whole

While we find each of these modes of representation reflected in Thomas Mann's work, it is *creative representation* that has been his first concern, the *self*-concern of the artist, narcissistic in appearance but religious in substance.[1] The scale of representation and with it the metamorphoses of the forms of being reach their climax in the creative genius. The artist is the representative *in persona*, devoted as he is to the pure and profound and perfect representation of the whole of being. To be sure, all of us live and move within a circle which describes both the range and the limits of our world. Notwithstanding its particularity, every perception emerges from a common background and has its universal reference, however vague this may be. It belongs to the world of this or that person, nation, or period, a world which binds it together with other perceptions in a peculiar, though mostly unaccented, way. On the other hand, it is precisely the "wordliness" of this world, its inner form, which expresses itself so strikingly in the *style* or idiom of a work of art. The artist's mode of representing the particular discloses his mode of representing the whole, and it is this coincidence that makes his work a symbol in the most literal sense.

The obverse side of the same fact appears in the symbolic bearing which Thomas Mann discovers in his own existence *qua* poet. He who knows how to represent the wholeness of being must himself be an embodiment of the whole.

Wär' nicht das Auge sonnenhaft, die Sonne könnt'es nie erblicken.

("Were not the eye sunlike itself, it never could the sun envision.")[a]

But his *world* is *his* world. Its scope will depend on that of his organs, on the sensitivity of his responding, with different degrees of clarity and distinction, to the claims from different realms of being. Thomas Mann has a gift of amazingly minute observation, above all, of data that are symbolic of inner states. His solitary inwardness knows, and knows that it knows, more of man than of nature, and more of individual man than of masses. Historical, social, natural events set but the stage and background to the inner drama which commands his human and artistic sympathy, notwithstanding the deep moral interest he has learned to take in political action and the eager curiosity with which his Hans Castorp, Leverkühn father and son, and even Felix Krull pry into the curiosities and secrets of nature.

World-Representation and Self-Representation

The world appears in the work "according to the mode of the recipient," which is 'worked out,' reflected, brought into the open. The symbolic value of his own nature as a poet was thus the primary evidence for the main tenet of Thomas Mann's *Weltanschauung*, viz., the unity of self-transcendence and self-realization of the particular being in its representation of the universal life; and it accounts, in turn, for the autobiographical character of his work even when he is not speaking of himself or of the poet as such. Elements of his own being come to the fore not only in the poets he portrays but in most of the main figures throughout his work. Reviewing his *Stories of Three Decades*,[2] he finds in nearly all of them "an allegory of the life of the artist" in his dubious grandeur, even though their mood and meaning undergo considerable change from period to period. It is not a question of any simple identity or external similarity between the artist and his figures, but rather one of a functional affinity between them, a kindred significance, a sort of cryptic reminder. He loses and finds himself in that productive contemplation wherein the ego is objectified and the object animated from within.

The proverbial "epic objectivism" is thus compromised in favor of a lyricism in disguise, and sometimes not even in disguise. In his passionate self-concern Thomas Mann sees in it the lyricism of all art. "There is in the realm of art no objective cognition, but only an intuitive and lyrical one." [3] The spirit of life is embodied in the product of art. Thomas Mann's incentive to work, his interest in its outcome, originates in its serving as a vehicle of self-examination, as a "creative mirror" of his own true being. "What I really am, what I actually will, or do not will, all this I came to know in the process of writing; and I came to know, at the same time, that the only way for a man to get acquainted with himself is to act" [4]: a sympathetic echo, this, from Goethe's *Wanderjahre:* "How can one come to know himself? Never through introspection, only through action." [5]

It is one and the same act in which the artist bares himself and his world; for *"How can I possibly uncover my whole self without at the same time uncovering the world which is my representation?"* [6] inquires the young novelist in a polemical essay of 1906. The phrasing of this question is reminiscent of Schopenhauer, but it is Leibnizian in substance. It is the formula for the "preestablished harmony" of representation even amongst windowless, uncommunicative monads. Just as the artist appears here in the image of his world, and the world in the highly personal, highly idiomatic expression which the artist gives it, so is Leibniz's monad, thanks to its "representative" nature, a true union of the individual and the universal, both mirroring its world and mirrored therein.

Thus it was in the realm of art that Thomas Mann first came to recognize the Janus face, i.e., the subjective and objective aspects, of representation. Soon this insight was generalized to extend beyond art and to apply to the "objective mind" as such, i.e., to products in every realm of human life. In this broad sense the theme is developed toward the close of *The Magic Mountain*, where Thomas Mann tells of the spell cast over Hans Castorp by Schubert's "Linden Tree": "To him the song meant much, really a whole world . . . which it represented and symbolized." For "a thing which is of the spirit, and therefore 'significant' [*bedeutend*], is so because it reaches beyond itself, and becomes the expression and exponent of a spiritual universe, a whole world of feeling and sentiment which is more or less adequately symbolized in it, and this 'more or less' is the measure of its significance. Furthermore, the love felt for such a thing is itself 'significant': it reveals something about the person who cherishes it, for it characterizes his relation to that whole—that world which the thing represents, and which, consciously or unconsciously, is loved along with and in the thing itself." [7]

The same holds true of whatsoever man "has mixed his labor with" and has thus made a part of his world. All of it bodies forth the creative effort expended upon it, though not in that pure and original, frank and uninhibited fashion which is the gift of genius. This distinctive freedom of expression issues from the artist's disentanglement from common life, the detachment, the ironical suspense of a vision which is committed only to itself and its own perfection.

This vision grows from a community of life which is effective even where it is not endorsed. Thomas Mann's Gustav Aschenbach and, in a precarious way, in his cynical remoteness, even his Leverkühn show and experience how, in time, the artist becomes the spokesman for his generation, even where he seems to speak against it. He gives clearer voice to his fellow men, and their problems, than they are able to do themselves. And fame is nothing but *reconnaissance*, the recognition of this common ground which the artist exhibits just because he is not bound to it. The feeling of this both close and strained relationship is what takes the place of the solitude to which he seemed doomed at the outset of his (also Thomas Mann's own) career.

Being and Representation

The principle of representation makes each individual being a potential candidate for universal significance and universal understanding. *Natura infinita est, sed qui symbola animadverterit, omnia intelliget, licet non omnino.* ("Nature is infinite, but he who is aware of the symbols will grasp everything, though not in every respect.") [8] It is the very secret of the growth of Thomas Mann's novels that the more he penetrates into the depths of his subjects the more they disclose, at the bottom of their individual being, their truly representative nature. And he is attracted by subject matters that somehow resound to his sounding, i.e., whose still dormant possibilities stir as he approaches them in his way. (In the case of the Joseph novels Thomas Mann himself has spoken of this process of the author's choosing and being chosen at the same time.)

As he advances in years, these symbolic references will come more and more into the foreground, absorbing all that is merely factual into their atmosphere of meaning and universality. "An event of our life," said the aged Goethe to Eckermann, "never counts as a mere fact, but only as a representative factor"—a symbol of human life as a whole.[9]

We have come back to our point of departure for this chapter. By now it should be clear why we are entitled to use "representation" as a technical term to facilitate the restatement of the artist's knowledge in the language of Leibnizian metaphysics. In its meaningful ambiguity, representation characterizes the nature of being in both Leibniz's and Mann's artistic visions of the world. Or, rather, the gulf that opens in *Buddenbrooks* between being and representation, the *esse versus repraesentare*, closes later on in the growing recognition that true being has its perfection in true representation—*esse est repraesentare* (a principle which this whole book will try to explicate). Representation is, at the same time, together with presentation, one of the pivotal concepts for the artistic process as such and Thomas Mann's art in particular. The convergence, between Thomas Mann and Leibniz, toward a singleness of truth aimed at by art and philosophy, though along different roads, is the more striking because it is unintended. (Mann, in a letter to the author dated February 3, 1944, writes that Leibniz's influence upon him is "quite indirect.") This influence has been mediated and considerably modified, above all, by Schopenhauer, Nietzsche, and increasingly Goethe, who was as much of a Leibnizian as he was a Spinozist.[b] And the power of the Schopenhauer experience in Mann's youth was of a catalytic rather than generative nature: it brought him into his own. In the works of writers such as Rilke and Thomas Mann metaphysics becomes a literary event. Art's metaphysical fictions are made rather than mirrored, even if they are made in the mode of *imitatio*.

As it appears in Thomas Mann, the process of representation is a dialectical movement, a dynamic that evolves not only within the various single works but in his work (and life) taken as a whole. This development, however, cannot be fully understood without some reference, at least, to the history of the idea of representation in the intellectual medium of Europe, and particularly Germany. Whereas the Christian doctrine has the rise of knowledge concurring with the fall of man, Leibniz and his time believe, without reserve, in the coincidence of the hierarchies of *representation* and *being;* one and only one principle of evaluation applies to both scales. The more clarity and distinctness of representation, the higher the rank, i.e., the greater the potency of being. In God, the supreme monad, omnipotence and omniscience are one; he is the absolute representative because he and he alone can adequately represent whatever happens in his domain. On the other hand, every restriction of power means a corresponding shrinkage in our capacity to give an account of the events within our world; and conversely, whatever impairs the lucidity of our mind weakens also our power of acting freely and appropriately.[10]

This notion of consciousness as power dissolved in the floods of anti-intellectualism which rose with Hume and Rousseau.[e] Thomas Mann sets out as a representative of that *German* form of this whole movement which has its roots in Christian thought, finds its idiomatic expression in Herder's early writings, reaches its climax in Schopenhauer and its breaking point in Nietzsche. A pupil of Rousseau as well as of Leibniz, the young Herder profoundly altered the latter's theory of representation by applying to it a twofold standard of value: for Herder adequacy of representation is *inversely* proportional to potency of being.[11] To him representation is originally a strong but inarticulate power; only in its higher reaches does it attain the doubtful privilege of enhanced clarity and distinctness. The topmost, sun-bathed branches of the tree of life no longer have the gnarled stoutness of the trunk.[12] Loftiness of spirit is associated with impotence of life; the fecundity of primitive passion is played off against the sterility, the sickliness, and the sophistry of modern culture.

Will and Representation

Just as Herder's early "Storm and Stress" attitude is the harbinger of Romanticism in Germany, so his revision of Leibniz (or, rather, one aspect of Leibniz) in the light of Rousseau may be viewed as a prelude to the radical denunciation of Leibniz's "vicious" optimism in Schopenhauer. But the different stages of objectification in *The World as Will and Idea* have by no means ceased to be a reflection of Leibniz's hierarchy, albeit a somewhat

distorted one. We can see the classical scheme underneath its
Schopenhauerian disguise—the transition from blind, strong desire
to more and more enlightened modes of representation.[d] And
though (with Schopenhauer as with Herder) the stability of being
decreases with its growing elevation, and sufferings make their appearance along with depth of insight, Thomas Mann insists that the
balance of this whole process is by no means merely negative.[13]
The spirit is supreme, pure, free, the great redeemer—notwithstanding the fact that in Schopenhauer redemption means but the ex-
piration of the will and freedom for Nirvana.[e]

The Will

The adoption from Schopenhauer of the subtitle of the present
work is justified by the importance of both will and representation
in Thomas Mann's artistic *Weltanschauung*. The formative power of
the will, expressing itself in diverse stages of representation, issues
finally in the work of art as the creative representation of the universe. The distinctive activity of the artist, representation, is still a
manifestation of the universal will that animates all reality. This
conviction comes out most clearly in a passage from *Death in
Venice*. Thomas Mann is speaking of how Aschenbach's whole
being was absorbed in contemplation of Tadzio's body and its
"tense youthful perfection": "The pure and stringent will which
had labored in darkness to bring this godlike work of art into the
light of day—was it not known and familiar to him, the artist? Was
not the selfsame will at work in himself, in the sober ebriety
wherewith he was wont to loose from out the marble mass of language those slender forms which he had divined in the spirit and
represented to men as the mirror and memento of spiritual
beauty?"[14]

The conception of the will as the formative power, as the
natura naturans, both within us and without is so congenial to the
artist in Thomas Mann as to constitute a kind of implicit, never dis-
puted faith. Being beyond doubt (though certainly not beyond
danger), this function of the will comes only seldom into the open
of a special declaration such as: "the material world is the work of
man's will," this will "on which man's life is founded."[15] It is
necessary, therefore, to insist on the fundamental voluntarism of

Mann's thought. The following pages will seek to clarify and elaborate on this idea, toward which we are favorably disposed by our awareness of Thomas Mann's deep indebtedness to Schopenhauer. The decisive intellectual experience of his youth—Schopenhauer's metaphysics of the will—confirms only what, according to his *Reflections*, Thomas Mann anticipates as the deepest thought he could ever grasp. But the centrality of the will as one of two poles is as inconspicuous as that of representation is evident in Mann's work.[*]

The strength of this basic presupposition explains for instance the assured manner of Mann's dealing with the personal union between *soul* and *body*. Embodiment, incarnation, not necessarily in the Christian sense, is the Alpha and Omega as well as the *mysterium magnum* of the philosophical tradition from Böhme to Schelling to which Thomas Mann belongs, somewhat obliquely, thanks to the influences of Schopenhauer, Nietzsche, Freud, and others. "All the ways of God end in bodily life," says Friedrich Ötinger, Böhme's apostle in eighteenth-century Germany. At bottom, Hans Castorp means the same thing in his little speech on the absolute value of personal stature: "No doubt, the bodily plays a part in that . . . in a mystical sense; as soon as the bodily plays a part, things turn mystic."[16] Truly, it is the will, the will to live, the will to existence, that builds the body up; and it is the will, the will to death and nothingness, that eventually dissolves it, as in Hanno Buddenbrook's case. It is 'inclination,' i.e., the condescension of the formative will within man, that ties him to formless matter.[17] For it follows from the fundamental premises of Schopenhauer's metaphysics "that the knowing subject, in and by itself, takes no interest in anything and does not participate in anything; to this subject the being or not-being of anything in the universe, itself included, is a matter of complete indifference. Why should this disinterested being be immortal? It ends up with the temporal appearance of the will—i.e., with the individual—just as it began with the individual. . . . Only the will endures, as it is the will only that is concerned with enduring; for it is the will to live." [18] This "creative power of the psychical," i.e., of the will, "in the world of matter" marks Schopenhauer's (and Schelling's) new version of idealism. Schopenhauer's view is revived in *The Magic Mountain*[19] as an idealism of the pathological, not to say a pathological idealism;

and it extends (as I wish to show in an anticipatory way) through-out Thomas Mann's work. "Everything has a soul," we read in "Lob der Vergänglichkeit" ("Praise of Transitoriness"); and the groundwork, the fond of this soul, Leibniz's *fundus animae*, is much deeper than consciousness, much "deeper than day had thought": the will has been passion long before becoming conscious and emerging as practical reason. We are "creatures of the blindly groping will." [20]

Like William James, Thomas Mann thinks that in the uncon-scious, those "lowest-lying and least enlightened regions of the individual soul," there are secret channels connecting it with an omniscient, omnipresent oversoul which is at the root even of the material phenomena. [21] This organic, unfathomed knowledge is intimated in such revealing phrases as "first the mind and, through it, also the body." [22] The cosmos itself is the expression of a universal striving for higher and higher order, and for the beautiful as its last result. Bent over the miracle of productivity, Thomas Mann recognizes (with Gustav Aschenbach) [23] in the most "precious form of nature" the secretly active will to pure and precise for-mation, and he dreams (with his Goethe) [24] of the "biological pre-history" of human beauty—how the "monad, empowered by Eros, finally attains its entelechy" in the process of nature's creative evo-lution.

In *The Magic Mountain*, Hans Castorp takes his stand for the integrity, the wholeness, of human existence. He is mediator, not only between the free-thinker and the spiritual fanatic, between Settembrini and Naphta, but also between the two physicians of body and soul, Councillor Behrens and Dr. Krokowski. In both cases he leans somewhat furtively toward the principle that seems metaphysically more profound but also more precarious to man, the principle that is advocated by the more dubious character, the psychoanalyst. Just as in the Berghof sanatorium a patient's fever rises whenever he grows excited or even when he anticipates some exciting event, so everywhere one's physical condition is determined by the *total* state of his appetitive being. Hans Castorp's, as well as Felix Krull's (and Thomas Mann's), "inner nature" fought against military service and knew how to avoid it. [25] Sickness, no longer altogether venerable, appears as a moral problem, a sort of de-bauchery. Even the brave Joachim's eagerness to serve may have been undermined by a more deeply rooted erotic passion that drives him into illness—that "indulgence in disorder"—and back into the sanatorium.[26] Again, Hans Castorp is detained on the magic mountain by "experiences that weigh upon him and stir him up," voluntary and involuntary experiences, surpassing his native powers.[27] And since genuine reason and pretext can scarcely be distinguished from each other, it may be true in Naphta's case also that his sickness is only an expression of his insubordinate leanings, "an excuse for the premature end of his career in the Order." [28] So far as the biographical causes of Hans Castorp's own ailments are concerned, he himself attributes both the "old scars" from his school days and his "newly acquired wounds" to his painful love for Pribislav Hippe and Mme. Chauchat, who in his mind are essentially one, since they induce fundamentally the same experience.[29] Lastly, Castorp's bodily salvation from freezing to death in the snowstorm is brought about through the stubborn will to live that proclaims itself symbolically in the young 'hero's' dream-vision and defiantly asserts itself against the lure of death.

From the later works we may recall how the old Isaac takes refuge in blindness which (without being feigned) makes possible the "good error" of blessing Jacob instead of Esau—the right son instead of the first-born. To give some other instances of this metaphysical oneness: the long-repressed sexual impulses of the "elegant saint," Mut-em-enet, at last transform her body into that of a beautiful witch.[30] And in *The Transposed Heads,* Shridaman's head, the locus of the spirit, assimilates Nada's body, that had been pieced onto it (and *vice versa*). But, by virtue of the unity of the whole being, there takes place also the opposite process, whereby the spirit is coarsened by the body—not, however, by any direct, physical influx, but rather because spiritual beauty is born precisely from the spirit's yearing courtship of sensuous beauty, and lasts only as long as this yearning remains unfulfilled.[31]

The *data* of our life are actually *facta,* products of our deepest desires. "The natural is the outcome of the moral," says Felix Krull—and makes of this insight an extensive, not precisely moral, use.[32] "Felix"—that is what he is and how he feels. Yet this felicity is not simply due to a gift of nature to one of her favorites, a born *charmeur.* Krull is a 'self-made man.' Even his charm is studied and turned on at will; he employs an iron discipline in improving upon nature, which includes his own sizable innate endowment.

Spirit vs. Will; Analytical Art

As a rule, the basic and universal importance of the will becomes patent only when its work is questioned by the sufferings and complaints of the mortals[33] and its foundations are undermined by the radical criticism of life in a spirit of *taedium vitae*—the fruit of (hopeless) knowledge (and useless) perspicacity. A famous passage in *Tonio Kröger* sees in this nausea "the case of Hamlet the Dane" and, thus, echoes a remark in Nietzsche's *Birth of Tragedy*.

Will and representation belong together. And since will is the creative principle of everything, everything is at bottom the *esse manifestativum*, the self-representation, the manifest presence of the will. So is art, taken on its level and seen in its positive aspect. We spoke of the lyricism of all art. It brings to the fore the substance of our being, i.e., the will in us. Hence the wording of a sentence quoted earlier is of a precision and significance which we did not immediately realize: Writing shows me "what I really am, what I actually will, or do not will."

The absolute will is the unconditional will to existence in the form of its manifestations. And the unconditional will is the will to form, the triumph over the torn conditions of the life out of which art is born. The splendor of art justifies the sufferings which issue in it and are endured for its sake. In Nietzschean terms: the Dionysian will is the will to Apollonian illusion.

The greatness of the masters, the perfection of their work, is, thus, bound up with the misery of the worker. And the actual life of the suffering creature may very well cry out against the specious appearance of life in the mirror of art. This cry is heard clearly in *Buddenbrooks* and *Tonio Kröger, Death in Venice* and, above all, *Doctor Faustus*.

This is a perennial and most distressing motif in Thomas Mann's work, distressing because it tends to deny the possibility of the work as such. In Thomas Mann we have no longer Herder's mere correspondence between a decrease of vitality and an increase of enlightenment, but a causal relation: the fruit of knowledge seems, at first, to make life a sham and acting a sin. The integrity of the spirit turns against that of primeval will, in the service of which the much younger intellect grew up—"a mere juvenile, who only came into being in what the earthlings call their tertiary age" (Hardy). Yet this new turn does not mean a quietistic annihilation of the will, as it does in Schopenhauer; it means, as Nietzsche saw it, a nihilistic will, the will to destruction, the negation of being, first of all for the sake of non-being itself—"the place has to be swept clear." [34] But this scathing cry of Turgenev's Bazaroff represents only the antithesis in that context of dialectical thought which is accepted even by Bakunin, father of that nihilism which swayed Europe's intelligentsia in Thomas Mann's youth. "Let us confide," writes Bakunin in a Hegelian vein, "let us confide in the eternal spirit that comes to destroy and annihilate only because it is at the same time the unfathomable, eternally creative source of all life. The delight in destruction is also a creative excitement." [35]

Destruction as the condition, even as only the other aspect, of creation—this is also the message Thomas Mann received from Nietzsche. In the drama of his own life and work Mann reenacts the intellectual struggle of a century. In the beginning, there is the contempt of the world as *"un défaut dans la pureté du Non-être."* A knowing weariness of life explains the early, unqualified emphasis on death. Death is not only the end longed for in the mystic allurement of *Tristan and Isolde,* the "drown in, go down in" a sea of deadly rapture; it marks also a final verdict on individual life carried out by that nonconformist and great destroyer, the spirit. Thomas Buddenbrook recognizes with Schopenhauer (and Charron) that life is an error, death its correction, the organism the "blind, thoughtless, regrettable eruption of the urging will." The will to nothingness and the delight of destruction lives in the improvisations of Hanno Buddenbrook and draws him into death; in *"Gladius Dei"* and *Fiorenza,* a fanatic spirit throws the flaming torch into the dwellings of complacent life; and Tonio Kröger, though "not a nihilist," and Gustav Aschenbach know the frenzy of the nil as well as of the sensory life.

The negation of life is characteristic, at first, of melancholy youth and the maladjustment of the artist to modern society; it is sustained by the *Todestrieb* of the aging man. The enticement of death does not cease to be felt, even though now the summons of life is heeded. To be through with all is the secret motive behind the desire to get through with one's work.[36] From the aversion to having a part in the delusive play and that bardic praise of life which is the natural trend of art grows a distrust of the work as specious appearance that threatens Thomas Mann's art and that of his time with, as it were, the Gorgon head of sterility. The unwillingness of falling in with creative life dooms Hanno Buddenbrook's music just as it insinuates itself, through the mouth of the Adversary, into the composer Leverkühn in *Doctor Faustus*.

To be sure, almost by definition, or, rather, as a matter of calling, the creative will prevails in the born artist over the will to destruction; and the paralyzing power of a lack of faith in work has its antidote in the moral faithfulness of the conscientious worker[37] and in a humor full of sympathetic understanding (*Tonio Kröger* already points at the unity of "humor and the knowledge of suffering" as the distinctive feature of *Buddenbrooks*).

Even so, the naïve upsurge of the formative will can never be fully restored. The capacity to know and still to act—in *Fiorenza* a flaming and deathly sword in the hand of Savonarola—becomes the expression of a noble compromise with life in the case of Joseph the Provider—where it has the color of resignation rather than of a pure and glowing ideal; and it is a thorny crown to the composer Leverkühn. The paradise regained of a second naïvety proves an illusion that delivers to the abyss a man like Aschenbach who resolutely forswears the abysmal knowledge of the spirit. (Connecting lines lead from here to the German catastrophe as depicted in *Doctor Faustus*.) The strength of the plastic will has to cope with a knowledge which is analytical both in the sense of scientific discernment and in that of actual decomposition. This is, indeed, the locus of Thomas Mann's oeuvre, which is at once a myth and a criticism of both great and wretched life, just as it represents a myth of art together with a self-critique of the artist. The cover of his works joins in a symbolic design the Heraclitean antitypes of lyre and bow.[g] This is in the tradition of Nietzsche, "who revived the use of both of Apollo's instruments, the bow as well as the lyre; he taught how to shoot, and shoot with deadly aim." [h] Art 'hits' life in this twofold sense: it penetrates into its depth and cuts into its heart.[i]

Representation as Travesty

'Reflective, critical, analytical art'—the very term implies the tension in the heart of a dialectical composition and indicates the paradoxical and precarious nature of this new enterprise.[38] The trenchant light of psychological analysis seems destructive to the enchanted mood in which myths are woven and preserved. This contrariety which Thomas Mann first diagnosed in Theodor Fontane's writings (and he loved him for it), fails, however, to obstruct artistic production as long as the naïve mythopoeic power of life proves still stronger than all intellectual censorship: and there is an unwearied fabulist left in Thomas Mann. By virtue of this naïve gift, he continues—however warily—in a community of life, moves in its medium, and communicates in the forms of an existence which, as an analyst, he tries to dissolve. This inner conflict is discussed in *Reflections of an Unpolitical Man* and cries out in *Doctor Faustus*. It leads the writer to the roguish, often joyous, often torturous diversion (torturous, at times, even to the reader, usually the beneficiary of the artist's pains) of travestying the forms of a great tradition in a spirit of reverent irony, a tender yet deadly love, and a piety without faith. The actual position of life betrays itself through the distance in which these forms are kept, i.e., both observed and respectfully disavowed. Frolicking as this sovereign use of given forms may appear, it is actually two-edged and may turn into a somber variety of that principle of *imitatio* we shall presently discuss.

Such imitation by way of travesty applies, moreover, to the contents as well as the forms of classical works such as Goethe's *Meister*, his *Faust, Hermann und Dorothea, West-östlicher Divan*, etc., which have their close analogies in Thomas Mann's production. This brings into his writing an ingredient of representation in its most dubious sense, as re-presentation of what is not lived any longer and without which, nevertheless, actual life cannot do. It is only in the disguise of the past that an otherwise mute, i.e., formless and uncommunicative, life can force at least a somewhat farcical indirect communication.

Humor and Travesty

Parody is the negative counterpart of *imitatio*. In life, it may be an *imitatio* that fails, or that succeeds only on a lower level, in a minor key, a false representation whose hollowness is sadly at odds with its splendid appearance. In writing, it is, above all, the seeing through the shabbiness of life, whose attire, while outworn, is still worn in a pretentious way. From there may derive a whole scale of humoristic moods, from the smiling recognition of human foolishness or the melancholy smile at the vanity and decay of noble human things (for instance in *Royal Highness*) to an indulgence in grotesque contrasts, as in the indecorous death of such elegant gentlemen as Thomas Buddenbrook and little Mr. Friedemann or the regrettable fact that the husband of the great poetess in *Felix Krull* is the very wealthy manufacturer of (of all things) flushing pans, etc. The disgust with life, or with the life of a certain society, comes close sometimes to disgusting effects *à la* Wedekind (whom Thomas Mann greatly admired)[39] or George Grosz. The frights in Thomas Mann's early drawings, the not very edifying *Bilderbuch für artige Kinder* (*Picture Book for Well-Behaved Children*) belong in this category, while the grimacing, Ensor-like death symbols in *Death in Venice* are powerful factors in the composition of the whole, particularly in their contrast with the gentle messenger of death—the young, Hermes-like Tadzio. In general, Thomas Mann's humor is warmed and animated by true sympathy with his figures and compassion with man and does not lapse into sneering laughter, into Swiftian cynicism. Even the icy nihilism of his Leverkühn revels in peals of laughter only to burst afterwards into tears.

The positive antithesis to this hellish and desperate laughter may be seen in the religious humor which is secured and cultivated by Thomas Mann's Joseph in his later life. We shall discuss it in the context of *Joseph the Provider*. The juggling and, still, holy play which Joseph enacts with a perhaps overly sophisticated consciousness of his role[40] turns into mere sophistry, the ingenious making of appearances, in the case of the fashionable swindler Felix Krull. The picaresque novel in which he appears in great style is a parody as audacious and high-spirited as is the life which narrates itself in it. We shall deal with it briefly at this point because its humor is the proper mode of this type of representation—a formal representation which takes the place of being, whereas in the Joseph stories the individual being finds in representation its real expansion and fulfillment.

These memoirs (the word "memoirs" offers itself because they are cut out of the same cloth with those of Casanova and the high-class swindler Georges Manolescu)[41] do not mark a new period in Thomas Mann's writing. Rather, they are a hilarious epilogue to the Joseph stories and, in a way, the satyr play after the tragedy of *Doctor Faustus*, which was, so to say, Mann's last word: the novel which he called his *Parsifal*. Leverkühn hates all beautiful semblance; Krull is just semblance in person, its very apotheosis. *Doctor Faustus* is the descent to hell of the absolute spirit. *The Confessions of Felix Krull, Confidence Man* comes close to an ascension of the flesh, in an exuberant and at the same time well-controlled sensualism, an astounding feat at the end of Mann's eighth decade.

The mood of a carnival (in the literal sense of this word) cannot conceal the fact that *The Confessions* offer just another version of his "World as Will and Representation," the world of the passionate will and the world of a highly artistic, boldly histrionic representation. Krull is, again, the artist, i.e., the anti-bourgeois, even though, for lack of personal substance, he cannot but long for the satisfactions and appropriate the value standards of the higher bourgeoisie. He admires, in breathless adoration, the heroic swings of the young trapezist Andromache, "*la fille de l'air.*"[42] She is of his kin: he, too, is a "floating existence," a *Luftmensch*, but anxious to be accepted on the firm ground of respectable society. If he succeeds, or succeeds, at least, for such a long time, it is because their own life has become a fraud. *Mundus vult decipi.* Deceptive in itself, this world wants to be deceived; it takes even a perverse pleasure in it, as the somewhat overdone example of Mme. Houpflé, *alias* Diane Philibert, shows (she herself instigates the jewelry theft in her room).[43] It is a world without true communication, a world of façades where one can put up long garlands of florid phrases without saying and committing himself to a thing.

This is an art in which Krull excels. He plays the roles of others better than they do themselves. Whereas in Thomas Mann's mythical world people are what they represent, whereas they have

and act their lives as an earnest play in the iridescent light of a
"this as well as that," the ambiguity in Krull's appearance is of the
evasive type of the "neither-nor": he is neither what he represents
nor anything apart from it. His representation is mere fiction; but
fiction is the element of his life. The human play becomes a farce
(even though the rules of the game are carefully observed).

The Dionysian delight in Apollonian illusion leads the formative will here to forge a pseudo-reality, making sport of the truth,
much to the pleasure of both the alleged and the real writers of
the *Confessions*. The creation of truth (*Wahrheitsschöpfung*) on the
part of the true artist is the translation into his language of the
truth which he suffered and of which the genuineness of this language gives convincing evidence.[44] It is not Krull's elegantly
worded disrespect for given facts, which has its *ratio essendi*, its
quasi-justification, only in the feeling that these facts are themselves
disreputable machinations fabricated for the use of a "public that
is served with what it believes in," the "*Schaumwein*," the sparkling,
frothy hock of his father.[45] Reality dissolves in a hoax—the hoax
of Krull's life and its story, where, just as in the childhood episode
of Langenschwalbach,[46] the movements of music are perfectly executed, while there is no real music made.

The bright coloring of this story cannot conceal the fact that
there is the emptiness of despair in the loneliness of the *charmeur*,
that the world he tries to fool (and with which he is infatuated) is
a bankrupt world and his memoirs are the looking back upon a
bankrupt life, the artifice of a proud yet ruined virtuoso. It is life in
retrospect, a hopelessly past life: if, blinded by its self-made splendor, Krull cannot see that, Thomas Mann certainly does. And this
brings into his merry-making (yet, in contrast with the Joseph
legend, no longer festive) story the secret bitterness of a travestying
mood. (It is the sad travesty of the classical educational novel, the
Wilhelm Meister. The rise *and* fall of the educational novel appear
in the novel of adventure.) From Faustus (*lucus a non lucendo*) to
Felix. After the inferno of *Doctor Faustus*, we are grateful for that
gift of gaiety in which man rises above the unanswerable questions
of life, the gift of "the light, yet knowing jest . . . , which may
bring a smile even upon God's, the great Unanswering's, face." [47]

Dialectics of Suffering

In difference from irony, that sublime indifference above the differences of life, humor is the comfort of the suffering soul, needed the more, the more sufferings the soul has undergone. It is the bitter comfort of consent, an ultimately religious consent, to repulsive reality. Its voice sounds through the threnody of the creatures which the ocean of creations hurls forth. Suffering is the destiny especially of the noble and tender souls. The activity of the will is taken to issue in ever higher representations, but also more and more in uprooted existences, exposed to suffering by the very refinement of their organization. Consciousness intensifies misery—and ennobles it. *L'homme est bien grand, puisqu'il connaît qu'il est misérable.* "Man is great indeed, since he knows that he is miserable." (Pascal)
The consciousness of misery implies both the excellence and the misery of being conscious. That on the scales of the world growth of perfection in one regard will be balanced by loss of perfection in another is a classical theme that can be followed from Aristotle through Lucretius to Goethe's morphology. The Preacher's saying that "in much wisdom is much grief; and he that increases knowledge increaseth sorrow" [48] finds a universal expression in Dante's

> *Quanto la cosa è piu perfetta*
> *più sente il bene, e così la doglianza.*
>
> ("The more a thing perfected is the more
> It feels bliss, and in pain the sharper sighs.")[49]

Yet it was left to the pessimistic wave of Romanticism to make this idea the principle of an elaborate system of tragic evolution. The generation of Byron, Leopardi, and Schopenhauer sees in the *distinction* of consciousness not only the eminence of man but also the curse of being different and singled out. Suffering reaches its climax at the lonely and icy height of genius, close to madness and martyrdom.[50] "The degree of suffering," says even Nietzsche, "is determined by one's position in the hierarchy." [51]

The fragility of the higher modes of being seems inherent in conscious representation and, above all, in the representation *par excellence*, that of the artist, condemned to the homelessness of a juggler who fakes, in the mirage of his work, a world in which he does not count. This feeling for the misery of human existence and the desperate speciousness in the life of the genius overcasts Thomas Mann's earliest writings. It is never dispelled, but is somewhat outshone by the growing recognition, apparent even in Schopenhauer himself, of the nobility in man's vocation for suffering and by the appreciation of the positive role of suffering in building up a new and higher life.

In this appreciation of suffering the Aeschylean wisdom of "to know through woe" [52] concurs with the Pauline "we suffer together, that we may also be glorified together" [53] and with the creed of the German mystics who were so close to Thomas Mann's heart. "Suffering," says Seuse, "is the narrow path which moves on right to the gate of heaven."

The unison of this conviction rang out to Thomas Mann from the Christian Hellenism of the Goethe-Hölderlin-Nietzsche tradition which he assimilated and made his own. The genius' way to *life*, such is Hans Castorp's discovery, is the way of the "twice born," the way through suffering and death. *Increscunt animi, virescit volnere virtus* ("the spirits grow stronger, valor grows virile through wounds"). He who descends unafraid into the hell of suffering will "emerge from it richer and mightier than before—filled with the bliss of a new and greater love." These are words of Nietzsche which are echoed by Thomas Mann and by his Prior (in *Fiorenza*) and Schiller (in "A Weary Hour"): suffering will make them great and give them fame. At a deeper level Thomas Mann's figures undergo and even provoke their fate with a bold willingness which is, partly at least, motivated by their secret knowledge of the loosening and purifying powers pain and even sin can have. The enterprise of the novelist is in itself a brave adventure, a "descent to Hell" as the Prelude to *Joseph and His Brothers* has it, full of the dread of the flesh but fuller of its rapture since, after all, the account is of the eternal history (the myth) of the soul, man's deepest concern.

The poet's story may be taken as a finale, the transfiguration of actual history into perfect form, yet also the form and tense of the perfect. We shall have to speak of both aspects, the sublime and the sinister. But, first of all and just where it seems to finish life, art, as critical analysis, is in itself a new and bold assertion of the will, the will to knowledge even where it hurts. Moreover, as pure art, it is praise; we called it a signal triumph of the formative will that composes the miseries of life into *schönen Schein*, fair semblance. (While, in *Doctor Faustus*, Leverkühn scorns such composure, his compositions are still expressions of that same creative will which his nihilism derides.) The writer's merciless dissection that cuts deep into the flesh of life shows the strength of the scientific will to truth, while the gracefulness of the artistic form, the growth of cosmos from chaos shows the thorough self-enjoyment of the formative will in its heroic playfulness, akin to Wilhelm Busch's little bird that warbles to its heart's desire before the tomcat comes to eat it.*

Hence, even as an indictment of life, art is never a mere preamble to death. If the will is that ultimate principle upon which everything else depends, it cannot disappear as its appearances do. The will to death, a nihilistic will, is conceivable; the death of the will is not.

There is no escape from the sufferings of the knower and from the knowledge of sufferings, the self-inflicted sufferings of the blind and restless will. There is only the way of taking up the challenge and giving positive meaning to human agony. Schopenhauer's complaints, in a way the grievance of all metaphysics, about temporal life cannot be overcome except by a productive reply and by embracing what they reject. Art, and especially the art of humor, is such a reply. Even more positive is what the Germans call *das Zeitliche segnen* (blessing this passing life even as we depart from it), as Rosalie does in *Die Betrogene* of 1953 (a *parergon* into which much of the wisdom of the old poet has gone). The elegy of the futility of life in the passage of time is turned by Thomas Mann as well as by Nietzsche into the "Praise of Transitoriness." With Goethe, Mann recognizes time as the very medium in which "the moment becomes eternity," and justifies death as a "means of life to have more life." [54] He sees death as a means to stronger and

---

* Thomas Mann's humor is as free a synthesis of tragic truth and specious beauty as is humor in the aesthetics of the most extreme and consequent pessimist, in Julius Bahnsen's *Das Tragische als Weltgesetz und der Humor als ästhetische Gestalt des Metaphysischen*, 1877 (= *The Tragic as the Law of the Universe and Humor as the Aesthetic Form of the Metaphysical Insight*).

more comprehensive life, the life of which in his one great vision Thomas Buddenbrook dreams, and of which the Prelude to the Joseph stories still speaks. This life not only is stronger but is also spiritually exalted, in the way in which Goethe (and also Thomas Mann's Goethe), conceives it.

With Nietzsche, Schopenhauer's lament over the painful boredom in the constant repetition of the same tragic farce of life is transformed into a hymn bespeaking the ardent will to the eternal recurrence of the same theme in ever new variations. And Schopenhauer's tragic antagonism between will and spirit gives way to the dream of their true cooperation, of a spiritualization of life, a vitalization of the spirit, the spirit's "break-through" into the realm of the soul (as it is postulated in the *Tales of Jacob* and fought for and against in the convulsive struggles of Doctor Faustus).

Enlightenment of the Will

We may now mention, once more, the rehabilitation of the Intellect, who begins his career as the vile servant of the Will, according to Schopenhauer's metaphysics. He still appears as a courtier, who attends upon the Will, in the *Reflections*.[55] In the turn—or return—from the unworldly spiritual self-concern of the *Reflections* (1918) to the qualified social humanism of *The Magic Mountain* (1924), however, Thomas Mann transcends a culture of uncommunicative inwardness and honors the instrumentality of the intellect in the melioration of civilized life.* Social reform carries the day over both reaction and revolution. The true victor, however, is neither the absolute mind nor the managerial intellect but an enlightened will that gives God what is God's and man what is man's.

Thus the tables are turned. The antagonism of being and being conscious is not final. Consciousness may still heal the wound which it inflicted. The (enlightened) will need not rage against the will to being and the forms it blindly produced. It will try to over-

---

* It is a mistake to think that Thomas Mann began as a German chauvinist. He began as a critical analyst of his time. The antidemocratic attitude of the *Reflections* is really a rear-guard action in defense of the absolute spirit and is preceded in *Royal Highness* by the critique, in *Felix Krull*—as early as the first fragment of 1911—by a mockery of the formal representation and the spurious pomp of the Wilhelmine era.

come the war of all against all, this "expression of the inner contradiction that inheres in the Will to Life and manifests itself in
the *principium individuationis*";[56] it will try to verify the pious
yet sceptical hope at the end of Hardy's *Dynasts*

> That the rages
> of the ages
> Shall be cancelled, and delivrance offered from the darts that were,
> Consciousness the Will informing, till it fashion all things fair.

Transcending the narrow selfishness of individualism, a new, holy
will may succeed, at least, in saving this "vale of want" from becoming "a sty of depravity." [57] On the one hand it will not indulge
in the "holy terror" of the anti-humanists Hieronymus, Savonarola,
Naphta, and (at some distance) Leverkühn, the fanatics of the absolute spirit to whom the forms of life are sinful as such, but will
confess to humanity without illusion about men and use analysis
mainly to dissolve the institutionalized forms of unjustified privileges.[58] It will be a charitable will, benevolent in Spinoza's sense,[59]
but also full of patience and pity, of a compassionate devotion to
our fellow beings and a collective effort to do away with the ignoble
sufferings we impose on each other through thoughtless and reckless demeanor.

Forms of Representation

The socialization of the illumined will is, from the human
point of view, the decisive way for the individual to break through
an isolation which is the more wretched the more splendid it seems.
It is the reconciliation of the individual and the universal on the
social level. Though restricted in its scope and fragmentary in its
results, it is the proper human contribution to the *Hen Kai Pan*, the
oneness of the whole. It is the ultimate responsibility of the person; to a civilization in the pangs of death it is the very order of
the day; and it has been increasingly recognized as such by Thomas
Mann himself. He has learned to see (here he is indebted to Walt
Whitman) that certain mystical and metaphysical vistas of unification, which first seemed to disparage the social view, are actually
able to complement and supplement it. Moral conscience can be
the point where metaphysical consciousness goes into action.

A stronger, deeper, more universal community of being may be cemented by a pioneering spirit which prefigures rather than mirrors life. Makers of their people, harbingers of the one world of man, Thomas Mann's Moses and Goethe struggle with the crude and unwieldy material they have at hand. Consciousness, being thus restored to its creative function, may succeed in laying the groundwork of a new human reality. The growth of knowledge is not exclusively the curse of growing solitude. And this bridge which social consciousness throws over the gap between individual and individual, between being and representing, is reinforced by new conceptions which make representation, not a break in the unity of being, but the very secret of its nature. The different aspects of representation in Thomas Mann's works are so many efforts to escape from the lonely drifting raft of individuation and to reach the coast of universal reality and coexistence.

In the second part of this book, we shall discuss the scale of representation in the chronicle of the Buddenbrook family and in the legend of the Jewish patriarchs. Under one aspect it is seen as decline, and under another as progress. In *Buddenbrooks,* the polarization between life and the different forms in which it is mirrored shows the decay of representation from the naïve class-consciousness of the born social representative through the wearisome representation of a role for the sake of family prestige to indecent histrionism and, in the end, dissolution of life in musical orgasm rather than musical composition. This is repeated in the solemn sphere of the patriarchs; but Joseph's individual representation of the holy patterns of life makes up by freedom of planning for what it loses in monolithic strength.

Still, the danger of the loss of substance never quite disappears. We shall not dwell on the noble, yet empty, *"formal" representation,* e.g., in *Royal Highness.* Cultivating as it does the mere technique of the dignitary, it would be deprived of substantial interest were it not for the silent tragedy it means to the older brother and for a growing sense of responsibility in the younger Prince Klaus Heinrich. In the crisis of Old World individualism, he awakens to a sincere, though still somewhat condescending, love for his people. This princely representation thus gains a deeper symbolic significance. "To stand for many . . . to *be* by way of representing: this too . . . is a modest kind of greatness." It reflects the poet's reflection of a common reality to which, according to the young author, he does not really belong.[60] On the other hand—in a negative aspect—the shabby genteelness of a German court and its unsound financial policy for saving face and stretching the dwindling revenues prelude the tricky game of semblance *versus* substance in the life of another *artista*, the swindler Felix Krull. Yet the motif does not die with that: it rises to a new, noble height in the moving figure of Potiphar (in *Joseph in Egypt*), exhibiting the sterile majesty and refinement of the eunuch. Somewhat less impressive, much less sympathetic Rüdiger Schildknapp, in *Doctor Faustus*, is still a distant relative of the same family.

We have mentioned before the sinister side of artistic *re-presentation in a mirror*—presenting once more in its reflection a life that belongs to the past and can thus be finished in a final analysis. To transfer a dictum of Hegel from philosophy to poetry: the owl of Minerva has its flight only when the works of the day are done. But the positive role of this transfiguration ought not to be forgotten. Art is a new and, in a way, higher manifestation of being. It is the definite account which being gives of itself in the medium of language, the climax of the ontological movement.

These perspectives blend in Thomas Mann's own estimate of the historical position of works such as his *Joseph and His Brothers* and *The Holy Sinner*. They all are products of a late phase of personal life and cultural growth. They recapitulate not only history but the same story which had been told over and over again. His may be the last and definite version, the full stop to story as well as history.[61]

The true artist responds to the call of things which appeal to the directive spirit as well as to the formative will within him. In this responsive and responsible contact he steps back into a reality to which he had long felt himself a stranger. *Artistic* representation becomes *personal* representation in the artist's anxious concern for the state and the future of the whole which his account has to account for. He stands for it in the form which he conceives and thus prefigures. He is to represent it not only *in figura* but in person. His work is a prologue as well as an epilogue.

Another type of representation enters in *The Magic Mountain*. It is an experiment in the universalization of the individual by way of *reflective* representation, i.e., by assimilating in their educational value the intellectual motives of the time. This is the receptivity of Hans Castorp, which does not yet reach the point of *artistic* representation in which receptivity and productivity are one.

Above all, representation can take on the form, or rather forms, of imitation. In the highest mode, this is exemplified in the *imitatio Christi;* but it may also appear in a perhaps playful freedom of personal appropriation and variation or else in the dull mood of slavish copying. It has its place in the sublimation of the spirit, but also in the cheaper version of a coarsening life.

Mythical Representation

Representation in this sense, as imitation, reaches in Thomas Mann's work the point of highest significance in the festive air of the myth. And while all other modes of representation can best be evaluated later on, in the analysis of the novels themselves, the idea of *mythical representation* branches out in all directions and needs a first, preliminary treatment here and now. This idea, the principle of a mythical world, is first enacted on the stage of the early Orient, the scene of *Joseph and His Brothers.* But the mythical note, the elative mood of the symbol is inherent in Mann's style, his use of the leitmotif, and is not restricted to the level of "primitive mentality," as is Lévy-Bruhl's concept of mystic participation, which it closely resembles in some other regards. Based as it is on the innermost experience and leanings of Thomas Mann himself and his appropriation of cognate teachings of Schopenhauer and Nietzsche, it rather serves to sift out what may be considered in Lévy-Bruhl's category as a perennial truth, the content of an experience which we, too, can enjoy. In Thomas Mann (so we shall see) it supports an understanding and conduct of life under the sign of the *imitation* of classical patterns and in the role of persons that perform their assigned parts.

Mythical representation is a way of overcoming the exclusiveness of space and time points, of things and events, without sacrificing altogether an articulate understanding of this world and identifying everything with everything else. It is, in other words, a way between the sheer manifoldness of the maya-world and the pure no-thingness of Nirvana, that ocean of Being in which all beings are drowned—the lure in Mann's as well as Wagner's

Tristan. It restricts the mystic *tat tvam asi* ("That thou art") to specific lines of phenomena that are different as temporal appearances while proving identical in substance. Each is the one thing present and, at the same time *something* (not *everything*) else. It is at one with the other since it represents the same ideal entity or the same recurrent motif, and thus means the same within the context of life.

While, throughout Thomas Mann's work, the inner richness of individual appearances remains unimpaired, a phenomenon gains its true significance through its symbolic function as a *pars pro toto*, a typical manifestation of a specific trend and mode of being. This shows how the yarn-spinning tendencies of the naïve formative will manage to stay alive even in the most critical artist and in what borders on the nihilism of a Lucifer. The early aversion from the world in time and space leaves the door open for the 'conversion' to the type and the species, this temporal unfolding of the timeless idea and the "most immediate objectivation of the Will to Life." [j] This artistic emphasis on the specific thus figures as a prolongation of natural trends, an extension of that concern for the elaboration of the idea and preservation of the species which classical metaphysics ascribed to nature's formative powers. Taken and shown in its substantial identity with idea and species, a phenomenon passes as it were beyond its own passing away in the passage of time.

The sym-bolism of this interpretation makes co-incidence, simultaneity, the open sesame to a mythical world behind the screen of historical sequences. This leads in different approximations toward the mystic's *nunc stans*, the Eternal Now*—the elixir Thomas Buddenbrook drinks from Schopenhauer. It is in its trance that Hans Castorp loses himself at the shore of timelessness. And *The Tales of Jacob* still takes this univeral tense of ever living presentness to be "the essence of life" to the initiated ones. [62] Who is closer to this mystery than the artist? It is, indeed, such equal presence to which artistic consecration brings and fugues the passing phenomena and the phenomena of the past. Artistic experience thus proves once more the key to the world's secret. The experience

---

* It is true that more recently, in his "Praise of Transitoriness" Thomas Mann has spoken out against the "stagnant now" and turned to the soil of time which man is called to till. But the harvest, that which is wrested from the transitory, is still the sempiternal. Cf. *Altes und Neues*, 266f.

of such simultaneity summarizes as it were those of *recurrence,*
repetition, and *imitation*—terms with which we shall deal in sub-
sequent sections even though their boundaries obviously overlap.

Recurrence

The identity of the content of a perennial present[63] is experienced, first of all, in the periodical recurrence of natural events. In
the mood of mythical thought all similarity borders upon identity
in accordance with the identity of the meaning it conveys. It calls
to mind a system of correspondences, i.e., of mutual representations
the feeling of which gives to life a certain familiarity with its world.
Thomas Mann, too, shares with Goethe the delight in "the rhythm
of the phenomena of nature and life," in the "alternation of day
and night, of the seasons, of blossom and fruits and whatever else
comes to view in periodic sequence and of which the healthy man
never grows tired." [64]

This order cannot but enter into man's intercourse with
nature:

> *Wenn Ihr Bäume pflanzt, so sei's in Reihen,*
> *Denn sie lässt Geordnetes gedeihen.*[65]
>
> ("Plant your trees each in its proper row;
> What is ordered well, is made to grow.")

And since human life and artistic creativity are continuous with
the life and the formative powers in nature, the artist recognizes
and loves also the element of almost vegetative growth, "the deeply
instinctive lawfulness, the silent harmony, the lucid correspondences
prevailing throughout the design of a truly productive life." [66]
This accounts for Thomas Mann's half-serious, half-ironical play
with numbers and numerical proportions regarding both his own
life and that of his figures. To the penetrating glance history loses
the semblance of arbitrariness and even part of its display of novelty
and falls in with the universal order. Thomas Mann walks here in
the footsteps of Goethe, who anticipated the young Nietzsche's
theory of supra-historical types:

> When one comes to know the doings and dealings of men as
> they have gone on for thousands of years, he will recognize cer-

tain universal forms that have continued to cast their spell over whole nations as well as over individual beings. These formulae, eternally repeated, eternally the same in myriad colors and guises, are the wondrous dowry provided for us by a higher power. Granted that everybody translates these formulae into his own personal idiom and fits them one way or another into his own narrow circumstances, mixing them up with so many selfish ingredients that it becomes hard to discover their original meaning. Unexpectedly, however, it springs up time and again, now in this people, now in that; and the attentive observer gathers from these formulae something like an alphabet of the world-spirit.[k]

Repetition

Goethe's mild wisdom does not go, however, to the extreme of Nietzsche's *eternal recurrence,* which, as the ghostly thought of a ubiquitous double, is repulsive to the historical sense. The hyperbolical character of Nietzsche's thought was itself the result of a violent reaction. It was conceived of as a defiant "So be it!" to Schopenhauer's commiseration of the creatures doomed "incessantly to traverse an orbit of live coals" or go through the deadly boredom of a "barrel-organ tune ground out innumerable times before, movement for movement and measure for measure." [1]

This is, of course, no new complaint. It is the story of Sisyphus, the plaint of Ecclesiastes, and it is in the Fathers of the Christian Church the recognition of this-worldly life as like a child's vain and endless playing in the sand, where the joy of building is as short-lived as the buildings themselves. The vicious circle of desire and disillusion is, according to Augustine, the circle of the vicious, who condemn their lives to meaninglessness. And Gregory of Nyssa tells how the circle opens to the wings of love, raising us to that place "where no satiety and disgust must be expected, where desire does not languish in fulfilment and longing keeps its ardor in the embrace." [67]

The power of this transcendence and the transcendent power which gives it wings are by no means absent in Thomas Mann's work even where they are present only in the feeling of their absence, in the experience of sin, in the passionate longing for grace and for the right love, a love so difficult to obtain in the attitude of artistic irony (which is only partly expiated by works in the service of mankind). In Thomas Mann's world man is not altogether the measure, and neither God nor the devil is completely "secularized." Neither, to be sure, does Mann assign to them absolute transcendence in the way a strict churchman would like. In this regard also he remains an heir of Goethe and Romantic humanism. His position has its nearest equivalent in the "turn toward the idea" in the sense of both Schopenhauer and Georg Simmel. The idea, above all the idea of the Highest, works its way through man, is worked out by him and has its reality in the absoluteness in which it lays hold of him and is empowered by him. Transcendence thus grows out of immanence and, in a way, outgrows it. It is no mere psychological phenomenon; it has an existence of its own which man helps to unbind and by which he is bound.[68]

While Thomas Mann, far from denouncing recurrence as deadly *ennui* or torture, rejoices in the aura of eternity around it, in the lifting of man's heart above the plane of transitory and disparate events, he does not consider it as a merely objective happening, accepted and, perhaps, exalted by an intoxicated will. It is prompted by the will, the soul of being and the motive power of representation. Recurrence thus acquires the more subjective note of re-petition, a recurrence, that is, which is qualified by inner experience and even active contrivance on the part of the person. So much so that, in *Tonio Kröger*, a mixture of real event and hallucinatory vision can have the meaning and strength of actual recurrence—of the reappearance of Hans and Inge, the idols of Tonio's youth.[m] From this episode, the way leads to all the mythical identifications of which the works from *The Magic Mountain* to *Joseph and His Brothers* are full. They are the metaphysical mainstays of Thomas Mann's technique of leitmotifs. To recognize a present event as the representation of an earlier one implies its grateful recognition (*reconnaissance*) and engenders the festive mood of an anniversary of life, full of the feeling of both past and future. Celebrated for its 'happy return,' the event is old and new at once—new, because now it is imbued by the flavor of familiarity. It wears, so to speak, our own coat of arms.

This concept of willed repetition originated in Nietzsche, who also universalized it on the basis of his aesthetic and metaphysical voluntarism: "no repetition in the things as such; all repetition has first to be created." [69] But it is rooted, of course, in the common ground of a voluntaristic metaphysics in which every fact will appear (and, perhaps, even be felt) as the product of an act of our will. The recognition of the object as a project of the formative will rather than conscious thought (this anti-intellectualistic version of German idealism) does away with the merely objective and accidental.[70] At bottom, everybody wills what he gets and gets what he ultimately wills. (He whose inmost will is success, for instance, will have success; [71] etc.)[n]

Thus the boundaries between *data* and *acta* become very fluid indeed.[o] Seemingly objective recurrences may turn out to be generated by a more or less unconscious will to repetition. Now the same recurrence which is willed by nature can also be willed by man. Nietzsche's fervent acceptance of eternal recurrence may be taken as aiming at an ultimate agreement between the deepest will within us and without, the universal will to repetition asserting itself on a higher and higher plane. Thus consciousness and subconsciousness permeate one another: conscious actions are borne by powerful natural impulses, and the natural urge is absorbed, mirrored, and transfigured by the human will. Repetition does not cease to be a product of the formative will that operates throughout nature (i.e., nature in the Spinozistic sense of *natura naturans*). As personal performance, on the other hand, it is close to Kierkegaard's category of repetition and thus not exposed to that *ennui* which is dreaded by Schopenhauer as well as by the Seducer in *Either/Or* and André Gide's Ménalque. While mere recurrences may be in a descending line due to a coarsening of life or a lowering of its spirits (we have examples of that from *Buddenbrooks* to *Lotte in Weimar*), genuine repetition is personal appropriation and rejuvena- of the past[p] and thus conforms to nature's transcendence into the spirit—this most admirable of all phenomena.

The story of the novelist itself is but a verbal repetition of the ancient history of man, not in every detail, of course (we cannot "drink the sea dry"),[72] yet a very conscientious realization of truth in the medium of fiction and the spiritual medium of language. Conscientious, because and as far as it is legitimated by a real continuity of concern between history and story, so that what proves the problem of the author's figures is at the same time a problem of his inner life. In this sense he is their contemporary and verifies for his part, and in an artful way, the idea of mythical simultaneity, while the ironical style of his narration is calculated to show, among other things, that all the *collectanea* of minute antiquarian studies come to life only in the strength of the artistic imagination.

The Creative Mirror (Mythopoiesis)

This procedure is, however, no mere deviation from the historical truth: it is a contribution to the perennial life which history has in the productive memory of the myth. "Myth is tradition, and to live in tradition means to live in the myth." [73] The artist deals with history, according to a comment of Nietzsche's, as "the Greek dealt with his myth: something he shapes and molds in a spirit of love and devotion, yet in the sovereign fashion of the creative mind. And just because for him history is more flexible and variable than any dream, he can embody in a single event the typical features of whole ages, and thus attain a truth of representation such as the historian can never reach." [74]

This transition into the myth is of the very essence of historical life. Since self-consciousness is part and parcel of historical reality, historical life cannot be seen as it is "in itself," i.e., apart from the relation which it entertains with itself. It sees and molds itself and stands out in relief in conformity with certain interests and intellectual perspectives which, for their part, are an offspring of life. They change as life goes on and, thus, reshape the appearance of the historical past. This is the way (prior to any scientific research) common memory works, in keeping alive, above all, the spirit of those in whom the community has learned to recognize its own permanent yet plastic nature. It accentuates certain symbolical features; it dwells on episodes which these geniuses themselves may have been the first to apperceive in their meaning and to elaborate in a perhaps dim and tentative fashion. The work of art only brings to an at least preliminary consummation that mythopoeic process through which a phenomenon of life grows into a monument of life's truth.

Thomas Mann himself has given us a sublime illustration of such a myth's birth. The peculiar fascination of *Lotte in Weimar* lies in the way the figure of Goethe takes on new life in proportion as he is mirrored by the individuals around him, all those, near and far, who are illumined and seared by the rays of his genius. In their almost desperate struggle to deliver, one after the other, the message they bear about the poet-king, we obtain glimpses of how reality issues into myth. Only after a long suspense, when the messengers have gone, does the hero himself take the stage (just as it was with the Prior in *Fiorenza*). Now we see Goethe in the mirror of his self-representation, i.e., his own thought and work, the product and fulfillment of a majestic self-concern. Last but not least, there is the mirror of the modern author himself, whose reverent irony is always present and always felt, catching all these reflections and transforming them into a new image, a new and wider vision, making of Goethe not only the historical figure we *know*, but a mythical presence we *feel*.

Déjà Vu

So it will be throughout for him who knows how to read the ciphers of history. What rises up out of the past, shrouded in the mystery of resurrection, is no external event, but rather a human experience fraught with meaning and emotional power. And what is present takes on significance as a reminder and, indeed, a new manifestation of the past, and, therewith, of the unity of life in all its stages. Hence, recognition, besides being the identification of a given experience with a certain datum from one's own past, allows this experience to play in different colors: "everything transitory" may be a symbol for many things it represents. The phenomena thus acquire a wealth of references which delight the meditative mind.[75] And finally, repetition appears also, in the manner of the *déjà vu*, as the sudden mysterious emergence of that which lies at the foundation of human being as such, its prototype or *a priori* form, the matrix of all actual forms (and even deformities) and of human experience and truly human culture as a whole. The knowledge of this aboriginal idea is intuitive and visionary in character, as in the case of Plato's "recollection."

The discovery of the inmost truth of human nature is vouchsafed to the young Castorp in his blissful vision during the snowstorm on the slopes of the magic mountain. And Hans Castorp *remembers;* he solemnly recognizes and recalls what he had never glimpsed in this earthly life and yet "had ever borne secretly and unwittingly in his heart; and this 'ever' went far back, immeasurably far back—as far as the open sea there to the left, where with delicate, violet shades the heavens came down to meet it." [76] Thus unfolds a heroic idyll in the softly glowing tints of an Italian bay (such as Hans Castorp never set eyes upon, though Thomas Mann knew it from a painting in the living room of his father's house). The shifting of the natural and human scene may be likened to the transporting of Faust from the Northern Walpurgis Night on the Brocken to the Classical Walpurgis Night at the Peneios. The waters of the Mediterranean and the Baltic begin to flow into one another. While the Italian landscape is painted, for the most part, in the hues and rhythms of the German pilgrims to Rome (the Marées, Ludwig von Hofmann, Stefan George), unexpectedly there creeps in a tender line from the Slesvig heath poet, Thomas Mann's beloved Theodor Storm, "a breath from the homeland" of his native plains:

> Die Luft war voller Vogellaut.[q]
>
> ("The air was full of winged song.")

Whereas North and South join hands in this recollection of an ideal state of harmony, the golden age of man and the promise of the future, the reminder shows in the same dream the demoniacal ingredients of human life as well. Thus humanity appears both in the fullness of its grace and in the barbarism that lurks beneath its surface. One is displayed against the secret, bitter knowledge of the other, hence in a style full of discipline and composure, or again in the ceremonious bearing of the dream figures—in short, in a spirit of cultured nature reminiscent of Goethe's "pedagogical province."

In symbol after symbol, cognition reveals itself as recognition. The Platonic element in this doctrine (mixed with certain Freudian ingredients) comes out even more clearly (though in a light and humorous vein) in *Joseph the Provider*. The chapter in question is significantly entitled "Pharaoh Prophesies." Pharaoh has been prepared for this task in a most ingenious way by realizing with Joseph's help that what he learned only recently about Hermes has, in reality, always been familiar to him in its typical outlines. In the ensuing reading of the king's dream, we find Joseph acting as a kind of midwife, very much like Socrates in Plato's *Meno*, where the slave boy is enabled to learn about geometry by himself.

Joseph's provocative questions elicit from Pharaoh himself the solution to the riddle of his portentous vision; the answer being as natural and convincing as the guesswork of the official interpreters had been devious and confused. Pharaoh indeed (to borrow a phrase of Schopenhauer's) has been "the stage-manager of his own dreams." He secretly knows their meaning because they are but the outgrowth of his own dutiful anxiety for the earthly (as well as the spiritual) welfare of his people. "Pharaoh is mistaken," says Joseph, "if he thinks he does not know. His servant can do no more than prophesy to him that which he already knows." [77] (That it is Amenophis who solves the problem in the end imparts a kind of dramatic life to the whole scene, making up for the fairy-tale facility of the task, in addition, of course, to bearing out Joseph's contention.) Throughout the Joseph novels there are many parallels to this story—among them the foreboding of Laban's fraud in a dream which tells Jacob only what he secretly knows and even more secretly accepts, and actually wills.

Stylistically, the mythical view, the divination of a symbolic meaning which slumbers in the appearances, creates a certain indirectness and ambiguity of expression. The individual figures become representatives of a history much vaster in scope and mightier in its cadences. Herein, the story told is but an episode,[78] a single tone almost disappearing in the whole score, yet capable in some mysterious way of suggesting the complete structure. "The Lord of the Delphic oracle neither veils nor reveals: he indicates" (Heraclitus). By this allusiveness life and narration take on something of the mystery play, festive and exalted, fusing many dimensions in one body, a veritable maze into which poet and reader love to penetrate with wonder and expectation. Being in this sense a play, life invites a certain playfulness of artistic diction, lightening the strain of solemnity, the long-sustained chords, the *chorus mysticus* of the universal drama. A new pathos, permeated by a new mirth and airiness, is what marks Thomas Mann's style in his mythical period.

"The Truth of Ages"

The understanding of symbols is retrospective and prospective at once. It establishes a substantial identity of past, present, and

future—a truth unfolded for us, however, in temporal and dramatic
forms. He who can uncover the meaning of the play will indeed
become prophet and historian at the same time, a mythologist in
the sense of Friedrich Schlegel: "Whosoever . . . may comprehend
that great act of universal rejuvenation, those principles of eternal
revolution, should be able to encompass the two poles of humanity
and understand the deeds of the first men as well as the nature of
the golden age that is to come. Then all the idle chatter would
cease, and man would come to sense what he really is and to know
the earth and the sun." [79]

In any such knowledge "the beginning would contract and
come together with the end." [80] It would mean an overcoming of
the distracted state of life in which the moments of time fall apart
into separate atoms. "Eternity," as men understand it, is at the
opposite pole from this flimsy life—a perfectly concrete unity, the
moments integrated into one capacious "Now." In the fullness of
this concrete moment

> . . . *wird Vergangenheit beständig,*
> *Das Künftige voraus lebendig,*
> *Der Augenblick ist Ewigkeit.*[81]

> (" . . . the past lives on for ever,
> The future thrives in actual endeavor,
> The moment is eternity.")

A myth is true in the same way that poetry is true—by reflecting that which is perennial in the passage of time. Regardless of its
literal accuracy, its external correctness, a poem reveals the truth
when it induces the feeling of "Yes, verily, so it *is*"; and the same
applies to the myth, whose form of narration is that of an "eternal
present."

> *Was sich nie und nirgends hat begeben,*
> *Das allein veraltet nie.*

> ("That which never anywhere has happened—
> That alone does never age.") [r]

Rightly is it said of Esau in the mythical "Conversation," not
that "he *was* Edom," but that "he *is* Edom," he *is* the Red: "Not
by accident is this statement cast in the present tense, for thereby

it is shown to be a timeless, supra-individual summary of the type."[82]

"The so-called motifs," declares Goethe, "are nothing but phenomena of the human spirit which have repeated themselves and will do so again, and the poet does but show them in their historical embodiment." All such motifs are variants of still more primitive ones which, like that of man himself, form the *a priori* as well as the entelechy of the present. They emerge from the "one day" of the myth—and advance toward the "one day" when their meaning shall be perfectly manifest. "The 'one day' [*Einst*] is thus a word of tremendous scope. It has two faces, the one looking back, far back into remote and twilit times, the other looking ahead, far ahead into the distances to come—ages no less solemn because they are bound to come than are the others because they have already come to pass." [83] It is into the dreamy twilight, the at-once of this twofold once, the source and terminus of all our obligations, that the myth beckons us. In a dreamlike state a synoptic vision of truth (i.e., of life's integrity) dawns upon all of Thomas Mann's main characters. It comes as reminiscence, as it were, of that primeval moment when, like Plato's souls, they too approached their destinies in the sight of the axis around which the universe wheels and whirls.

Imitatio

Are experiences of this kind the source or the outcome of man's burning desire to break through the isolating walls of the empirical moment and the empirical ego? They are both. They open up the freedom of infinite horizons and give the single event true significance by making it the sign for a whole of individual and superindividual life. They have us, in the course of our existence, walk on, as it were, "transparent ground consisting of innumerable crystalline courses illuminated by lamps which shine between them" and thus spatialize time in the mythical figure of simultaneous presence of its moments.[s]

There is a pensive delight in recognizing the unity of substance in a variety of reflections, in realizing the "inner universality in everything representable, howsoever particular it may be, from the stone up to man; for everything repeats itself, and there is literally nothing in the world that exists just *once*" (Goethe).[84] And this enchanted recognition is inseparable from the productive urge to make and remake one's life in the image of an ideal prototype. Repetition enjoyed in this recollective mood will by itself turn into *imitation, mimesis* in the spirit of Pythagorean-Platonic-Aristotelian tradition. The sense of life is not merely that of a linear progress. In one of its aspects, it is a round of births, a "rotation of the sphere"—a process, above all, in which man works on the image of God, remakes himself in this image and may even be removed to the gods, just as God descends to earth; in this cycle something real attains an ideal status and an ideal entity becomes naturalized and somewhat lowered by its enfranchisement here below, much as we strive to preserve its purity. Thus the upward path of sublimation and idealization becomes one with the downward path of realization. This is the mutual relationship between history and the myth, apotheosis and anthropomorphosis, the dialectics of incarnation, sacrificial death, resurrection, and transfiguration. Immortality has as prominent a place in Thomas Mann's thought as it has in *Buddenbrooks:* the ardent confession to it, by a little schoolmistress, would be endorsed by the author himself, though on his own terms.

In this intercourse between the ideal and the real there is no room for the Platonic gap between the two worlds; even the Leibnizian thesis that essence tends toward existence is transcended and can be converted. The species and the individual coincide in a subphenomenal sphere of which the aesthetic consciousness knows as well as that of 'primitive' men. The real needs ideation as much as the true needs realization:

> Der Schein, was ist er, dem das Wesen fehlt?
> Das Wesen wär' es, wenn es nicht erschiene?[85]
>
> ("What is appearance when true essence fails?
> Would essence *be*, if it did not appear?")

This round-dance in which the ideal emerges from life to merge into it over and over again, brings a certain relativity into our speaking of the timelessness of the ideal type. First of all, it may (but need not) come from times immemorial and be eternal in mocking all our attempts to trace it back to its origin. "The stuff of becoming is being, which is itself a product of becoming and derives from far distant life." [86] Just as even Plato's ideas presuppose a designer (the *phytourgos*), so each archetype in Thomas Mann is destined to function as a classical solution of a problem and establishes a historical *a priori* since it owes its existence to a history-making act, even though we may never find its original author and must be content with groping toward him by plunging deeper and deeper into the history of imitation. At home in an unfathomable depth of time, the myth founds the primeval, qualitatively timeless "forms and norms of life." [87]

The original formative act sets a new pattern but is also qualified and conditioned by the particular situation it has to meet, and by the peculiar impulses and limitations of its first performer, as well as his successors. Notwithstanding its qualitative eternity, such a motif has a definite history—a birth, a struggle for existence, an eventual victory and fulfillment, perhaps an ultimate degeneration and death. In its mythical significance, in setting an example or following it out, life becomes exemplary: it experiences the assurance and elation of being *dans le vrai*.

The definite setting of a type is more than merely envisioning it. Yet the forerunner himself constitutes a special type—Amenophis being cited as the prototype of those who have not the strength of their own insights.[88] They too show what life can be like, and thus disclose one of the forms in which the fellowship of men may be realized. In the very shipwreck of their existence and even in the perversion of the image of man for which they die, they present a spectacle "profoundly to be revered as something mythical, a poem and a tragedy of life." [89]

Living Tradition

While to acquire substantial worth and weight life must be lived under the sign of one of the great human prototypes, this relation may not be exclusive of others. A man may qualify his imitation of a personal model, may change his orientation and enjoy even a limited freedom of moving into a different constellation.

This is eloquently demonstrated by the way *imitatio* figures in Thomas Mann's own inner and outer life. After Schiller, his *heros eponymos* is now Schopenhauer, now Goethe, and now, in a mingling of passion and compassion, enchantment and fright, Friedrich Nietzsche, who (before *Doctor Faustus*) "had not yet found his artist, as Schopenhauer did" [90] in Wagner and in *Budden-brooks*. Mann has seen and enacted his own life in the light of great archetypes. He has "projected his own being into the forms of their sheer perfection," [91] or the heart-rending and sinful, yet cathartic, tragedy of their vicarious suffering. How much love, praising and withholding, even rejecting love, how much enthusiasm, irony, and even travesty, how much play and labor, imagination and thought, transposition and transformation have contributed to making these intricate works of "free dependence" and "indirect communication" possible and matters of deep—smiling and painful—delight! (Pastiches to be pierced only in *Faustus*, by the "wild directness" in the outcry of the bare, tortured creature.)

Personal ideals of man's youth may be deposed later on (as Thomas Mann actually did with some minor deities) by enthroning the true paragons of human existence. The radical search for the genuine founders and foundations of our present life will often prove its great masters to represent only rather advanced phases in the life of a motif which rises from, perhaps, unfathomable depths, imitations themselves within the one great imitation, mankind's *imitatio Dei*. (Hence the mixture of joy, curiosity, and "pale apprehension" in the adventure of the poet's epic journey, in his descent to the "mothers" or, as *Joseph and His Brothers* has it, to hell.)

In addition to all this, the leitmotifs of life lead into the future as well as into the past; and life molds them just as well as it is molded by them.[t] The "truth of ages"—"*das alte Wahre*" [92]—must be embraced in order to keep alive, insinuate itself into noble hearts, and form the bond of the spirits. It persists in these processes of genuine renewal so that

> *Keine Zeit und keine Macht zerstückelt*
> *Geprägte Form, die lebend sich entwickelt.*[93]
>
> ("Nor time nor might are able to dissolve
> Forms firmly coined which living on evolve.")

By virtue of their historical plasticity types may be changed almost past recognition. The notion of the historical genesis and movement of the ideas (corresponding, in his scheme of things, to the belief in God's own development) distinguishes Thomas Mann's conception of history as myth and *mimesis* from mythical consciousness in pre-historical times and from the artificial fundamentalism of modern mystagogues like Breisacher in *Doctor Faustus*. "In primitive societies, as we know them," says A. J. Toynbee, "*mimesis* is directed towards the older generation and towards dead ancestors who stand, unseen but not unfelt, at the back of the living elders, reinforcing their prestige. In a society where *mimesis* is thus directed backward towards the past, custom rules and society remains static. On the other hand, in societies in process of civilization, *mimesis* is directed towards creative personalities who command a following because they are pioneers. In such societies 'the cake of custom' is broken . . . and the society is in dynamic motion along a course of change and growth." [94] Imitation thus becomes what it is in Thomas Mann. It is, in its magic charm, a mythical and aesthetic issue, and it is a moral task in response to the challenge of both the past and the future.

In this "conservative revolution" the law of the new world is validated without abrogating that of the old: instead, the dynamic of that old world is caught up into the new, richer movement that thus unites the force and constancy of nature with the verve and lightness of the idea. Like the dark daughters of night, the guardians of the maternal soil in the *Eumenides* of Aeschylus, the old world is honorably received into the procession of the new historical life.

Entelechy

The mutual turning into one another of the temporal and the timeless, together with the inner awareness of types as standards of life, prevents them, in Thomas Mann, from being restricted to the pure transcendence of Platonic ideas. It gives them, in their realization, the position of Aristotle's inherent forms, i.e., of *entelechies* as formal, formative causes embodied and more or less individuated in personal and historical life. In every being there is a secret principle, a plastic power, the law (a *lex seriei*, to speak with Leibniz) that orders the whole course of its existence. "Operating from a region far out of the reach of the individual's conscious representations," [u] it constitutes an inner teleology, hidden in most cases, but patent in those great, original natures in which even the seeming detours will at last stand out as steps essential to the appointed end.[v] Contrariwise, this formative power may be felt *in absentia,* when individual and social life disintegrate and surrender to outer circumstances and blind chance.

Attracted as he is by his inmost possibility, spurred by the power of love, man, even Goethe's homunculus, manages to realize the entelechy of the monad he is.[95] In *Doctor Faustus* this inner form appears literally as entelechy and as "the Angel, the Genius of life in whose knowing guidance the individual sets his loving trust": Plato's and Goethe's Demon, but also the Angel of Stefan George's *Tapestry of Life.*[96]

While in a life that is given to reflection this formative principle may, at times, come to explicit attention, its birthplace is not in consciousness proper; its domain is neither the mental nor the physical realm exclusively. As a principle of the whole, it holds sway over both. *It is one of those mysteries of life which the poet reveals without probing or dispelling. He leaves it to philosophy "to deal with them as she sees fit"* [97] *by transforming them, by hook or crook, into philosophical problems. He speaks out of the heart of our being, from the source of becoming, the center where everything is still in the state of formation, but whence all the specific human activities branch out.*

Intelligible Character

The *a priori* nature of this formative power is what the Kantians call a man's *"intelligible character"*—a moral term which serves to indicate rather than explain one phase of this mystery. In Schopenhauer it is linked to Platonic and Brahmanist teaching[98] and his own voluntaristic metaphysics.

Schopenhauer's view puts necessity in the realm of function (*operari*) and freedom in that of substance (*esse*).[99] Our empirical nature and behavior, with all that pertains to this bodily life of ours, are considered the necessary results of the will's metaphysical decision to assume the form of this particular being. "The responsibility," says Plato, "rests with the chooser. God cannot be made responsible." [100]

Both in the *Reflections* and in his Schopenhauer essay Thomas Mann stands by the profound mystical truth of this doctrine which but confirms one of his own earliest and deepest convictions.[101] As a poet he proclaims it, e.g., through the mouth of Nanda in *The Transposed Heads:* "Ultimately there is no distinction between that which is 'given' and that which is freely 'assumed' " (i.e., accepted, and even taken up on one's own initiative).[102]

Amor Fati

Themselves darkly aware of this original free choice, all of Thomas Mann's principal figures willingly shoulder its consequences. Their fate is their fault; their deeds and misdeeds, their doing and undoing follow from their having willed themselves into this life. *Operari sequitur esse.*[103] ("Operation is dependent on being.") "Profounder, more secret sins there are than those which we consciously, empirically commit," so confesses Goethe in *The Beloved Returns.*[104] And "can it be that I am responsible for your act by my very being, though not through any actions of my own?" asks Nanda over the lifeless body of his friend.[105]

One's ultimate entelechy is in his steering toward man's ultimate end. It may be good to illustrate this *amor fati* by some examples drawn from the long series of characters from *Buddenbrooks* to *Doctor Faustus* and *Felix Krull.* It is, indeed, this final readiness that ennobles Thomas Buddenbrook in his enchanted moments of metaphysical insight. It inspires Savonarola, who loves the fire that is to consume him. It appears in Gustav Aschenbach's meeting death "with a gesture of welcome, a calm and deliberate acceptance of what was to come." [106] Hans Castorp's knowing way of testing his fate and grasping man's destiny shows in his challenging the elements in that crucial scene where "the mad youth" climbs into "the misty naught," "the wild silence, vast and foreboding" of the endless snow in the high mountains, into "an ever deeper solitude," pathless, without posts and staves.* A challenge to the 'elements' is

---

* *Zauberberg* II, 233. The whole scene and its grotesque counterpart in *Doctor Faustus*—the imaginary adventures of Adrian Leverkühn and Professor Capercailzie *alias* Auerhahn—are reminiscent (and intentionally so) of Faust's descent to the realm of the "mothers":

No way. To the Unexplorable
Never to be explored; to the Unimplorable
Never to be implored. Art in the mood?
No locks there are, no bars are to be riven.

implied also in his provoking the wrath of the monumental Mynheer Peeperkorn. What seems at first sight mere forwardness and playing with fire is really the advance toward that extremity in which the meanings of life and death shine forth.

And what of Joseph? In his dealings with his brothers and with Potiphar's wife he, too, tends to arrange things with a view to experiencing his fate, if only to pass through into a higher state of life.[107] He bends over the well of death to capture not merely the sweetness of losing but also the strength of finding himself (and his brothers) in the infinite depth.

In a similar vein of "blissful craving," of "die and rise" in flames, of immortality through sacrifice both made and imposed the dream vision at the end of *Lotte in Weimar* concludes, the imaginary dialogue which dissolves Lotte's lifelong, painful uncertainty about the great experience of her youth. So, eventually, she too will be able to acquiesce in her destiny, in the creation and sustenance of her role.

Another sacrificial flame, melting the particulars and their guilt in the *Holy One*, a "flame of life," flares from the stake in *The Transposed Heads*, when the fire unites Shridaman, Nanda, and Sita after all their strayings and yearnings, their griefs and delights. They embrace their fate, plan their own deaths, and prepare their funeral pyre after having quenched the thirst of their violent loves.[108]

"Wander through transforming shade and shine"—*Geh in der Verwandlung aus und ein!* (Rilke).[109] The unity of life runs through the procession of figures. The Beloved of Goethe's youth does not truly "return" in the aged appearance of Frau Councillor Kestner, but in the rejuvenated, spiritualized form of the love between Goethe and Marianne Willemer. And either love passes, through transfiguration by the genius, from outer through inner life into the ideality of the poem—to fecundate life and become real again in loves that are richer for their previous rehearsals.

Through solitudes you will be whirled and driven.
Canst thou imagine wastes and solitude?

. . . .

Naught will you see in that vast Void afar,
Nor hear your footstep when 'tis pressed.
Nor find firm ground where you can rest.
—*Faust* II, 6222-27, 6246-48 in Priest's translation

It is our hope (and Mann's) that this dialectic will also apply to the tragedy of Nietzsche—repeated as it is by that artistic progeny of Thomas Mann himself, Doctor Faustus. He too knows his hour, cries not for help, and does "not resist evil" or protest against undergoing the torments of hell. Perverted as it appears in the travesty of Nazism, this agony of solitude, this desperate striving for integration, need not end altogether in madness and despair, as it does with Nietzsche, Leverkühn, the German people, in all their adventures and aberrations in the flesh and the spirit. All these pains, morally deserved or not, may be stages on the way to redemption through the purifying power suffering can—*can*—have if it is truly undergone.

A daring parable of this truth is offered in the story of the Holy Sinner Gregory and his no less sinful mother and wife Sibylla. They both take 'in good grace' a fate they have conjured up by their own inmost nature. There is unconscious, yet willful repetition in the incest Sibylla commits with her brother's son, just as there is a secret imitation of the Oedipus pattern in Gregory. Since he goes out to seek his mother, he will find her in his wife. Knowledge of the unity of mother and wife "runs in his blood" (as it does in ours): each wife represents the mother of all, Mother Earth. (It is appropriate that Mother Earth sustains his life by her milk—the ancient motif of "earth-milk" was graciously supplied by Thomas Mann to the medieval legend.) She sustains Gregory throughout the seventeen years of his repentance on the lonely rock in the lake, the repetition of the seventeen years of his childhood on the remote fishing-island in the North Sea.* He knows himself elected to both sin and grace; both are excessive; but so is his repentance which leads him from a worse than pariah state to the Holy See.

In the array of those in whom will and destiny are one, there is finally Felix Krull, this somewhat dubious but none the less decorous variation of the "favorites of heaven." He cultivates his gifts as a swindler, a maker of appearances, with an earnest passion, a strict discipline, and an almost religious devotion to the world he cheats

---

* Thirty-four years altogether in which the time of history stands still. We shall deal with this magic number later on. *The Holy Sinner* teams with seventeens in its time computations. But the same bisection of thirty-four—in a vaguely analogous situation—has already appeared in *Joseph der Ernährer*, 621 = *Joseph the Provider*, 1195.

(or improves?). While the average citizen may think all this effort worthy of a better cause, Felix places it with great solemnity in the service of his devious calling. He is (and feels himself to be) an *artista* in an appearance before the footlights which is both flimsy and heroic; as flimsy as each artistic pseudo-existence and as heroic as the formation of illusions, the playing above the abyss, is seen to be by Nietzsche and his successors. He is true to his fraud.

The ambiguity, the chiaroscuro of Krull's life is but a witty variation of that ambiguity which is peculiar to man. Man is always "between." He always labors as a member of two realms to neither of which he belongs exclusively; heaven and earth, spirit and nature, being and non-being. Each generation has both to acknowledge this ambivalence of human existence and to try to overcome the tension between above and below, light and darkness.

The truth and fullness of all human life is in some unity between day and night, in some, however delicate, identity of the opposites. (This accounts for the dialectical way Thomas Mann characterizes his figures through contrasting yet complementary features, and groups antagonists together or around the center of the composition.) The form of heroism he understands, the way to greatness he sanctions is through weakness, suffering, and sacrifice, ultimately self-sacrifice. Both Aschenbach and, in an even stricter sense, Leverkühn are "heroes of their age":[110] they carry the cross of their time to the height of Calvary. Just as the light of hope rises in the very darkness of despair, there is no full-toned gladness except his who has drunk from the cup of bitter pain. Even Joseph, Leverkühn's antipode in the scale of the human, verifies Schopenhauer's: *In hilaritate tristis, in tristitia hilaris.* Rejoicing and resignation are coupled in his life. He pays for his worldly enfranchisement, his social honors and blessings by being removed from the dynasty of those who, in the tribulations of their flesh, are bringers of the blessings of the spirit. To preserve the creation as a prince of this world and to serve the divine spirit in absolute devotion prove incompatible tasks with him as well as, in the reverse sense, with Amenophis. "You know it?" asks Jacob, and Joseph answers: "I know."

Predestination

Hilarity and sadness mingle in the destiny of the mediator as Thomas Mann sees it. It is the dual nature of his own writings. But this mediation between nature and spirit is the lot fallen to man; and the artist stands out just as an outstanding example, a marked representative of mankind. It is therefore only the artistic variety of a fundamental human experience which appears in the bipolar form of one of Thomas Mann's book titles: "Greatness and Misery of the Masters." The same ambivalence which, in ancient languages, applies to "being singled out"—the twofold sense of *sacer*—is felt by Thomas Mann in the form of the blessing and curse of the artist's calling, but not of the artist's alone.

The dogma of original sin, hanging over our present existence, has its counterpart in Goethe's no less paradoxical thesis of "innate merits." [111] Both seem to have reference to the afore-mentioned crucial act of the will, proceeding as it does from a depth far beneath that of individual, empirical life and consciousness, and thus giving a mystical justification to the otherwise pitiless doctrine of predestination, that there are "vessels fitted to destruction" and "vessels of mercy afore prepared unto glory." [112] Here as elsewhere, we see Jewish-Christian (and more specifically Protestant) ideas being reformulated in terms of modern metaphysics and being verified in the actual experience of the artist. The awesome mystery (*mysterium tremendum*) of God's unfathomable grace, that he has pity upon those whom he chooses to pity; that he alone will be blessed who is already blessed; that to him only is it given who already hath —this is a leading motif of the Joseph novels, just as it is an elemental experience of the artist.

This is one of the secrets which well up into our lives while our intellect penetrates into them "no more than into the ocean penetrates the eye" (Dante). Yet Mann is eager to give it its proper place. What is in question is the blessing of man in his twofold nature. That blessing is never a mere biological fact. The right of the first-born can be forfeited, it can be lost, and it can be overthrown according to a decree we do not understand. And it is no mere emotional issue either. To be sure, a child's bodily and intellectual charm and even the peculiar circumstances of his birth may

become a source of predilection on the part of his earthly (and—
so it seems—even his heavenly) father.[113] But however arbitrary or
excessive this favoritism may seem, particularly from the moral point
of view, it is not identical with the ultimate order of election to that
ecclesia invisibilis in which, through the anguish of suffering, humiliation, and sin, the kingdom of God is destined to ripen. In the
last instance, however, the "two swords of the empire," the wise
ruler—for instance Thomas Mann's Roosevelt—and the martyr,
the witness to the spirit, are both needed and employed to serve
the purpose of the Highest in this creation and in the sphere of
humanity.

The Human Play

The strong feeling and faithful acceptance of one's destiny,
molding man's life, directing his aspirations, cautioning him against
straying away, make the embodiment of an ideal type the more or
less conscious enacting of a given role in the drama of life. The
interpretation of life as a performance before God or the gods appears as early as in Plato's *Laws* (803ff) and in Proverbs (8:31f), and
as late as in Goethe's *Faust*,[114] in Nietzsche,[115] and even in Russell.[116]
The philosophy of life of Thomas Mann's Joseph can be well sum-
marized in the words of Angelus Silesius:

> *Dies alles ist ein Spiel, das sich die Gottheit macht;*
> *Sie hat die Kreatur um ihretwilln erdacht.*[117]

> ("All this is but a show that on God's stage is played
> —For him who for himself the creatures planned and made.")

And this is still a valid symbol of Thomas Mann's own view of the
spectacle of life. The world of the theater, the world of the poet, is
but an abstract of the theater of the world got up by the *poeta
mundi.* "All the sacred plays of art," says Friedrich Schlegel in
his "Dialogue on Poetry," "are but faint imitations of the infinite
play of the world—this work of art which eternally performs itself." [118]

That the very earnestness of life is in the spirit of play is a
humble acknowledgment both of finite human existence, which in
itself is not worthy of absolute concern, and of the seriousness

which none the less accrues to it by its relationship to the absolute, by its being performed and celebrated as it were in the festive mood of a re-presentation, the present renewal of a perennially valid, exemplary form of life. To consider the realization of a human type as the reenactment of a role is, of course, a treat to the playful narrator; but it is more. Under the disguise of an ironical style and a bantering language, under the garment of the myth beats the heart of religious experience. It is the experience of life in the presence of the absolute, as an answer to a calling, an account in view of our being counted upon. It is this experience that goes into the metaphor of existence as the performance of an assigned role, as a spectacle before a divine spectator. To be counted upon means somehow to be known. The *cogitor ergo est* reaches into deeper ground than Descartes's *cogito ergo sum*. The subject *finds* itself as an object of higher knowledge in what ought to be a worthy appearance.

As to the human contribution to the play, it is the distinction of man to be not only, and at his best, "a plaything of the Gods," as Plato has it, but an actor and agent at the same time—an agent who, in his very acting, knows himself as a *persona*, i.e., as sustaining, creating, or re-creating a certain role. As such, he is neither a dupe of his role as Schopenhauer[119] sees him, nor Nietzsche's poetical fool, mottled and masked, "a mask to himself," [120] nor a histrionic exhibitionist like Christian Buddenbrook. He grows through his role, and his role grows through him. He passes beyond the limits of trifling, inconsequential, disoriented individual existence, joins a tradition which he lives and revives, and, like Peeperkorn, makes his exit when he can no longer live up to the demands of his part.

Overcoming the feeling of artistic representation as a mere shadow of original and integral life, Thomas Mann himself has learned to live up to his own role in kindly administering his fame as a representative, advocate, and, indeed, paladin, at first of his own generation, and then of the German, the European, and finally the human spirit as such. At the same time he must also be a mediator between these spheres, representing Germany *in* the eyes of the world and *to* its eyes: this German Lucifer who could stray so far and fall so deep because he ventured so high in his proud and lonely flights.

Mann's characters play and know their roles just as their author does. Embodying their types, being what they represent, they may even be taken for one another or pass themselves off for the other with whom they are substantially one. This happens on a lower level to the successive servants in *Joseph and His Brothers* and *The Beloved Returns;* in the highest sphere the 'Lord's' majesty is variously represented to Joseph by his God, his father, and Potiphar—adumbrations of the same principle, which, at times, may melt together in one pluridimensional vision.

While in this interplay the specific distinctions prevail over the individual ones, they do not lead to a rigid and unilinear hierarchy of higher and lower ranks. The different types complement and, therefore, call for each other, so much so that (as we saw), in a mutual longing rather than jealousy, the representative of one type is always tempted to betray it in favor of the opposite type. Moreover the "how" of the performance, its spirit, is just as important as the "what," the content of an actor's role. Their indispensability to the whole levels thus, in a way, the differences between rewarding and unrewarding parts, the roles of the angel and of the villain, the lucky fellow and the wretched man. This is another aspect under which the offense of predestination, the incomprehensible distinction between the elected and the rejected ones, may be mitigated. Men in what Nietzsche called aristocratic ages have always believed in their predestination for their roles.[121] Whatsoever is implied in their roles and thus inscribed in their selves is felt to be a matter of obligation—down to the innocently dangerous tricks of beautification employed, for instance, by the handsome youth Joseph, as it were in "obedience to his pleasant role, and devoting to his natural excellences a service which may be interpreted (and therefore approved) as having a religious connotation."[122] Even little Sita's art of eyebrow-penciling expresses a subconscious sense of duty imposed upon her by beauty itself, through whose sensuous appeal the spiritual charm of the soul may be called into play.[123] (Notice the Christian Platonism coming out even in this Indian guise.) *"Elle doit se dorer pour être adorée"*—to speak with Baudelaire.[124]

God's favorites, as well as those who, in the lineage of Cain, are stigmatized by the Almighty, honor the knowledge of their hearts as to "who the individual essentially is, apart from time, in a mythical and typical sense."[125] This is true to the spirit of Hellenistic-Jewish-Christian mysticism which (being grist to his mill) Thomas Mann worked into his Joseph novels. They echo the mood of the medieval miracle play as Hugo von Hofmannsthal, his "brother in the times" (so Thomas Mann called him),[126] revived it in *Das Salzburger Grosse Welttheater* (1922). "What here takes place," proclaims the First Angel in that play, "similitude is it, and not reality; and good or bad—thus shall be called the playing rather than the role, that day when all things shall have reached their end." Indeed, it is just the most wretched role, so we are informed, that presents the most heavenly privilege, the greatest challenge to a superbly free, creative performance: man's descent to hell as his offertory for mankind's ascension to heaven.

Part II THOMAS MANN'S WORKS

Chapter 3 THE GENEALOGY OF THE ARTIST: THE PERIOD OF *BUDDENBROOKS*

. . . Plus encore que la vie
La Mort nous tient souvent par des liens subtils.

("... Even more than life
Death often holds us fast with subtle ties.")

BAUDELAIRE[1]

The Problem of the Artist

"No problem under the sun is more tormenting than that of artistic existence and art's effect on human beings." [2] This assertion of Tonio Kröger originated in Thomas Mann's early experience; and his Goethe, a product of his later years, still speaks of art as "this utterly unique and therefore most entrancing of phenomena." [3] "Why should not the workman think about his own working, if another work comes out of it, and since ultimately, perhaps, all work may be nothing but the profound vanity of being absorbed in the phenomenon of the worker—nothing but a highly ego-centric performance?" [4]

Many other issues have confronted Thomas Mann—problems insistent in their bearing upon current history and therefore clamoring for immediate solution. He has always stood his ground, and valiantly tried to fight his way into the open. But within an ever larger setting the enigma of his, i.e., the artist's, existence has always remained his most personal concern, from *Buddenbrooks* to *Doctor Faustus*.

This problem arises whenever an artist is compelled to assert and to question his own existence. It may be described as an iridescent problem, for it imperceptibly shifts, changes, and comes round, assuming ever fresh nuances and overtones. In Mann's early works the relationship between artist and man is shrouded in doubt, and indeed almost completely effaced by that youthful melancholy which feels so strongly and so ironically the discrepancies between the artist's inner being and his *mise en scène*, between the conditions of pro-

85

ductivity and the product of these conditions.[5] In the following decades, however, it is drawn into a movement toward a point where it seems to be wonderfully clarified and resolutely affirmed. But just before reaching this climax and, as it were, the poet's enthronement on high, the ascent suddenly falters, the movement recedes in disillusion, resignation, and all but despair. *The Transposed Heads*, the finale in *Joseph the Provider*, the Moses story *The Tables of the Law*, and *Doctor Faustus* are stations on the way of the Cross to which the artist returns in the agony of his soul.

Being and Representation

In its disparity between being and representation, the initial stage displays a tension which is both agonizing and productive. For, in the last analysis, only those questions are fruitful which lead us far out to the boundaries of human existence. At the heart of life the curse and blessing of being an artist are felt to be one.[6] The artist is stigmatized by his very distinction and exposed by his very ex-sistence, i.e., his "out-standing" being.[a]

This ambivalent feeling of being singled out drives him back and forth between an arrogant isolation from his fellows and a nostalgic yearning for communion with them, between scorn and veneration of healthy everyday life. Uprooted from this common life and condemned to represent it only in the mirror of his work, he assumes that the integrity of being is preserved and represented bodily by the unsophisticated people around him, though this latter representation more and more reveals itself as limited, dull, and even insincere. That is why the young poet's passionate admiration of the 'common' is tinged with irony, irony with respect to the others, irony with respect to himself who, in his veneration of the vulgar, disavows his own eminence. (This is the mainspring of Thomas Mann's ironical style.) "What," so asks Nietzsche, "what does he know about love who has not been compelled to despise the very thing he loved?" But "some day" such a lover "will grow tired of his solitude" and "will not see his grandeur any longer." [7]

Since it is to the world at large that the artist bares his heart in his writings, he likewise wants to be loved and admired by all mankind.[8] Is he not their redeemer from a life that is unconscious of itself, from commonplace, unheeding reality? Does he not transfigure this life of theirs into the fairest of forms and the clearest of representations? But all the while, at the bottom of his heart, he is aware of the pitiless isolation to which his dreams and meditations condemn him, aware of his frightfully abnormal relationship to his "brothers." More and more there dawns in him the consciousness that such isolation is not only to be borne as imposed by outer destiny, but atoned for as a result of guilt. In the favorites of nature this guilt resides in their very perfection, which means their 'excommunication' from never ending human strife. In artists of Thomas Mann's type it comes from what the Christians call the root of all sins—the pride of a spirit that cannot love—and leads to a quasi-metaphysical short circuit. Thomas Mann's artist, the artist and metaphysician in Thomas Mann himself, not the burgher in him who fights for humanity and honors the order of the day—the pure artist sees through the whole and represents it without illusion. He laughs at this whole blunder of existence in which he does not want to have a part. And yet he is allured by the spectacle of life and consumed by his envy of those who are strong and naïve enough to enjoy acting in the play, unaware or, sometimes, even aware of its outcome.

Eagerly pressing his face to the windowpane, he sees the "others" at work, and play, and yet he does not open the door in order to join them in the dance of life. This Theodor Storm motif[9] (a version of a characteristic nineteenth-century image) reaches far beyond *Tonio Kröger*, on into *Death in Venice*. It reechoes in *Disorder and Early Sorrow* and is discussed anew in *Lotte in Weimar*. It reveals the contemplative love of the stranger and spectator who is rich but in want, the nostalgic and renunciatory love of Schiller's Philip II, of *Royal Highness*:

> . . . des, der angetan mit der Könige Purpur
> das schwere bleiche Angesicht senkt auf den Purpur.

> (". . . of him who, clad in the royal purple,
> bends down his grave pale face to the purple.") [b]

The artist's remoteness and self-dependence are not mere willful isolation. By the young Thomas Mann, at least, they are felt to result from a decay of life, from an exhaustion of vital energy, which marks, at the same time, the birth-hour of the artistic spirit.

The once well-rooted vitality of the Buddenbrooks is exhausted in proportion as their sensitivity refines itself; the more Tonio Kröger's health is weakened, the keener grow his artistic and analytical powers.[10] Dependent on mastering life in art, the artist endures as long as he succeeds in balancing the impact of the most violent impressions by his sovereign power of expression. Spiritually awake and serenely composed in the midst of suffering and passions, he enjoys "that clairvoyance even through the tearful veil of feeling and emotions" [11] which he may feel as both a heavenly and a diabolic power. Life is enabled to embrace itself retrospectively, as it were, in the recollection but also the loving betrayal of its past. Thus it enters the wide-open eye of the artist.

Autobiography as Research into the Origins

It is the artist's privilege to realize the typical in the particular, the essential types and universal laws of being in the single instance. No one has ever been more tireless than Thomas Mann in observing the minutest features of outer life, or more astute in reporting and representing them. The almost unbelievable wealth of human content in *Buddenbrooks* earned for its young author the emphatic 'recognition' of a world which in this account recognized its own rise and decay. This account was so full and perfect a rendition of life that the cup of bitterness was presented and could be enjoyed as the pure wine of art. A melancholy rejection of the world is suspended in the medium of irony. And the few shrill dissonances, such as the unseemly death of dignified Thomas Buddenbrook, serve only to enhance the awareness of the *sotto voce* style in which this slowly developing *danse macabre* is set. The miracle of the artistic transubstantiation of heavy suffering into composed language is in moving contrast with the wild eruptions in *Doctor Faustus*, the work in which the writer returns to the old German town and its musical climate, while flinging away the comfort of temperate, well-measured form.

As a sum total of personal experience, *Buddenbrooks* does not leave out any trait that may contribute to the meaning and actual presentation of the past. But, here as elsewhere, Thomas Mann is far from the chimerical aim of objective completeness. He registers what found a positive or negative response in his own existence and thus took on validity as a symbol of, or as a contrast to, his own inner being. Conversely, only because he felt his own development to be of universal significance does that development emerge both as subject matter in his single works and in the way they complement one another. What takes place here, under the guise of telling a story about a Lübeck family, is a bringing forth, through a selection of autobiographical material, of the conditions of the artist's existence. This impulse marks the scope of artistic representation and determines its limits. *Buddenbrooks* is no mere bourgeois novel. Significantly enough, it had its germ-cell in the story of little Hanno. It tells the growth of the citizen into an artist and is developed, therefore, from the point where Thomas Mann's poetic ethos is still in contact with the quondam Protestant ethos of work and its everyday hero, working "at the brink of exhaustion." "I have never depicted it"—this modern bourgeois type—"as a political-economic phenomenon. For that I had neither the sympathy nor the knowledge. But the truly poetical—this I have always considered to be the symbolical." [12]

The Scale of Representation in *Buddenbrooks*

However real and palpable they may appear, the four generations of Buddenbrooks are essentially symbols, representing stages of existence. In each successive stage, more and more breaks and fissures appear on the placid surface of sound bourgeois life. There is the old "radical" Buddenbrook, who can afford to be Voltairian. Born a representative of his class and his city, he does not need to be elected as such. Then there is Consul John Buddenbrook, representative of the Restoration era, who already needs religious justification for his business transactions and feels under obligation to the firm—and God—to make a dignified showing. This dignity is in jeopardy in the following generation. John's chubby daughter Toni is still full of bourgeois instincts and ambitions, but they miscarry one after the other in an ominous way.[c] Of John's sons, Thomas and Christian, the latter disgraces not only his family but his very name. With him, Christian self-concern degenerates into the shameless exhibition of petty grievances, and genuine life into a disreputable show. But even with highly responsible Senator Thomas Buddenbrook the almost heroic struggle against fate assumes the nature of a spectacle. Social stage-acting becomes to him at once an aesthetic need, an idiosyncrasy, and a stratagem. He must "worthily represent" what he no longer really is; he "represents" in order to keep up the façade, without any real belief in what he officially stands for.

Boundless Representation

At the same time Thomas longs to be released from this wretched, painfully limited kind of representation, to escape the boundaries of his individuality and attain a universal representation, the power of selfsameness with the whole of life. Through a reading of Schopenhauer he is eventually assured of just such a blessed state of boundless life which corrects the blunder of this individual existence.[d] "The walls of his native city, in which he had consciously and willfully shut himself up, were thrown open to him and to his gaze disclosed the world, the whole world, of which he had seen this or that little piece in his younger days, but which death promised to bestow upon him whole and entire." [e]—as one perennial present.

This whole experience—the beatific, yet fleeting vision of a single night[f]—is reported almost literally in the words of Schopenhauer. But it is Schopenhauer's doctrine without Schopenhauer's asceticism; it is Schopenhauer in a Nietzschean interpretation, asserting a "fuller, stronger, happier" existence.[13] While a family's will to life may be drowned in the lust for death, for instance, in the drunkenness of musical excesses, life as such, immortal life, will march on triumphantly through the various forms, the strong self-assertions of the creative will.

It may well be that Thomas Buddenbrook does not fully decipher the meaning of the Indian gospel—the "That art thou" (tat tvam asi) and "I am Brahman" (aham Brahma asmi)—in Schopenhauer's interpretation. The substance of his experience must be distilled from the rather cloudy form in which he is able to grasp it. But the ecstasy of his "That is me," "I am he as well as I" [14] is the first recognition of Thomas Mann's lasting credo that the boundaries between ego and non-ego are fluid, that man reaches beyond his individual self into other, greater existences and they into his. It is the metaphysical version of the ambiguous mythical formula—

the "I am it"—out of which Thomas Mann's Joseph is to make so much capital in his profoundly knowing play.*

Thomas Buddenbrook's is the mystic unification wherein "the deceptive forms of knowledge, such as space, time, and consequently history" break down, and the *nunc stans,* "enduring eternity," is certain. As Indian mysticism thus filters into German Critical Idealism—a trend initiated by Schopenhauer—time and space are existentially annihilated, and history loses its character as ultimately real. This is what occurs in *Buddenbrooks:* "Nothing ever began and nothing ever ceased. There was only one endless reality." And for the last so-called representative of the family, Hanno Buddenbrook, as well as, later on, for the young Hans Castorp, human salvation lies in an escape from the "flatland" of busy, everyday life with its social responsibilities. It lies in a trancelike state of metaphysical absorption. Only on his descent from the magic mountain did the poet achieve the consecration of life in all its temporality.

We shall follow the long way that leads from Mann's captivation by the eternal to his recognition of the enmity to life in the frozen formations of snow, quartzes, and pyramids in *The Magic Mountain*[15] and *The Beloved Returns*[16]—geometrical forms that lack the very principle of life, the "Die and rise" of integration and disintegration, representatives of "dead eternity," "dreary duration," the "altogether uninteresting" in its lifeless persistence. Over against this crystalline timeless being, the "Praise of Transitoriness" enhances human activity that wrests from the passage of time perennial results. We have indicated, and we are going to point out again, how in Mann's later works the myth is destined to mediate between time and the timeless, eternity and history.

Historical feeling is bound up with the sense of individuality. Inasmuch as he is painfully aware of the bounds of individuation, Thomas Mann's attitude in *Buddenbrooks* cannot be described as unhistorical; rather it is *counter*-historical, not only in principle, as

*"The flight of the lone one toward the 'one and the whole'" (to use a famous phrase of Plotinus) is to Thomas Mann, even in so late an essay as that on "Heinrich von Kleist and His Stories," the proper expression of "metaphysical longing"—the longing for a union which is anticipated by the unity of the individual and the universal in art: the poet finds the self in the heart of the selves and reveals mankind in the guise and disguise of men.

an offspring of Schopenhauerian metaphysics, but also as a revolt against the torn conditions and idleness of the historical life of his time. Somehow it expresses his (and Nietzsche's) aversion to the glitter of the Wilhelmine era and his early apprehension of the imminent catastrophe of the whole historical system. Throughout the decades, from *Buddenbrooks* and *Death in Venice* to *Joseph in Egypt* and *Doctor Faustus*, there is the nightmarish feeling that chaos will come again, that it lurks within the bulwarks of our civilization and threatens the whole defense mechanism, the rigid self-discipline we set up against it. Thomas Buddenbrook is weighed down with "anxiety for maintaining the prestige of the past," and filled with dread "of some eventual historical dissolution and decomposition."

The hope of finding "in nothingness the Whole" soon dies in Senator Thomas Buddenbrook himself, but it gains tenuous realization in his son Hanno, who has inherited from his mother a musical gift not present in the Buddenbrook strain. The "metamorphosis of the *bourgeois* into an artist" [17] is the descent from the world of convention into the realm of origins, but also (to speak with Goethe) into the realm of mere shadows in which actual being is prefigured in an eternal process of "formation and transformation." [18] Thus the sick little artist moves toward translating being into pure, creative representation,[19] the redemption of life through its pure expression, "a unique dissolution . . . a melancholy modulation from one key to another." A tiny motif of one and one-half beats, "a nothing," grows in the course of its development into an expression of the Absolute. "It brings resolution, dissolution, fulfillment, perfect satisfaction." This is a renewal of Thomas Buddenbrook's Schopenhauerian experience on an incipient creative level, as though "curtains were torn apart, doors sprang open, thorn hedges opened up, and walls of fire sank down." [20]

The unbounded "will to ecstasy and decline" [21]—the merging and submerging of the one in the whole, the Tristan motif—here reaches its appointed end in the death and transfiguration of a series of generations. The life of the Buddenbrooks negates itself at last in the fever that consumes Hanno's delicate, boyish frame.[22] The play of life thus ends in the (qualitatively) eternal life of play. With a gesture, whose symbolic meaning he did not fully realize, of course, but which was not wholly foreign to him even so, the little

Johann had already drawn the final stroke under his name in the family album. "I thought . . . I thought . . . nothing would come after that," he replies to his father's reproof. Later on, *Lotte in Weimar* is to show the even more disheartening lot of the epigones, whose play has become an afterplay, whose imitation runs a tortuous course between pure reflections and silly parroting, and whose representation costs them their souls.

This development from rootedness in society, with all its limitation, toward de-radication and liberation through art brings to the fore a fragility concealed in the most luxuriant finite life. To be sure, the youthful romantic melancholy of *Buddenbrooks* and *Tonio Kröger* is soon replaced by a mood more serene and self-composed. Nevertheless there persists throughout a frank recognition of the radical misery of finite existence, so that compassion, *caritas*, embracing "what is doomed to decay," is present in all passion, even of the wildest or most reverent kind.[23]

To this abysmal knowledge corresponds a deep and lasting desire to break through the limits of individual selfhood and henceforth to live in beings of a higher and freer order. This metaphysical yearning, intense though still inarticulate in *Buddenbrooks*, was developed and clarified as Thomas Mann went on to show how the individual enlarges his being through universal reflection and creativeness, through mythical identification and active social solidarity.

But the attraction by boundlessness, no-thingness, the lure of Nirvana remains—for "is not the Nothing a form of perfection," and the perfect the tense of the past? [24] Still, Thomas Mann—the worker, the artist—has never been an addict of the Hindu narcotic (much as he distrusts the overly definite form; a great composer himself, he nevertheless has no taste for the obsession with purity of style in writers such as Flaubert). His viewpoint is not the clear, unequivocal Greek rejection of the "measureless" as that which is not truly being; but neither is it the Hindu's wholehearted embracement of Nirvana. He feels the nothing to be ambiguous in its irresponsible appeal; he both seeks and shuns it, sees it glorified by spirit drunken with speculation and vilified by practical reason. Such unequivocal espousal of a highly equivocal position is characteristic of Thomas Mann.[g]

Spirit Contra Life

Art is a divine gift, giving what the artist needs. It composes his inner chaos.[25] Poor Hanno, however, is not vouchsafed this grace of the sons of God. He is not permitted to stand "underneath God's thunderstorm" and "grasp the Father's shaft" without being burned by it.[26] His life does not find redemption in art. Rather does art redeem him from life. Art leads him out of life, by catering to his will to boundless nothingness. On the other hand, it would be wrong to assert with Schopenhauer that herein a power, enhanced by knowledge of the world's essence, "at last tires of playing and takes a serious turn." [27] Hanno perishes not by reason of his power, not by the tension between life's lust and art's law; he knows only the lust of death; and his music (an offshoot of Wagner's) is but a discharge of this lust. He perishes of weakness, due to the disproportion of spirit and life in his own personal make-up. He lacks the vital energies for real work. Only with the strength of life can art grow beyond it.

In *Buddenbrooks* Hanno's end is still interpreted in Schopenhauerian terms, namely, as the spirit's withdrawal from life's summons, from "this bright, cheerful, slightly derisive warning to turn and come back," which "may reach the spirit on his fevered, alien path, that leads into the cool shades, the peace" of Nirvana.[28] The spirit's *taedium vitae* becomes again a fatal trait in *Doctor Faustus*. In the meantime, however, it is supplanted by the spirit's more or less unhappy wooing of life and its growing readiness to fulfill life's obligations. (It is almost a palinode when Thomas Mann's Goethe anticipates "the horror of death as the spirit's despair when life fails him." [29]) The way of the living spirit, the true way of genius, leads through that inferno of knowledge, the knowledge of Hamlet the Dane, which dooms action as absurd, toward works which are deeds, works of a man whose writing is action, not in spite of all knowledge but because he knows—a knowledge both pitiless and compassionate.

Chapter 4 THE DOMINION OF MAN: THE PERIOD OF *THE MAGIC MOUNTAIN*

> *Le vent se lève! . . . il faut tenter de vivre!*
> "The wind is rising . . . life has to be tried!"
> —PAUL VALÉRY[1]

"Representatives"

Again we start with the problem of the artist, the contrast between art and life, being and representation, such as Thomas Mann saw it in his earlier years. Perhaps it would be better to speak of a contrast between bodily representation by one's whole being and mere representation in the mirror of a work from that mental distance in which the community of being is suspended. The artist does not 'belong'; he is a civic nonentity. From the viewpoint of the burgher, the fellow citizen in Thomas Mann as well as in Tonio Kröger, there is "something utterly ambiguous, utterly disreputable, utterly dubious" in the extra-ordinary which is of the very nature of artistic existence.[2] This verdict applies to all art even though it has to be qualified in accordance with the other dualisms that overlap with that of art and life, namely, the polarity between nature and spirit and, within art itself, between the naïve and sentimental types.

Hence Thomas Mann's concern with the problem of the artist has a sceptical and even somber keynote from the time of *Buddenbrooks* to that of *Doctor Faustus*. His radical suspicion of this mode of existence shows itself early in the exhibition of a whole gallery of poets most of whom (such as Spinell in *Tristan*, Martini in *Royal Highness*) cut rather pitiable figures.

Yet, even a representative writer of the stature of Gustav Aschenbach (in *Death in Venice*) is deeply problematic—in his very dismissal of subversive problems. His is an abortive attempt to overcome the predicament of the modern artist. The reputable author of a canonic art, Aschenbach conjures up the rebellious powers which he abjures, and which take revenge by pulling him down into the abyss. There is prophetic insight in Thomas Mann's rejection of a new classicism whose noble appearance is paid for by the suppression of the unruly spirit. For there is a temptation to 'go beyond' enervating moral and intellectual doubt, to put up the façade of a beautifully integrated life and to adopt the air of a hale and healthy, yet undialectical and artificial artlessness. While Mann cannot help feeling the lure and logic of this development toward a naïveté regained, he parts company with Aschenbach because of a deep respect for the inner chaos, the pressing demands of opposed powers within man, as the ferment of human productivity. Still he acknowledges the identity of his and Aschenbach's existential problems by describing the figures in Aschenbach's earlier works after the model of his own Senator Buddenbrook, Lorenzo Medici, Savonarola, the prince Klaus Heinrich, and the swindler Felix Krull (and in this sequence).

But besides these direct portraits of the creative artist we have, above the realities, the meeting places, and the battlefields of human life, a whole array of utopian existences and pseudo-existences wherein the artist both recognizes and conceals himself.

As early as 1899, we find in "The Wardrobe," a significant, almost surrealistic short story, the figure of the wayfarer who is initiated into life's mysteries just because he is estranged from its conventional order and distinctions.[a] On a different plane—or, rather, on different planes—we encounter the buffoon, the operetta star, the rope-dancer, the fashionable swindler Krull, whose reality is transmuted in the luster of his fake representation.[*] Other features of the artist come out in those glittering "formal existences"[4] who seem to fulfill their duty in mere representation. Such are the mercenary, the courtier, the prince, and in a certain sense even the Olympic gods with their (not altogether enjoyable) freedom from destiny and their "divine indifference." Far removed from humanity, they still represent the human in a deceptive supra-terrestrial splendor and perfection.[5]

High and low parasites, they prey upon life, but also provide it with a brilliant representation of itself; dangerous and endangered natures, they swarm about life, attract it, and are attracted by it;

---

[*] It is symptomatic of Thomas Mann's 'lyricism in disguise' that Krull's careful distinction of a life *like* a soldier from life *as* a soldier appears also in Thomas Mann's own, very personal *Reflections*.[a]

seize upon it for sensuous enjoyment and aesthetic contemplation, and still do not assume any of its common obligations or feel at home within its borders;[b] indulge in irresponsible play and yet may "often be sick to death of representing the human without sharing in it." [6]

Throughout his life, Thomas Mann has been haunted by the nightmare of the artist's ghostlike existence. First of all, he suffers from his inhuman segregation from man, the dark counterpart to that contemplative solitude which is of the very essence of any higher productivity. And he is both seduced and frightened by the uncanny power which is bestowed upon the artist. Is not the charm of art, at the same time, the deadly magic which captures life and disposes of it by giving it the finish of a perfect form, a form which is not of this world? The lust, the horror, and the indictment of vampirism run through Thomas Mann's work from *Tonio Kröger* to *Mario and the Magician* and *Lotte in Weimar* and reach their climax in *Doctor Faustus*. While adhering to it, Thomas Mann has never been fully satisfied by the soothing metaphysical idea that, after all, being reaches its final and definite state by way of pure artistic perfection. The painful ambiguity of this 'final' and 'perfect,' which know no beyond and hold no promise, is a permanent thorn in his flesh. But it is also a goad, inciting ever new attempts to bridge the gulf between art and life.

The arch of this bridge may be thrown from one bank by the artists and their like. Love will enable Tonio Kröger as well as His Royal Highness, Klaus Heinrich, to espouse the cause of a life which, at first, they only represented. But the same process may also take place in the opposite direction. Life may discover its original powers and embark on the way toward genius.

This is, in *The Magic Mountain*, Hans Castorp's good—yet not wholly undeserved—luck. An "average lad," he is not born for the intellectual rank he is going to occupy. He is born for this role even less than the simple but affable and well-intentioned Klaus Heinrich was born for the throne which his elder brother, a true yet weary nobleman, would abdicate in his favor.

Thomas Mann places his young friend on a magic mountain and lets him thus transcend the world of the plain[c]—the *cités infimes*[7]—and, in a way, transcend himself as well. Mediocre though he is in his appearance, he gains the most unusual experience. Not exactly a hero, not so noble a creature as, in his silent heroism, his friend and cousin Joachim Ziemssen, he becomes worthy of being chosen the hero of *The Magic Mountain* because he is venturesome enough to create himself. To be sure, this *se faire* is not a *creatio ex nihilo*. It is due to the conscientious use of the materials of his world, to a deep-seated instinct for the nature and situation of man, and to the moral courage to feel the lust of death and eternity and still decide for the future of life.

The choice of this inconspicuous hero marks the difference between *The Magic Mountain* and the romantic and psychological novels of the nineteenth century. No psychological detail is neglected. What counts, however, is neither what the individual is nor how he came to be it, but what he does with his life, what he personally represents, and how seriously he understands his role. Castorp is not outstanding as an individual, and what happens to him is not extraordinary from the outside. What is alone extraordinary is the sense he develops for the outstanding place of human existence as such.

That he is modest as an individual and significant as a representative makes *The Magic Mountain* an ontology of human life and shows the way Thomas Mann has traveled since *Buddenbrooks* and even *Royal Highness*. While the prince, the formal representative, shares with the artist the melancholy privilege of being born on the heights of mankind, and while, behind his appearance as a political functionary, he is meant to be a symbol of the artist, Castorp must find his way himself, must create his distance from the flatlands and, at the same time, grow into the role of a catholic representative of mankind. No longer is the genius of representation considered the monopoly of a unique and somewhat monstrous being. The narcissism of art is left behind. Hans Castrop is not the poet in disguise. He exhibits the extraordinary possibilities, the genius slumbering in the common man. In his eagerness to understand men and things he rises above the anonymous state of a seeming nobody; he not only earns the distinction of becoming the center of a great composition but centers within himself the forces around him.

The Genius of Malady

Hans Castorp comes from the Hanse town of Hamburg and the family of the blond Hanses, the exponents of life in *Tonio Kröger*. But he is more than this. He is also "Hans the dreamer," a figure out of the German fairy tale. In him life has overcome its own bluntness, its indifference to the spirit, but is also giving up the shelter of time-honored conventions. A child of life, he is to become its problem child. And, as so often happens with problem children, it may be that life is kindly disposed toward the young man just because he boldly embarks on the perilous course of the spirit.

In his mountain abode Hans Castorp is sundered from the busy world of active life and elevated far above it. He is in an expectant mood. At this time the spiritual stimulant of disease takes hold of "the rather simple, though attractive young man" and ennobles him, just as it is to ennoble the modest overseer Mont-Kaw, Joseph's benefactor in Egypt. "Strength is made perfect in weakness." [8]

Illness shares, however, in the ambivalence that marks all of life. Even healthy life subsists only by restoring itself all the time. "Of themselves the elements of our being drift toward disoxidation. Life is enforced oxidation." [9] Hence, Hans Castorp's curious wisdom is no automatic result of the anomalous state which sickness produces. "The agency of the agents is proportionate to the disposition of the patients." [10] The truth of this Aristotelian wisecrack on the part of the erudite devil in *Doctor Faustus* is proved already by the behavior of the guests of the Berghof sanatorium. While Christian, mystic, and Schopenhauerian sympathy with suffering induce man to consider disease in and by itself as a patent of nobility, it actually depends on the individual soul whether malady, shaking as it does the fabric of our being, will help to break the fetters of conventional thought or merely express and favor a bent toward disorder and lasciviousness.

In one of its aspects illness is ignoble and shameless, a product of lustful dissipation. In this capacity, we see it at work in the feverish sensuality of the common males and females who populate the pleasure grounds of the sanatorium and lose themselves in surrender to their libidos. Indeed, the same secretly nihilistic lust becomes fatal even to the valiant Joachim Ziemssen and is the pathological element in his cousin Castorp's love for Clavdia Chauchat. And yet suffering is also man's noble distinction.[11] "The same reasons," declares Nietzsche,[12] "which cause men's depravation, drive the stronger and unusual ones upward—even toward greatness": a phrase that can serve as a guide through the twilight that prevails on the magic mountain. "Illnesses, especially chronic ones, are years of apprenticeship in the art of life and in the formation of personality." [13] Finally, to trace this line of thought back from Nietzsche and Novalis to Goethe's *Wilhelm Meister* (whose godchild the story of Hans Castorp proves to be): "All transitions are crises, and are not crises a form of disease?" [14] In Hans Castorp, disease and the atmosphere of disease serve to bring out a real depth from behind that surface naïveté with which he had contented himself before. The magic mountain becomes his abode just because at bottom he is weary of the seemingly purposeful yet fundamentally meaningless life of his time, weary of its relativities, its unashamed finitude.[15] "The secret of our disgust lies in the futility of the ends that are assigned to our activities": these are words by Barrès, whose intellectual temper, problems, and artistic motifs were very close to the author of *Death in Venice*.[16]

Crisis

This complaint against our own time still rests on a criticism of time as such. The criticism appeals from time to eternity, whereas the complaint appeals from the present to the past and the future. In his 'higher education' man feels the tension between the cultivation of death and the organization of life. Hans Castorp is torn between Naphta's religious, metaphysical principles, the holy obligation of piety, and the technological, humanistic ideas of progress advocated by Settembrini, the "September man." He experiences the encounter between culture and civilization, medievalism and the Enlightenment. He tries to steer a middle course between these two extremes; but, since both he and his creator 'incline' to the precipice of metaphysics, they both, for the sake of balance, will have to lay a certain deliberate emphasis on man's tenancy on earth and loyalty to life. Just as in *Wilhelm Meister*, the watchword "Remember to live!" relegates the *memento mori* to the background of the soul.

The new life is to be communal life. "Perfect form springs up from common soil." [17] But this soil is today no longer that of *Buddenbrooks*, of nineteenth-century society. No longer do we see the bonds of comfortable, healthy, everyday life loosened and untied in *one* family, merely to reappear in another, knotted with the old firmness. Rather are all these ties and privileges of class-citizenship forsaken in the search for something higher, which is ultimately not Hans Castorp's mystical trance but the true world-citizenship, the loyalty to earth and man, for which he is secretly fitted by his education on the magic mountain. His story has "a certain universal significance" [18] also in this regard, that his *déclassement* is not the exceptional one of the artist-outsider and outcast. The whole process of his social uprooting and losing face (at the end, he sits in the sanatorium dining hall at the "poor" Russian table)[19] comes about not because he himself fails to satisfy the bourgeois standards but rather because, in spite of his "commonplaceness" and social normality, he is not really satisfied with bourgeois life. Stale as this workaday world has grown with the decay of the patrician order into that of big bourgeois management, the old Protestant ethos of work meets his needs even less than it does Thomas Buddenbrook's. The religious certainty is a thing of the past, and nothing has come in to take its place. Yet, almost without his knowing it, the depths of his soul cry out for certitude, for a firm foothold somewhere on absolute ground. He must go down into the 'lower world' of the mountain cave in order to be reborn.

Hans Castorp and Wilhelm Meister

Hans Castorp's years of apprenticeship resemble those of Wilhelm Meister. Never quite satisfied with the career of a technician, a bourgeois specialist, he moves out into a richer and wider realm, trying, like Meister and Faust, to assimilate within himself what is assigned to all mankind. The infinite within man proves itself by leading him into all dimensions of life. As prerequisite for this course of education, Hans Castorp and Wilhelm Meister share what seems to be an unbounded receptivity to impressions of all kinds and from all quarters. "It takes all men to make up humanity, just as it takes all forces to constitute the universe." [20]

The relationship between the two novels can be most clearly illustrated by the fact that, in describing Wilhelm Meister, a literary historian of our day, Korff, gives a characterization that also applies precisely to Hans Castorp: "This kind of man pursues the universal, which is life in general—not a particular aim or station within life. He strives for inner totality and development of all his gifts—not for any special competence or specific profession." [21]

Hans Castorp and Wilhelm Meister are both transported into a new and magic world that fills them with wonderment and stimulates their powers of assimilation. Each comes to be "a mirror of the universe, faithful yet by no means merely passive" (to use Schiller's words regarding Wilhelm Meister); "he gathers, as it were, the spirit, the meaning, the inner content of whatever goes on roundabout him, transmutes every dark, inarticulate feeling into a concept of thought, gives each single item a universal form, brings the significance of all things nearer home to us—and thus realizing his own nature, he subserves the purpose of the whole." Both figures are placed in the midst of "imposing authorities," and recover but slowly their self-consciousness against these odds. Neither Meister nor Castorp ever succeeds in making the world outside conform to that within. So far it holds true of either that "his value lies in his own nature and not in any outer efficiency, in his aspirations and not in his accomplishments." [22]

The Growth of Genius

Wilhelm Meister found the half-hidden but ever dominant purpose of his life in the Leibnizian formula of making himself the man he is—which is but a calmer version of Goethe's own titanic urge "to spear up into the air as high as possible the pyramid of my existence, whose base has been given to me, settled and firmly founded." [23] This ethos of self-realization is equally strong in Castorp and Thomas Mann himself. And there are many additional evidences of Hans Castorp's affinity with his creator and the artist in general. It is reflected in his estrangement from time—his own time. And it is reflected in his propensity (at first vague and inarticulate) for the Unconditioned—hence for death, which looms up before him in the snowy grandeur of the high mountains and figures as his intimate in the sanatorium. As Castorp develops, additional proofs of this resemblance turn up: e.g., his universal capacity for mediating between extremes, an attitude akin to poetic justness and artistic irony; the gradual shedding of his bourgeois respectability, a process that makes him brother to all the "lost sons of their class," the poets especially; and other kindred traits to be mentioned shortly.

Hans Castorp, that modest, retiring young man, at last receives from the poet himself the right to characterize his own way to life—the detour that leads through death—as the way of genius. For what is genius but the creative gift of recasting old forms into new, passing through dissolution to order and through non-being to being?

Hans Castorp's growth is the growth of his formative powers as signalized by his mounting imagination, by his visionary dreams and daydreams, culminating in the magic séance at which Joachim Ziemssen is conjured up from the dead. In this weird scene, we find the "clairvoyant, somnambulistic" element in Hans Castorp and his yearning, quasi-Faustian aspirations in an uneasy alliance with a prying, disgusting occultism that smells of the witch's kitchen. If indeed our own existence is regarded as springing from an act of will, should not a supreme concentration of will power avail to summon up the spectral presence of *another's* shade and form? (And is not the artist himself, in his own descent to the "mothers," uncannily akin to the "daring magician," another Doctor Faustus, a nefarious necromancer?)

The growing strength of Hans Castorp's formative skill shows up most conspicuously in his new gift of formulating his thoughts in an easy, elegant fashion. It becomes evident in the new liveliness, versatility, and plastic power of his speech, which eventually gains sway over his native North German reticence, over that unwillingness and incapacity of the solitary individual to speak out and share his thoughts and feelings with others. The silence into which both Hans and Joachim tend to relapse in the face of what they regard as the meddling of other people signifies not only a distaste for idle chatter (this Hans Castorp scorns to the very end) but also a refusal to partake responsibly in the conversation of life. Settembrini, Hans Castorp's social conscience, is outraged at this "German peril," the failure to *respond*—that speechless, stolid insulation, storing up a charge which some day may explode in deeds of fearful violence.[d]

From Schopenhauer's point of view (one which, we may be sure, is never quite absent in Thomas Mann) any such withdrawal into silence can only be considered a gesture of despair, acknowledging man's fate of individuation in the body. To break through—*"Durchbruch"!*—remains, for all that, *the* very craving and watchword in German life. Hence, each new work of Mann's is a fresh attempt to break down the walls that separate being from being. His earlier visions, the divinations of Thomas and Hanno Buddenbrook, by no means lose their validity. Hans Castorp, too, is a metaphysical dreamer who takes a voluptuous "musical" delight in feeling his individuality dissolve in the ocean of the one and the whole. On the other hand, certain motifs come to the surface in *The Magic Mountain* (not all of them for the first time) that are to play a dominant part in Thomas Mann's later thinking.

Hans Castorp's ideal of a fair community of life is but a new way of breaking the fetters of individuality. Others that were foreshadowed as early as *Buddenbrooks* and *Tonio Kröger* are more strongly emphasized in *The Magic Mountain* and will be brought to a climax in the Joseph saga and to a tragic paroxysm in *Doctor Faustus*. The Joseph novels are dominated by the motif of solidarity with the past through tradition and imitation; but *The Magic Mountain* was the first to introduce symbols of such solidarity—the baptismal vessels—bowl and plate—handed down from generations past and inscribed with the names of earlier owners, immortalizing, as it were, their very lives. For centuries the same ceremony had taken place over this bowl, so that in the onlooker there was aroused "a strange, half dreamy, half apprehensive feeling of something transitory and permanent at the same time, of subsistence and change, of recurrence and dizzying monotony." [24] But the idea of repetition and mythical identity goes far beyond the range of historical continuity. Thus, the two great erotic experiences in Hans Castorp's life are first described in rational terms as merely similar and reminiscent of each other, but come more and more to be recognized as mysteriously yet really identical.[25]

However relevant all these factors may be to the story of Hans Castorp's life and growth, the real feeling and atmosphere of the narrative arise from its subtle, far-ranging dialogues. Conversation is the pedagogical and stylistic medium of *The Magic Mountain.* The education of Hans Castorp proceeds by way of conversing and reading (a special kind of spiritual intercourse). His growing inclination and capacity for putting his feelings into clear, coherent form attests to the socializing, humanizing influence of the *littérateur* Settembrini and at the same time brings our hero to the brink of artistic expression. Nevertheless, the work remains a novel of education in the fullest sense. Like his predecessor, the second Wilhelm 'Meister' continues to be an apprentice to the very end. Assimilation is his *modus essendi,* not activity or productive enterprise. If he travels the road of genius and at the end comes close to being a genius himself, it is by reason of his unusual capacity (so familiar to Thomas Mann) for absorbing the ideas of others, that "cunning, sympathetic interest in life, which causes him to find everything worth listening to." Strangely enough, this susceptibility comes to exercise a social function. Serious, attentive "listening" is shown to have a certain magnetic force which draws more and more of what had been a mere aggregate of patients into his circle and, through his eager personality, serves in some measure to bind them together.[26]

The Magic Circle of Reflection (Reflection as Universal Representation)

Although Hans Castorp is not a poet, he nonetheless evinces a trait belonging to a poet's very essence, namely, pure receptivity. In this substratum of the artistic a certain satisfaction is already given to man's yearning to unite his individual life with the life of the universe. The individual is not altogether swallowed up by the universal; but just as art is capable of representing the particular in its universal significance, so Hans Castorp's openness to ideas and impressions of every kind helps him to acquire a universality within his own being. The monad's representation of the universe is here achieved in the sphere of reflection.

This is the real 'plot' and the inner form (*forma formans*) of *The Magic Mountain.* Essentially this is a *philosophical* novel. On the other hand, it is philosophical *poetry* because the universal never appears in its purely abstract form, but always as the consummation of a concrete experience. The universal is embodied

by men and women; it is entangled in their conflicts and endowed
with the grace and life of poetic communication. The unity of the
work is defined by the magic circle of reflection which the young
Castorp spins for himself. From this circle there can be no liberation in the work itself; when the poet releases his metaphysical
dreamer into life—and death—he must forthwith write "Finis
operis," in accordance with the economy of the whole.

Hans Castorp's ecstatic visions and his metaphysical frenzy,
the individual's penetration into the whole, cannot be explained
away as mere excitement caused by a bit of fever. Like the remoteness (at once actual and symbolical) of the high mountains,
the physical state merely occasions and furthers that spiritual deepening and loosening of his human being for which he must have
had a latent desire all along.[e] He is ripe for this experience as the
fruit of his studies and meditations, but also because certain vague
but powerful impressions of his childhood have prepared him for
insights to which man is blinded by life in the "flatlands," the
everyday of existence. Things happen to him because he needs and
cares.

The Way of Genius

While not a genius, Hans Castorp has an original, elemental
relation to the "principle of genius"—to *death*.[27] As for every
genuine poet, so for Thomas Mann death appears in as many forms
as there are types of life. Death is more than the mere *factum bru-
tum* of life's end, and only one of the meanings and interpretations
of which it is susceptible is that of the entrance to Nirvana, the
way into the Absolute, the release from all limitation and bondage
in this earthly life, redemption as privation of any particular form.

This formlessness of death is appreciated by nobody more than
the artist, that misfit in the ordered pattern of bourgeois life; and
no one feels more strongly its seductive power. But this appreciation and feeling are complemented by the will to form, inherent
in the artist as such. The *goût de l'infini* is tempered and set off in
the work of art by the order of its composition. The artist creates
order because he knows chaos, and he is permitted to know it because he knows how to exorcise it.

Death, however, acts in still another way to suspend the form of life proper. For death implies not only formlessness but also the opposite—a kind of lifeless "super-form," [28] which is strict beyond measure. This is the form in which Aschenbach tries to shut himself off from life's disorder. Just as in Leverkühn's austere constructions, the perfect and the definite of which the artist is enamored may appear in a state of petrifaction. The perfect may thus be represented in the tense of the definite past and conform to the words of Baudelaire's "Beauté": "*Je haïs le mouvement qui déplace les lignes.*" [29] This form is as pure as it is unethical, since its face is averted from life. In *The Magic Mountain* it finds a cosmic counterpart in the deathly silence and eternal snow of the high mountains, whose "stony dream, eternal and silent," forms the hostile background for Hans Castorp's dream of humanly beautiful life. Again, in *The Beloved Returns*, the aged Goethe holds up to the sun an opal whose clarity seems too pure for this world and thus symbolizes a state of final perfection in which life itself is eternally stayed. And he is reminded of the pyramids in Egypt's land of the dead.[30] This Egypt, the Egypt of the Joseph legend, not only harbors the lifelessness of what is foreign to life and soul—the crystalline forms—but also piously preserves, in the sacred forms of human tradition, the relics of what has ceased to live.*

In *The Magic Mountain* death thus appears in the forms of rigidity as well as dissolution. In one of its roles it wears the stiff ruff of the Spanish grandee or of the Hamburg or Lübeck patrician on which the chin can rest. This is one of Mann's favorite leitmotifs. Life with its "fear and trembling" needs the inner security and outer support that come from pure and noble form and formal bearing. But Death (the Death in Venice) may also tempt by the vague, alluring gesture of the "pale and lovely psychagogue"—out toward the shoreless eternal sea. "*Homme libre, toujours tu chériras la mer.*"[31]

Death's messenger is beauty, "the holy dread that invades a noble heart at the appearing of a godlike countenance or a perfect human body" [32]—this is Thomas Mann's version of the theme that occurs, at about the same time, in Stefan George's Maximin experience.[33] Beauty is the earthly manifestation of unearthly perfection, a form of being that contradicts itself and is therefore "transitory," marked by death and marking out for death—like Tadzio:

Wer die Schönheit angeschaut mit Augen
Ist dem Tode schon anheim gegeben.

"He whose eyes have once encountered beauty
Cannot live: he is to death surrendered."

Thomas Mann subscribes to these initial lines of Platen's "Tristan," a poem that anticipates the union of love and death in Wagner's opera,[g] giving the aesthete's variation of the Biblical saying that nobody may see God's face and live.

But this is only one aspect of death, just as it is only one aspect of life. Life is neither in hermetic preservation nor in dissolute change. Life is preserved in its decomposition. Death, the *res bina*,[34] is both a cradle and a grave, and a means rather than an end to life. The appeal of death which Thomas Mann never ceases to hear is to be heeded only as it calls for a euthanasia of old forms of life and their rebirth in new and nobler ones.

Just this is the heart-warming knowledge to which Thomas Mann leads his young hero in *The Magic Mountain*. Only "death and lust," *la mort et la volupté*, go together, whereas "the old romantic formula of 'death and love'" (found even in Walt Whitman) [35] is now replaced by the better and truer rhyme of "life and love." [36] Tearing himself away from the lure of white death in the high mountains, that sea of snow and infinite nothingness which reminds him of his "native dunes," Hans Castorp, the dreamer, returns to the trusteeship of life. In a climactic yet fleeting moment, he envisions and espouses a life that is deepened by the sense of responsibility for man's future and by the apprehension of death as the fatal spell and the murderous cult of the past.

The dark seductiveness of death had been familiar to him from early childhood, particularly in the figure of his beloved, half-Slavic schoolmate Pribislav Hippe,* whose Kirghiz eyes "would at times glance sideways and shroud themselves in mysterious darkness." Hans Castorp spoke to him but once[h]—a single occasion corresponding to his single night of love with Mme. Chauchat, the "charming, feline" Russian whose very name suggests the cat and

* "Hippe"—the very name suggests death (The German word *Hippe* means "scythe"). A shadow and a skeleton—an X-ray picture—such is the image Hans Castorp keeps of his other love, Mme. Chauchat.

whose voice has the timbre of Pribislav's, the fatal, compelling magic of "a harsh and sweet enshrouding."

In Thomas Mann's anthropology, Mme. Chauchat is the embodiment of the Slavic, with its dreamy vagueness, its sense of the infinite and the demoniacal, its worship of holy prostitution, its unrestrained caprices and 'deadly' charm. For years Hans Castorp, the well-mannered North German youth, will be under her spell, just as the master-artist Gustav Aschenbach yields to the enchantment of the beautiful Polish boy Tadzio, of the dim gray eyes and "tenderly blurred" speech. In him, Hellenic and Slavic traits are enthrallingly fused into an acrid sweetness that conveys the intoxication of death. Italy's teeming but spiritless *bellezza* and elegant rhetoric have never exerted any lasting influence over Thomas Mann or his main characters.

For a long time these characters were German, above all in that fundamental sense in which Thomas Mann liked to consider himself a *German* artist.[37] They are men of the mean (so he thought), attracted by the extremes of pure form and absolute formlessness, but intent on reconciling them in a work that is no less an expression of the soul for being a construction of the mind. (This is still Leverkühn's passionate desire.) The way through lust, decadence, and even death[38] is the way of genius: the perfect representation of the old life comes from a sphere superior to it and prefigures, with a new perspective, a new form of existence. But this position has to be paid for: Thomas Mann knows with Nietzsche that "each decisive thing grows 'in despite.' "[39] Gustav Aschenbach's art was such a thing, splendid 'in despite,' born "in spite of grief and torture, poverty, desertion, frailty of body, vice, passion, and a thousand hindrances,"[40] So too had Tonio Kröger sunk into adventures of the flesh, into lust and fevered guilt, and in so doing had suffered "unspeakably."[41]

Unspeakably? Did he not have to suffer, in order to speak as a poet? For Thomas Mann, the real task of art coincides with that he once assigned to the German man—to draw order out of chaos "which is wealth." This is the insight he lends to Schiller in the story "A Weary Hour";[42] this is the insight in default of which Aschenbach's art atrophies. "One must have chaos within himself to give birth to a dancing star"[43]—out of the need for an order that composes the disorder of the soul. Lisabeta Ivanovna may disparage Tonio Kröger as a *bourgeois manqué*, and Mme. Chauchat may with equal good nature deride her young German friend for being *un joli bourgeois à la petite tache humide*[44] and make fun of his authentic German combination of *bourgeois, humaniste, et poète*.[45] In the end, however, these Slavic women simply do not know what they are about. They do not understand how the will to form functions as an inner compulsion, winning victory over the *douceur vertigineuse*[i] that besets man, over the "seductive pull toward the inarticulate, boundless, and eternal—toward nothingness."

Though it knows the "enticement of death," Thomas Mann's work becomes increasingly "sympathetic to life." [j] Only in relation to death does the sense of life in its totality, its joy and sorrow, its pleasures and seriousness, reveal itself to the spirit. This revelation occurs first as in a dream, the dawning of life's proper end. "The meaning and value of life consist in its leading us to knowledge—viz., to that knowledge that awaits us at life's conclusion." [46] This saying of Fontane's has been adopted by Thomas Mann and has been given a more and more positive interpretation. Life is embraced with all the more care, tenderness, and compassionate understanding if it is seen against the background of death and with the inner freedom which the true knowledge of its ultimate outcome provides. "Two ways lead to life; one is the usual way, simple and direct. The other is grievous, it passes through death—this is the way of genius." [47]

In this second way attachment and detachment of feeling are united into a power of seizing life's sum total in the mirror of pure, intense experience. This power lies at the basis of all artistic creation and yet, as we are now in a position to see, is no monopoly of the artist's.

Dialogue and Dialectics

The road from death to life, from death's trance to life's wakefulness, runs directly counter to the road of *fin-de-siècle décadence*. This latter looks for a resurrection from life's dream into the awakening of death.[k] The "sympathetic horror . . . insatiably desirous of the obscure and uncertain," Mme. Chauchat's experience of voluptuous self-abandonment, is here "suspended," though not disparaged. It will have to find its place within an order of life in which man himself gains dominion over the so-called contradictions of life and death, nature and spirit, health and disease.[48] This viewpoint enables Castorp freely to appropriate the element of truth contained in the Slavic praise of death. Thus Mme. Chauchat's expression of Christian libertinism, *"Qu'il est plus moral de se perdre et même de se laisser dépérir que de se conserver,"* [49] echoes back to her from Hans Castorp's mouth. The echo is tranformed, however, into the praise of a brave, simple soldier (his cousin Joachim Ziemssen), ready and willing to serve his fatherland.[50]

In this whole development, Hans Castorp's thought moves from a pre-dialectical to a supra-dialectical stage. He sees that, exposed to the solicitations of nature and to the call of the spirit, man must weigh both in the scales of humanity, if he is to "have dominion" over them. Man is not merely the stage on which spirit and nature vie for supremacy; he is himself the protagonist who decides the struggle.

This polarity, inherent in man, permeates every sphere of his existence and sets the tone for his dialectical, dialogic situations. Man's being is a dialogue, inner and outer, within himself, with his fellow beings, and with the powers around, below, and above him. From such interaction between the different spheres of the inner and outer worlds emerge various spiritual types, the *homo Dei, homo humanus, homo faber,* etc. Thomas Mann's fondness for discussion and dialogue, which pervade so much of his work, is explained by the radical significance of the dialectical factor in human life.[1] Social life itself is based on the duality, even the tension, of self and others. This dualism is sharpened to the point of tragedy in the duel between peoples as well as between individuals. The duel between Settembrini and Naphta, for example, is a symptom of the nervous excitement preceding the First World War, one of the premonitions (not understood by Hans Castorp) of the approaching catastrophe.

Thomas Mann's artistry is revealed in the way he depicts the growth of this conflict as it proceeds inevitably toward the breaking off of personal and quasi-diplomatic relations between the two men (representatives of two human powers) and the outbreak of open hostilities. While retaining all their intellectual brilliance and intensity, the disputes between Naphta and Settembrini lose more and more of their vital interest. Not prompted by a sincere desire for mutual understanding, they resemble an exchange of notes followed by a futile and somewhat artificial trench warfare. At the same time they appear more and more tortuous and confused, because in the last analysis the two contestants have more in common than either of them is willing to admit. They fight a civil war within the realm of the spirit. They bear out contradictions which each one bears within himself. All this remains mere play-acting, so long as it takes place in the isolated, hermetically sealed area of the magic mountain. Real discussion can occur only where there are real responsibilities in life, to give the controversy a proper bearing and relevance to our daily existence. Here, however, we are dealing with a pair of uprooted beings (their sickness serving merely to symbolize this deeper fact). How ghostly is Settembrini's "International League for the Organization of Progress"! And, metaphysically speaking (as we have seen), Naphta's illness is simply a pretext to gain him an honorable leave of absence from his Jesuit order.

The Great Pan

The eleventh-hour introduction of the monumental figure of Peeperkorn is artistically justified because, purely through the aboriginal force of his personality, he disarms the two combatants and lays bare the flimsiness of their mental stratagems. The discussions and debates, with their intellectual fireworks, sputter ineffectually against the eruptions of this volcanic nature, awe-inspiring even in its extinction, a figure who subsists, as it were, beyond the opposition of body and spirit. Here we see the personal unity which man fundamentally *is* holding sway over the contradictions which he *has* within himself, and to which he so often succumbs. At the same time we have a presentiment that the final decision between the competing ideologies will be a *personal* decision, made not by way of eristics but by staking one's very existence in life's deadly struggle.

Not only are the shots in the Naphta-Settembrini duel a prelude to the "thunderbolt" of the First World War; the things for which they both stand are intimately related to its conflicting ideologies. One cannot say that the disciple of Carducci, the Freemason and Italian patriot Settembrini, represents the democracies pure and simple; still less that Naphta, the Jewish convert, Jesuit, and amateur Communist, stands for conservative Germany; the relationships cannot be formulated with any such rigidity. Nevertheless, the controversies of *The Magic Mountain* are really an artistic transcript of the polemical *Reflections of an Unpolitical Man,* in which the idea of democracy is bound up with a kind of enlightenment that claims a monopoly on human dignity and complacently moves in sweetness and light, while Germany proper stands somehow for an acute sense of the dark, underlying ground of our existence, revealing itself in the cult of the past and in a trenchantly anti-liberal metaphysics.

Hans Castorp would not be a true German if the voice of this metaphysics did not fascinate him more strongly than the admonishing word of moral order and progress—a word, however, to which he cannot help but listen. In reality he needs both teachers; but, in the early stages of his career, Naphta's influence seems to drown out the "barrel-organ music" of the rational moralist Settembrini. Here too, Peeperkorn's advent marks a decisive change. Castorp, whose being (even when he was in love) had been filled with the cultivation and ecstasy of death, now comes to know the cult and ecstasy of life, comes to know that this pagan joy too has its devoted service and wants its deep eternity.

The master of life comes upon the scene as a mortally sick man from the very beginning—like Lorenzo Medici in *Fiorenza.* Originally, however, his cult of life was not, like Lorenzo's, a compensation for physical weakness. While writers like Tolstoy, Walt Whitman, Gerhart Hauptmann (all dear to Thomas Mann's heart at that time) have contributed to Peeperkorn's make-up, he is also a Dutchman who might have stepped out of the drinking scenes of Jan Steen, Jordaens, or Rubens. *Le roi boît.* But his impassioned life is swallowed up by the fever contracted in the tropics: just as in Lorenzo's monologue,[51] elegiac words from Gethsemane reecho in the wearily sustained pagan mood of Peeperkorn's banquet.[52] The talk about the "great Peeperkorn" reminds us of the fable of the "great Pan"—and his death. Passionately clinging to life as it glides inexorably away from him, Peeperkorn is a man possessed— like Naphta, though in precisely the opposite sense. And like

Naphta, he dies a suicide. The frenzied love of life must "abdicate," like its frenzied hatred. To complete the picture, however, we must add that although that "clear-eyed mentor," the liberal human-ist Settembrini, seems to have gained the day, even he stands "at the end" on very shaky legs, literally as well as figuratively speak-ing.

The lust of the senses fails, like that of the spirit; from neither one comes the liberating word. The Venusberg opens to dismiss Hans Castorp; the magic mountain of metaphysical seclusion does not yet let him go. At this point, we have to come back to the dan-gerous implications of German egotism even in its highest form— religious and speculative self-concern. Such a concern has as its counterpart a thirst for self-abandonment that yields the shudder of voluptuousness, but not the happiness of self-donation. In their incommunicado existence, Thomas Mann's heroes know the silent craving of disorderly love rather than love's sacramental order and brotherly Thou. (The Thou remains a prerogative of the Wal-purgis Night with its dissolute revels.) Here Peeperkorn is of no help, for he embodies only the masculine, imperious passion. Just as Hans Castorp ventures into the language of love only in a foreign tongue and when he is "beside himself," so Peeperkorn's stammering is a stammering of passion, a rhapsodic soliloquy rather than a genuine communication, destined at the last to be swallowed up by a roaring cataract.

The Voices

Real communication, which is the dialogue of love, can occur only when life joins life in communion and with full acceptance of human responsibilities. Such communion issues neither from abso-lute spirit, nor from the cult of the senses, nor again from the pragmatic outlook of sheer intellect; for none of these proclaims both the freedom and the finitude of men in their relations to one another.

Nor does our young hero's thirst for experience, his eager ab-sorption of all stimuli of whatever kind, lead out of this hermetic story. He dreams and ponders about a perfect state of mankind, and he remains in the magic mountain. From his "seven-sleepers' meadow" he neither sees nor hears the signs and admonitions of the time. The contradictions over which he had hoped to gain dominion clash in the duel between Naphta and Settembrini that takes place in the very domain of his seclusion, "blooming with summery blue." From the infra-historical realm of "the mothers," these warning symbols obtrude themselves upon him. They stir his slumber, but they do not awaken him. In a spiritualistic séance, there appears to him the figure of his cousin Joachim Ziemssen in field gray with a steel helmet. Strangely enough, the watchwords of reality reach him even through the somnambulism of music. But while the phonograph records from *Aïda, Carmen,* and *Faust* (of which Hans Castorp had taken charge in the sanatorium) herald our duty to serve on life's battlefields,[m] fundamentally, music is a seductive power, metaphysics in disguise,[53] luring us into a "boundless land" of "laughing liberty" and "happiest enchantment"; thus the voice of duty is drowned in ecstasy and trance.

Hans Castorp knows what he does in succumbing to the siren song of German romanticism.[n] In Schubert's "Linden Tree" he is able to recognize that inward, metaphysical yearning for the calm of death which was to attain its most exalted expression in the "soul magic" of *Tristan.*[o] This little song becomes to him a symbol of his world, the world of metaphysics. It stands for all that was deepest and deadliest in the German character and, largely as a result of its influence, in the whole prewar world.[p] For this reason Hans Castorp loves it very dearly, with that passionate yet "sceptical love" which knows its own inclining toward the fair and homesick song to be the soul's decline into the dark mother-country of death.[54] He has fallen prey to this nostalgia, just as his nation has, the nation of Schopenhauer and Richard Wagner. He has this song on his lips—singing it unwittingly—when he fades from our sight on the battlefield amid the storm's tumult.

The Return to Life

But he dies, so we are to believe, not only *with* it, but *for* it as well. That is to say, he is ready to atone for his loving it, to atone with his very life and in the midst of his brothers. His confession of sin is, at the same time, a confession to the earth, the challenge of which he and his like had failed to meet in their metaphysical flights. "Thus he sank upon his knees, face and hands raised to heaven, which, however dark and sulphurous, was no more the grottoed roof of the mountain of sin."[55] Such conversion is not discredited by the fact that it lies in the shadow of tragedy and is the "yea" to life uttered by a man who is marked for death; nor by his joining a community that yearns for death and is drunk with blood, though Hans Castorp's dream of a fair state of mankind living in serenity and courteous composure cannot come true in so unholy a time.

Thus at last, on death's very threshold, the way of genius comes for Hans Castorp to its proper (and bitter) end. This way, long since recognized by him, leads through the passion for death to the love of life. So "life's problem child" finds his way back from the heights of metaphysical solitude into the plain of common struggle and social responsibility.

They are *fleurs du mal* that thrive on the soil of a metaphysics drunk with death. The voice of duty, the "order of the day," cries out against drowning in the infinite inane. Though such an absolute may imply the coincidence of all opposites, life compels us to make a choice, to take a position on one side or the other. At the bar of human conscience, of the categorical imperative, and of the "critical principle" of the primacy of practical reason—before these, the metaphysics of decadence stands condemned as "*the* evil." [56]

Speculation, reflection, passion—these are the complementary intoxicating powers that dominate *The Magic Mountain* and prevent the dream of man's real kingship from coming true. To be sure, sexual passion and metaphysical reflection seem *prima facie* identical with Schopenhauer's Will (focused in sex) and its antagonist, Representation (culminating in pure spirit). But Thomas Mann's thought, having been heterothetic (bipolar) in his youth, veers more and more to the dialectical view that all antitheses derive from and tend toward an ultimate unity. Faithful to his mission as a mediator between extremes, Hans Castorp speaks of his "phlegmatic passions," [q] passions curbed by philosophical patience, considerateness, a sense of justice and understanding. Passionate reflection and reflective passion both make for the universalization of our being and experience, i.e., they teach man to realize the universe within himself by way of inner expansion and to grasp a universal significance in the individuals with whom he enacts the drama of life. Yet, vigorous as this inner realization of unity and universality may be, it is not matched by the capacity for giving the idea of man an objective existence. Neither universal passion nor universal receptivity and reflection have the virile power to bring such a world of man into being. And when the field of active life opens up in the very end, it is the battlefield where the vision of an integrated humanity dies in the murderous flames of hatred, and European life, the life of the world's youth, is torn to pieces. "Can it be that out of this universal feast of death, out of this evil, feverish conflagration—Love shall rise some day?" [57] While fervent hope and resolution grew in the soul of its author, *The Magic Mountain* must literally end upon this note of interrogation and dismiss the reader into life with a personal, all-important question destined to burn itself into his conscience.

The universal life so ardently desired by Thomas Mann and the creatures of his imagination cannot be gained by any metaphysical leap over the concrete, particular items of everyday living. It can be gained only by entering into these particulars with the sense for a universal communion and community of existence, shown in action and proved in sacrifice. Words of love like "humanity" and "democracy" in the Thomas Mann of today stand for some such attitude, whereby life's conditions are transformed by unconditional acceptance of the risks and responsibilities which they involve. Slowly and grievously learned, these words speak not of a passionate (and hence painful) love for man in his actual state but of a considerate, resolute, and respectful love for mankind, i.e., the idea of man. Defamed in Nazi Germany, they were far from popular in the earlier Germany of 1914 or even 1924. Yet Thomas Mann felt that he who "consumed his life in self-conquest" and at last "swore allegiance to the flag" of brotherly life, like his Hans Castorp, lifting himself above the abysmal passion, the metaphysical frenzies of Wagner and Schopenhauer—that such a one had in his heart already "the new word of love and the future which he did not yet know how to pronounce." * [r] This does not mean that Schopen-

---

* These formulations go back ultimately to Nietzsche's psychology and to the moral of his fight against Wagner. This is why in a parallel passage—in the speech on Nietzsche in 1924 (*Bemühungen*, 331-335)— almost the same words recur with reference to him. The very fact, however, that at the same time they were meant to apply to Hans Castorp (even though with Nietzsche in mind) shows the mounting esteem which our simple hero has won for himself in the hearts of both author and reader.

hauer's yearning to escape the bounds of individuality is thwarted or denied, but rather that it begins to bear fruit in the soil of human society. This attitude, reached only after a long struggle against German, patrician, artistic self-concern, marks Thomas Mann's penance and that of his hero, Hans Castorp. Historically speaking, it was a call to the German people, who read and praised his work but declined to follow his ideal of social humanism.*

---

* The role which the problem of *time* plans in Thomas Mann's writings will be studied in connection with the Joseph saga. For that survey we reserve our account of *The Magic Mountain* in its character as a "time novel."

Chapter 5 THE MYTH OF THE SOUL: THE PERIOD OF THE JOSEPH NOVELS

A. From *The Tales of Jacob* to *Joseph in Egypt*

All the world's a stage.

—SHAKESPEARE

Gestaltung, Umgestaltung,
Des ewigen Sinnes ewige Unterhaltung

("Formation, transformation,
Eternal meaning's endless recreation")

—GOETHE

Impotence of Formal Representation

The Muses' grace, falling upon their chosen favorites and promising eternity in the form of the spirit, is not freely bestowed. It is the fruit of *renunciation*, the reward of that "creative self-limitation which is of the essence of a work of art."[1] Wholeness of life comes to him, and to him alone, who in freedom of spirit has learned to sacrifice his life as a whole.[2] This is the Goethean motif of absolute resignation. Such resignation is more than an artistic phenomenon or a token of weakness; in Goethe it is an act and state of abundant life. His artistic discipline reflects that self-discipline which is a part of his civilizing, educational mission. Following Goethe, Thomas Mann comes gradually to recognize the social function and moral obligation of the writer. Hence he feels more and more estranged from artistic asceticsm, in both its romantic version and its anti-romantic counterpart.

In its romantic form, devotion to art means abdication from life, an idea that springs from the romantic's quarrel with modern life as such. This mood appears in protagonists of romanticism like Jean Paul, and even in the anti-romanticist Flaubert; it lives on in Wagner and Ibsen, Rodin and Cézanne; it dominates at least one period of Rilke's life; and in the early works of Thomas Mann it is responsible for that paradoxical, haughty, and envious attitude to-

ward life which combines the praise and affirmation of art with suspicious criticism of it.

The artist in little Hanno Buddenbrook senses "how beauty
hurts, how it plunges one into depths of shame and yearning despair,
and eats up his courage and fitness for everyday life." [3] "The representation of life absorbs *all* one's energies. . . . Renunciation is our
pact with the Muse . . . and *life* is our paradise lost"—thus the
poet Martini coughs out a confession to the prince who, in the
seclusion of his royal highness, shares the fate of being at once a
brilliant representative and a poor phantom of life.[a] "One must
have died, in order to be purely creative"—this had been said already by Tonio Kröger.[4] And the figure of the noble martyr
Sebastian is "the fairest symbol" of Aschenbach's art.[5]

All this, however, expresses only a partial truth. Its inadequacy
becomes apparent in just the degree to which the poet works his
way back into life and comes to recognize that in giving himself to
art he has not lost but realized himself—as the mouthpiece of his
people.[6] The more concrete experiences of later life restrict youth's
absolutes to their relative values, leaving them, however, the function of extreme possibilities. Since it remains true that "the sense
of sacrifice is the sense of all art," [7] creative potency in the *representation* of life is always in danger of being purchased at the cost
of impotency in real life, and the more so, the more rigorously the
artist persists in his cultivation of pure and mere form.

Why does the poet Spinell in *Tristan* never need a shave? [8]
Why does Tonio Kröger touch upon the ticklish motif of the
"prepared papal singers"? [9] "His Royal Highness" recoils at the
chilly and empty life of devotion to a formal role which, like the
cold silvery hall of his castle, is "beyond convenience and comfort"
—pure representation for its own sake.[10] And *Joseph in Egypt*—
three years after the temporary collapse of Thomas Mann's hopes
for a new and better order of man[11]—presents a new figure cheated
of any true efficacy, the eunuch Potiphar (Peterpê), "pure . . .
but wholly sterile," a clay colossus of high, mild, and charming nobility, yet without substantial function. Futile though stately, he
stands forth as a melancholy symbol of all specious representation,
within a world built on representation as the rock of being, the
early world of the East which sets the stage for *Joseph and His
Brothers*. Potiphar is "pure form," "purposeless adornment," a

superfluity of smiling conversation that scorns any concern with
serious matters and remains aloof from the business of settling things
with one another.[b] The atrophy of nature in Peterpê presents an
affinity to the artist, to all that is suspect in his creating of beautiful
appearances, all that is unsubstantial and fruitless in his relation to
the real world. His is the game which Goethe occasionally ascribes
to the poet: the sowing of kisses, and not children, butterflies and
glowworms of the spirit whose light soon fades, instead of "solid
things" that endure.[12] Peterpê's smile has the melancholy that comes
from a feeling of "hollow dignity." He ever requires support from
the courtliness and devotion of those about him.

The delusiveness of his appearance and formal perfection is offset by young Joseph, the poetic dreamer, but also the coming man
of an age to come. Potiphar is merely a victim in the expiatory
sacrifice that his parents, out of the darkness of old Mother Nature,
offer to the light and spirit of a future age, as if the strength of the
spirit could ever come from the castration of nature. Joseph, on
the other hand, dedicates his youth to chastity in the pride of
the spirit and in obedience to a higher call—perhaps also in expectation of his "time of enfranchisement." He himself braids the
wreath of myrtles, the herblet touch-me-not, as a symbol of his
sacred destiny; and he guards the purity of this mission against the
temptation of a love that he views as licentious and forbidden.[13]

Power of Mythical Representation

Thus Potiphar exemplifies only one side of the artist's existence.
Even so, his significance transcends that of mere impotence. Both
courtier and artist may be impotent and in need of assistance;[14] but
is this not only the shadow and the human travesty, as it were, of
divine supra-sexuality—or bisexuality[c]—and the divine need of love?
Amid all his worldly splendor, Peterpê suffers from this solitude
just as do the lovelorn poet and the jealous god.

The divine has correspondences in the human. "Fluid is the
bond beween earth and heaven, and you have only to dwell upon a
single phenomenon and it will break into a double image." [15] Hence
both Thomas Mann and his young hero, Joseph, see and depict in
Potiphar a number of grades and transitions from impotence to
omnipotence. Joseph's relation to Peterpê, and to others as well, is

first of all determined by his relation to God. For him, God's countenance shines through that of Peterpê, though the two faces do not become one. Both are "the Lord." When Peterpê takes his after-dinner walk, it is—as in Genesis 3:7—"the Lord who walks in the garden, when the day has cooled." [16] "Lovest thou the Lord?" asks Mont-Kaw, Potiphar's major-domo, and Joseph replies by uttering the profession of faith: "with all my heart and with all my soul and with all my mind." [17] The alliance into which both enter on Peterpê's behalf is for a Joseph a kind of holy covenant.[18] In the countenance of the Father who saves Joseph from succumbing to temptation, the paternal features of Jaakob, Mont-Kaw, and Potiphar are strangely interwoven. Yet this face "bore still other features transcending these similarities and altogether more powerful." [19] And the trial scene of the last chapter, in spite of all the ironical lights playing through the narrative itself, somehow foreshadows the mood of the Last Judgment. Potiphar adopts the role and even employs the imagery suggested to him by Joseph on their first meeting. Allegedly he does not allow the human heart to interfere with his sentence. The *pater familias* acts as God-Father and feels his word to have the animating power of the divine spirit.[20] He is the Lord who judges, the Lord in whose sight everything lies naked and open, and who silences the foolish gossip that he "pays heed to nothing on earth, except perhaps the repast. . . ." [21]

This mode of representation, which has in it something of parody, lends itself to the content of the novel and may be justified in a threefold way—from the world represented by the artist, from the traditional interpretation of the Bible, and above all from the very nature of artistic vision. For Thomas Mann still regards as valid his early insight that poetry means self-exhibition and universal representation at once.

In the spirit of the myth, as well as in that of Schopenhauer, Thomas Mann is prompted to make a new attempt at abolishing those boundaries which the intellect erects between one being and another, between the ego and the non-ego. These sharp divisions have their footing neither in primary experience (e.g., that of children or of primitive peoples) nor, e.g., in the moral or aesthetic life, both of which presuppose an original communion between being and being. "Is the human ego a thing imprisoned in itself and rigidly shut up within its borders of flesh and time . . . ? Not al-

ways has the distinction between spirit in general and the individual
spirit had such a hold over men's minds as it does in our day, which
we are leaving behind" [22] to trace the course of Biblical history and
thus to renew our own life at its historic sources.

The Principle of Simultaneity

By himself the mere individual is but the result of an internal
decomposition of the common spirit; in this state of exclusiveness
and isolation from the whole he cannot be truly understood. "The
concept of individuality is . . . continuous with categories like
unity and totality, the Whole and the All." [23] The prehistoric,
myth-making Near East, which is the scene of the Joseph epic; the
mystical interpretation of the Bible, the way for which had been
paved in the Old and New Testaments themselves, and especially
by St. Paul; and finally the structure of poetic experience, as understood by Thomas Mann—they all recognize such continuity. All
three are dominated by the principle of *simultaneity*, whose vehicle
is representation of one in the other. Thus representation, the poet's
forte, is rediscovered as the formative principle of that ancient
world re-produced and glorified in the Joseph novels. The aging
Goethe of the *West-Eastern Divan* entered into just such a primeval
world and was entranced, rejuvenated, and greatly strengthened by
this "recognition as in a mirror, this dream-play of metempsychosis,
mystic and serene." [24] In like manner Thomas Mann was struck
by the Old Testament world as it lives, for instance, in the Agga-
doth of Talmud and Midrash, because there he found the mode of
his own activity, i.e., representation, recognized as a general law of
human conduct, and its universal significance dimly anticipated. But
this Jewish-Hellenistic mysticism is in itself a sort of modernistic
version of an even more ancient mode of thought. "In the life of
the human race the mythical marks an early and primitive phase, but
in the life of the individual a late one, fully mature." [25]

Thomas Mann thus views this mythical world partly as its
commentators have understood it for many hundreds of years: [26] as
pointing backward and forward, giving rise therefore to the method
of concordance between the Old and New Testaments; a world in
which one and the same being makes its appearance in various
figures; a world of magical identity between the son of God and the

son of man; a world of ancient prototypes to be kept as the very standards of actual life; a world in which "the same eternally repeats itself and flows eternally" (Goethe). In this way, all appearances come to be symbols of other things, and form a world of relationships at once mysterious and manifest. "Whithersoever he turned, his soul was struck by allusions and correspondences, diverted and lured so far afield that past and to come were mingled in the present moment and his gaze was blurred and broken, as in states of deep reflection," says Thomas Mann of Jaakob, in whose world "spiritual rank and 'significance'—this word taken in its strictly literal sense—depended upon the range of mythical associations and their power to permeate the moment." [27]

In this structure of Oriental life Thomas Mann hails the feeling for what his beloved Novalis had called the "utterly forgotten" doctrine of "mutual representation throughout the universe." [28] "Everything used to be considered a manifestation of spiritual forces; today we see nothing but deadness and mechanical repetition, which we do not really comprehend. The meaning of the hieroglyph is lost; we live on the fruits of better times." [29] The aim of the Joseph saga is precisely that of making repetition vital and meaningful once more.

But Novalis is not altogether right. History and myth, historical and mythical consciousness pervade one another. The mythopoeic powers (and pseudo-mythic machinations) have grown stronger again with the anti-individualistic tendencies of our own time. Mythical identification, however, need not be a regressive feature. Its place is not only in infantile and primitive mentality. As *imitatio*, it is a constituent of all living tradition. Thomas Mann is eager to point out not only that Jesus may have interpreted and arranged his life and death in the image of the "suffering servant" of Deutero-Isaiah and the 22nd Psalm, but that chains of mythical identifications, reaching back to Miltiades, also run through Alexander's and Caesar's lives and from there to Napoleon; and that Cleopatra is Ishtar-Astarte-Aphrodite in person and acts in life and death the role of the Egyptian Ishtar, namely, Isis. She is *bedeutend* (significant) in the sense of antiquity: she is and knows what she represents.[30] And our own existence becomes symbolic through the image in which we see and make ourselves.

Excursus on Time: The Degradation of Time

In Thomas Mann's Early Writings

It is the poet's peculiar gift to create symbols which show the universal in the individual and the essence of things in their impact on man. He brings to a focus the elemental and historical forces dispersed in time and space. Hence every view of things must be congenial to him which overcomes this dispersion in some such way as mythical participation does. Kant and Schopenhauer had taught that spatio-temporal order is appearance and not ultimate reality, a doctrine confirmed by Thomas Mann's early feelings and impressions. Schopenhauer and Nietzsche, moreover, reverting to the Greek example, had changed the symbol of time from a straight line to a circle, the figure of eternity always turning back upon itself. In this way, the coincidence of the time-pattern as such with the pattern of its contents was brought to light. For it was precisely the recurrence of content that first suggested the circle as an adequate symbol of time.

The fading of our consciousness of time and space had been depicted by Thomas Mann in the traveler of his short story "The Wardrobe," as early as 1899. This Albrecht van der Qualen got off the same train (did he not?) that brought the young Thomas Mann to Italy. He lives, he really does not know where, for "everything must be up in the air." Actually he lives in the world of the story. "He had no watch. . . . He did not like to be reminded of the hour, or the day of the week, and even with the calendar he had no truck. Some time ago he had dispensed with the habit of knowing the day of the month, the month of the year, or even the year itself."[32]

In The Magic Mountain

The last but one stage of life on the magic mountain is precisely a metaphysical dream-state in which Hans Castorp (not so young any more) goes farther and farther astray from the order of normal life. "He no longer carried a timepiece. His watch had fallen from his night-table; it did not run any more, and he had not bothered to have its measured rotation restored—for the same reason that he had long since given up using a calendar, whether to keep track of what day it was or to foresee a coming holiday—namely, for the sake of his 'freedom,' his strolling on the strand of eternity abiding now and forevermore. . . ." [33]

Taken as a whole, *The Magic Mountain* is certainly a "time novel," [34] above all because time is its theme, the object of a thoroughgoing experiment and the victim of a shrewdly conceived plan of annihilation. Time's claim to being self-subsistent is challenged; its structure is shown to depend upon our way of dealing with it; thus, its contraction or distension is a complicated function of human concentration or distraction.

As a bourgeois, young Castorp had been familiar with time in the form of a straight line, a course no longer directed by divine providence but laid out in the plains of human life; the way of a finite being striving to obtain the means for certain temporal and always preliminary ends. To such a being time is precious, a commodity not to be wasted or squandered. Even up in the mountains time appears, at first, as weighty and fraught with interest. There are many new things to observe, the telling of which, it seems, will never end. But then, all at once, time begins to shrink and grow empty, thanks to a technique of living that makes boredom and diversion "hard to distinguish sometimes." For "What we call boredom is rather a pathological waste of time resulting from monotony" and the tiresome routine of existence. [35]

In the sanatorium pastime serves to kill time. The medical regime, on the other hand, articulates the day and cuts it up into small pieces, with the result that every day is of the same pattern as every other. Time thus loses more and more of its inner distinctions, as the individuality of its component elements is blurred. While the minutes are counted, e.g., when taking one's temperature, time as such no longer counts. It is spent ever more carelessly. Life's progress is suspended in the circle of repetitions described by the hands of the clock. This repetition is no longer *experienced*. It lapses into mechanical, "outer recurrence." [36] With all this monotony, such scrupulous care is taken to keep people occupied that this pseudo-life comes to absorb all their attention. At the beginning, the noisy machinery of life in the plains, protesting against the lofty existence of the 'mountaineers,' had still sounded, though faintly and afar off; but now at last it has died away. To go back once more and serve in everyday life, one must "desert to the colors." [37]

To all appearances, life has become carefree, because every other care is swallowed up by caring for one's bodily well-being, whose real precariousness is never admitted. All this would be of no more than pathological interest had not, in Hans Castorp's case, the whole process of loosening life's bonds led to a true "ecstasy" and separation from the world. Obsessed by *"le goût de l'éternel,"* under the growing spell of "hermetic magic," [38] he sees opening up to him a medium of life both new and deeply familiar, the medium of an aimless but strangely significant wandering:

> *Du zählst nicht mehr, berechnest keine Zeit,*
> *Und jeder Schritt ist Unermesslichkeit.* [39]

> ("Time does not count, nor dost thou count the tide.
> Immeasurable is thine every stride.")

Lost in the sand dunes, the damp, salty taste from the sea of eternity on his lips Hans Castorp is completely sidetracked from the normal march of time.[d]

Time varies with and is determined by the time sense, while the time sense varies with and is determined by the sense of life. The very contents of time gain their temporal structure in accordance with one's basic outlook. In like manner the *nunc stans* of eternity is a mode of our experiencing things, of our taking them under a definite aspect, *sub specie aeternitatis*. In accordance with this mode, "the eternal lights begin to sparkle" when "the din of the day's battle has died away." Out of enlightenment and intoxication grows Hans Castorp's sensual-supersensual vision of life; out of the polarities of existence grows his vision of man as a whole, man as both the source and the master of the oppositions between sense and the senses, liberty and piety, intellect and spirit.[40]

But the growing breadth and depth of Hans Castorp's understanding remain within the sphere of his inner life and the "pedagogical province" of *The Magic Mountain*. Neither his primarily receptive nature, nor his scientific studies and metaphysical experiences, nor the milieu of the sanatorium can supply that power of initiative which converts an idea into action and reality. Almost to the end, until the thunderbolt of the First World War awakens him from his mystic trance, the world remains for him a matter of 'intellectual representation' rather than a challenge to his responsible will. The Platonic man, having found his way out of the cave and into the light of day, goes back to share the discovery with his brethren. But the metaphysical dreamer is prone to continue his stroll along eternity's shore. Hans Castorp "makes bold to take shadows for real things and things for shadows." [41]

This "simple youth" [42] turns into a kind of legendary figure, inhabiting a world of fairy-tale arithmetic and fairy-tale space-time. Like the Seven Sleepers (Hans Castorp spends seven years on the magic mountain), he forgets about actual time, and so do we, as we become immersed in the legend. For the world and time of the story as such are unreal—an imaginary world and an imaginary time, conjured up by the story-teller, "the rounding conjurer of times gone by." [43] The story draws forth ideas and elements that were scattered in the past, and welds them into the immediate presence of a dream. "De-realization," removal from reality, and realization of a new and wondrous order of life are here involved, both in the form of narration as such and as one of the themes in this particular story. It is a form of serious play, a revision of ancient wisdom in the light of modern analysis.

The metamorphosis of time, so characteristic a device of Thomas Mann's generation, occurs throughout his work. With him it is an evaluation of his philosophical heritage and leads into the myth. The magic of *Death in Venice*, for instance, lay precisely in its power of mythical transformation, a kind of holy distortion of the world in which we normally live.[44] So it is in *The Magic Mountain*. What began apparently as a psychological time novel can pass almost imperceptibly into the realm of the mythical and mythological.

In *The Magic Mountain* the mythical time-form and the mythological categories of time transfigure first of all the recent past. In the medium of Hans Castorp's dream life his outer world recedes from the daylight of practical consciousness into the twilight of the myth. In addition to this, the mythical epoch as such is already taken into consideration—experimentally, so to speak. The chapter "By the Ocean of Time" contrasts two viewpoints, the microscopic view of the insect and the "bird's-eye view that borders on the divine, where a thousand years are as a day." "It would not be hard to imagine creatures, perhaps living on one of the smaller planets, whose time-economy is a miniature of ours, creatures for whose abridged existence the brisk, tripping gait of our second-

hand would have the sluggish, thrifty proceeding of the hand that
marks the human hours. Contrariwise, one may conceive of people
in a world so spacious that its time-system, too, has a vast, majestic
stride, and the ordinary distinctions between 'just now' and 'in a
little while,' 'yesterday' and 'tomorrow,' cover an immensely wider
range." [45]

In Joseph and His Brothers

One sees how a wide time span is associated in consciousness
with a spatial span of comparable breadth. In latter-day "little
Europe," with its delicate organization, its finely meshed patchwork
of countries, and its peoples crowded together, nobody ever has any
time, whereas the "children of the East" can afford to be "bar-
barically grandiose in their time-consumption." [46] In the early days
of life, under the wide-arching Eastern skies, mankind had a fabulous amount of time; hence the fable-telling poet loves those leisured
ages and spacious lands. He is glad to linger with the men from the
edge of the Arabian desert, to bear them company on the long,
weary journey over the gleaming sands, the well-nigh endless
journey through the almost endless space that lies between the
patriarchs and their primeval world, and the highly sophisticated,
"contemporary" world of late Egyptian culture. To the impatient
modern reader the account of this journey may seem a bit long-
winded; but the author's very aim was to give his story the length
and breadth of those periods that dispose of infinite time with a
simple but imposing gesture. The poet's technique consists in the
reproduction of that time-feeling that is akin to timelessness. And
Thomas Mann's true reader is the one who freely yields to eternity's
spell.

" 'At the same time'—that is the very nature and essence of all
things; they appear in disguise, one in the mask of the other; yet
the beggar is nonetheless a beggar for the fact that a god may possibly be dissembled in him." [47] In those far-off times, "there was
no call to decide between being and significance." [e] When identity
of being is determined by identity of meaning and function, the
various distinctions introduced by time as *principium individuationis*
fall by the wayside.*

* In a passage of *The Magic Mountain* in which the poet ventures
farthest out beyond the limits of everyday life, we find the time-se-

Thus, Abraham, ostensibly Joseph's great-grandfather, is in reality a multiple appearance who wanders through time, typifying the homeless man of God. Thus every generation is again given the same wise servant Eliezer; and thus Jacob's wicked brother, Esau the Red, is to be identified not only with Edom, his people (even as Jacob-Israel is one with his people); in addition he always reappears as foil or counterpart to the protagonists. He was Cain to Abel, Ishmael to Abraham and Isaac; he was Seth-Typhon, the murderer of Osiris; he will be Judas to Christ, and Hagen to Siegfried;[48] he is Moloch, and in the starry heavens he is blood-red Mars, the fire-planet; he prefigures Goethe's Mephistopheles; he is the serpent, standing for Evil as such, not necessarily evil in his individual nature, but the Evil in the universal function assigned him as his role.[49] Even today we use the singular exclusively in referring to such natural elements as the air and water that we breathe and drink, or the demon fire haunting this place and that. Just so, the old but ever new stories know nothing of individuals, but only of powers and potencies in different manifestations, powers that stage the same play over and over again.

In this way, the repetition of beings and events is clearly more than the mechanical swing of nature's pendulum. Certainly the idea of this recurrence is not wholly foreign to Thomas Mann. It is part and parcel of his creaturely feeling, as well as of his inheritance from Schopenhauer and Nietzsche, and appears as a structural element as early as in *Buddenbrooks*. This work begins (to mention but one or two instances) with the banquet in the spacious old house on the Mengstrasse, which the Buddenbrooks have just acquired from the Ratenkamps, that "family, at one time so prosperous, who had built and lived in the house until a fatal decline and impoverishment forced them to move away"; and the book ends, again "in order that fate may be fulfilled," [50] after the sale of the house to the *nouveaux riches* Hagenströms, with Gerda Buddenbrook moving to Amsterdam: "she took nothing with her and left as she had come." [51] In like manner, the precarious relationship between the brothers Johannes and Gotthold is to a certain degree recapitulated in that between Thomas and Christian: but the whole

---

quence overthrown by means of purposive anachronism. In the spiritualistic séance mentioned before, we saw Joachim Ziemssen conjured up from the tomb in a strange guise—wearing the uniform of a soldier in the coming World War.

treatment is so objective and delicate that only very slowly does it dawn upon the reader that he is witnessing the same drama with a different cast of characters and in different settings of political economy. In both *Tonio Kröger* and *The Magic Mountain* an additional step is taken. Here the *hero* himself senses the typical in all appearances; he feels a more or less extensive identity between seemingly different persons of his world. But not until the Joseph saga are the figures themselves aware of their own identity with others who have played the same role, and of the obligations thus incurred.

The Rehabitation of Time

But is it not obvious that the character and the phenomena of life do not remain the same when colored by however secret an awareness of recurrence and contrived by however dark a will of repetition? Following Schopenhauer, Thomas Mann insists, as late as 1943, in *Joseph the Provider*, on the present as being the very nature of life and on presentation as the very work and offering of art. The tenses of the past and the future are said to be only the mythical and even popular appearances of life. Now it is quite true that the living past and the living future are the depths which belong to the fullness of the present moment and into which this present (a *praesens de praeteritis*, a *praesens de praesentibus* and a *praesens de futuris*)[52] extends. The development of the Joseph stories into the activism of *Joseph the Provider* belies, however, a ruling out of time in which time as passage and, therefore, the preciousness of the passing moment are definitely denied. What Thomas Buddenbrook once experienced is still true in the Joseph legends, in the dim realm of mythical consciousness—that in reality "nothing began and nothing ceased"[53]—but it is no longer the entire truth. If one wants to cling with Thomas Mann's Goethe to the circle as an image of time, the circle will be, at least, the symbol not of changeless eternity but of a permanence which is, at the same time, "restless intensification, enhancement and perfection."[54] This would account for the time which yields results, though not fully for the stretch of time within which the works of the day have to be done.

In fact, *Joseph and His Brothers* shows just this duration in change and change in duration. While "the well of the past" is certainly "unfathomable" and some of the typical roles of the figures of the play, as for instance that of "the Red One," go back to times immemorial, some others are newly created either within history or at what Jaspers calls the "axis time of world history," when the foundations of our modern world were laid. (Thomas Mann's Abraham is one of the founders of this new type of man.) And, as we mentioned before and shall see presently in more detail, they are all in a process of perpetual re-creation and more or less free personal renewal. Joseph *is* what he represents ("I am it") and he is it *not* because he is it in his own individual way; "the general and the typical form vary when they find their fulfilment in the particular. . . . This is the very nature of civilized life that the taking and binding ground and the outlines of a classical pattern are filled out in the God-given freedom of the I; there is no human civilization without both, the one as well as the other." [55] *

This is the insight Thomas Mann lends his hero; he has it "since 'he' came to years" [57] and grew beyond the raptures and twitches of his youth; secretly it is a personal confession of the author himself. The principle of individuation is still in disrepute. But the historical person represents more than the single individual is. We are our history in response to our personal and historical calling. History and the myth do not exclude one another. History passes into the myth, and the myth provides the ground patterns which history molds in their personal appropriation. Understood in this sense, the myth bridges the gap between universal and individual life and between eternity and time. The plasticity of the mythical patterns does away with the rigidity of the *nunc stans*, the timeless now, and accounts for the enhancement of the moment in its both eternal and unique content and significance.

The rest of this chapter will be devoted to the verification, within the framework of the Joseph stories, of this general thesis.

Repetition and Reproduction

The internalization of recurrence into repetition, and in so far reproduction, is not restricted to the peculiarly knowing way of

---

*Joseph and Amenophis are truly contemporaries in the free treatment of a given tradition, a freedom which has not only a religious expression but, in the art of Tel Amarna, also an artistic one. [56]

Joseph's life, for instance the way he understand his repeated descent into the pit as the recurrence of a set pattern which implies its own promise and is, therefore, secretly conjured up and willingly entertained.[58] Jacob, too, had to spend a whole lifetime (so to speak) in the "land from which there is no return," in Laban's "realm of the dead." The being past of the past is here denied. Just as is the case in modern art, re-presentation means renewed presentation. "The experience consisted less in something past being repeated than in its becoming present again." [59] Repetition becomes substantial identity by being internally conditioned and internally sanctioned. Men act in a way "corresponding" to their predestined role in life. They act in a proud and festive mood; for even the saddest role can be acted well. Thus Esau passes by, "still in his honored estate," "arrogant, gay, and highly puffed up," "striding high and handsome," though in his heart of hearts he knows already that he is one of those doomed to the world below, with its weeping and gnashing of teeth. "He did all this because it lay in his role to do it, and he devoutly believed that every happening is precisely a coming true, and that the happening happened because it had to happen according to its established prototype." [60]

Like all the rest, Joseph has his role assigned him; but it is left to his initiative to cooperate with "the scheming Lord of his dreams" and assure an adequate performance of his part.[61] On the whole, therefore, and in his case above all, the correspondence between this world and the other world must already be described as a largely free and personal correspondence—a covenant in which both God and man fulfill their true selves in concord with one another; "a bond . . . in whose very establishing God's sanctification and that of man are understood to form a double process, whose two sides are most intimately bound together." [62]

The presentiment of his role and an erudite sense for the patterns of life, the meaning of events enable Joseph to embrace the past, to comprehend the present (i.e., to realize "what 'actually' happens"), and to project his gaze into the future. But this future will be of his own making—though not entirely so. In the dreams that direct his expectations, the state of things to come is prophesied as a fact—a fact, however, that needs interpretation and enactment, calls for a moral effort, and does not exclude surprise and 'dis-appointment' when it finally occurs. These three ways of understanding time—attentive present-mindedness, depth of retrospection, and responsible foresight—belong together, and combine to give the present moment its absolute significance. In such a moment everything is placed in jeopardy; everything can be lost and ruined "in a moment." [63]

Joseph's awareness of the moment's cruciality charges the decisive scene before Potiphar's wife with high dramatic tension. This tension attaches not to the action as such but rather to its universal implications. Joseph exemplifies the Hebrew care for both past and future, a care that contrasts sharply with the Egyptian cult of the past, as well as with the Greeks' devotion to the timeless and with the carefree hilarity of the Olympians, and stamps the very face of this Hebraic world and its God. It is the world of 'Cabala,' i.e., of a tradition which is handed down and has to be handed on.

Tradition and Artistic Reproduction

But what of Thomas Mann's story itself? Does it really belong to this context of tradition, drawing the reader personally into its orbit? The answer to this question depends on the way in which the poet takes the legend and leads his readers to understand it. Is the whole Joseph saga a fantastically clever piece of artistry, executed with all the refinements of modern scholarship, and with lively colors painting a spectral past? Or is there a real bond between that early moment of human history and the motives animating it, and the life of our own times, the issues it presents and the resolution it demands? Only where such a bond exists, only when the two historical contexts are linked by the same motive operating in each so that one is able to represent the other—only then will any such concern with the old story be fruitful and compelling in its results (and hence justified from the human point of view).

Thomas Mann's habit of now and again interfering in the course of his narration is often tinged with irony and may thus be taken as evidence that he is fully conscious of the "distance" that separates us from Biblical times and makes our concrete decisions ultimately our own. But it is also prompted by his feeling that the far-away, ancient resolves are at the same time classical solutions that have contributed to the formation of our life and world. In this sense they are close to us and bear vitally on our own problems.

The Myth as Research into the Origins

In venturing out into the exotic lands of Canaan and Egypt, the poet remains faithful to the world of his soul. Far from seeking only the antiquarian's truth, the Joseph saga is a new phase of that 'archaeology,' that research into his own origins, the idea of which has inspired Thomas Mann's work ever since *Buddenbrooks*. At that time he had thought he could penetrate to the source of his being by tracing the ancestry of little Hanno. Into what bottomless depths must he now plunge to accomplish the "descent into the hell" of self-knowledge! But this concern is not confined to the autobiographical even in a deeper sense of this word. It goes beyond the Narcissus-like absorption of the artist in his own image, in the nature of his art and the source of his queer mode of being, and takes all this as a pointed expression of the human problem.

"Whatsoever the path thou takest, thou wilt ne'er explore the soul's far reaches, so ineffable are its depths." [64] Thomas Mann's delving into the historic depth of his own being stops with the Jewish patriarchs; thus the full and complete story of the human soul and its living past is far from being presented, while vistas into its still deeper strata are opened up at every turn. His singling out of this one epoch, however, is fully justified. For this is the point where myth becomes history while history keeps its mythical significance. It is the point at which the outlines of our historical world were drawn by way of resolutions that have gone on renewing themselves time after time, so that we are still bound by them today, in spite of all we have experienced since.

Thus, in the hour of its sorest trial, Thomas Mann has given his adherence to the Jewish-Christian tradition. Not that he accepts it in any dogmatic or ecclesiastical sense. He embraces it rather as a tradition of *our* world—a historical world, dominated as it is by what, despite their mythical connotations, I would call the categories of historical understanding: simultaneity in the sense of contemporaneousness and virtual presence, etc.

It was a stroke of genius for Thomas Mann to show the ingredient of perennial truth in mythical consciousness just by choosing the theme of the Joseph novels. With the old commentators, he sees the dawning of a new order in the life of Joseph's forefather Abraham—the moon-wanderer, the deeply disquieted man of the spirit. Abraham appears as the mythical and mysterious father of historical consciousness, the finder and founder of man's very own world. In the history of the patriarchs man emerges from the mother realm of anonymous life in the collective and goes away from his kinsmen, the servants of idols, and the country of astrologers, the Chaldean Ur. He ceases to consider himself a mere part of nature and to think of his destiny as subject to the astronomical constellations. He dares to become a partner in a covenant with God, subject to no one but the Highest, he who is not only the architect of the set patterns of nature but above all the ruler of history, the principle of the future, the patron of man in his needs and aspirations.

Abraham's decison for the God of the future and personal life is the prototype that will be freely renewed by Joseph in the face of fleshly temptation. Thomas Mann's Joseph acts not as a solitary individual but rather under the warning auspices of his father and God-father. He is tempted, not simply by an individual woman, but by Eve who tenders him the apple. Through the demonic power of sensuality Potiphar's wife, Mut, is re-transformed, as it were, from an elegant saint into what her name signifies—the great mother, Isis who wears the vulture's hood.[65] Amun, whom she serves, is a god of dark, tribal, reactionary instincts (quite different from the blithe and versatile Aton, then coming into favor with the court); and the woman's courtly composure is devoured by the *flammes noires,* the wild, dark forces from the depths of earth that engulfed Gustav Aschenbach's hard-won classical order and are forever seeking to strangle man's true selfhood and undermine the sense of responsibility to his calling. Not merely two individuals but two epochs stand in opposition to each other, in a duel to be fought out between God and Amun.[66] Will the young God be overpowered by the black magic of the old?[67] The answer given in the Joseph saga is the same answer that Thomas Mann himself gave in act and deed to the idolators of blood and soil.[f] Like Abraham following the command of the Most High, he went out into a strange land (into "misery"—*Elend,* as the German has it).

Like Joseph, he went down into the pit of the old life and the well-spring of the new. A refugee, like the patriarchs, he became a messenger to mankind.

The autobiographical element at which I have hinted in these last words has been explicitly acknowledged by Thomas Mann and developed, with due restraint, in a lecture on "The Joseph Novels." Here he interprets his *magnum opus* as the fulfillment of a longeval urge firmly embedded in his own personal existence. "A work must have roots deep in my life, secret threads must lead back from it to the dreams of earliest childhood, if I am to consider myself entitled to it, if I am to believe in the legitimacy of what I am doing." [68]

A mighty bridge is thrown across the abyss between the past and the present. The wheel has come full circle, and we have the problem of *Buddenbrooks* all over again—man in search of himself. But now everything has been elevated to a new plane, that of the eternally human, in the festive atmosphere of reencounter and recognition. This is no form of escapism, no desperate retreat into the dim and distant past. It is the presentation of a perennial movement of life,[69] or, to speak with Goethe, an entering into the original depths of our human world.[70]

World Literature

The passionate research into the genesis of human types and motifs, the enthralled view of that ocean which "rolls and swells with ever higher forms," [71] passes beyond any particular data and loses itself farther and farther in time and space. Since each phenomenon thus represents an inner universality, it has to be rendered in the language of the world wherein it originated. The writer is drawn beyond the word of his own language toward the linguistic realization of a universal literature (*Weltliteratur* in Goethe's sense) in which all things speak, as it were, in their own native tongue.

The increasingly rich orchestration of Thomas Mann's works draws forth its voices not only from the German past, the epics of the Middle Ages, Luther, Goethe, and the Romantics, and not only from the foreign literature of the nineteenth century, but also from the ancient world of Greece and the Near East, the cradle of our civilization. From *Death in Venice* radiates the golden light of Plato's *Phaedrus* and filters through the mock solemnity of its classicistic style. The hymnic voluptuousness of Walt Whitman as well as the languor of the French *décadence* have their echo in *The Magic Mountain* (together with a whole system of allusions to Goethe's Walpurgis Night). In a somewhat ironical vein, *The Transposed Heads* employs the magical overtones and luxuriant imagery of Hindu scripts. The stories of the fifties glory in linguistic caprioles from all over the world, including American slang, and even from the world of Mann's own imagination. Above all, however, the great Joseph novels are an enthralling symphony of tones and overtones from the Bible, the Midrash, Babylon, Egypt, Arabia, and Persia, a confusion of the tongues which is not the seal of human disparity but a reminiscence and promise of human unity and cooperation toward the one world of man. In the medium of this work humanity has learned to speak German and the German adopted the language and languages of humanity. Tragically enough, this has occurred at a time when political Germany had foresworn this language and reviled this word.*

Myth and History

But this universalism (which has just one of its expressions in a universalized language) emphasizes a concrete universality rather than an abstract one. This means that the individual is not taken as a mere particular instance of the prototype or of a specific type of man, but as a member of the human community, as a person who, in the chain of generations, performs his role with a growing amount of freedom. To be sure, freedom is always precarious. It offers new possibilities and exposes one to new dangers. In Thomas Mann's eyes, its positive sense seems to lie in the new content it gives to a universal form, its negative sense in playing truant and

* The decisive importance of this issue has been stressed by Thomas Mann himself. "More and more, while at work at the novels, I got used to considering them a linguistic composition of many strata. Obviously, this linguistic form is but the symbol and the expression which belong to its inborn humanism" (letter to the author, February 3, 1943). Cf. the lecture on the Joseph novels, published in *The Atlantic Monthly*, February, 1943, 96f, 99 (= "The Theme of the Joseph Novels," Washington, 1942).

perishing in the boundlessness of Nirvana. His novels show the ways of emancipation—toward liberty or toward libertinism.

Just as the first generations of the Buddenbrooks live in a certain medium of universality, the restricted one of a class society and its ethos, so do the patriarchs, the forefathers of Joseph, have about them the aura and specific universality of the myth. In spite of their emancipation from Babylonian star worship, they are, according to Thomas Mann, like Rodin's sculptures which only half emerge from the block of stone.[72] Joseph, on the other hand, is given the place though not the fate of Hanno Buddenbrook, who oversteps the confines of collective life for the liberty of an art which is also the liberty of death. In a risky yet promising version, showing all the signs of 'modern' individualism and artistic narcissism, Joseph carries on a process already begun in the patriarchal Jacob. Still knowing the truth and power of the myth, he yet ventures to play freely with it and to use it as material for God's— and his own—ends and schemes. He thus advances beyond the incognito within a whole in which true individuals have not yet been carved out, and beyond the insolation of the ego, toward a real community of free, responsible persons. The road leads from the thesis of natural collectivity through the antithesis of the single ego toward the synthesis of solidarity with his fellows whose worldly needs are to be satisfied in a 'new deal.'

This will dispose of the objection that we have escaped the charm-circle of metaphysics in *The Magic Mountain* only to become entangled in a similar circle of myths and mythical correspondence. With Thomas Mann, as in the tradition whose course he is tracing, the myth is well penetrated by an ethos, without by any means being dissolved into mere morality. Thus (to cite just one other instance) God intervenes and prevents Abraham from complying with the ancient pattern, wherein the son has to slay his father but also the father may have to slay the son.[73]

The Magic Mountain had conjured up the dream of "a fair community of life based on kindliness and mutual understanding, with a silent glance toward the gory meal," the nightmare of the world's youth slaughtered on the altar of age-old barbarism. But the real community to which Hans Castorp returned at last, aroused by the thunderbolt of the First World War, was dominated more than any other by the ecstasy of blood which befogs the senses—

the order of the "old" Empire, the "remotest past" (as it appeared in 1924 to the wishful thinking of the author). Castorp came back to join in a "world-festival of death" perpetrated by men who had the "sympathy with death" in their bones, and whose "ineffable longing" was for a return into the womb of Mother Earth.[74] Out of this "evil, fevered passion" will "love ever arise"? With this question *The Magic Mountain* dismissed us—from death into life.

With a confidence that seems glowing at first, then more and more tempered as time and work go on, this question, too, has been answered by the Joseph saga, which tells a moral parable in the form of a historical legend. If not a world-festival of life, peace on earth (perhaps) or at least a passable truce will take place when Joseph and his brothers are reconciled, when spirit, endowed with the grace of nature and enriched through suffering and love, comes to be the "provider for life," the Zophnat Paneach (Joseph's name as ruler in Egypt), and life's brute forces bow before a spirit which will not misuse its newly won secular power. At a time when the cult of the blood and the exaltation of primitive instinct ran rampant,[75] Thomas Mann brought us back to the old Biblical story, which is the archetype for the reconciliation of matter and mind, in order that we might behold its meaning and hearken to its precept. Without much lecturing, though not without friendly and polemical allusions,[76] he refers life to the providence of the spirit— a spirit of knowing love, not unworldly, but not entirely of this world either. This employment of the myth in favor of historical progression runs counter to that worship of primitive mentality, that playing off of the unfathomable soul against the alleged shallowness of the spirit, which had become fashionable with more or less sophisticated mythomaniacs and obscurantists in Germany. With Freud and against the blind admirers of Bachofen,[77] he sees in the elucidation of primitive states a new opportunity for human enlightenment rather than a refuge for reactionaries, or, to use his own words, he seizes their position and turns their guns against them.[g]

Repetition as Rejuvenation

It is by virtue of personal imitation that a temporal fact becomes a perennial motif and that an ideal form is remolded in the

fire of historical action, giving worth, poise, and direction to the individual being. It is one constituent in what we may call the
threefold *responsiveness* of life as understood by Thomas Mann:
discipleship in the sense of following out the past and linking it with
the future, *companionship* in compassion and cooperation, and personal *confrontation*, i.e., the recognition of one another's claims and
needs. In other words, a mutual "backing," a shouldering of common tasks, and man's facing man form that triune human relationship, a relationship which is displayed in a significant scene of
Joseph in Egypt, though we formulated it in our own terms. Joseph
sees, for the first time, the future king, the weak and tender Lord
of the future, the "God" with whom he may sometime work together as the representative of mankind, a mediator between
heaven and earth. But he must first mature, to be worthy of this
promise, the promise and privilege accorded to man. He must
"grow from his place" into both the depths and heights of life "before there is even the slightest, vaguest chance that his dream will
come true—the dream of standing in the face of the Highest and
even at his side." [78]

When, upon the strength of such imitation, the past is summoned back in the present, the past comes to be felt not as a dead
weight pulling us down but as a nourishing undersoil, essential to
our growth and development.[79] "The deeper our being strikes its
roots into the grounds of bottomless history [*ins unergründliche
Geschichte*] . . . the richer in meaning is our life." [80]

The linguistic transformation of the temporal process of history
("*die Geschichte*") into a quasi-spatial structure with its various
strata ("*das Geschichte*")[h] is characteristic of an art that seeks to
overcome life's distractedness in the spirit of the 'all at once.' That
is why the stream of history seems dammed up in the "well of the
past." [81] Hence the poet's method of narration time and again
takes a regressive turn, dipping deeper and deeper into the past and
enriching what happens to be present with the contents of memory.[i]

But the presence of the past is a new presence, a re-presentation, and—in its positive mode—a rejuvenation in the more refined
atmosphere of a later period.[j] As a typical grandson, Joseph is
"easy-mannered and witty, problematic and fascinating," and
withal an artist. The volatile air of Amenophis' Egypt is his *milieu*.
Here in the cities he can make his fortune, and not among his

father's shepherds. In his flight from his brothers, in his death-like existence in foreign lands, in his rising upward from servitude, in all this (as in other things) he retraces the history of his father, but always on a new plane. The same elements occur in new configurations, and quite a few things in Joseph's own life and apparent death seem rather to point farther backward to Adonis and Gilgamesh, or forward to Moses and Jesus.[82] "Repetition is variation." [83]

Hegel once remarked that the idea of new life rising out of death, the idea of resurrection, was the greatest achievement of *oriental* metaphysics. Distinctively *occidental*, however, he declares the further notion "that the spirit arises not only rejuvenated, but heightened and transformed." [84] If this were indeed the case, if the idea of repetition on a higher level were really limited to the Occident, then the Joseph novels stress certain features that must be regarded as foreign to the Biblical outlook. The real distinction, however, is not between the oriental and the occidental views of time, but rather between the Judaeo-Christian and the pagan traditions. The time between the creation of the world and its redemption cannot be understood on the model of a circular movement, as it is in Plato's *Timaeus*. To be sure, Hegel's interpretation is not expressly excluded by the Old Testament, whose philosophy of history is never very articulate, being a matter more of stylistic implications and allusions than of abstract doctrine. More explicit statements, however, are to be found in the prayer books, the commentaries, and the philosophers (concerning our special problem, e.g., in Bachja ibn Paquda).[85] Abraham's break with Chaldean astrology, strongly emphasized by Thomas Mann himself, the Lord's revelation to Moses in the burning bush (the Bible's *Eheye asher Eheye* is the very opposite of the *sum qui sum* of our Aristotelians)—these and kindred features bear witness to a spirit in which the past and the future are not suspended in favor of the eternal present and its contemplation, but contributive to, and affected by, a present decision. Hebrew conceptions of return by mending one's ways (*teshuvah*) are as different from that of periodical recurrence as is the Hebrew concept of *zikaron* (personal remembrance of decisive facts in human life) from Platonic *anamnesis* (recollection of eternal essences). Similarly the relationship between the Old and New Testaments has been viewed from the very beginning as one of hidden promise and patent fulfillment, the Old being recognized in the New as the foreboding in the finished revelation. The post-Biblical mysticism upon which Thomas Mann drew for his mytho-historical concepts is a hybrid grown from Jewish and non-Jewish stocks during the mingling of cultures toward the end of the Roman Empire.*

It is an atmosphere favorable to that thoughtful confusion between high and low, future and past, which floats around representation in the circling of the sphere.[k] By way of a *locum tenens*, representation subrogates one being, one activity, and one suffering for the other. Vicarious suffering takes place in sacrifice, whether it be the sacrifice of God, man, or animal. Isaac is saved through the offering of the ram: thus he himself has become the ram, lives its life, and dies (in "the Primordial Bleating") the animal's death. This theme of sacrifice permeates the whole Joseph legend. Abraham is ready to sacrifice the son he loves. Jacob, not feeling strong enough to bring a like sacrifice,[86] does nevertheless the very same thing, acts the very same play.[87] He sends Joseph, his own beloved son, adorned as a sacrificial lamb, to his brothers; he makes him a mediator for mankind,[88] thus virtually giving him the part of Christ. At the bottom of their hearts and in fulfillment of a higher command, both Joseph and his aged father had laid plans for this sacrifice. "Together they had brought the lamb into the pit." [89] Torn by wild beasts, the young and handsome, the gods of fertility, Adonis and Osiris, had perished—to rise once more from the abyss, wrapped in glory. Just so Joseph, divested of his garment, the veil of maya, and therewith (as he takes it) of his life[90] by the bestiality of his brothers, raging against him tooth and nail[91]—Joseph later on escapes the cistern and prison. To him the cistern has been prison from the outset, and both are "the pit into which the true son descends, he who is one with his mother and wears her garment in exchange." [92] And later, so the old legend continues, his coffin, like Moses' little basket, is drawn up out of the Nile, which he now "represents"; for Osarsiph, the name he assumes in Egypt, may well mean "Osiris in the rushes." [93] Joseph's sacrificial "death" takes place under these auspices and authorizes him to see his own life in the image of "beneficent deities bearing the bliss of comfort and redemption to mankind." [1]

Joseph knows that "the mystery of the substitute is implied

* See Appendix IV, "Novel and Midrash."

in the constellation of man, God and beast, and is the mystery of vicarious being. . . . It is written: a god shall they slay"—the very words babbled forth in the ram's role by the dying Isaac—"and the beast actually means the son who knoweth his hour as he does in the feast and knoweth also when he shall overthrow the habitation of death, and come forth out of the cavern." [94] Isaac, in the hour of his death, had actually prophesied the new sacrifice of the lamb, the vicarious death of Christ, whom he always represents in the concordance of the two Testaments, each having carried his wood to the altar: "Verily I say unto you there shall be slain the man and the son instead of the beast and in the place of God, and again ye shall eat." [95]

The theme of the sacrifice is repeated while the individual subject of the sacrifice varies. Man, God, animal, father, and son— all these distinctions turn out to be reversible owing to the "Die and rise" in the "rotation of the sphere." [96] At the same time, the motif itself is intensified in the process of repetition. From the remotest times (not only in Isaac, "the spared sacrifice," and Joseph, who acts twice "the snatched-away and uplifted lamb"), we find a prefiguring of what is considered the peak of the development and its fullest, most sublime manifestation—the Christian sacraments.* Just as well, pit, jail, and tomb are mutually related, so the angel, who sits at Joseph's pit, speaks to Reuben, who hearkens to him in bewilderment: "All this is but a play and a feast—a beginning only and attempt toward fulfillment, and a present that is not to be taken quite seriously. . . . Perhaps this pit is only a grave produced by a lesser cycle, and your brother is still growing and far from being fully grown, just as this story is still growing and not yet fully grown." [97]

Thus the circle opens up into a spiral, and we see the twofold perspective that makes Joseph's case so fascinating. Not only is the world-view of Jacob and Joseph akin to that of the poet, not only is their world in the last analysis the projection of the poet's own representative nature into the world at large; but within this whole magical, poetic mirror world, Joseph in particular, even

* To the author of the *Reflections* as well as of *Doctor Faustus* vicarious suffering as the way of salvation is more than a recondite idea— it is a most real experience; it is one of the most deeply rooted Christian motifs in the message of his life.

more than his father, comes to represent the poet himself. Like
Hanno, he is the poetic epilogue to a closely bound family life.
Now, however, this life does not deny itself. It becomes the prelude to the history of a people and to a new era of human life. To
be sure, by the same token it is *only* a prelude, not the ultimate
fulfillment of its grandiose motif. We have here an early and subtle
suggestion of the resigned finale which will form the end of the
novels and determine the rank of the poet as well as of Joseph.
Only the ultimate sacrifice will yield the ultimate reward. The
true crown of life, the crown of thorns, will be reserved for the
martyr. New vistas open here: the way to Gethsemane; may we
add: the way of Doctor Faustus? But all this remains allusion.
Lightly ironical, sceptical lights play over the darker, melancholy
side of the tale, somewhat in the manner of an Alexandrine novel. For
the new style enjoys the mysterious transparency of the myth, with
its representation of a typical form in an individual appearance—
and thus reaches for a time the "serenity of insight reserved as a
privilege for the later years of life." [98]

Such is the end to be aimed at—a facility that is the fruit of
labor. The young Joseph's power of intuition ripens in the school
of suffering, rising from the early stage of irresponsible story-telling
into that keen, creative imagination that marks the active man in
his full maturity. Poetry grows beyond life, just as it grows out
of life's disintegration, but also sums it up, reaches a new point,
and prefigures what is to come—the life which is to outgrow
poetry.

Like all the main characters in Thomas Mann's works, Joseph
owes his personal significance to his role as a representative. His
way of representation is, to speak with Leibniz, that of a "creative
mirror." In contradistinction to Hans Castorp's inoperative vision
and Peterpê's merely decorative speech, vision and word become
in Joseph's life more and more the organs for both shrewd and
responsible action in the fulfillment of his personal task. The dialectic of representation thus leads to an *active representation* in which
the individual stands for the universal by *taking* his stand for a
universal cause and *partaking* in the development of a perennial
motive.

Projected upon the plane of Goethe's novels, the passage from
The Magic Mountain to the Joseph saga appears as the transition

from *Wilhelm Meister's Years of Apprenticeship* to his *Years of Travel*. In the sphere of myth and enhanced ideality, Thomas Mann's narrative fulfills anew what Schiller had recognized as the law of movement in *Wilhelm Meister:* "equally far from vain fancy and from philistinism," Wilhelm "passes from a vague and empty ideal to a life of resolute activity, without losing, however, his innate power of idealization." [99] This is the humanly perfect state of "spiritual health" [100] which, springing from error, passion, and sufferings, puts to shame the "dull health" of mere animality.[101] The idea of "spiritual health" would have been a *contradictio in adjecto* to Thomas Mann in his earlier years. Now it has become the sign wherein man shall conquer.

Yet it will have to be, after all, a conquest in a human way without boasting and flourish—disillusion and resignation being mingled in the blessing and victory. Or is there no victory at all but merely endurance? A sobering voice which we shall hear in *Joseph the Provider* grows bitter and almost shrill in *The Tables of the Law* to blend in a unison of passion and agony in *Doctor Faustus*. Still, the middle register of Thomas Mann's language is not to be entirely silenced by the "wild directness" of the human cry. The silvery sound of a pain-begotten irony rings forth again and again, in his last writings just as it did in his first ones—an irony which applies to his work as well as to the world, the irony of a man who is faithful to his vocation without owning a solid faith and truthful in rendering his account of human life without possessing the truth which deletes the question marks from the margins of man's diary.

Chapter 6 THE MYTH OF THE SOUL: THE PERIOD OF THE JOSEPH NOVELS

B. *Joseph the Provider*

(The City of God and the City of Man)

> Heaven and Earth combine: the symbol of peace.
> Thus the ruler aligns and perfects the courses of
> Heaven and Earth,
> Promotes and orders the gifts of Heaven and Earth,
> And assists the people.
>
> —*Yi Ching* I, 11

Dilemma

In the second half of *Joseph the Provider*, we have the sense of coming into a blind alley. The poet's art of *imitatio*, deftly conjuring up the past, has presented for us (rather than re-presented merely) that fabulous meeting between Joseph and Pharaoh, a pearl which many years ago shone temptingly from the bottom of the story's well, when Thomas Mann first had to overcome the "shrinking of the flesh" before venturing into the regions below. Following this new triumph in the art of the dialectical dialogue, this portentous conversation between the God-drunken king Amenophis and "Osarsiph," the adept in the monotheism of his forbears, we witnessed the laughter and tears of the greatest recognition scene of all time. This is the scene in which Joseph reveals himself to his brothers, and the mystic "I am He" in which he had wrapped himself is turned into the humble "I am your brother Joseph." But what is to happen after these high points of the tale have been reached? Should not the curtain fall upon this "happy ending" of the famous success story?

Or is it no success story after all, and is the great surprise still to come? Those "marvellous correspondences," "so pleasing to the mind" will indeed be carried through, but in a spirit for which, blinded by the brilliance of Joseph's career, Thomas Mann's reader may prove much less prepared than our charming hero, the teller and interpreter of dreams himself.[1] And what began as a loving encounter between Jacob and Joseph when he flirted with strange gods at the well of Hebron will end in Joseph's final, though loving and mitigated, rejection by his earthly and heavenly fathers. The original author of our story, whom Thomas Mann does but "imitate," always "knows how to obtain his effects in due gradation." [2]

Climax as Anticlimax

But the climax itself is disguised as an anticlimax. Just as in *The Magic Mountain* the effects are gradually toned down and the dialectical fireworks of the two disputants, Naphta and Settembrini, are destined eventually to peter out, so is Joseph's splendor somewhat dimmed and overcast before the end. The dream of heaven in *The Young Joseph* comes true in actuality, as regards every one of its parts—the "vanishing out of sight," the "lifting up of the head," the brothers bowing down to him to earth, and the "making to come after"—but it does not come true in essence; i.e., not in heaven, but only in the "lower world" of Egypt. How disappointing for all of us! Have we not, like Benjamin, smelt and loved "the fragrance of myrtle" emanating from Joseph, just as the "scent of the divine" hangs about Thomas Mann's Goethe? And do we not know how he himself cherishes the ideal which both his Joseph and his Goethe embody, the united blessings of spirit and nature? Will the charm of Joseph's life turn out, after all, to be nothing but the glitter and vanity of this world?

The "Withholding Love"

In answering these and similar questions, we can set at discount any deviations from the original plan and spirit of the work, such as are inevitable in an undertaking which took almost twenty years (and what years!) to complete. To be sure, the new chapter of our book tallies with a new chapter in Thomas Mann's life and writing. There are seven years between *Joseph in Egypt* and *Joseph the Provider*—not the fabulous years of the fairy tale but infernal years, years in exile, years of sadistic slaughtering of man, the suicide of humanity—and only one great star of hope in the Western world: one single man, the Hermes-like psychagogue, whose mild and shrewd ruling is the sign into which Joseph's later life moves, and who alone, in a world debased by the mania for power, seemed to teach in his person the compatibility of human power with human grace and kindness.[a] The mildew of bitterness could not but taint the colors of original feeling. This shows in the sometimes colder brilliance of Thomas Mann's narrative, in the growing facetiousness of his playing with both motifs and figures, and in the curbing of human aspirations so as to fit the needs and measures of this world.

Yet, Thomas Mann's account of Jacob's withholding love and Joseph's calm resignation is implied in the ancient story itself, which he follows faithfully, though in a way so personal that its wisdom is made to confirm and sustain his own. The outcome (foreshadowed by earlier hints and remarks) is also necessary for stylistic reasons, i.e., the peculiar character of the work as a whole.[b] Lastly, it is intended to point to an order that transcends even the harmony of nature and spirit in Joseph, and so to open up a new view of the summit beyond all summits.

In the Bible

As for the first point, it will be sufficient to note that the Biblical Jacob, too, while lavishing his blessings on Joseph's head, reserves the highest, that of the election of the first-born, for Judah, his fourth son. "The sceptre shall not depart from Judah." Joseph, on the other hand, though promoted to the rank of a minor patriarch, does not appear as a name-giver of any of the tribes of Israel ("him who prevails with God"). His place is to be taken by his sons, Ephraim and Manasseh who have been adopted by Jacob as his own children ("like Reuben and Simeon, they shall be mine").

In Joseph the Provider (*Joseph and Amenophis*)

The receding of the hero in Thomas Mann's narrative is, however, motivated by other, spiritual and artistic reasons which cannot adequately be set forth without a few preliminaries. These center around Thomas Mann's bold innovation in identifying Joseph's Pharaoh with King Amenophis IV, the royal dreamer and revolutionary who proclaimed Aton, the god of the sun, his heavenly father and the only God. Egyptologists have outdone one another in stressing the Christlike features of Amenophis' teaching, character, and ultimate fate. And in his *Akhnaton, King of Egypt*, the Russian writer Dmitri Merezhkovsky (to whom Thomas Mann pays glowing tribute in his Goethe-Tolstoy essay and, above all, in *Pariser Rechenschaft*) has eagerly seized upon these analogies and interpreted Amenophis' rise and fall in terms of a philosophy of history which (like so many of the other Russian philosophies of the time) has its roots in Schelling. (This is one of the roundabout ways in which Schelling has influenced Thomas Mann.)

Merezhkovsky had also stimulated Thomas Mann by his earlier attempt at reconciling Christianity and paganism after the manner of patristics like Clement of Alexandria, and thus bridging the dualism of flesh and spirit. Thomas Mann's distinction between the Goethe-Tolstoy and the Schiller-Dostoievsky types is apparently drawn up along the lines of Merezhkovsky's *Tolstoy and Dostoievsky*. Indicative of this close relationship (and instructive in many respects) are passages like the following, taken from the Introduction to *The Birth of the Gods*, a book that leads straight to the threshold of Akhnaton's (*alias* Amenophis') Egypt:

"The historical development of mankind," writes Merezhkovsky, "is a mystery-play, a sacrament of crucifixion in which all peoples take part. The path from Bethlehem to Calvary is the path of all 'pagans,' of all pre-Christian humanity. The peoples are many but the mystery is one—the mystery of God who dies and rises again from the dead. The myth of the suffering God refers not to an event that happened once, but to an event which is happening always and which is lived over and over again in the life of the world and of mankind. 'Universal history is an acorn, the eternal content of which, the beginning and the end, the cause and the aim, is Christ' (Schelling). The human world is the geometrical space in which the Body of Christ is being formed."

"Osiris of Egypt, Tammuz of Babylon, Adonis of Canaan and the Aegean islands, Attis of Asia Minor, Dionysus of Greece—all these contain Him. They are the shadows, and the Body is of Him."

Take away the element of stolid orthodoxy which brings Merezhkovsky to overdo his historical analogies, and add the fine flavor of Thomas Mann's searching, sceptical mind, his art of chiaroscuro with its dreamlike, fleeting allusions, and there still remains a large area of agreement between the two writers. We may sum it up under the word "universalism," the same metaphysical trend which puts Thomas Mann's work (and even his language) into the category of "world literature." In religion it leads to methodical syncretism, the basic principle of which is the idea of repetition.ᶜ This principle makes for a universal concordance far transcending the limited *concordantia novi et veteris testamenti*.

With the same artistic play upon the leitmotif "I am He" which Thomas Mann uses in the case of Joseph, Merezhkovsky elevates his Akhnaton to the status of a Christ before Christ. No wonder Thomas Mann also touches upon the theme of "Christ" in dealing with the priestly king; he does it, however, in a very delicate, slightly ironical way. And he is careful to point out Amenophis' limitations which make him as well as Joseph a mere prefiguring of higher reality. In Thomas Mann's novel his teaching anticipates the mood of Johannine Christianity and some of the sayings in the Gospel of John; but this is done at the end of a chapter entitled "All Too Blissful." He preaches a religion of pure love and peace in which the *mysterium tremendum* of God's transcendence and the harsh realities of a world in arms have no proper place. In vain Joseph tries to show him that meekness and kindness alone will not prevail, and that God's peace needs "strong hands" if man's world is not to become a disgrace in His sight.

The truth of Joseph's words, corresponding to the actual historical difficulties and appeals for help on the part of Amenophis' governors in the provinces of the Egyptian empire, was borne out by the Pharaoh's fate and that of his premature reform; but these words are also a thinly veiled admonition to our own time. They are based on a wisdom dialectical in form, Heraclitean, averse to naïve immediacy of any kind,[3] and critical even of the immediacy of love. As Merezhkovsky's high priest Merira says to King Akhnaton: "Day and night, mercy and wrath, peace and war, Son and Father—all of these opposites are in God. . . . We say 'peace,' but there is war; we say 'love,' but there is hatred; we say 'light,' but there is darkness instead." [4]

With his new deal Joseph is able to succeed where Akhnaton is doomed to failure. The king is so passionately addicted to pure Light that (sick and weak as he is) he is without any genuine feeling for the fertile "blackness below." The priest in him is sorely at odds with the king; he is unable to carry the sword of God's deputy. Joseph, on the other hand, has the blessings from below as well as those from above. The former (though inseparable from the latter) make him just the man to provide for Egypt's material welfare.

We are now in a position to understand Joseph's eventual eclipse in the holy story, and how it is made necessary by the artistic design of the whole. Joseph's separation from his brothers is not meant to be the seclusion of the saint, the heavenly transport of God's favorite (as in the youth's dream), but a worldly estrangement from the center of life, in accordance, however, with God's own plans. Throughout the narrative, which significantly ends with Jacob's death and obsequies, the central religious role remains that of Jacob. The Joseph story, irresistible as it has proved to so many writers, is but a necessary offshoot on the tree of redemption.[5] Amenophis and Joseph, one harmless as a dove, the other wise as the serpent, stand flanking the figure of Jacob, in whom shrewdness is one with saintliness, who knows the ways of the world and "respects its greatness" (for "it too comes from Him"), without forfeiting the dignity of the man of God.[6]

This symmetry, however, is not a mere matter of form; it is also psychologically convincing. Pharaoh's unworldliness needs to be offset by the calculations of a "wise and prudent man." The uneasiness the reader may feel with regard to some of Joseph's scheming will be somewhat lessened when he takes into consideration that, after all, Joseph's God is a scheming God, that calculation is an element of providence, seemingly indispensable to the Lord himself as well as to "Joseph the Provider." Such provision, moreover, is in agreement with "the nationwide Egyptian passion for thrift and foresight";[7] thus he comes to be the ideal mediator between Pharaoh and his people. True, Joseph also watches carefully over his own future and that of his family, on which so much depends for the future of mankind; but since in Abraham's "seed shall all the nations of the earth be blessed," [8] even this family policy is not devoid of religious justification. Just so his relation to the godly king is not only a result of worldly ambition but has also a moral and religious coloring. They both serve ultimately the same cause; and Amenophis is the one whose kiss wiped off that of Judah in the valley of Dothan when Joseph was sold to the children of Ishmael.[9]

Accepting his earthly mission, Joseph throws himself between Amenophis and the abyss. By assuming this charitable office (though not only for the sake of charity) he sacrifices the blessing of the first-born to which he had once aspired in secret league with his father. As Joseph repeats on a grand scale the success Jacob once had in Laban's "lower world," the star of his life moves into a new constellation. The associations that previously had gathered around his being, and therefore also about his name, the tentative identifications with Adonis and Tammuz, Dionysus, Jesus, and Osiris (Osarsiph, the name he adopted in Egypt, being a compound of Osiris and Joseph), all these now fade into the background, to be superseded by the identification with Thomas Mann's "favorite god" Hermes,[d] another amphibious deity, a go-between with links to both the upper and the lower worlds. The winged messenger of the gods (but also the god of tradesmen and seafarers) is a somewhat mischievous mediator, full of artful wiles, of "shrewd, persuasive speech that shrinks not even from deceit, yet deceives with the greatest charm" [10]—an art which, after all, is not unknown in Joseph's family (and which is excessively practiced by Felix Krull). Thus Joseph is "*tâm*," in the sense in which Thomas Mann would have this Hebrew word understood, a versa-tile, many-sided agent; [11] somehow divine in what he represents, yet not standing altogether for Deity in its highest sense, the sense of the Highest.

In Thomas Mann's Weltanschauung (The Worldly and Spiritual Blessings)

Our ultimate concern, however, is not with justifying Thomas Mann's procedure from the historical, artistic, and psychological points of view. It is rather with the scope and meaning of his humanism, the validity and limits of the ideal for which both his Goethe and his Joseph stand, and which is succinctly expressed in the oft-repeated phrase about the twofold blessing that rests upon both men.

To be sure, this union of nature and spirit, beauty and wisdom is still a kingdom of *man*, not the Johannine kingdom of God which, according to Christian philosophy of history from Joachim of Floris to the school of Schelling, will at the last supersede the dominion of Peter and of Paul. But was not man's sovereignty over the opposites the goal Thomas Mann had been driving toward so far? This development may well be summed up in the words of

Richard Wagner, who was a potent influence on Thomas Mann's spiritual growth. Beyond the longing of the solitary individual on the lonely heights of the spirit for the beloved sensuous reality below, beyond this Wagner saw only one still higher summit of feeling: "the complete unity of spirit and the senses, the one really joyous element of the life and art of the future in their highest capacity." [12]

Indeed, the whole Joseph tetralogy and especially *Joseph the Provider* seem to be aiming at just this "art of the future," when suddenly the ideal of such a unity is put under the verdict of "withholding love" (*absprechende Liebe*). This is the main theme of the concluding chapters, "the final and profoundest motif of the Joseph-polyphony. It is indeed the most human one in this work which aims at embracing as much of the human as possible, and it is closest to my heart." [13] "You are blessed indeed, my dear child," murmurs Jacob, "blessed from the heavens above and from the depths that lie beneath, blessed with blitheness and with destiny, with wit and with dreams. Yet it is all a worldly blessing, not a spiritual one. . . ." [14]

Apparently there is a seriousness above the play of irony as well as below it. To the venerable old man who stood before God throughout his life and is now come face to face with death, Joseph's nimbleness and versatility appear idle jesting and "flowers of speech." [15] Joseph's thoughtful "lightness of the spirit," the spirit of a "glad-sorry man," may be the last word in human wisdom in its smiling resignation before the Infinite, just as his guarded yet unrelenting attack upon human misery represents a union between religious consent to and moral dissent from the status of man. (Joseph is different in this regard from the autonomous perfection, the phenomenon of "unchristian harmony and human grandeur" in Thomas Mann's Goethe.[16]) But man's last word is not God's. Thomas Mann's ultimate love is with those who do not compromise with the flesh, but suffer unspeakably under its yoke—a vicarious suffering in the faithful performance of their roles—and who will be justified by the grace of heaven just because they do not expect anything but hellish condemnation. He stands with those "restless, active natures, the sons of the spirit, afflicted with the sacred disease" (like Schiller, Nietzsche, Dostoievsky, even like Leverkühn), rather than with the favorites of the gods, the complacent or faithful representatives of harmonious order and of the quiet unfolding (*ruhige Bildung*) of natural powers.[17]

The Divine Men and the Men of God

It was Wagner who wanted "to erect the altar of the future, both in life and in living art, to . . . Jesus who suffered for mankind, and to Apollo who lifted it to a plane of joyous nobility."[18] But can these two figures stand unrelated in the temple of the future? And if not, what is their true relationship?

It was possible for Mann to answer this question by referring to the totality of human being, which needs the Apollonian as well as the Christian tendency, while leaving undecided which of these two great types "may be called upon to make the supreme contribution to the well loved image of perfect humanity." This seems indeed what he did in 1922, endorsing Merezhkovsy's "religion of the future" which sanctified the flesh as well as the spirit, and setting up the Goethe-Tolstoy type against that of Schiller and Dostoievsky.[19] In this essay on "Goethe and Tolstoy" he confesses even to a certain predilection for Goethe and his like, the favored children of the gods; and in his *imitatio Goethe* this preference finds an expression both practical and artistic.

In a rather furtive way, however, the same essay discredits not only this predilection but also the equilibrium of the two types of humanity. Mere emotional preference cannot tell the whole story; our deepest sym-pathy must be with those who suffer most deeply, and our final loyalty must be to the spirit. This is why Thomas Mann intimates that, "with a special liking" for them, he had to turn *against* the "children of nature," the geniuses of whom he does not cease to be so fond.[e] And we can now realize what is implied in the predilection for those who will not be elected. This is the germ of what will come out quite clearly in *Joseph the Provider* as "withholding and rejecting love." In the meantime Thomas Mann had been tortured by the sight of mankind hanging on the cross of unprecedented suffering, inflicted by those who reviled the spirit. For this spirit, therefore, he was to crusade, tasting in its service something of the sweet bitterness of martyrdom. The laurel crown of the poet is not the highest. Even while he admired the charming power of 'hermetic' mediation, Thomas Mann revered (and experienced in a foretaste) the holiness of the mediator who suffers and dies for mankind. In this recognition art transcends itself. Though being life's very panegyrist, art attains its highest function in bringing life before the tribunal of pure spirit and arousing the dread of God in its breast.[20]

Greatness and Resignation

No doubt mankind as such is best glorified by the great pagans, through the works of those pure artists in whom (to speak with Merezhkovsky) the "god-beast" is mightiest. But may not the outcry of a tortured soul reveal the truth of human existence as well as, or better than, any number of placid contributions to "the well-loved image of humanity"? [21]

Old voices, once heard in "A Weary Hour," the agony of a spirit in torment, rebelling against a man like Goethe, "radiant, sense-endowed, divinely unconscious . . . serene and free from self-torture, a gushing spring"—these voices are subdued, yet not silenced, in *Joseph the Provider*, while all hellhounds are to be unleashed, the spirit's despair to be united with the agony of the creature in the lamentation of *Doctor Faustus*.

Yet, comedy and tragedy blend in life as well as in Thomas Mann's work. There is resignation in bliss and hope beyond hope in despair. It is impossible neatly to separate the plus and minus sides in the human enterprise, this *imitatio Dei*, this emulation of the Highest in whose image and to whose image man is created. To imitate God means to follow in his ways, and this following constitutes man's service to God. But this service means humiliation, the surrender of human pride. Dostoievsky's "Humble thyself, proud man!" points the way toward God as well as to a deeper self and a higher glory. Just when he is most pitiably prostrated do the heavens open up to the unhumiliated depths of Thomas Mann's Jacob.[22] The servant of God is the "man of sorrows," and the man of sorrows is the man of promise.[r]

Sadness and gladness mingle also in Joseph's life, the life of a man which is defined by the idea of God and lived in his presence. Joseph, too, "was brought as a lamb to the slaughter," "taken from prison and judgment," "cut off out of the land of the living," [23] to be resurrected, though only to a somewhat melancholy secular glory. He is "removed into this world," to use a phrase which is as paradoxical as Joachim Ziemssen's "desertion to the colors." Even so, he is not altogether a child of this world. He "enjoys life" in the land of the dead, in Menfe, on "the other side of the stream," in "the sprightly metropolis of the tombs."

Still, he enjoys it. For all his comeliness and beneficence, his profound sense for death as well as life, Joseph does not belong to those religious heroes who wrestle with God all night and, though wounded in the encounter, extort a blessing from him at last. As a matter of fact, we were forewarned as early as *The Tales of Jacob* not to expect too much from the combined blessing of heaven and earth. "When earth and heaven are mingled, heroes and great kings may emerge, but not God himself" [24]—so Jacob had spoken to the divine beast-man Anubis, Osiris' son, a descendant of Geb and Nut, the god of the earth and the goddess of heaven, and, significantly, a Hermes *in statu nascendi* (Hermanubis).[25] True, "what is sweeter than the double and the doubtful?"—so the same Jacob muses on his deathbed as he renders the blessing of heaven and earth to Rachel's son, the "Lord of the Land of Egypt." Yet "the double is not of the spirit for which we stand." [26]

One cannot have both the worldly favor and the spiritual election; one cannot have the kingdom without the yoke. Divine predilection and election are not so indissolubly united as Joseph had thought in his boyish, arrogant dream.[27] The dogma of predestination becomes acceptable only if the election is free from predilection, and if God has mercy on him who craves for mercy and compassion on him who groans with passion.

"Studying God's Soul-Life"

Graceful as he is, the "enfranchised" Joseph is not "quite seriously called and admitted" into the pages of the holy story. Having flirted with the world, he is to be "elevated and rejected at once." [28] Even with the Highest Joseph's dealings have been of a shrewd and worldly order. To be sure, one of man's earthly duties is to study God's ways in the world, i.e., to develop a sense of the highest values that may be wrested from the historical moment. "For, wisdom is His, but shrewdness is man's entering thoughtfully into God's intentions." [29] This involves what in his drily humorous way Thomas Mann calls "studying the soul-life of God" [30] in his designs for the world, in order that we may help him carry them out. It serves to familiarize man with the God of the future; it estranges him from the tremendous mystery of the *Deus absconditus*. In his playful, precocious way Joseph loves to look behind the scenes of the "divine play." He understands almost too well the plot and the design of his own life, and is almost too confident of its final outcome. "One can very well be in a story and not understand it. Perhaps that is the way it should be, and I was wrong in always knowing only too well what the play was all about"—so he confesses at the end.[31]

In the many ups and downs of his career, in the very darkest hours when he sat in the pit, weeping as befits man, the "child of the moment"—in all this, does he ever really despair? He "knows" even his tears; knows that they, too, are in order. "Gilgamesh wept when he scorned Ishtar's desire, and she 'prepared tears' for him." [32] Joseph always succeeds in finding hints and correspondences which bring his life into step with a greater rhythm, with universal motives, and so elucidate its meaning. Thus he cannot fail to be happy, whatever may happen to him. "A transparent situation, by its very nature, is saved from being entirely somber." [33] Yet "he lives not aright," says Thomas Mann, adopting a saying of Goethe's, though not quite in the Goethean sense, "he lives not aright who cannot truly despair." [34]

Sacred History

The Protestant and the poet in Thomas Mann are at one in making him cling to the Bible and reserve the election, the inheritance and blessing of the first-born, the bequest of the highest promise—that of the savior—for Judah, for the sinner, who "in fear and trembling" knows only the scourge of the flesh, and nothing of its blessing. Judah (to be sure, a somewhat recalcitrant subject for Mann's religious constructions) is among the chosen ones who, unlike Joseph, are full of doubt, humility, and self-reproach, desperately reluctant to believe in their own election. Through him, the Judas who with a kiss sold his father's son into slavery,[g] through the plagued one, the slave of Astarte, through the sinner and the "man of conscience" [35] shall the blessing be transmitted—yet not to his legal sons, for there is no legalism in the religious lineage. No, it will rather be transmitted, through him, to the descendants of a Canaanite woman, Tamar, who like him hates Astarte and the unrest she arouses. Herself Astarte-like, she is full of a nobler unrest, searching for truth and for salvation.[36] Resolute, "erect and almost somber," she stands on the threshold of the great story into which she has wormed herself with so much tenacity.

From Tamar's son Pharez will come Boaz, "husband of a lovely one," Ruth, whose story repeats that of Tamar, so that Thomas Mann can put into Tamar's mouth words which Ruth 'repeats' in the Bible.[37] Ruth is to be the ancestress of the house of David the anointed king, and of the Anointed One, Christ himself[38]—he who is said to be the Messiah in whom the Bearer of the world comes also to bear our sins.[39]

Not that we would commit Thomas Mann literally to the dogmas of the Christian Church, much as he loves and admires the Bible's wisdom.[40] Thomas Mann's universalism implies a "primacy of the positive," i.e., a belief that there is an element of truth and genuine insight, a communion of grasping and being grasped at the bottom of every living tradition. No real experience is lost. It works its way through human history and finds a more and more adequate expression as it goes, claiming our recognition and calling for authentic re-creation of its meaning. Thus it is with the idea of God. The approximations of polytheism find their true fulfillment in Elohim, the almighty God of Abraham, Isaac, and Jacob, while in the story of the thoughts of the patriarchs themselves there dawns the conception of the triune God of Christianity.[41] The perspective leading toward Christ, the Holy Lamb, is suggested over and over again, e.g., in the traditional correspondences that prevail between Isaac, Joseph, and Jesus (the tearing of Joseph's coat, his descent into the pit of the lower world, and his resurrection to splendor and glory), even though the outcome of Joseph's story has not the eschatological significance, and his kingdom has not the painful spiritual majesty of the Christian Messiah.

Instead of concluding on the reconciliation between God and mankind, the inmost mystery of the gospel, the Joseph story ends on the note of reconciliation between man and man, brother and brother, a union celebrated under the stars in the spirit of mutual forgiveness. This motif first appears toward the end of *Joseph and His Brothers:*

"Father, do you forgive me?" are Joseph's first words on being re-united with Jacob; and "I forgive you" is the dying Jacob's last assurance to his beloved child. At the last the author dismisses us with the words of forgiveness extended by Joseph to his brothers, or rather, with his declaration that pardon should be asked of none but God alone. For in the last analysis, all our sin is the sin of our particularity, and therefore a sin against the holy spirit of the whole. Men do not need to be forgiven by their brothers. They are recon-ciled one with another just as soon as they are reconciled to their roles. For they are all needed as actors in the same play, and their actions and reactions are so interwoven that everyone is co-respon-sible for the guilt of his fellow beings. ("The tempter or the tempted—who sins more?" inquires Shakespeare in *Measure for Measure*.) They all may be assured that whatever they do in play-ing their parts will serve a purpose other than their own, and may thus be ultimately right, even if it is not morally good.

The Sacred Play

Joseph and the Poet

The autobiographical character of Thomas Mann's whole work suggests the question of what Joseph's destiny means with respect to the poet. Following Thomas Mann's lead, we have more than once hinted at parallels between Joseph and the poetic genius. Are not the poet's work and the life he invests therein, like Joseph's life, a "sacred play," but only a play after all? Thomas Mann has come a long way since his youthful denunciations of the artist as a charlatan, a strolling player, an ape who acts the great man; but even now he looks upon Joseph's life not much differently from the way he viewed art in the *Reflections*, "this enigmatic being with the thoroughly cunning look, which is serious as far as its play goes and playful in making serious things the mere stuff of its sovereign forms, this being which through delusion, brilliant imitation, and whole-souled jugglery, shakes man's breast with unspeakable sob-bing and unspeakable laughter at once." [42]

Is not Joseph's ingenuity at interpreting dreams really one with the poet's 'hermeneutic' gift? In Wagner's words, so familiar to Thomas Mann, is not

                        even this the poet's work,
                    to find in dreams what meanings lurk?

so that all poetry, at bottom, turns out to be *Wahrtraumdeuterei*,
the interpretation of significant dreams? [43] Is not the poet, just when
he "deals" with the spirit, again like Joseph (and Hermes) a kind
of rogue and an ironical friend of both spirit and flesh, betraying
each to the other? "When he becomes an ironist, the artist is both
melancholic and modest; the great passion, the great gesture, great
phrases are denied him; in a spiritual sense he is not even truly dignified." [44] The figure of Joseph is drawn as if to illustrate the theory
of the artist which Thomas Mann's Aschenbach adopts from
Phaedrus. In his "mediating task, his hermetic and magical role,"
the artist appears—like Joseph and like Plato's Eros—as a broker
between the upper and the lower worlds, between idea and phenomenon, spirit and sense. Thus is established art's "unique mission
in the world, her high dignity—which flings dignity away." [45]

The "easy poise" of art is still insisted on and makes for an insistence on the "right measure." But all human measure as well as all
emotional surge must needs fail when confronted with the measureless and absolute, which proves to finite man a burning and consuming flame rather than the golden glow of love envisioned by a
sickly Pharoah in his Johannine ecstasies. "He is as He is, and cannot make Himself more moderate for the sake of our weak hearts." [46]
Joseph's own sphere is the sphere of the poet in the Goethean succession, i.e., "the sunny middle mountains" (to borrow a phrase of
Gide), which he prefers to the "superhuman summits of the sublime." It is a sphere which even Jacob cannot help loving. For
he too, besides being a priestly character whose solemn language
stands out in bold relief against the middle-register colloquialism of
Joseph and of Thomas Mann himself, is a dreamer and poet: "Called
to the heights and to the sight of diamond-sharp crags, secretly I
loved the gently sloping hills." [47]

In these words of Jacob can we fail to hear, once more, the
trembling voice of the artist himself? Is not the high pedestal to
which Joseph withdraws in resignation the very abode of the poet
who, like Joseph, has been "set apart" both from mere life and from
pure spirit? His strength is his weakness: to be *perfectly* human
means to be *all too* human. Have we not here a repetition, on a

much higher plane, of Aschenbach's warning against the poet, "for whom the path to the spirit must needs go through the senses, and who cannot walk the way of beauty without Eros for his companion and guide"?

Worldliness of the Poet

To be sure, the alignment of forces has changed since *Death in Venice*. On the one hand, by weaving the particular into an ever denser maze of significant relations, Thomas Mann's art has grown more and more spiritual. On the other, the senses have been vindicated more and more in their original innocence and their positive function. And even where sensuality loses its innocence in the eyes of the spirit (spirit being the sense of sin), not only does it add to artistic sensitivity (as in Aschenbach and Tonio Kröger) but, paradoxically enough, it may become the vehicle of religious salvation. In the pure ones like Judah (and "one can sin only against his purity" [48]) the sin of the senses arouses the thirst for purity and is thus hell and purgatory at once.

Moreover, the poet (or is it only the poet endowed with Joseph's ambiguous charm?) is no longer suspect in the sphere of common life. Here too Joseph has stood the test magnificently. His dreams bear real fruit (and so do his words like the words divine on the day of creation) on the exalted but no longer solitary heights of life where "king and poet are enthroned together," to quote the saying which underlies the symbolism of *Royal Highness*. The artist is not threatened any longer by frail little Hanno's fate. In the later parts of *Joseph the Provider* the visionary has grown into a respectable, somewhat corpulent "little uncle" whom Pharoah slaps on the back (as Karl August may have done with Goethe[h]). Joseph's "fragrance of myrtle" has become a childhood memory.[49] In one of its aspects the worldliness of the poet is bound to grow with the experiences and commitments, successes and duties of a representative life. We are not permitted to keep faith with the unworldly chastity of our youth. Even Joseph must marry. (Everything seems easy now—too much so for us to feel at ease.)

But the poet's worldliness is not merely the result of the human communications which he inaugurates and sustains through his writings. Contrary to the flaming protests of the young fanatic in *Gladius Dei* it is rooted in the very nature of art. In cautioning against the dangers of poetry, Jacob makes use of Aschenbach's term, the "profligacy" of the poet—"song rhymes all too easily with wrong";[50] but it now stands for the will-o'-the-wisp, capricious aspect, the "playful spirit" of poetry, so long as the poet is not fast grounded in the "holy spirit," i.e., so long as his fancy is not "bridled by concern with God." [51] Even then a work of art remains essentially a *document humain*. It speaks the language of man groping for God, not the language of God revealing himself through the mouth of his prophet.

The Mysterium Magnum

The writer is the teller of stories, but there are no such stories to tell about God as about the gods of the heathen.[52] He is a man of imagination, but there is no adequate image of God in this world; even man is a mirror rather than an image of the Deity.[53] The limits of the world are the limits of representation. To be means to represent, whether one is aware of it or not. But, says Thomas Mann (through Joseph, who in turn reports what is said to be Abraham's thought), all particular being means ultimately the "Being of being" (*Sein des Seins*). It somehow derives from the *superens* "which is greater than its works, and outside of them," [54] the *Creator Spiritus*, prior to all being and maintaining his freedom over against it, just as the writer does over against his work. (This is one reason for the lightly humorous, ironical vein in which Thomas Mann handles his characters.) Yet, while a spark of this transcendence may be alive in man, and, above all, in absolute art, the story-teller cannot deal with pure transcendence. He can only put his work against the foil of eternity, showing how life faces death, yet perennially overcomes it by way of repetition, a sempiternal *logos* prevailing amid the flux of appearance. In the case of man more especially, he may explore what Amenophis ponders, the problem of the Universals—whether human being is "only a meeting-place between non-being and ever-being, and our temporal existence but the medium of the eternal," or whether the individual gets and gives value through its own uniqueness.[55] In the creative freedom of the spirit he realizes that "all that passes is but a symbol"; but as an artist as well as a man of action he cannot part with the world of passing appearances; he loves it in its transitoriness, and in this sense he remains, like Joseph, a worldly man.

Though absorbed in a working partnership with the God of his fathers, Joseph is by no means unaware that God is both near and far, and that "while the world is in Him, He is not in the world, but in heaven." [56] In view of this transcendence, we can but move toward that eternal light "which no man can approach unto," which is beyond all human power and abides calmly above human stress and strife. It is only in this world of ours that the unbroken light of being breaks up into the opposites of day and night, life and death, nature and spirit, good and evil. In the complementary nature of these opposites, in their "longing" for each other, we see a longing for their primeval unity in God.

What in abstract, inadequate terms one may call Thomas Mann's own faith in this all-embracing, everlasting unity, from which all things have departed and in which they all shall be united again "one day," has its most direct expression, perhaps, in Thomas Buddenbrook's ecstatic "I shall live." The will is certain of its eternity. It is this intuition—Schopenhauer militating against Schopenhauer himself—that is usually disguised in the forms of "indirect communication," speaking of the ineffable now in more dogmatic, now in more speculative terms. Carried through all the doubts and temptations of reason, there is yet, in the very last words of *Buddenbrooks*, the burning creed of tiny hunchbacked Sesemi Weichbrodt, a quivering, avenging little prophetess who dauntlessly hurls her Christian faith in an immortal life against the sad story of a family's decay.[57] Her viaticum is what becomes for Amenophis an incandescent yet static vision of eternity—not "a coming and going, becoming, passing away, and becoming again, not a life facing death and thus phallic, not life at all in the sense of a life which is life unto death, but the changeless source of light, subject to no rising and setting," "the Being of being, that looks not into the face of death, that does not become and die, but *is*, the abiding light, neither rising nor setting, the unchanging source out of which flows all life, light, beauty and truth." [58]

The freedom of the will to believe assures sympathy (indeed, an "immeasurable sympathy" [59]) to the naïve directness of a living faith, however dogmatic, just as freedom of thought does to the lofty flights of the religious metaphysician. But all this with the ironical reservation that every such expression is only a symbolic paraphrase of life's ultimate secret rather than a precise solution of its enigma.

This transcendent One, being beyond the system of being, beyond the system of dialectics, and beyond the specific unity of an artistic composition, is the well-spring of the religious credo, the philosopher's truth, and the artist's beauty; but like Plato's Good, it cannot be grasped in any of these modes of representation. Being the source of life, only life can bear witness to it and verify it by verifying itself.

Religious Humor

What is of ultimate concern thus seems not a matter of adequate artistic objectivation, and what can be objectified artistically is, in itself, not a matter of ultimate concern. To deal with things in a playful manner, to show them, for instance, in that broken light in which they lose their identity with themselves, is to indicate that the locus of proper seriousness lies elsewhere.

Irony, the superior air of the master to whom everything serves indifferently as a material that derives all its value from its artistic treatment and its position in the work, goes together with *humor*, the loving amusement at the weaknesses of things in this vanity fair, and with that *pleasantry* that yields some sort of stop-gap relief as man shrugs his shoulders and resigns with a jest in view and open acknowledgment of the insoluble riddle of the universe.[60] Art and religion speak of one and the same though in different languages, at the edge of silence.[61] The artist's play, if performed in due respect for the holy spirit, is itself a *holy* play; the lightness of its treatment is not a sign of frivolity. "A certain divine indifference, a certain illicit hilarity on the poet's part at the cost of all the 'important' things," [62] may issue just from his recognition of the *unum necessarium*, the all-important One.

The specious appearance in art thus becomes the *splendor veri*, the refulgence of truth; and the artist is vindicated at least as the *joculator Dei*, God's own jester. Throughout the decades, Thomas Mann's work has drawn its effects from the ambiguous nature of a *comédie tragique*. Of the two ingredients, tragedy has emancipated itself in *Doctor Faustus*, while *Joseph the Provider* (like *The Transposed Heads* and *Felix Krull*) proceeds in the sprightly mood of high comedy.

The element of the humorous will always be comprised in a conception which envisages life as an enactment of roles, the more so, the more the *dramatis figurae* themselves enjoy the consciousness of their acting a play and acting it well. The picture of human life which results in this way is no mere farce. All true humor has its dimension of depth in a subdued grief, overlaid by a thoughtful and reconciled smile. To understand all that is transient as but an imitation shifts the real seriousness from the action to the acting.[i] The insight that whatever comes and goes is nothing in itself, is a source of comfort as well as of mourning. The whole last volume of the Joseph story is full of tears and laughter, but the tears are themselves sweet with the fragrance of remembrance, relief, and compassion. Warm sympathy with poor man distinguishes the humorist in Joseph from the cynic in Faustus-Leverkühn, whose laughter is that of nihilistic irony, the diabolic laughter of a Lucifer seeing through the ridiculous blunder of the whole and, above all, of the futile strutting of man, comical and wretched, wretched and comical, just as it appeared to young Tonio Kröger.

Humor's smile is mild and warm because it borders on religious feeling and consent. It is not obsessed by the experience of an utter and unmitigated nothingness of being, but realizes it only against the background of the really real, the absolute before which appearances pale. It is not of the humorist's competence to bridge the gap between the human and the divine. Yet he exhibits the unsubstantiality of earthly things, not in order to annihilate them in the frost of sneering contempt, but smilingly to show their suspension over the abyss of the nil, their relativity to something other than themselves, and to open up the possibility of their relationship with the divine in person—a relationship which only faith may be able to ascertain as a fact. Thomas Mann may have thought especially of *Joseph the Provider* when in 1944 (a year after it had been published) he recognized in his diary the "sublime cleverness" of Kierkegaard's characterization of the humorist such as he found it in the second part of the *Unscientific Postscript:* "The humorist does not cease to put the idea of God side by side with something else and thus produce the contradiction. Yet, he does not relate himself in religious passion to God (*stricte sic dictus*); he transmutes himself into a jesting and thoughtful intermediary for such a transit, but he personally does not enter into this relation with God." [63]

The airiness of the humorist's mood may express a confidence that the solution of problems far too difficult for us is in good hands, after all; and it may thus relieve the pressure exerted by the whole upon the individual being, and brighten the mood of his world. This is what Joseph experiences. "Lightness, my friend, and the artful jest are God's very best gifts to man, the finest stratagem of the heart in the face of that intricate, highly questionable thing we call life." There are questions which life puts to us, but which we cannot answer in dead earnest. "Only in lightness of spirit can man rise above them, so that with a tender jest at the Unanswerable confronting us we may bring a smile even upon the face of almighty God, He who answers not." [64]

This transcendent One is the backdrop before which both the real play of the world and the world of the artist's play are staged. Everything points beyond itself and takes part in a 'uni-versal' orientation, a common orientation toward the One. So does the artist. He does it in his way. In his concern for the world of the phenomena, their relations and, thus, their significance, he observes ultimately their ultimate reference. With Tonio Kröger he still "stands between two worlds without being at home in either one." But these worlds cannot even be symbolized any longer by the anti-thesis between *bourgeoisie* and *bohème;* and this "between" is not that of an outcast but a mediator—like Joseph a benefactor, though not a redeemer of mankind.

While he glorifies (*ver-herrlicht*) the world in the veil of Maya, the artist lets the One shine through the manifold and thus contributes secretly to the greater glory of the Lord, the Being of beings. As an artist, he never quite ceases to be of this world: he cannot help but embrace the appearances of the world with a "child-like, naïve and faithful look." But this same look witnesses them as being themselves witnesses to their creator. They "enjoy the state wherein it pleased God to create them; they look out cheerfully and can expect to be looked at the same way in return." [65] The true artist fulfills this expectation by following out the hints which lead from one to the other and lets them all converge toward the One. Thus he may succeed in doing what Amenophis urges one of his artists to do: "he may help a little to all becoming one in Him. . . ." [66]

Joseph the Provider does this very thing in a both roguish and conscientious way. This way of life defines man's position toward the One by redefining his position toward his brothers. It provides bread in the City of Man, but it fills the heart with longing for the City of God and for a majesty that outshines even Joseph's exemplary stewardship of this world. It is the document of a humanism that knows of what is higher than man. Thus it may be likened to the way of Dante, who also braved the "descent into hell" in his own lifetime, not to convey the highest speculative wisdom or the blessing of life beyond, but "to remove the living, in this their earthly life, out of the state of misery and to set their feet in the way of beatitude" (*"removere viventes in hac vita de statu miseriae et perducere ad statum felicitatis"*).[67]

Through all the clang and blares
Of Tartar legions
Rises our song and dares
To near thy regions.

In thee we're live and strong,
Bold our endeavour,
Thy life may last for long,
Thy realm for ever.

—GOETHE[1]

From Schiller Toward Goethe

On revient toujours à son premier amour. Thomas Mann grew up under the auspices of Schiller rather than Goethe. There are exactly five decades between the early Schiller story "A Weary Hour" and the "Essay on Schiller," "dedicated in love to his memory" in 1955. The very "subjective short-story of 1905"[2] is a glowing personal identification with him. And, *vice versa*, it is a reading of Schiller in the light of the main problem that harassed Thomas Mann from *Tonio Kröger* to *Doctor Faustus*—the all but impossible combination of critical analysis, pitiless and, hence, heroic knowledge with divine and naïve creativity (all creativity is naïve), "the direct calling by name with godlike lips the things bathed in sunlight."[3]

We knew from *Tonio Kröger* of Mann's youthful enthusiasm for Schiller's *Don Carlos*. We now know of Mann's "first literary love" for one of Schiller's early works, "Semele," "a lyrical operetta in two scenes,"[4] a prelude to Kleist's *Amphitryon*, to which Thomas Mann devoted one of his most inspired essays. We spoke of the decisive influence Schiller's aesthetic writings, particularly the classical treatise on "Naïve and Sentimental Poetry," exerted on the formation of Mann's aesthetics and his theory of human types.[a] The twofoldness of his own work is mirrored in this twofold indebtedness to Schiller.

The *imitatio Schiller* applies also to the slightly disdainful nostalgia in the comparison with Goethe. "A longing and melancholy envy" leads slowly to that loving self-betrayal which is equally characteristic of Thomas Mann and of his human types, i.e., to the adoption of a second nature, an *imitatio Goethe*, which finally allowed him "to see in his own life and work a personally molded contribution to Goethe's immortality." [b*]

In this *imitatio* occurs a growing osmosis of two personal substances so that, in a way, Goethe becomes in Thomas Mann what Thomas Mann becomes in Goethe. Like Grillparzer, Stifter and Keller, Nietzsche and Hofmannsthal, Barrès and Gide,[5] Thomas Mann enters into the Goethean tradition and thus partakes in the creation and life of Goethe as a mythical figure. Goethe's style is assimilated, remolded, but also travestied in Mann's works; and the correspondences between these works and Goethe's are listed with the same care as are those between the origins and the outer and inner lives of the Frankfort patrician on the one hand, the Lübeck patrician on the other.

With *Lotte in Weimar*, the main work in the interval between the last two volumes of the Joseph quartet, the sun of Goethe, which had long lingered on the horizon, reaches its zenith in Thomas Mann's world, shedding upon it a bright and all-pervading, if sometimes rather frigid, light.

It is significant, however, that in 1935 Thomas Mann had placed two centenary addresses in Goethe's honor in a volume on the *Sufferings* (!) *and Greatness of the Masters*. The wartime *Reflections* and the "Goethe and Tolstoy" essay of 1922 already bear witness to the fact that their author had become aware of the problems involved even (and just) in the lives of the favorites of the gods.

At the same time Goethe's life has grown into a myth representing, not in legendary Canaan, but within our historical compass, the personal embodiment, on the human stage, of Thomas Mann's dearest idea, the union of nature and spirit. While, following the inborn trend of the sentimentalist type, Thomas Mann moved toward "the lucid world of the other," he came to realize that, in a

---

* The growing assimilation of Goethe into Thomas Mann's own being allows us to interpret Mann in the light of leading motives of Goethe's life and art. That is what I shall try to do in the present chapter. Such an interpretation will prove helpful, above all, in shedding light upon Thomas Mann's never fully evolved ethical thought, which feeds upon Goethe even more than upon Nietzsche.

spiritualization of his existence, Goethe himself had gone beyond the naïveté of a darling of nature—though, unlike the sons of the spirit, he did not need to long for natural perfection, the unattainable goal of those "sentimental starvelings" (*"sehnsuchtsvolle Hungerleider"*).[6]

To be sure, as in Joseph's case, this conspiracy of the two factors implied some curtailment of the leadership principle of the spirit, a principle which points as far above the human sphere as mere life does below it. In its ambiguity Goethe's perfection is specifically human perfection, and so is the perfection exhibited by art. While it is qualified by its way through the senses, it is by no means discredited by it, as Gustav Aschenbach was inclined to think. Thus Goethe, the artist, became a symbol of man, in his dual nature the standard-bearer of Thomas Mann's humanism: the most wonderful human possibility—still, a human possibility only.

Spiritualization

As Thomas Mann understands it, this mythical quality of Goethe's life is not merely our way of viewing it but the perspective under which Goethe learned to experience it himself. Like Joseph, Goethe sees his life ruled by the mythical category of repetition. This repetition is no longer distributed over several generations, as in *Buddenbrooks* and even in the saga of the three patriarchs. It is also felt as the law of an individual existence if only the hero grows old enough to observe, as Joseph does (and Mann loves to do), the mysterious correspondences between the different epochs of his life. Even in Gustav Aschenbach, who, like Schiller, after a dissolute youth is "duty-bound to his work," (*ein Moralist der Leistung*), we sense a good deal that seems to go back to Goethe as prototype and points forward to the Goethe novel. Like Goethe, Aschenbach longs "to become old," "for he had long been convinced that only that art is truly great, truly comprehensive and worthy of honor, which has been granted the favor of gathering fruits from every season of human life." [7] Gustav Aschenbach's favorite word had been "Hold fast!" [8] And Thomas Mann's Goethe says: "All heroism consists in endurance. . . . True greatness comes only with old age, when things become ever fairer and more significant, mightier and more solemn." [9] Thus the exuberant sensuousness of youth is refined through the years, and heightened by mature powers of insight and contemplation. "Less life than at first, but again more life, on the spiritual level." [10] "Life in its immediacy is dull; it needs reiteration and enhancement by the spirit." [11]

The significance of life's phenomena grows richer and richer, the more references they comprise within themselves and the deeper their roots strike into human feelings and emotions. The disclosure of new and deeper affinities is the poet's forte and his special task. "I love the word 'relation.' . . . The significant is nothing but what is rich in relations." [12]

By reason of his sensitivity to these forward- and backward-pointing relations, these anniversaries of life, the poet gains an exaltation of spirit in which the whole of life merges into the atmosphere of a high festival.[13] The present becomes a celebration of the past, re-producing and transforming it, and elaborating its eternal content. "Strange," muses Goethe, "how it is always the same thing . . . the same thing at different levels. . . ." [14] *The Tales of Jacob*, by diving into the well of the past, aimed to uncover the preconscious, original sources of present existence. Just so, Goethe's life renews itself by going persistently back to the springs whence it came; by "making contact, like Antaeus, with the elements and nature";[15] by searching for the permanent foundations beneath the fateful changes and vicissitudes of the present; by attending to the actual moment as transparent for some epochal experience of former years.

The Werther period has come to life once more for the aged poet of the Goethe novel, not so much because of the bodily (yet, to him, somehow spectral) reappearance of Charlotte herself, as—independent of it—by the significant recurrence of what may be called the Werther configuration. Indeed, the young Goethe's hopeless love for Charlotte, already engaged to Kestner, is at once matched and sublimated by the elderly man's love for Marianne, the betrothed of Willemer. We have essentially the same relationship embodied in different events of the phenomenal world.[c] For "when a cloud takes form in transformation, is it not still the same cloud as before?" "There is no past for which one needs to have a nostalgic yearning; there is only the eternally Now, formed out of the expanded elements of the past"—so Goethe exclaimed in a famous outburst against the cult of remembrances.[16] This is "the

gift of life's renewal by the spirit" as the *life* of life.ᵈ "Man is conscious of *repetition* in the states of his life," Thomas Mann's Goethe
reflects. "To him it is given to live over again what has been lived
before, but in a manner spiritually enhanced; his is a heightened rejuvenation." [17] As a corollary of this law of life and experience,
art likewise presents the same problems over and over again, yet
with a meaning that keeps growing in range and profundity.

Repetition in a Minor Key

This law, however, points to no mere matter of fact; it bears
witness rather to the personal gift of creative fidelity. Hence, as we
have seen in the case of the Buddenbrooks and the Hagenströms,
repetition does not necessarily mean sublimation. Even in Goethe's
life sublimation represents only the dominant soprano, ringing out
over the darker, melancholy underparts. In him, the family heritage
is strengthened and transformed and brings joy to the world;[18] but
in his son—even in his outer appearance—Lotte discovers to her
distress "life's persistent, not quite successful effort to repeat itself
in a slightly modified form, to come up once more in time, to be
once more present actuality." [19]

The whole story of *Lotte in Weimar* centers around Lotte's attempt (unavailing, outwardly at any rate) to repeat and get to the
bottom of the unfathomed experience of her youth; but Goethe
too seeks, by means of an insidious "emotional illusion," not only
to revive what was real in his past, but also to carry out certain of
its possibilities which he had definitely forfeited. (And here, just as
well as in *The Holy Sinner*, we reach uncanny, morally dubious
deeps of mythical identification.) He seeks to escape the finitude of
life and revoke the sacrifice, to cancel the very renunciation which
made his life-work possible.[20] He marries his son to "the little one,"
Ottilie von Pogwisch, because he sees in her a daughter, an offspring
as it were of his love for Friederike, Lilli, Lotte, and Marianne, who
gave him poems instead of children; he wants to gain her for himself in the person of his son and thus make her captive in his "upper
rooms." The marriage is hence to be a kind of brother-sister affair, as
Lotte dazedly recognizes; when finally (and somewhat indulgently)
she gives it her blessing, it is just because secretly she longs for a
similar kind of vicarious fulfillment.ᵉ

"Die and Rise!"

The master's knowledge of the "heightening of life through repetition" allows him to look beyond any present experience for its return and enhancement. This applies, first of all, to the phases and stations, deaths and resurrections within an individual life—such as Goethe's Faust. It is the claim and privilege of the spirit to rise above the finite positions of actual life. Learning how to "resign ourselves altogether once for all," [21] we become free from partiality, and open to new possibilities of existence. It is in this sense that Platonic philosophy teaches man how to die,[22] and that Shakespeare's sublime admonition ought to be understood:

> Be absolute for death; either death or life
> Shall thereby be the sweeter. . . .[23]

Freedom is, according to Thomas Mann's Goethe "to give up existence in order to exist." [24] Thus might the passion-way of life "mount upward to eternity," if only the Phoenix-like "Die and rise" would hold good forever, and if the vital energies were as inexhaustible as the spiritual aspirations seem to be. "The dread of death is the idea's despair when life runs dry." ᶠ

But even this termination, seemingly so final, does not remain absolutely such. In Goethe—the Goethe of our novel—its horrors are banished by the not altogether fickle hope for a purely spiritual life to come, in which he would fain believe wholeheartedly, "were he not afraid of being counted among the pious herd." [25] Even so, this hope is hardly wholly vain in Thomas Mann's eyes. Goethe's presentiment in Lotte in Weimar is the spiritualized counterpart of the vision that gladdened Thomas Buddenbrook's heart so long ago, the vision of a life that recognizes itself and lives on in each strong and joyous self-assertion of man. This, at least, is one way of interpreting the allusions on the last page of Lotte in Weimar, where two chains of thought really intersect.

The one chain depends on the conviction that suffering and death bear living fruit, and links the Christian doctrine of immortality with the philosophical theory of life and death as circularly recurrent. In reviewing Gide's Si le Grain ne Meurt,[26] Thomas Mann himself has brought together John's saying about the grain of wheat that must fall into the earth and die in order to bear much fruit, with Goethe's "Die and rise," and the whole of the Joseph novel may be regarded as a verification of this outlook. *"Le coeur a ses raisons que la raison ne connaît pas."* In *Buddenbrooks* the flaming proclamation of faith in a reunion after death is too significantly placed at the very end of the novel to be completely discredited by the fact that, in his ironical manner, the poet puts it in the mouth of that spinsterly midget, Sesemi Weichbrodt.

In like vein, the Goethe vision of *Lotte in Weimar* concludes with the question: "Death, final flight into the flame, what else could it be but transformation in the All-in-One?" and with a slight variation on the last lines of *Elective Affinities:* "Peace hovers over their places, bright forms of guardian angels look down upon them from the vault above, and what a joyful moment it will be when one day they wake up together!" It is true that in one of the 1932 essays on Goethe,[27] Thomas Mann (almost) disposed of the same words somewhat lightly as the "gracious, ornamental" expression of that condescending attitude which is so typically Goethean, one of his attempts to get reconciled with the common people. Still, as these words form the last, solemn cadence in both novels, they may well convey a deeper import in either case. Otherwise we cannot take seriously even the chorus of the Penitent Women at the end of *Faust* and Gretchen's joyful prayer, words which are themselves a most moving instance of repetition and transfiguration:

> *Neige, neige*
> *Du Ohnegleiche,*
> *Du Strahlenreiche,*
> *Dein Antlitz gnädig meinem Glück.*
> *Der früh Geliebte,*
> *Nicht mehr Getrübte,*
> *Er kommt zurück. . . .*

> ("Bend, oh bend now,
> Matchless, attend Thou,
> Thy radiance spend now,
> Look on my bliss in charity.
> My early love,
> His troubles over,
> Comes back to me.")[28]

All this would be in no way expressive of Goethe's own faith, but an insignificant (though supremely beautiful) flourish of poetic periods, or else the sign of a cheap currying to popular beliefs.

There can be no doubt that these and similar passages, if taken symbolically, as the words of a poet must be taken, give embodiment to a truth which Thomas Mann holds in common with Goethe. Here is where the second of the two chains of thought of which we spoke is linked with the first. In anticipation of death, the Goethe of Thomas Mann's novel recalls the saying of Tasso that, whereas other mortals are dumb in the throes of pain, a god has given him the power to say what he suffers.[29] And the same "favor of the Muses" holds out the pledge of immortality:

> Wisset nur, dass Dichterworte
> Um des Paradieses Pforte
> Immer leise klopfend schweben
> Sich erbittend ewiges Leben.

> ("Know ye: Poet's words arise
> Soaring around Paradise;
> Knocking at the door they pray
> For eternal life and stay.")[30]

The poet lives on in his works; and he lives on in the hearts of those in whom his poetry lives and breathes. This may sound familiar to the point of triviality; and it is always in danger of being discounted as merely a palliative, or as "just talk" and sham enlightenment. But there is a difference. Thomas Mann's early yearning for death as the dissolving away of individual bounds and limitations, as a blessed return into the All-One, this longing, curbed by the mature man, but never wholly extinguished, makes of death a reuniting of what terrestrial life has put asunder. This metaphysical *tat tvam asi* is now anchored in the experience of mythical representation and renewal of perennial motifs, whereby past, present, and future melt into a higher identity. Substantially, a man is not defined by what he is as some-body, but by what he embodies and represents *qua persona*. He enjoys an immortal life somewhat similar to the eternity Plato envisioned for those who become at one with the eternal ideas.

Immortality in varying degrees (as Goethe took it) may thus be attained and a victory over time's flux scored wherever what is substantial in earthly life warrants eternal existence.[31] It would be wrong, of course, to take all this for a philosophical or religious doctrine. It is the offspring of a living motif which, at times, prevails in Thomas Mann's mind, whereas at other times it is overcome by waves of cold despair. The life-work of an artist bears witness to this encounter of quasi-mythical, divine and demoniac, powers in the human soul. Its very liveliness and emotional appeal derive from contradictions which would have no place in a philosophical system. In playing them off against each other, the writer embarks on serious play. Sincere in his expression, he is faithful to his experiences, even though he may not commit himself to any firm status and statement. This mixture of earnestness and playfulness is the source of ever new delight and ever new irritation to Thomas Mann.[32]

Artistic Symbolism

The spiritualization of Goethe's life makes itself felt and is properly enjoyed in the spiritualization of his art, life's finis and crowning finale. Yet a similar refinement and transfer is characteristic of Thomas Mann's own growth as man and artist. His works show the welter of appearances transfigured into the transparency of an ever more meaningful context and drawn together into a multiplex unity of symbolic relations. Thus naturalism and symbolism enter into a well-considered synthesis. Only in some more parabolical short stories has Mann taken the opposite road and given embodiment, subsequently as it were, to a general formula of human experience, somewhat in the way Franz Kafka has thought out wondrously precise symbols for man's tormented exposure in this world.[g]

To be sure, all art is symbolic in that it makes one thing visible in and through another, in that here the single phenomenon coincides (*symballei*) with the whole, which it represents through the mode and mood of its appearance. "All that happens," says Goethe, "is symbolic: in fully representing itself, it points toward everything else." "Wherever the universal is represented by the particular, not in dream and shadow, but as an actual, lively manifestation of what cannot be exhausted in thought, there is symbolism at its best."[h] This applies to art in all of its phases. But what is a primitive unity in more naïve times is the result of subtle contrivance at so highly advanced a state as Thomas Mann's. The restoration of this symbolic consciousness in Goethe is what drew Thomas Mann closer and closer to him and created a community of mood between their writings, a stylistic affinity which Thomas Mann worked out with a pinch of irony, fully aware of the fact that times had changed and a Goethean deportment in language ceased to be legitimate. This style, however, gives *Death in Venice* the decorum which its hero needs. In *Felix Krull* (of the same year, 1911) the often quaint phraseology of the writer with its circumstantial formalism and the assiduous cultivation of well-rounded periods add to the droll revival of a past which is *passé* even in the make-up of its beauteous language.

Artistic Irony

This element of parody does not detract, however, from the real proximity to Goethe in life and art. Both life and art become ever richer and richer in meaning. But this is the same as to say they are always gaining in poise and serenity. For the bulk and thing-like solidity of actual being are more and more transmuted into a circle of lightly hovering, ideal relationships. "Light as it is, the light is weighty though." [1] "Profundity shall smile." [33] The representation of life is absorbed by the thoughtful playing with appearance, the appearances of *one* essence, the variations on life's primal motifs which are ever the same.

Secretly Goethe portrayed himself in his Ariel-like "Genius Hovering over the Earth's Globe": [34]

> *Zwischen oben, zwischen unten*
> *Schweb' ich hin zu muntrer Schau . . .*
>
> (" 'Tween above and 'tween below
> Gaily poised, I feast my eyes . . .")

This equilibrium and this blissful view of the whole constitute the nature of Goethe's *irony*, the many facets of which Thomas Mann describes with the passionate concern of the artist whose very being and cause are here at stake.

Since his doing consists in formation and transformation, the artist deprives subjects and objects of their substantive status, taking them as mere materials to be molded in the playful way of his imagination. They derive their new value from their new, symbolic form; hence it does not matter whether the genius indulges in "making pots or dishes," "counting peas or lentils."[35] This is what Goethe calls "spirit," spirit in a sense which comes close to wit and to that delightful intellectual brand we found in Joseph, the late product of an early culture: "the privilege of older age and an aging historical period, able to survey the ways of the world and distinguished by irony and the free employment of all talents."[36] Overriding the party lines, doing away with the fixed and one-sided views and claims of separate things and isolated moments, poetical justice succeeds in giving everything its relative right, its right in the whole.

In defining this attitude of the poet toward the particular as such, Thomas Mann goes back to a passage in Goethe's *Poetry and Truth*, regarding the ironical mentality of Oliver Goldsmith, which was "able to raise itself above external objects, above fortune and misfortune, good and evil, life and death, and so come into possession of a truly poetic world."[37] (Goethe speaks in a similar mode of Prosper Mérimée, as of an author who treats his objects "in an impartial way and, as it were, with irony."[38]

Art is a spirited and lightly ironical playing with one's subject matter: "What is matter? Matter is what lies by the way."[j] Spirit is the "higher guide" that "warns us to view the sensuous as simply a disguise for subtler relationships."[k] These relations permeate every sphere of existence; hence their pursuit involves a complex weaving and interweaving of elements from widely distant fields. Thus in the imaginary dialogues and soliloquies of *Lotte in Weimar*, we find reality and unreality so intermingled as to constitute a free fantasy and at the same time an entirely faithful portrait. The farewell conversation of Goethe and Lotte, for example, hovers mysteriously between dim reality and dreamlike hallucination as the vehicle of truth.

All this shifting play of correspondences by which everything, as it were, is cheated of its individual self creates a mood of pensive jesting, spirited allusions, and even sublime travesty.[39] Thomas Mann's Goethe toys with this notion in a flippant yet tender vein: "The old, the sacred, the beloved, the lofty pattern—to repeat this on a plane and with a kind of subject-matter that set the stamp of parody upon it—a product approaching the late, loose, ironic forms of post-Euripidean comedy. . . ." [40] "The state of the genius," says Nietzsche, "is that in which man both loves and mocks one and the same thing." [41]

Thomas Mann has seen his own *Magic Mountain* in just such a double light, as involving in style and content certain ambiguous relationships to others of his works, as well as to other literary sources. Just like *The Tales of Jacob* later on, it appears as a repetition of *Buddenbrooks* at a new stage, both in his own personal life and in that of the German nation; it had been intended as a satirical counterpart to *Death in Venice,** and as an "almost parodylike renewing of the old Wilhelm Meister theme—the novel of education." [42] That "book of childhood," the *Confessions of Felix Krull,* had all the enticement of travesty for our poet: it transferred "an element of a well-loved tradition" (viz., the aristocratic Goethean autobiography) and the story of *Wilhelm Meisters Theatralische Sendung* "into the criminal realm," so perilously close to the artistic with its glamorous atmosphere and its studied use of deception.[43] In the same manner he compares his *Gesang vom Kindchen* with *Hermann and Dorothea:* "Love for a mode of artistic expression which is felt as irretrievable past, gives birth to parody." [44] On the whole, the free imitation of the past *qua* past implies both pious reverence and an element of superiority. And, again, masterly artistic reproduction gives to the related experience a touch of a past that is well in hand. In particular, the mosaic of quotations in *Lotte in Weimar* as well as the iridescent play of lights in the Joseph saga, the deftly ironical treatment of the events, and the whole allusive method employed, all produce an effect that verges on blasphemy and is only justified because it combines sympathy and distance, and, in Joseph's case, reflects the chiaroscuro of this paradoxical "late though early epoch." From its prologue, the "Descent into Hell," the Joseph saga never ceases to evoke the kind of feeling described in a waggish paralipomenon to *Faust:*

---

* *Death in Venice,* for its part, has much in common with Goethe's "Der Mann von fünfzig Jahren." The artificial rejuvenation by way of cosmetics to which the heroes of both novels subject themselves is but the most conspicuous instance of this relationship.

Man wittert wohl Mysterien, vielleicht wohl gar
Mystifikationen, Indisches und auch
Ägyptisches, und wer das recht zusammenkneipt,
Zusammenbraut, etymologisch hin und her
Sich zu bewegen Lust hat, ist der rechte Mann.

("One may scent mysteries, may even scent
Mystifications—ingredients these, from
India and Egypt, and who concocts and brews
Them well, with etymological moving
To and fro—he is the proper man.")

Is the bloodhound-philologist simply mocked and summarily rejected in these lines? Is he not at the same time (albeit ironically) put upon the scent?

Even religion thus becomes mere material for the free activity of the artist, and enters into the blithe yet serious playing of absolute art. Illustrating the playfulness of the artist, the carnival scene of *Faust* II shows Plutus with the boy charioteer and with the tongues of flame shooting from the latter's hands, in what Mann considers a suggestion and secular parody of the Christian Trinity. By varying slightly the words of the New Testament—"In thee, dear son, I have much pleasure"—Goethe here indulges in a sportive imitation of the holy. "Gentle destruction, smiling farewell," [45] issues in the new embodiment of a motif that has outlived its old life, and of whose "familiar image" one may now "avail himself quietly yet significantly, to make visible and palpable some general aspect of the spirit." [46] To absolute art nothing is sacrosanct, for art itself sanctifies everything.

Following Goethe, the author of the Joseph legend takes delight in mingling sacred and profane motifs. He and his figures like to use quotations in such a way that what was originally said of God is now applied to man.[m] This merry-go-round of devaluation and revaluation will not stop before Thomas Mann's own productions. Final and definite as the newest realization of the Joseph story may seem, it remains part of a tradition whose very nature is to re-form every given form, to mediatize immediacy at every stage.[47]

This attitude is in tune with the superior irony which the old

Goethe was inclined to adopt toward his works, these "mere farces," as well as toward every particular item of his world: [48] "How do they know," he asks in *Lotte in Weimar*, "whether it isn't poetry that's the dabbling, while the real concern is elsewhere—namely, with the Whole?" [49] "What matters in life," according to him as well as Meister Eckhart, "is life itself, and not its results." [n]

As against the growing formalism of the "art for art's sake" movement in the nineteenth century, it must be emphasized that Goethe's notion of pure activity, too, even though no longer rooted firmly in the religious soil, has a distinctly religious origin and mystical significance. Like Thomas Mann's, it makes art a moral symbol of life. As the articles of indenture in *Wilhelm Meister* put it: "Words are good, but they are not the best. . . . The spirit in which we act—this is supreme over all."

This sovereignty of the spirit in handling its subject matters is, moreover, supported by the artistic experience as such; by the superiority of the artistic mood, the inner freedom of the master whose composition breathes a divine composure in the way he rules over the turmoil of life and derives the cosmos of his work even from the chaos of passions. It is as if he worked from a vantage point which is not yet dragged into the torn conditions of man.

Under the spell of this experience, Goethe is eager to point to a primordial unity which, having divided itself within itself, [50] still subsists as the source of all our striving for unification, as the eternal peace at the bottom of all temporal differences, as "the naïve ground from which all sentimental poetry grows." [51] Thomas Mann is inclined to keep company with Goethe up to this point. At the same time, he has us notice that, wonderful as this intimacy with the whole is, its effect is to illumine rather than to inspire. [52] It leads to a derogation of all higher desire. One has arrived before having started. Hence, and this is the reverse of the divine blessing, one is without ends and ideals, without particular attachment and clear orientation, perfectly (though not permanently) at one with himself, but necessarily at odds with a world of imperfect, needy beings. [o] There is too much sun in the Goethean type of life. No human life is fully human without the thorn and the spur of longing.

In vain Thomas Mann's Goethe tries to make up for this incongruency by way of supercilious equity and condescension [p] and even an indiscriminate flirting with anything and everything. [53]

All this betrays the unreliability of a Protean nature that does not always enjoy halcyon days but often falls into illness and weariness, often into moroseness and cold despair. "Bitter apathy, like a cloud, hangs over his brow." [54] Familiarity with all the secrets of nature engenders a mood of "cruel dispassionateness," a kind of naïve yet demoniac sensuality which is foreign to the spirit's ethos—"neutral, elementary, and maliciously confusing, in short, elfin." [55] This is a depth into which one cannot help diving—but with eyes closed; an atmosphere superhuman and inhuman at once.[q] Uneasiness, apprehension, feels Thomas Mann's Lotte, are the mood in Goethe's "artistic home and the magic circle of his life." However graciously their host may welcome them, his guests cannot breathe comfortably in an air so full of bewitchment.

In this atmosphere, the "democratic" proverb that "the great man is a public calamity" [56] arouses a laughter that is too loud to be sincere: it betrays the resentment on the part of people that have become mere tools and materials for the poet, to be used and burnt up in the creative process. Such protest of the exploited, repeatedly launched against Thomas Mann himself, has to be assuaged by making them realize that the poet personally makes the sacrifice which he imposes. He is the candle, he is the butterfly.[57] He dies in the flame of his work.

The Yoke of the Kingdom

"Above all peaks" may be "rest" from the problems of life. But as a place in life this 'above' seems utopian; and as a phenomenon of human life such dispensation from its problems is problematic in itself. The joint blessing from above and below marks a state of being which is superhuman both by nature and in the superhuman effort which the seeming effortlessness of its execution implies.

Still, the result is glorious, a wonderful equipoise of nature and spirit. "Man being situated at nature's summit," we read in Goethe's essay on Winckelmann, "views himself as another nature, that has to build up a second peak within itself." [r] Thus it comes about that "the Universe takes on a human outlook while man looks out with starry eyes." [58] Nature confides its secrets only to him who is himself a nature, "the one reflecting cosmos in the cosmos of nature." [s]

The image of an equipoise between nature and spirit in the genius, who "unites and fully expresses in himself all hitherto scattered and undeveloped tendencies" of his ancestry,[t] may have its origin in Goethe's own well-weighed recognition of "the double nature in man, both sides of which have equal rights and should be held in careful balance." [59] As adopted by Thomas Mann, however, it is bathed as it were in a different light. There Goethe sees his own life as "a feat of equilibrium as precise as it is necessary, a delicately balanced stroke of nature, a difficult and supremely skilful knife-dance, an all-but-impossible achievement." [60] The tone of overstrain in these words comes from Schopenhauer, who speaks of such a delicate balance of being as distinguished from Leibniz's "this best of all possible worlds"—this world which would actually be destroyed by the slightest deviation from its course. "Even nine-tenths of the human race live in permanent struggle with want, on the brink of the abyss, keeping their balance above it but precariously." [61] In *The Magic Mountain* Thomas Mann had dwelt on the miracle of organic life, "the existence of that which by all logic cannot exist: and still, in a feverish process of, at once, decay and renewal, it keeps its poise on the needle point of being with a grace which is, at the same time, a painfully needed precision." [62] And at its peak, with the artist, life is "a difficult and perilous knife-dance." This metaphor appears as early as *Tonio Kröger*.[63] The "suspension" of nature and spirit in a unity far above the oppositions of average life is miraculous in the sense both that thought cannot grasp it and that it seems incompatible with the conditions of human existence: "Just try the trick, but do not break your neck." [64] The same Goethe who is sprightly like Ariel is also the Atlas who groans:

> *Wo ist einer der sich quälet*
> *Mit der Last, die wir getragen?*
>
> ("Is there any who is burdened
> By the load which we have borne?")[65]

The perpetual creation of an always vanishing unity is an almost hopeless Herculean task, which can be pursued only by way of iron, fatiguing self-discipline and an almost pathologically elaborate system of protective devices (not quite unknown to Thomas Mann himself). From this point of view the balance of nature and spirit, richness of life and unity of form, appears as a desperate damming up of order *versus* chaos and madness.[66]

Out of his sufferings, the artist distills the incense of his praise. The storms of creation which rage through the outer and the inner worlds shake the foundations of his own being. But "I must leave the world as it is, and like St. Sebastian, bound fast to my tree, with arrows in my tendons, I must laud and praise the Lord. Hallelujah! Amen." [67] Is it too far-fetched to see in this exclamation of the young Goethe the seed of the Sebastian motif as it has been used by Thomas Mann in *Death in Venice* to symbolize that art of "holding out" which is represented by Gustav Aschenbach's writings? [68]

To him who knows the inseparable "Die and rise," everything will chant the praise of being. "Be it as it may be, it was ever so fair" is the confession of the seer, the Lynceus in every artist. In his work he takes up and extols the process of production and reproduction in nature. Thomas Mann shares with Goethe the vision of how "in the infinite the same flows onward in eternal repetitions" (*wie "im Unendlichen dasselbe sich wiederholend ewig fliesst"*); and, in a way, he can subscribe to the aesthetic credo of the Goethean school in K. Ph. Moritz's famous essay: "Death and destruction themselves are swallowed up in the concept of eternal, creative imitation . . . by virtue of a life that is constantly being rejuvenated by its own power. It is through this permanent self-renewal of being that we ourselves have come into existence. This, that we *are*, is our highest and noblest thought. And of beauty mortal lips can utter no more exalted word than: She is." [69]

Beyond Good and Evil

This saying "yes" to the whole in all its manifestations applies to moral phenomena as well as to the course of nature and is likely to drown the voice which discriminates between the two realms. It will have the line of demarcation run between the noble and the base rather than between good and evil. "I see the antithesis to the good," Thomas Mann writes in 1941, "not so much in the evil as in the vile and vulgar by which, in my opinion, each decent artist can very well be disgusted to the point of making him ready for martyrdom." [70] While having nothing but scorn for foppish immoralism such as the Renaissance hysteria and the Cesare Borgia cult,[71] he is affected by the genuine motives of that German tradition which leads by way of the pre-Weimar Goethe to the Nietzsche of *Beyond Good and Evil.*

To do justice to Thomas Mann, the writer and artist, it will be necessary to see him *in concreto.* This means, on the one hand, to see him in the nexus of an intellectual life in which he is rooted, whose language he speaks, but in which he also shifts his ground. (After 1918, his relation to Nietzsche's aestheticism became more critical from the viewpoint of a critical and pragmatic ethics and more compassionate by virtue of an ethics of compassion.)[u] It means, on the other hand, to see him in his artistic practice and to study his problems in their proper setting. Absorbed as he is by concrete phenomena in the fullness of their relations, the novelist does not offer an ethics *in abstracto.* The moral aspects of his topics blend with the aesthetic, religious, and metaphysical ones and will have to be presented in this unison.

But what is concreteness in the artistic context may seem confusion in the context of thought. It may, therefore, not be overly pedantic briefly to analyze the texture of the phenomena in question before exhibiting them in their total appearance, in the artistic and historical interweaving of their strands.

With regard to morals there is in Thomas Mann a healthy synthesis between absolutism and relativism. The difference between the meaning of good and evil as ideas of positive and negative moral value is absolute. This discernment—moral sense—is the gift that distinguishes man as a personal agent. In this "moral sense" man "possesses the Absolute," is "as one of us." [72] The Good is in Thomas Mann (as it was in ethics from Plato to Kant) the principle of unification, just as the Evil is that of destruction. In this capacity it is related to mankind (and *vice versa*) without being relative to man or a group of men. "Nothing is 'good' . . . which does not weigh 'upon the scale of humanity.' " [v]

But whereas the distinction is self-evident and absolute, its application to a particular case in a specific situation is not. In scholastic terms, synderesis and conscience are not identical. While the meaning of "good" remains the same, the locus of its appearance, the things that are good, is constantly changing. In the dialectics of human history, the evils of today may be the goods of tomorrow.

And immoral is that status of moral stagnation in which certain things are honored or stigmatized once for all. The absoluteness of the good implies the relativity of many goods.

It is, however, not sufficient to say that things or actions which are evil in themselves may nevertheless have a relative and instrumental value in procuring future goods. Metaphysically speaking, the real good, the absolutely absolute, the holy is actually in none of these single states and products. It is in the productive process, in that power of creativity, in the manifestations of that eternally formative will, which is both mild and cruel and of which construction and destruction, good and evil in this sense, are complementary and equally necessary aspects. The greater the power of creativity, the more radically will it demolish what is still a matter of piety even to the destroyer himself. Though not without precedent in India, this is, in the present context, a confession of modern dynamism. Now such dynamism may degenerate into a cult of power as such, and the aesthetic sense will always incline to bow before "aesthetic greatness," the impressive manifestation even of barbaric power. Not so the truly creative mind. It will not allow dynamism to run idle or wild, in a shameful waste of vitality; it is directed by the spirit as the last word, the free self-criticism of life; [73] it knows of the creative as the common element in which nature and spirit originate; and it has its model in the image of God as the principle of creative goodness.[74]

Seen from within, the Promethean mood of human activism has the deepest religious implications. Necessary as the evil may prove in a metaphysical view, within the economy and the dialectical development of the whole it does not cease to be offensive, impious; it causes suffering from the sufferings it inflicts; it is sin. But sin such as is experienced by the spirit (not only in the temptations of the flesh but in those of the spirit itself and, above all, in the tragic conflicts of life, inevitable conflicts, conflicts that cannot be solved without guilt)—such sin and such suffering are the purifying flames of life; they alone can give to life that depth from which it can grow to new heights. They are far more moral than "bourgeois morals," the cheap moralism of the philistine and the pharisee who live within the precincts of a given order and anxiously observe its *dehors*.

These are, in very general terms, Thomas Mann's ethical convictions. They have the flavor of personal truth, however, only with regard to his whole historical *ambiente* with its means and challenges and with regard to their artistic embodiment in his work. These regards converge in his artistic account of the moral problems involved in Goethe's and Nietzsche's existence. We shall, therefore, go in quest of these problems, first in Goethe's life as they are seen through Thomas Mann's eyes and recognized and treated as very much (though not altogether) his own problems in *Lotte in Weimar;* later, in *Doctor Faustus,* the Nietzschean problem and tragedy will be shown.

But the main motif, even in *Doctor Faustus,* is that marriage between heaven and hell in the medium of the absolutely absolute, the common abode of both good and evil which has its legendary expression in the Faust saga and its personal evincement in many utterances of the young titan Goethe, utterances to which Thomas Mann proved particularly sensitive.

I mean, for instance, Goethe's defiant confessions to friends like Lavater and Sophie La Roche: "My soul is constantly being purified, and yet I confess that God and Satan, Hell and Heaven, are indistinguishable in my nature. . . . Or, rather, the stuff whereof man's soul is formed and wherein it has its being may be called a purgatory, a mingling and interplay of heavenly and infernal forces." ᵂ "Fire that lights and warms, you call blessing from God; fire that burns and consumes, you call a curse. Blessing, then, and curse! Am I under obligation to give you more than nature feels obliged to give me? Does it not warm, does it not enlighten me and feed upon me at the same time? . . . Really and truly, it is all one." [75] "Fair and foul, good and evil . . . all these exist side by side with equal right," so he defends the grandiose, but chaotic spectacle of elemental forces against the "effeminate" taste of French and Swiss esthetics.[76] The same creative indifference he claims for Shakespeare: "What brave philosophers have said about the world, goes for Shakespeare too: what we happen to call bad is nothing but the other side of the good, belonging to it and to the whole as inevitably as scorching heat to the torrid zone and freezing cold to Lapland." [77]

It is this coexistence and coalition of the divine and devilish in him which frightened even Goethe's friends just as it often scandalized the world. Heinrich von Kleist's adored friend, Captain

Ernst von Pfuel, could not help feeling that "out of one of Goethe's eyes looks an angel, out of the other a devil; and his talk is nothing but irony about all things human." [78] These words not only are quoted in Thomas Mann's "Goethe and Tolstoy" but are also reflected in a remark his Riemer makes in the novel—to wit, that Goethe's outlook, the outlook of pure art, combines in one glance the vision of two eyes, the eye of "absolute love" and that of "absolute indifference and annihilation." [x] "The coupling of enthusiasm and irony," thus Thomas Mann ponders himself, "constitutes the secret of productivity and its native ground. Enthusiasm means to be filled with God; hence what is irony?" [y]

But since Thomas Mann's conception of God makes him the principle of the whole, the devil can be as little an extraneous adversary power as the good and evil in man are foreign to each other. *Nemo contra Deum nisi Deus ipse.* [79] No one can be against God except God himself. "Since God is the whole, He is the devil as well." [80] Both the Joseph story and *Lotte in Weimar* are as it were built around the idea that "the contradiction inherent in a world of life lies in the very fact of divine greatness, that He, the living God, was not simply good; rather, He was both good and evil. The compass of his life embraced the evil—and with all this He was holy, the Holy in person, demanding holiness of others." [z]

The notion of a dualism within the unity of God is not without precedent in Jewish and Christian traditions. In the development of the "*Zedakah*" (justice) concept, the Bible shows a gradual fusing of God's righteousness and his mercy. Like the Lord's names, Jahveh and Elohim, they belong together. And in a *Midrash*, [81] reproduced on the very first page of *Joseph the Provider*, God feels compelled to create the world in the image of both his mercy and his sternness in order for it to endure, just as the *Zohar* joins the *Sephirot* of strict judgment and forbearing love in the soul-life of Deity.

The Christian version of the same theme runs from Augustine to Böhme, [aa] from Dante (God's love creates the city of his wrath) to Shakespeare's *Merchant of Venice* and *Measure for Measure*, and from Goethe to Gide. [bb] The old mystical doctrine of the correspondence between the upper and the lower realms comes out in Dante's modeling of Satan after the divine Trinity and in Goethe's intention to set up, in the Walpurgis Night, Satan's tribunal as a counterpart to that of God; but also in God's tolerance and joviality toward and contract with the devil, and in the reconciliation that was planned for the end of *Faust*. In the "Classical Walpurgis-night" Goethe takes the diabolical element as indispensable to the godly in their asceticism, as well as to the wicked in their excesses. The antics of both serve only to amuse the Lord.[cc]

In the same ironical vein Thomas Mann's *Magic Mountain* fuses the elements of the holy and the devilish in both Settembrini and Naphta: the revolutionary moralist is introduced as "Satanas" and banters in the Mephistophelian tongue, while Naphta, this "man of God," shows definitely satanic features. And the Joseph saga stresses the contrast between moral rigor and that supra-moral goodness and compassion the light of which is freely shed alike over the just and the unjust. The moral alternatives and their symbols, heaven and hell, coincide, perhaps, in the one greatness which transcends the boundaries of the human realm. Thomas Mann's Dr. Riemer (and, through him, Lotte Kestner) conjecture that "seen in the proper light, the diabolical is but one side (the obverse, if you will—yet why the obverse?) of the divine. . . . One cannot draw near the divine without also approaching the devilish." [82]

Dialectics of Good and Evil

The secret of divine irony is revealed to the artist by virtue of his share in the secret of creativity, the complementation of vital and spiritual grandeur. Thus the absolute finds its place in experience, and the artistic experience its sanction by the absolute. "We must be on our guard," warns Goethe in a conversation with Eckermann, "against identifying the formative with what is perfectly pure and moral. All greatness has formative power. We must only be ready to see it." [dd]

Still, this vindication of irony is not to be the last word of either Goethe or Thomas Mann. After all, is he not against the good who fails to stand up for it? The answer is again in the holistic pattern; it is in terms of the universal movement. Without the *élan vital* spirit must give up in despair; yet, without spirit life would be lacking in the unity of direction. The evolution of the whole, the self-transcendence of nature has its climax in the self-transcendence of man and, consequently, in a moral dialectics in which the antithesis, the destructive factor, breaks the ground for the constructive work of a new thesis. But only the growing totality of life will decide about the ultimate value of a particular action. A man may be drawn toward his true vocation without being able to justify his way according to established standards or even formulate the personal law which he obeys.

Thomas Mann has little patience with the so-called moral order. He has always shared Goethe's contempt of those who are

> . . . pure through and through
> but eternally sterile too.[83]

Just as Goethe's God has his dealings with Mephisto, so in the Joseph novel God shows more sympathy for Shemmael than for the whispering angels of the upper circles. And just as Faust in all his strivings and strayings, in spite of his contract with the Devil, does not cease to know the right way and be "the good man," so will Judah, the slave of Astarte, be blessed with the blessing of the first-born. Sin, suffering, and grace belong together: the elected ones are the 'holy sinners.' That applies to Judah as well as to Pope Gregorius. Evil is included in the law of rising life; not until he finally ascends to heaven can Faust rive the "old-enswathing bond of earth."

Thomas Mann's dialectical ethics is, thus, the counterpart of the religious metaphysics we studied in the first chapter of the present book. Just as in Schelling, to whom, as a powerful, though hidden, source of Thomas Mann's thought, we have repeatedly referred,[ee] sin as the fall of man means also his rise and universal mission—a breaking away from God without which a free identification with him could not be achieved.[84]

> Whence does man come? From nature, bestial nature—and that is just the way he behaves. Nevertheless, it is in man that nature first comes to consciousness. She seems to have produced him, not only to make him her master—that is merely a crude expression of something more profound—nay, in him she lays herself open to the spirit. She admires, questions, and judges herself in this being who belongs to herself as well as to a higher order. To become conscious means to obtain a conscience; it means to become aware of the distinction between Good and Evil. Sub-

human nature does not know this; it is innocent. In man it becomes guilty. Man is the fall of nature; only, this "fall" is also
an elevation, just as truly as conscience is higher than innocence.
What Christianity calls "original sin" is no mere priestly trick to
suppress humanity and keep it under control; it shows the deep
feeling of man as a spiritual being for his natural infirmity—the
very state which he overcomes in the spirit. Is this a betrayal of
nature? Not in the least; it is the fulfilment of her own deepest
urge. It was for her own spiritualization that she produced man.[85]

Sin, *qua* violation of the old order, is at the same time the labor
in which a new world, a new man, are born. The tree of human
life cannot grow upward without striking deeper roots in the
dark depths of evil and pain.[ff] Suffering and even sin are liberators
of the spirit—in those who are of the spirit—and *vice versa:* "spirit
is the sense for sin"; "hell is for the pure ones"—for those who
suffer from seduction, not for the callous herd.[86] The way through
hell and death, the familiarity with the principle of negation, is the
way into the open, the way which frees the genius in man. This
is the moral of *The Magic Mountain* and, in the garb of religious
language, of *Joseph and His Brothers* as well as *Doctor Faustus.*
But long before this Tonio Kröger was subject to the experience
that "good works come only from the pressure of bad life"; and
that greatness derives from "grief and pain, poverty, destitution,
vice, passion and a thousand other obstructions" is the "very formula of Aschenbach's life and fame, the key to all his work." [87]

Thus, throughout Thomas Mann's writings, there prevails the
old mystical insight that he who has not suffered does not know,
and will not attain greatness; and he who has not sinned does not
crave for redemption. The very "complaint" of sin, according to
Eckhart, becomes an incentive to virtue. "For everything is for
the good of the good man (as saith St. Paul and likewise St. Augustine)—yea, even sin"; so that "he who is fast established in God's
will cannot desire that the sin into which he has fallen should never
have occurred. . . . That is why God hath drained the cup of suffering to the bottom, and why He hath inflicted the gravest sin and
the most grievous suffering on those whom he has chosen to rear
up for great things." [88]

The young Nietzsche adopted Meister Eckhart's saying that

"suffering is the quickest steed carrying us to perfection." [gg] Thus a whole strand of German thought leads over Luther's *iustus simul et peccator* (the sinner who is accounted just) and through Nietzsche's active sin as Promethean virtue to Thomas Mann's own defiant plea for sin. Being itself a religious category, sin is close to religiousness as Thomas Mann understands it: "freedom which is a way, not an end; which means openness, tenderness, willingness to accept life, humility, attempting and tempting, doubting and erring." Sin is "the bend toward the forbidden, the desire for adventure, the propensity to lose oneself, to surrender, experience, explore, and know; it is that which tempts and seduces"; but it is also "more fertile and humanly more liberating than morality, dignified reason, the Philistine's conceit at commandeering the truth." [89] "Morality?" asks his Schiller, "What was, after all, behind the fact that just sin, surrendering to what hurts and consumes, seemed more moral to him than all wisdom and temperance? Neither of them, nor yet the contemptible knack of keeping a good conscience were truly moral; moral were strife and stress, pain and passion." [90] Mme. Chauchat's Christian libertinism is cast in the same vein: *Les grands moralistes n'étaient point de vertueux, mais des aventuriers dans le mal, des vicieux, des grands pécheurs qui nous enseignent à nous incliner chrétiennement devant la misère.*[91] The injunction of Matthew 6:39 ("resist not evil") was interpreted by Nietzsche and, in his wake, by writers like Thomas Mann and André Gide as a challenge to provoke evil directly,[92] to expose oneself to it, whether it comes from within or without. It is in this sense that Thomas Mann calls Jesus' saying "the Gospel's supreme ethical maxim." [93] *

"Great is the course of the world," he says, "and since we cannot wish it to stop quietly, we cannot rail at the passions that keep it going; for without guilt, there would be no headway." [hh] This realistic philosophy of history (which, as a matter of fact, Thomas Mann shares with the German idealistic school, with Kant and Hegel) is but a fruit of his philosophical holism. As an artist, he loves the double of Joseph's blessing, "this ancient mighty spell," [94]

---

* He would have had less and less patience with Tolstoy's quietistic interpretation of this maxim, which made it—according to Chekhov— a mere example of "reactionary phraseology": cf. *"Versuch über Tschechow," Neue Rundschau* (1956), 16.

the divine poise of chthonic and spiritual powers in Goethe; he excels in playing off against one another the representatives of opposite parties; he "leans instinctively toward the left when the boat threatens to capsize toward the right." [95]

The phrasing of the last sentence is symptomatic: Thomas Mann has moved farther and farther to the left. Whereas during the First World War historical piety prompted him to retract somewhat from his earlier criticism of the old regime and come to the defense of the organic growth of life against the schemes of abstract reason, he soon had to realize that the excesses of the utilitarian intellect are but ridiculous and relatively harmless in themselves. Pernicious is only the running amuck of brutish or rotten, perverted life. To side with the whole means to give up the suspense of supercilious irony and to side with the laughable Don Quixotes, the zealots of the spirit.

But such spirit can be no longer the absolute spirit of a remote, irresponsible metaphysics. One does not cease to be an idealist by crusading for a material life in which the spirit, no longer aloof, can feel at home. Sincere and serene, art may advance the cause of human freedom. To be part of a "sacred life and a heroic activity" [96] need not remain the monopoly of that holy Russian literature which Tonio Kröger and Lisaveta praise so fervently. In a modest way, at least, through the soft voice of a symbol, all true art may prove the guide and provider, not only—as Goethe has it—the companion of life.[97] For art is just this: "the fairest and strictest, serenest and most faithful symbol of all suprarational striving for the good, for truth and perfection." [98] Thomas Mann has summoned these suprarational powers against the irrational powers of "blood and soil."

Through the 'naturalization' of the spirit in its care for earthly life, the gap between the two main types of Thomas Mann's typology of man—the favorites of nature and the devotees of the spirit—as well as that between the subtypes—the working intellect and the absolute spirit—has been narrowed down, though it does not disappear. In Thomas Mann's Joseph the spirit is intellectualized, the intellect spiritualized. Naphta and Settembrini were enemies, Amenophis and Joseph are allies. Hence, resuming again his own line in adopting the cause of the spirit, Thomas Mann does not part with Goethe at all. He recognizes that Goethe is not merely a darling of nature, unproblematic or blind to his problems. Instead of exploiting his "barbarous advantages," he has made himself the product of a civilizing and liberating spirit. He transcends the limits of a psychological type and countertype. The moves are toward a new and higher totality, though from different starting points.

It would be ludicrous to see only the unfaustian features in the creator of Faust, the incorrigible metaphysical starveling,[99] and to set the author of *Wilhelm Meister* against 'Meister,' the eternal apprentice. As an individual, a suffering human being, he knew of the heart-rending tension of the two souls within him as well as of their aboriginal harmony. He not only experienced how the infinite bliss was balanced by infinite pains but accepted this lot even as the privilege of God's favorites.

> *Alles geben die Götter, die unendlichen,*
> *Ihren Lieblingen ganz,*
> *Alle Freuden, die unendlichen,*
> *Alle Schmerzen, die unendlichen, ganz.*

> ("All things give the Gods, the infinite,
> To their dear ones in full,
> All the joys, the infinite,
> All the infinite pains, in full.")

"He who has not been skinned will not be schooled." The metaphor of skinning used in this proverb, which stands at the head of *Poetry and Truth*, was frequently employed by Goethe, not so much to denote a facile stripping of outer forms as to mark the renewal of life from within, through labor and pain.[100] It is through pain and death that the Brahmin's wife in Goethe's Indian "Legend" is transfigured into the goddess of the pariahs, the symbol and advocate of suffering mankind, which, like her, is subject to the antinomy between head and body.[ii]

Goethe himself has been deepened by the experience of his youthful offenses and the pangs of conscience and bitter despair which lend a dark background to the radiant colors of his palette and heighten his work above the rococo elegance of his early writings. Mephistopheles works as God's adjunct on earth. And Faust and Gretchen obtain salvation through error and sin. Thus a

Christian element is infused into the praise of creative power and its sovereignty over good and evil. Reverence for suffering and even sin as hallowing powers is solemnly proclaimed by "the Three" in *Wilhelm Meister:* it is the distinctive virtue of Christianity to "recognize the divine in poverty and degradation, scorn and contempt, disgrace and misery and to be able to love and respect even sin and crime as promoting rather than impeding a holy life" [101]—the life of the "holy sinner." And some lines which Goethe wrote in 1827 can well serve to indicate the sum total of Thomas Mann's own wisdom; they send a ray of hope into the deadly night of *Doctor Faustus:*

> *Also muss die Feuerquelle*
> *Sich im Abgrund erst entzünden,*
> *Und die Niederfahrt zur Hölle*
> *Soll die Himmelfahrt verkünden.*

> ("Ever must the fiery well
> Spring from chaos and declension,
> And the descent into Hell
> Shall annunciate the Ascension.")

Chapter 8 LAST JUDGMENT:
DOCTOR FAUSTUS

Die Wüste wächst: weh dem, der Wüsten birgt!
("The waste land waxes: woe to him who harbors wastes!")

—NIETZSCHE[1]

The Locus of *Doctor Faustus*

The descent to hell—now it no longer means one's meditative losing himself in the abyss of the past. It means to be thrown into the abyss of the actual moment and to suffer its agony. There are no roses of Goethean extraction wound around the cross to which Thomas Mann's Faustus is nailed. It is the day when the veil of the temple is rent in twain from the top to the bottom; and the earth doth quake, and the rocks rend.

It is the day of Golgotha for an Antichrist on the cross, for the German composer Adrian Leverkühn, doomsday for Germany, day of judgment for Thomas Mann himself, accuser and defendant at once, because it is truer of this work than of any other that "to write is to sit in trial over oneself."

There is an inner limit to the *imitatio* Goethe, both as an ideal and as a reality. For a long time the lines Goethe-Thomas Mann tend to converge; they do not coincide. After having reached the point of their closest proximity, they seem to part again. After *Lotte in Weimar* comes the anticlimax of *Joseph the Provider* showing the merely secular character of the double blessing (which is similar to Goethe's blessing—"*le plus bel example, à la fois souriant et grave, de ce que, sans aucun secours de la Grâce, l'homme de lui-même, peut obtenir*").[2] With the election of Judah over Joseph, the Schiller-Dostoievsky nature in Mann comes to reassert itself in one whose curse is to be transmuted into a blessing. And *Doctor Faustus* will emphasize the (not entirely) un-Goethean, anti-Goethean, Mephistophelian element in Faust—another Judah who may be of the lineage of Christ. (Symptomatically, there is no Goethe poem among the many whose words the German composer Adrian Leverkühn, the "hero" of this novel, weds to his music.)*

In the monstrous *débâcle*, the hellish descent of Germany in 1945, Thomas Mann felt, in love and shame, abhorrence and pity, the *mea causa agitur*, his own lasting concern and involvement with the German cause and fate. He had enough humanism, enough of the Erasmus, Holbein—and Zeitblom—within himself to "flee in the dread of conscience from his country's guilt";ª but also enough of the boundless depth, the demoniacal pressure, enough from the heritage of Luther, the young Dürer, Wagner, Nietzsche—and Leverkühn—to feel his consubstantiality with that element in the German soul which lured it into crime and ruin. The nihilistic pull toward the abyss, sometimes retarded by the antidote of a strict and even hypertrophical form, runs its fateful course through the lives and productions of most of Thomas Mann's main figures from Hanno Buddenbrook to Adrian Leverkühn. If Joseph and Goethe are spared this fate, it is because of Joseph's playful shrewdness, which does not expose him to the excesses of the flesh and the spirit, and because of the wonderful though ever precarious equilibrium of these two powers in Goethe, which is a legendary miracle and promise, as well as a matchless effort. In *Doctor Faustus* the nihilism of the demoniac spirit reaches dimensions of world-wide significance and a tragic grandeur which keeps the humanist in Thomas Mann and the reader, but also the Catholic humanist, who is credited with writing the whole story, bent over the pages of this life and death, spellbound, breathless, and horrified.

The Two Types Again

This classical philogist is *Fausti famulus*, a Wagner *redivivus* on a higher scale. He is no "dry sneak," but would be not much more than a duly installed schoolmaster with a weakness for music were it not for his friendship with Leverkühn, which makes him a traitor to the type he himself embodies, and the passionately devoted disciple of a magus, satan and cherub at once, of a meteoric spirit whose rise and fall he depicts with a trembling hand. Serenus Zeitblom—this is his revealing name: its meaning and even its linguistic forma-

---

* The aspect of the devilish in Goethe derives from his elemental, titanic nature, not from the lovelessness of the ab-solute spirit.

tion suggest a counterpoise to Adrian Leverkühn. Just as the first name, Serenus, is indicative of the native mood of its bearer, so is the second name identical with that of a Swabian painter toward the end of the fifteenth century, Bartholomaeus Zeitblom; and this master's calm and solemn style is in a strange contrast—and, in view of *Doctor Faustus*, a significant one—both with the themes of his own works and with the wild expressionism of the contemporary Franconian school; witness, for instance, the composed mood of Zeitblom's "Cure of the Possessed," a world apart from the tumultuous visions of the young Dürer and from the whole air of ostentatious candor in early Protestantism.

Whereas Zeitblom stands for catholicity rather than Catholicism, Leverkühn is a late fruit of this volcanic Protestant ground. His father bears exactly the features of Dürer's Melanchthon, his uncle those of Dürer's Hieronymus of Augsburg, while his mother, like the mothers of most artists in Thomas Mann's works, has a *Roman* touch. She is modeled after Dürer's picture of the "German Woman from Venice" (1507). (Adrian has her brownish complexion; and the musical temperament, instinctively restrained in her and revealed only by the charm of her voice, will break all dams in her son—more precisely, her second son.) Dürer's engraving "Knight between Death and Devil," an object of cult to the young Nietzsche and a symbol of Nietzsche's life to the younger Thomas Mann—this work is mentioned only in passing. Much more akin to Leverkühn than the knight's manly vigor and steadiness is the sinister brooding genius of Dürer's 'Melencolia,' surrounded by mathematical bodies, the compasses in her hand, overhead the magic square, and a wreath of nightshade, the flowers of loneliness, in her hair. Out of the depression of this close air will burst forth the storm of Leverkühn's oratorio "The Revelation of St. John the Divine." Its spasms and unheard-of eruptions originate in that sphere of tradition which reaches from Ezekiel and John of Patmos to the frenzied ecstasies of Dürer's "Apocalipsis cum figuris."

In different forms, *Doctor Faustus* reiterates the dialectical interplay between the two antagonists, nature and spirit. But it is not done any longer in a playful, ironical way and in a middle register. It is done in the agony of a soul which cries out in despair. The motor of the dialectical process is still loving self-betrayal in Zeitblom's case; the mild and equitable, well-grounded nature of the humanist is thrown out of balance and enthralled by the grandiose spectacle of the spirit's perilous flight (toward heaven or hell?). This lifelong love—Zeitblom's instrument is the viola d'amore—this love full of frightened admiration is, on the one hand, exonerating. It can plead its cause as that of the never rewarded, yet never swerving, friendship to the German genius, as the unselfish attendance upon the "significant" life of Leverkühn. It is incriminating, on the other hand, as a surrender to the fascination of the evil, an evil which has greatness and all the elements of the tragic in the trinity of Faust-Nietzsche-Leverkühn, but which shows even there the stains of murder and the germs of the travesty known as Nazism.

The self-betrayal on the part of the other *personae* in the play, however, is sheer sacrilege and prostitution in different guises and disguises and cannot but lead to the revengeful betrayal of their fellow beings as well. There are, modeled after the fate of Thomas Mann's own sisters, the sad histories of Ines and Clarissa Rodde— their misdirected and unsuccessful attempts to find their way out of the dubious mixture of a somewhat shabby patricianism and a "housebroken Bohemia" in their mother's home at Munich. Clarissa sets out for Bohemia proper. Her choice, her career as an actress, demands, however, a versatility of *representation* to which her noble, unpliant being does not lend itself. Inexperienced, she succumbs to sexual abuse on the part of a theatre roué and sycophant. And Ines tries in vain to go the opposite way and neutralize a melancholy knowledge of suffering and futile existence by a specious bourgeois well-being as the wife of a manikin with a worship for Cesare Borgia natures. She betrays him, as well as herself, with the type of man they both admire. She ruins herself in an essentially illegitimate liaison with life—laughing and whistling, flirting and deluding life in the person of a blond and blue-eyed 'Hans.' His name is now Rudi Schwerdtfeger and he is a violinist, whose charm in both play and human intercourse is, by the way, not quite equaled by his strength as a male and musician. He dies as a victim of the children of spirit, who had been infatuated by him—Ines and Leverkühn, secret allies in these dialectical and treacherous entanglements of nature and spirit. Just as, to compensate for her pessimistic moralism, Ines throws herself upon the paragon of happy naïve life, so Schwerdtfeger's not mean but minor and elfish nature hails and woos the spirit; hence he obtrudes upon its frigid solitude in Leverkühn. And whereas the latter would usually sneer at the Tonio Kröger type of sentimental longing for hale and healthy nature, he too is homesick and has become hungry for a community of life and with life from which he is excluded by his haughty and loveless heart. Now he surrenders in a weak moment to such an assiduous siege, such a hearty temptation, but only, soon after, to send his lover to death. This is as it must be under the devil's dictate. The devilish pride in Leverkühn cannot bear the idea of being humiliated by a love which is contrary to the law and below the level of the absolute spirit. Thus even here and here again life and spirit meet only in a fleeting kiss which will soon be betrayed. It is openly so in Rudi's snatching away from his friend the "exceedingly sympathetic" Marie Godeau—this girl with the eyes of Shakespeare's "Black Beauty" (Sonnets 127, 131, 132), but also with the eyes, the complexion, and the musical voice of Adrian's mother. Adrian looks always 'homeward.' The final treachery, however, is his, not Rudi's. He acts like Nietzsche in his love for Lou Salomé and entrusts the *charmeur* with the unnatural task of being his matchmaker with Marie. He thus condemns him, first of all, in the failure of this mission, to "break a twofold truth." * Yet the all-too-happy suitor is thus *ipso facto* also condemned to death; he is delivered up to the jealousy of his forsaken sweetheart, Ines Rodde.

Behind all the illegitimate and outright criminal intercourse between type and anti-type, however, there still lives Thomas Mann's own nostalgic desire for another and better love and the compassionate resolve to propitiate the nightly demons and join their cult with that of the upper gods; there lives the desire for the metamorphosis of the Erinyes into Eumenides through the medium of the soul, for the blessing, if not of peace, then of an armistice, a fruitful junction of two opposite trends. The contraries are to complement one another. At the "one day" of God's and man's dream the personal union between Leverkühn and Zeitblom, stern spirit and cultured nature, will take place. Then genius will no

---

* In this way he arranges a cunning imitation of Shakespeare's plots; does it even in Shakespeare's words: actually, the moral twilight and the twisting and smuggling in of phrases from the Sonnets and such comedies as *The Two Gentlemen of Verona, As You Like It, Much Ado About Nothing*, and from *Love's Labour's Lost*, which he has made into an opera, belong to the lurid atmosphere, the thicket of ambiguous 'representations' in which he speaks, moves, and hides.

longer stray into the icy void of the nil, and earthly humanism no longer be caught in a stagnant philistine order.

Tragedy and Travesty

The complex problem of man as both spirit and animal becomes a crucial German problem in *Doctor Faustus* because, failing to find its solution, the German people had first allowed and condemned spirit to abide in its absolute domain, to stay uncommunicative, and thus indulge in an irresponsive, disengaged existence. This was Dostoievsky's judgment and Mme. Chauchat's verdict regarding Germany. Meanwhile, defamed and mauled by itself and weary of its analytical power and critical mandate, spirit had given way to a sadistic perversion of the crudity and cruelty of mere life. The animal in man was brought down to the level of the bestial.

The phrase "repetition of an earlier state" had a festive and solemn tone in the Joseph and Goethe novels. Now it sounds hollow and cynical. According to a Marxian dictum, history repeats itself in such a way that farce follows tragedy. An execrable farce —that is what, in Thomas Mann's eyes, Hitler made of the grandiose and queer German tragedy of Nietzsche's life.[b] To be sure, the potential drop between model and caricature is so big that, in the analogue of Thomas Mann's novel, Leverkühn's works could not be performed in the Nazi-state. In contrast with the hellish bluster of Nazism, Leverkühn's descent to hell is a way through bitter suffering, sin, and death. It is still the way of the German, all too German, genius of which Hans Castorp spoke; even in forsaking God it is still negative religion.

"Spirit is the sense for sin." Being an inner reality, sin cannot exist without this sense. In Adrian it takes on the form of a short circuit between spirit and flesh—a savage intercourse almost without the soothing mediation of the soul.[c] It becomes the expression of an uncompromising and even arrogant, but also delicate and vulnerable, mind, the revolt of a painful and cynical perspicacity against the sentimental, yet procreative, self-deception of the German *Gemüt*.[d] Man, as seen in this light, is still the man of Tertullian, one of the ancestors of Protestant theology: an angel riding, without saddle, on the back of a beast, a Christian image instead of that of the charioteer who has to rule over a pair of winged horses, in Plato's *Phaedrus*. The rider thrown off, the beast will run amuck. The "lechery and frenzy of decay," the nightmare which Aschenbach already *enjoys* in the dream in which he surrenders to the demon[3]—this *débâcle* will have its way and hurl man into ever lower depths of guilt and corruption.

Myth and Reportage

"Man," says Pascal, "is neither angel nor brute, and the unfortunate thing is that he who would act the angel finishes by acting the brute." What begins on the lonely heights of the haughty spirit (pride being the root of all sins) ends in the inferno of Nazism. Thomas Mann's book, Zeitblom's report, moves throughout on two levels. It embodies the mythically sublime, as the mystery play of Doctor Faustus, a spectacle of heart-rending beauty and sadness; and it exhibits the lowly burlesque, as reportage of what in its vulgarity is below the dignity and in its devastating effects actually beyond the strength of Thomas Mann's heart and pen. And it is the grotesque, the even absurd truth that nevertheless one is made to *represent* or, rather, prefigure the other. The tragic significance of the disdainful genius in Leverkühn consists in anticipating through the dictatorial strictness of grandiose yet reckless musical constructions the law of the lawless, the brutal totalitarian control and the regimentation of the mob.[e]

Just as Plato's later world-view shows a complicated unity which encompasses the irrational as well as the clear rational proportions of the cosmos, so is *Doctor Faustus* a work of incongruous congruity, almost too much akin to the work of its hero. For just as in Adrian's twelve-tone system the dissonances become absolute and as it were unredeemed within a despotic order, so is Thomas Mann's book a work of compression and dissolution, chaos and cosmos at once. It is a striking mixture of highly artistic composition and no composition at all, of myth-making and modern collage technique. In its opening up to the raw material of crude reality, in the wildness of the seemingly uncomposed cry, in the professed dilettantism of the story-teller who feels in no way equal to his task and is always afraid to make a pretty mess of everything—in all this it is no longer a self-contained work of art. And still, it is just this and in the highest degree. So cunningly is this disorder arranged, in so masterly a way are the cataracts of these cries displayed (*vide*, e.g., the concerted disconcertment in the beginning of Chapter XLIII), and, above all, so densely knitted is the net of references between myth and diary, that in this novel the news appears as the epilogue to the myth, whereas the myth becomes an entreaty of life, runs counter to the mythical law of repetition, and tends to resolve into a fervent "never again."

Types and Themes

It is in keeping with the mythical tenor of this period in Thomas Mann's writing and with the specific implications of the Faust motif that more than ever the individual counts only by what he represents. And he ultimately represents universal powers, the powers of heaven and hell as they have their battlefield in the human soul—more precisely, in our souls and in this historical hour. This is no *roman à clef;* and although even the names of our contemporaries are freely and sometimes maliciously used, they have only illustrative value. They mark very real and only too actual possibilities of human existence. We are face to face with typical phenomena of our time rather than portraits of any single person.

Leverkühn, above all, is neither simply Mann himself, though he is not foreign to him either (even less so than Zeitblom), nor 'really' Nietzsche or Hugo Wolf or a concoction of them, and of others in the bargain. While occasionally indulging in a parody of romanticism, his art is the very opposite of Nietzsche's dream of a Socratic music, luminous and transparent like an autumn day; but it is just as little a faithful, enhancing, or detractive copy, for instance, of Schönberg's music. It is the music of this novel, the artistic equivalent of a precarious mood of our age, which cannot but present the stylistic character of today's art. Thomas Mann's work shows the spasmodic pains of the time in the countenance of its artist and describes time's tragedy in the way of the cross, the way which Leverkühn travels in the *imitatio* of Nietzsche, like him "a good and a bad Christian," [4] Christ and Antichrist at once.

To secure their symbolic significance, the two protagonists, Leverkühn and Zeitblom, are characterized only as manifestations of the powers which they embody, while their individual features are purposely effaced. Conversely, the persons with whom they are in mythical identity are so absorbed in their artistic reappearance that, for instance, any mention of Nietzsche had to be carefully avoided.[5] (This happens even in a passage[6] which obviously refers to him as the one source of moral and aesthetic tendencies which were destined to diverge later on: the novel lends them, therefore, to that ill-matched couple, allotting one to Ines, the other to Helmut Institoris.) Thanks to the same Nietzschean, dialectical unity between opposite types and, consequently, between Leverkühn and Zeitblom themselves, facts and factors of Nietzsche's existence can be attributed to Zeitblom: for instance, Nietzsche's military service in Naumburg, and above all, of course, his classical philology, while the study of "alas, theology" is incumbent on the new Doctor Faustus (though he turns away from it—a little later in his life than Nietzsche did).

To make up for the physical anonymity of the two friends, the figures around them, the truly novelistic figures, stand out as it were in a sharp and pitiless spotlight which gives most of them a somehow ghostlike, surrealistic appearance; they are made participants in the dance of death of an epoch, actors in the frightfully bizarre play of a German Walpurgis Night, in which, following a great example, Thomas Mann does not spare his whip. They alone remain the bearers and almost victims of personal leitmotifs of a peculiar shrillness. For the rest, the characterization by leitmotifs recedes in favor of so dense a symphonic texture that, as in Leverkühn's music, almost every phrase has its thematic significance as mere variation of one basic identity. Such is the law of the "magic square." [7]

Here too, the sharp contrast with the playfully festive mood of *Joseph and His Brothers* ought to be noticed. The playing of roles—always the same roles by different individuals—creates in the Joseph novels an identity prevailing throughout its variations and externally similar to that which we have in *Doctor Faustus*, but with the opposite meaning. The smile which recognized and celebrated identity in the rendering of the Biblical story is now quasi frozen into a painful grimace; identity appears as stagnation and as the hopeless monotony of a life and world devoid of sense. It is obvious that the principle of "eternal recurrence" implies both alternatives and evaluations—the festive and the sinister one—as possibilities which may assert themselves with different strength in different situations. The first formerly exalted possibility is not wholly disparaged in *Doctor Faustus*. The idea of mythical *imitatio* cannot, without remainder, be reduced to that of hopeless travesty; it does not cease to mean repetition as a productive process of renewal and sublimation. After all, sheer stagnation is the aspect of Leverkühn's rather than Thomas Mann's artistic world. On the other hand, Thomas Mann cannot but recognize features of his own magic constructivism in the deadly logic of the art which he describes and denounces in so far as its pitilessness is not seasoned by mercy and charity.

The Signature of Our Time

The strict and thorough symbolism of a music wherein each part represents and varies one and the same dominating musical phrase has in itself symbolic value. It is expressive of the violent desire of our time to find its way back (find it at all costs) from the open spaces of personal selfhood, but also from the void in which the individual is lost. The death of liberalism marks the bend on a total and even totalitarian order, on the subjection of the merely subjective, the redemption from the yoke of unavailing freedom. But this is a two-edged thing. Thomas Mann, the disciple of Schopenhauer, Wagner, and Nietzsche, knows only too well the dangerous temptation to forgo the distinction and responsibility of the person together with the introversion and isolation of the individual. His whole literary career is directed by the effort to steer clear of this reef and to reintegrate communal life by way of restoring the universal significance of the person. Yet the problem is of European and even world-wide scope. The period of the heroic self-sufficient Renaissance individual has had its day. Napoleon, Goethe, Beethoven are its last mighty expression; and in *Wilhelm Meister's Travels* and the words of the dying Faust as well as in Beethoven's sonata to end all sonatas and in Whitman's democratic hymns and vistas, a titanic self-assertion moves over into the mythical and collective,[8] where the particular is but the symbol and organ of norms and powers beyond it. "Would you have in yourself the divine, vast general law? Then merge yourself in it." Thomas Mann's own symbolism is a branch of a broad and

deep stream which comes to the fore in poets such as Blake and
Brentano (two of Leverkühn's favorites), in which Baudelaire is
carried together with Wagner, Hardy with Schopenhauer, and in
which Yeats and Joyce, Pound and Eliot concur with the German
epic of our time. As it is, this symbolism is not yet *dans le vrai*,
in the state of the new, unambiguous truth. On the contrary, in
turning against the futility of the present state of things, it is
tempted to choke life by handing it over to the specters of the past.
Such symbolism is a current of the truly mythical with dangerous
undercurrents of the magic and the primitive. A sophisticated fundamentalism, a morbid bent for a pre-moral or decrepit naïveté are
phenomena which parallel the relapse of our world into the uncanny
and demoniacal—ghosts conjured up by the very expansion of our
technical power and civilization.

Man has ceased to be the measure of his world even while
measuring it by all sorts of technical means. The astronomical numbers through which he reaches out into the infinite as well as into
the infinitesimal in the realm of matter are incommensurable with
himself and the dimensions of his wonted life. "The eternal silence
of these infinite spaces" had frightened Pascal. To the religious
humanist in Zeitblom it seems not overwhelming but just a devilish
mockery of man, whereas Leverkühn dives into it with a gusto
which is nihilistic rather than reverential. The idea of a physical
universe expanding with a fantastic speed, an exploding universe,
in other words,[9] is the counterpart to a both expanding and exploding historical world. Monstrous numbers whose bombardment
deafens our imagination, monstrous dimensions so vast as to cir-
cumscribe no human habitat any longer, they engender a spooky
world, a world full of demonic pranks and—like Adrian's music—
of shrieks and convulsive laughter, a world which breeds terror and
black magic as a desperate means to 'fix' things—and men.

This night of human existence, a feeling of utter hopelessness
and nothingness, aggravated by the artist's utopian position in a
system of bourgeois calculations and a world of soulless technique,
cannot but drain the joy and vigor of creativity and paralyze the
flights of art like those of Mallarmé's virginal Swan frozen in the
agony of a sterile winter. "Virginity is well, yet must to motherhood" [10]—this admonition on the part of his musical mentor meets

in Leverkühn with the knowledge of sterility as the threat and even signature of the time and, therefore, with the presentiment of the dreadful price such 'motherhood' will exact.

The running dry of art and the frustration of the artist are depicted in the figure of the translator Rüdiger Schildknapp, who is so dangerously akin to Adrian. In fact, he sees the world out of the same eyes as Leverkühn, gray-blue-greenish eyes with a rust-colored ring around the pupils; and he shares with him the indulgence in an uproarious and, indeed, diabolic laughter, a laughing to tears, out of a nihilistic sense for the utter vanity and ridiculousness of everything. This sense contributes to the delicacy of his taste but causes also his impotence in more than one respect. He is found wanting and refuses to serve wherever he is needed. The absolute potency persists in the state of the potential.

If, on the other hand, in Leverkühn the spirit begets in the flesh, art thus conceived will not be a child of warm natural love, but an incubus out of the devil's laboratory, a hybrid of superform and deformity, of calculation and intoxication, of a feverish mania contracted as an antidote to the icy nihilism of the spirit. This in itself is the contracting with the devil, the blood contract which Adrian enters by taking upon himself the *cross* of a *hellish* sacrifice and having his blood poisoned by contagion from the whore. *Le transparent glacier des vols qui n'ont pas fui*—"the transparent glacier of flights which are not flown"—melts in the heat of the sickened, but also loosened, mind, which now, together with all the pains of hell, experiences also all the transports of illumination and euphoria.

In Thomas Mann's work the enhancement of genius by way of intoxication had a comparatively harmless prelude, above all, in *The Magic Mountain*. Its great, its often literally imitated historical model is, of course, the tragic poem of Nietzsche's life. From this angle new light can be shed upon the sequence of tragedy and travesty. The hectic color of pseudo-vitality in Nietzsche's writings, the boundless ecstasy of a vision which so often checkmates his admirable power of critical analysis, an extremism which sneers at moderation are the bold and ravishing, yet ominous, work of real inspiration, heated by feverish and even delirious dreams. Sober ebriety may be the token of genius, the matrix of art. But to abandon the soberness and poise of responsible thought altogether the better to revel in drunken flights of the spirit proves disastrous not only to the philosopher; it is prompted by malady and must end in madness. In the hands of the mob, Nietzsche's cult of the excessive and orgiastic could not but lead to uninhibited excesses and orgies of shameless barbarism.

The alchemy which produces the gold of music in the witch's kitchen of a poisoned mind is not an exclusively German art, nor is it Thomas Mann's personal invention. The *fleurs du mal* grow in France and Ireland as well as in Germany. 'Magic' and 'magician' have become almost stock phrases for 'art' and 'artist'; they mean the artist's superior, but also disdainful, power over the materials of crude reality, materials which acquire their worth only as inlays in the jewelry of his work; but they have also undertones of his shudder at sacrificing all reality to the moloch of this work, this monster whose claws fasten into the flesh of its own begetter and high priest.[11]

The German Scene

Faust, the German

Having shown Adrian's fate against the background of a time whose sand has run out and of an art whose voice is choked because what had been genuine expression before sounds trite and spurious now, we must acknowledge that, after all, *Doctor Faustus* is a distinctly German tragedy, the heart-rending *De Profundis* of the German soul—even though Leverkühn himself has no (or little) soul and, with Nietzsche and many other great Germans, all but derides the German temperament which he so conspicuously represents.

Faust as the representative of the German—this in itself is of the stock of German tradition. *"Nicht Faust wär' ich, wenn ich kein Deutscher wäre."* ("Were I not German, I would not be Faust!") This is an exclamation from Grabbe's *Don Juan and Faust*.[12] Faust as Protestant recluse, Faust as a musician, priest and victim of a high-strung mentality which is both revolutionary and reactionary, both nihilistic and ecstatic—this shows what, as a German, Thomas Mann has discovered as the truth about German nature.

German Medievalism

Not his earthly birthplace, to which his numbed body will return in the end (*so durchlauf' ich des Lebens / Bogen und kehre, woher ich kam;* "So I describe life's circle, returning to whence I came"),[13] but Adrian's spiritual hometown is Kaisersaschern. This is allegedly a place south of Halle an der Saale, in the middle of Germany and in the heart-center of Lutheran reformation, but it is actually a ubiquitous German city, to which Lübeck as well as Nuremberg, Naumburg as well as Aachen have acted as godmothers. Under the thin varnish of the modern, it is the very embodiment of the timeless old town. Here Otto III, Emperor of the Romans, a prize specimen of German self-contempt, is said to be buried. The main buildings are still medieval, and the air is pregnant with medieval sorcery, devilish tricks and freaks, all the morbid neuroses of the decaying Middle Ages which never died in Germany,[f] but were stubbornly preserved by a never reformed reformation, the work of a man who, all his life, indulged in an intimate struggle with the devil.

Lutheran Air (Daemonologia Deutsch)

It is this stagnant atmosphere, in which Satan is so much better known than the *Deus absconditus,* that stays with Leverkühn from Buchel, his parents' farm, to Pfeiffering, the Bavarian estate, a second Buchel which is his workshop in the years of his artistic maturity. Such brooding air fills the study of his father, who ponders piously over his bulky Luther Bible, but also, like the father of Goethe's Faust, feasts on "speculating the elements" by way of somehow equivocal and tempting 'trials.' Hans Castorps *Placet experiri* is quite innocent compared to the secret satanism which animates the experiments of this strange, slightly sentimental dilettante in the sciences. He pries into the ambiguous realms of nature and the senses, realms where opposite phenomena—visual and acoustic, organic and inorganic appearances, the healthy and the sick—confusingly blend, and the fair is foul and the foul fair.

Adrian's music feeds on the element of the necromantic in his father's inquiries as well as in his own courses in theology at the

Lutheran University of Halle-Wittenberg.* Thus it is always the
same spooky air which surrounds him. In Halle appear, together
with the first premonitions of his fate, the first prefigurations of
the devil, thinly disguised in professorial garb, the same devil who
will finally visit him in person under Italian skies in the small town
of Palestrina (which, together with Rome, was the cradle of *Buddenbrooks*).

The immovable pressure of this intellectual blanket is *linguis-
tically* realized in Leverkühn's Lutheran German, the natural as well
as ironical disclosure of his spiritual locus and personal struggles[14]—
not a mere aping of Luther's hearty voice as in the professional
play-acting of Dr. Kumpf in Halle. And it has its artistic equivalent
in the law of Leverkühn's composition, i.e., the rule of simultaneity
in which the opposites coincide and the free flux of time is transformed into a system of concentric waves "without any dynamic
and dramatic development." [15]

The mystic's insistence on the *nunc stans*, the motionless present of myth and metaphysics, shows here its demoniacal implications. It is not without deep purpose that Thomas Mann concludes
his Goethe essay of 1948 with Goethe's "actually last word," which
is also a holy resolve: "The only thing that counts in the end is
progress." Progress, the bliss of "perennial striving" of Goethe's
Faust, is outlawed in Leverkühn's work which turns against time
because it is without hope, love, and faith. In its arresting of time
this work appears as the grandiose intensification of the all too
modish cult of the primitive, the less sublime yet not less perilous
tendencies and discussions in the milieu of (Thomas Mann's and)
Adrian's Munich contemporaries, and as the sinister variety of that
metamorphosis of passing time into a kind of spatial presence which
occurs in Rilke as well as in the Joseph stories. The modern Faust,
much more medieval than Goethe's, is detained in the circle of his
own magic. He descends from a reformer who hated and anathema-
tized progress, a category of the social sphere which is said to lack
the inwardness of the 'unfathomable' German soul and seems to

* "It is highly significant," says Heine, to whom Thomas Mann owes
more than one of the perspectives of his novel, "that Wittenberg, the
residence of Faust, is at the same time the cradle and laboratory of
Protestantism" (*Werke*, ed. Elster, VI, 501f).

tamper with the absolute significance of man's relation to a merciful God.

Leverkühn's music, religious as it is in a negative sense, is the work of a theological musician in the wake of the musical theologian and expert exorcist Martin Luther.[16] In both men we have the mania of embracing sin though only Luther experienced justification and adoption by a gracious God. Luther's fateful imperative *Pecca fortiter!* ("Sin bravely!")[17] is echoed in Leverkühn's arguing with the devil: "A stepping in sin, so hopelessly far that it makes man radically despair of salvation is the truly theological way of salvation." [g] And while consciously to speculate on the attraction which great guilt exercises on divine mercy is the vilest guilt, it is at the same time and for this very reason "the ultimate and most irresistible challenge to the boundlessness of grace." [18]

In the Lutheran view our world, the world of history as well as of nature, runs the risk of being left to the devil. But, to speak with Kafka, prayer, i.e., true communication with God, is identical with man's relationship and communication with his neighbor and atrophies with it.[19] Religion in Nietzsche's sense, as the exclusive concern for one's own salvation,[20] a concern without regard to the redemption of the world and without laboring for it, issues in words without the right love, words which will "never to heaven go." [h] Debarred from living communion with the life of the whole, art ceases to communicate as either prayer or praise.

Adversary to Works

The unbelief in, and defamation of, works is a profound motif of the Pauline-Lutheran tradition. But if it is not restricted to the *opus operatum*, or work for outer reward, if it is not directed against the idolization of the self-contained and self-sufficient work at the expense of life (human life at large, not solely the realization of the self), then such inveighing against works is in line with the devil's fight against the works of divine love.[21] It is a token of a sinful state which the contract with the devil will confirm rather than create. Leverkühn's alienation from man (an experience which Goethe's Faust was spared) is in itself his alienation from God, his falling away from the source of love, the sun of Deity; it is the dark wood, the *selva oscura* of sin. "What is Hell, oh my brothers?" asks Dostoievsky. "Is it anything but this, that one has become

incapable of love?" Man's dialogue with the divine Thou thus
turns into the talk with the devil, the end of which (on p. 386)
forms exactly the center of Thomas Mann's book (773 pp.).

The feeling of the gap between creator and creation, emphasized in Ockhamism and deepened in Protestant thought, could not
but affect the "creative imitation" (*bildende Nachahmung*) of
nature. The celebration of the "Marvels of Creation" (this is the
title of one of Leverkühn's symphonies) has not only the elements
of parody of his early fantasy "Ocean Lights." It is a sardonic mockery of the 'cosmos' as such, that of art as well as of nature. In a
world where love has ceased to be the golden chain which unites
the creature with both the creator and its fellow beings, the work
is 'out of commission'; it becomes a solitary, somewhat dubious en-
tertainment, not made to be heard after its first conception.[22] "The
work of art? It is a fraud." [23] Beauty is something unsubstantial like
the azure, or dull, or half and half tedious like the beauty of certain
prostitutes among the lepidoptera which father Leverkühn likes
to show, gorgeous in their appearance but unpalatable by reason of
their secretions. Is it mere chance that Adrian will be fatally attracted by one of their sphere? He knows, as such an artist must, of
specious, melancholy, pariah beauty.

The Silent Protest

Yet, his destiny is not that of the artist pure and simple. His
demoniacal isolation is not identical with the productive solitude
of the genius, but mirrors also the refractory way of the German
people. The great idea of a silently protesting and in this sense
Protestant Germany (one will notice how the Thomas Mann of
Doctor Faustus uses both terms 'Catholic' and 'Protestant' in a symbolic as well as historical sense) had its sinister implications even
in *The Magic Mountain* (see above, pages 103-104). Since then, bad
had grown worse, irresponsiveness degenerated into irresponsibility,
seclusion from mankind turned into a murderous all-out attack
on humanity.[1]

Art as Prostitution

Sin as the corruption of the original community of human
beings has always had its most adequate symbol in the sexual sphere.
By merely capitulating to the *connubium* with the senses, Lutheran-

ism has not rehabilitated earthly love as a poem of life, as a work of the soul in which spirit and physical desire interpenetrate and enhance each other. Thomas Mann's definition of the artist as the man in whom all powers conspire, of art as "sensuality spiritualized, spirit informed and made creative by sex," [j] applies also to Leverkühn, but in a frightful, altogether unhealthy way.

The inhibitions of the German Protestant and the haughtiness of a spirit which originally scorned to beget forms in the realm of the soul and the senses[k] pillory art in Leverkühn's eyes as a sort of exhibitionism. The warning of the "*O homo fuge*" ("Man, flee, oh flee!"), the inner voice entreating him as well as the Faustus in Marlowe and the German puppet-show—this warning is to be passed over only by way of transgression (*ein "Schritt vom Wege"* [24]). And the chastity of a homeless mind, not destined to enjoy the "enfranchisement" of a Joseph, leads, at first, to a pure constructivism—an art immune to the "cow-shed warmth" of animal feelings and their expression.

In its nihilistic clairvoyance, which is the perspicacity of a Lucifer rather than a Goethean Lynceus, in its total alienation from the world, spirit cannot overcome all inhibitions without the help of the never extinguished formative will and without an act of utter prostitution (perhaps not altogether without charity, but certainly without human attachment). Art as a product of such prostitution—this is the way in which music appears to pure spirit, another Kundry to the Parsifal in young Leverkühn. Adrian's choice of theology before he surrenders to music—the German fate—is not so much a matter of self-discipline; it seems, above all, a result of his pride, in which he is willing to bring the sacrifice of the intellect to make even philosophy and music ancillary to his own spiritual profession; it is a feast of self-humiliation after the model of Tertullian.[25] His flight to God is a flight from his destination, while conversely his final acceptance of his destiny, this ultimate *amor fati*, means his apostasy *in* faith rather than *from* it.[1] In the hell of lust, he drinks the cup of poison which Shemmael presents to him, and which is not to "pass from him." The hot and cold of the fever thus imbibed instill that naïveté regained which carries him beyond the inhibitions of criticism and nihilism, the fear of the trivial, the qualms of reticence, and the palsies of an "unhappy consciousness."

The Black Magic of Art

Thus is engendered a demoniacal art in which, nevertheless, a wide-awake intelligence holds its own against passion so as to bring the fruit of creative impulse to a subtle and strange identity with the constructions of a trenchant musical calculus. As if to atone for the very fact of its shameless existence, this art withdraws into the recesses of an utterly esoteric style. Willed to be understood rather than to be heard, it contrives all kinds of obstacles to its performance. Representative of its time as this art is supposed to be, it goes without saying that it shows analogies not only to contemporary music but also to the thematic texture of recent literature, as well as to the conceptual patterns of cubism, patterns which add the language of knowledge to that of perception. It will be appropriate, however, briefly to dwell on the technique of indirect and even "inaccessible" communication which Adrian's father had read into nature, and which is 'repeated' in the musical cryptograms of his son, intricate devices for saying things— to nobody. This effort gives rise to an allegorical and often only visible music vaguely reminiscent of the visual acoustic of Chladni (another celebrity from Wittenberg), figures which Jonathan Leverkühn had demonstrated in Adrian's childhood. We thus have cipher writings at best for the eye and thought of the thoroughly initiated reader, who is compelled literally to spell the notes in order to grasp the leitmotifs, which are sometimes kept in the character of merely private allusions such as the ominous cipher h/e/a/es, for *hetaera* (i.e., prostitute) *esmeralda*, which floats through Leverkühn's works.[26]

This method has its parallels not only in the allegories of spiritualistic ages such as early Christian art. There a Christus-formula ("Jesus Christ, God's son, the Saviour"—*Iesus Christos, Theou Hyios, Soter*), for instance, can be represented by a fish because the initials of the Greek words of this phrase constitute the noun *ichthys*, i.e., "fish." But a similar symbolism of numbers and letters can be found in Thomas Mann's own works and, to give only one instance from recent music, in Max Reger's B-a-c-h fugue (after the precedent set by Bach himself). To Leverkühn it serves not only mystagogical purposes but also a desperate urge to wrest from mute inwardness an expression which, still, will not give away his secret.

In his recourse to old ideas and in his bold inventions of new schemes, the reactionary and the revolutionary, ultra-refinement and ostentatious simplicity enter into a not always holy alliance. The ideals of humanism are discarded. The revolting experience of a time in agonies of pain, registered in advance by the sensitive seismograph of art, gives the lie to all striving for harmonious beauty and mediation between the opposites. Unredeemed dissonance is proclaimed the absolute of the time. The harmonics of the humanistic age is transcended in two directions, by means of medieval polyphony and brand-new atonality. But the breaking down of classical traditions does not even intend to break ground for a new freedom. It does not find the way back to the elemental freshness of a vernal season; it is fatally attracted by the artful artlessness, the fantastic logic, the frozen smirk, the guileless corruption of senile primitiveness in the *Gesta Romanorum*. (Yet so is Thomas Mann.)

The tendency of Leverkühn's music is toward a style of absolute power to construct a quasi-astrological constellation of tones, a pseudo-mythical 'at once' in which life is strangled by musical logistics, and everything is exchanged for everything and, with supreme indifference, tricked out of itself.* Witness the imitation in the strict movement, for instance the retrograde imitation (whose revival was announced as early as in *Buddenbrooks*), the role of quotation and travesty, the fusion of the horizontal and the vertical, the neutralization between harmony and melody, the primitive and the hyper-modern, between instrumentation and vocalization and, again, between voice and speech, speech and howling (by way of the gliding voice, the glissando), the identification of the harmonious and the devilish, the dissonant and the angelic, of the hellish laughter and the heavenly children's chorus: take all this together, and you have the uncanny affinity between the earliest and the last utterances of a civilization, a con-fusion such as was systematically exploited and propagandized by the fascist wire-pullers among contemporary intelligentsia; you have a fascinating spectacle, indeed,

---

* This is the intensification of a process we have already observed in the absolute art of the old Goethe, and it has its counterpart in Thomas Mann's own Representationalism.

and, more than this, you can experience an abysmal temptation to which none of us has proved quite immune.

This gives the sadly obvious explanation of the fact that Thomas Mann could 'write' and literally bring to life Leverkühn's not altogether fictive music, which, as a responsible moral agent, he abhors. He knows of it not only by listening to voices from outside. He practices it as the magician he is, in his own musical writing. It is, in a perverted form, one component, but only one component, of his ironical art. He enjoys its fatal charm, and suffers from it unto death. What has become of this play of metamorphoses of which his Goethe can still speak as something "dear and familiar" to him, because the artist is its very high priest—the "seduction" and transmutation of all things moral and natural, past turning to present and *vice versa*, the solemn sacrifice which the part in the play imposes and makes? In the hand of gamblers and prestidigitators, cynics and desperadoes it was to reveal all the hideously perverse features of black magic while keeping nothing of its original pensive grandeur.

A bitter presentiment of this fate already lives in the story of *Mario and the Magician* (1930), which, in its parallelism between fascism and magic art and, actually, the personal union between them in the dirty sleights of the hunchbacked fascist Cipolla, foreshadows *Doctor Faustus*—on a much lower level, it is true. Yet Adrian's forbidding and abstruse art contains the same elements of nihilism and cynical tyranny which Cipolla employs in the vulgar abuse of mass hypnosis to prostitute human beings and travesty human love.

But there is something inhuman in all performances which use living subjects as subject matter according to the pitiless dictate of the work in which they are both quasi transfigured and laid at rest. And our novel reaches the most frightful climax of this process, a process in which art "finishes" life and the formative will triumphs over the human heart and depletes the resources of human strength. The artistic interment comes literally and hyperbolically true in this novel when Thomas Mann's own and most beloved grandson has to die *in effigie*, in the angelic figure of little Nepomuk. He dies of meningitis, in heart-rending agonies of pain—prey to what seems the poisonous climate of artistic sorcery. It is a correct, but somewhat philistine, distinction to observe that, after all, Leverkühn does

not really kill his little nephew, and that the murderous influence
of Adrian's "evil eye" exists only in his hypochondriac imagination.
It is of the peculiar nature of this story, even more than of other
works of Thomas Mann, that its vision transcends the boundaries
between inner and outer reality, the mental and the physical, fact
and imagination. If it were different, what would become of the
contract with the devil? The devil's existence here as well as that of
Abraham's (and, in a way, Thomas Mann's) God in the Joseph
saga are beyond the alternative of matter of fact and mere chimera.
The same holds true of whatever happens under their signs. And it
applies also to the so-called real world and the world of the novel—
they are not ultimately distinct. The sacrifice he makes *in effigie*
is a real sacrifice to Thomas Mann; it is his way toward Mount
Moriah. It is the way Jacob felt unable to go—and still went by
sending Joseph to his brothers and thus into the pit.

The personal sacrifice and self-accusation in this dreadful offering, made as if to pacify the dark deities, ought to remove all semblance of pharisaism from the book's accusation of the German
people. It reveals the most dismal ingredients which enter into the
conditions of an art that grows at the barren brink of nihilism; and
it allows us to understand more deeply and with a boundless sympathy the last words of *Mario and the Magician*, spoken over
Cipolla's dead body: "a horrible—yet, after all, a redeeming end; I
could not and cannot help feeling that way." Not only society has
been freed from its oppressor. Cipolla, the magician, himself has
been freed from the convulsions of the restlessly suffering, restlessly
working will, from the strain and martyrdom of the will to power—
an inhuman power.

Eschatology

The presence of both Leverkühn and Zeitblom in Thomas
Mann makes him the martyr as well as the *testis*, the witness and
narrator, in this oratorio, this cantata of the last judgment, which
is, at the same time, a recantation of the past. The *mysterium tremendum* of the whole consists very much in the fact that the fear
and trembling, the admiration and terror, the pity and rejection are
those of a bystander whose own cause is at stake.

Thomas Mann writes what he has experienced as the great and horrible possibilities he has in common with his people. He writes it at the foot of the cross; he speaks from the cross itself. In reality he undergoes all this during the same days, weeks, and months in which his Zeitblom reports and denounces the execration and defeat of his country and recalls, at the same time, the portentous overture to the present German deluge in the life and death of his "representative" friend, he who was so "frightfully visited, lifted up and hurled down."

In the alarum trumpets of the void, in its howling and rearing, bleating and crowing, Leverkühn's "Apocalypse" anticipates the cataclysm of our historical world. And that this is the end toward which "everything rushes and tumbles, under the sign of the end stands the whole world"—this is the refrain which, beginning with the Dante motto *Lo giorno se n'andava* ("The day drew to its end"), recurs throughout the book.

There is one farewell after the other. These adieux commence in the musical sphere after what amounts to a tuning of the instruments in the delightful, Chardin-like still life of uncle Leverkühn's music shop. The first leavetaking occurs in a tender, unspeakably moving dirge, the translation from music into language of Beethoven's Opus 111, in which the form of the sonata reaches its end and transfiguration.

But music means "everything" in this musical novel. The end of the sonata has a symbolical bearing. It marks the end of an epoch. The form of aesthetic idealism, the ideal of individual universality is destined to pass, and in Beethoven's and Goethe's last creations *has* passed, into a new myth, that of a moral and social era.[m] That God is no longer "great in us"—as one of Thomas Mann's paraphrases of the sonata's arietta-motif has it, that (to speak with Nietzsche) "God has died," means, in human terms, that the highest norm and form of man's former existence has lost its binding power and that in such a world, forsaken by God, we do not know for what to live and to die. In this vacuum of lovelessness the devil becomes the most real experience. The *"Eli, Eli, lama sabachthani?"* in "The Lamentation of Dr. Faustus" is the outcry of one who feels condemned to hell, with no resurrection and ascension in sight.[n]

God—the God under whose sign Thomas Mann's Joseph conquered the temptation of a culture of graves—is the God of a coming age, an age of men who have a future, coming up as they do to the Highest, whom they can choose and by whom they are chosen (just as to reject and be rejected are one). In opening our hearts to the Lord of the future, we know that devotion to the Thou which gives fulfillment to the self. The deadlock of this fundamental correlation of I and Thou—and Leverkühn (and not he alone) shrinks back from the very word "Thou"—marks the suspension of the covenant of life and is in itself a liaison with the powers of hell.[27] It is exactly right that to one like Adrian, whose life has lost the true support of the Thou, the devil appears in the guise of a *souteneur*, as the friend of the whore whom Adrian gives the name of that butterfly, Hetaera Esmeralda. Hetaera means companion, and apart from the prostitute there is only one real "companion" to Adrian, the untouchable: his nihilistic chum,[28] the chaste and sterile virtuoso Rüdiger Schildknapp. Intercourse without love, existing together without sharing existence, such is life in such a world—a desert illumined by the St. Elmo's fires of an icy burning art.

This is the end and burial of an era. In *Doctor Faustus* an old man looks back to his own life, that of his friend, and that of his age. And what he sees is death—death in the majestic exit of a great tradition, but also in the barrenness in which it issues; in the pseudo-life of travesty, the "aristocratic nihilism"—so well known to Thomas Mann—in which old forms are perpetuated, reverently or not; in hollow mimicry instead of true succession; in the defilement of the holy by the vomit of the serpent's poison; in a spiritual and intellectual obstruction to work, which only the sin against the purity of the spirit and the befuddling of intellectual conscience seem able to overcome; in the self-betrayal and corruption of a culture which glories in diagnosing its own decline and death and throwing itself to the wolves.[o]

The end of all things—Zeitblom experiences it in 1945, terror-struck like the disciple of the Apocalypse, just as, with the deep apprehension of the humanist, he experienced its prefiguration in the "Apocalipsis" of his friend. And Thomas Mann himself? The answer cannot be given in a few simple words. To the admirer of Schopenhauer and the romantic the idea of the end is alluring rather than frightening. Throughout his life he has sympathized with his Gustav Aschenbach in feeling nothingness to be a form of the perfect, a repose for his melancholy; to use a Nietzsche dictum on music of which the passage in *Death in Venice* reminds us: music and the deep, drowning sea, they belong together. "The truly noteworthy and pleasurable is death," so he writes Karl Kerényi in 1938, words in which both Schopenhauer and Freud are alive; "one strives and desires all the time to finish his works and does not realize that, at bottom, he strives to be finished himself and be dead." [p] "To be chosen to stay" (*"zum Bleiben erkoren" zu sein*) is a charge and duty rather than a gain.

It is a duty. Mann does not allow himself to indulge in voluptuous death dreams. In opposition to the promptings on the part of metaphysical knowledge, he has resolved, in *The Magic Mountain*, to side with life, not in any blind enthusiasm, but in a spirit of sympathy and compassionate loving-kindness. This resolution he has followed out through a network of restless activities for the cause and the causes of struggling humanity. Without love and care, so Hans Castorp intuitively realizes, there can be no genuine form.[29] And in the last hour of his conscious life even Leverkühn confesses to the ideal of the "beautiful work" as the expression of an order of life which we are in duty bound to restore.[30]

But *Doctor Faustus* would not be what it is—a passionate, wild, and agitating confession—in fact, there would have been no personal necessity for it at all, were it a fruit ripened in the new social climate. Thomas Mann has not ceased to stand, as Tonio Kröger did, "between two worlds without being at home in either one"; and it is a typical understatement (which is corrected in the Faustus novel) that "for this reason things are a little bit difficult for him." [31] The choice is no longer that between the bourgeois and the bohemian who comes in such a questionable shape. It is not ultimately that between naïve and sentimental. It is that between the aesthetic and the social attitudes, between the solitary work of the magician and the working for human communion. It is just as much a German question as a question put to Thomas Mann himself, as the master of an art magical to such a great extent.

To Break Through!

To break through! This is, indeed, what the book itself intends, and (like Leverkühn's "Lamentation") in a way achieves: a German break-through, as a solution of *the* German problem,[32] much more promising than the famous break-throughs at the military fronts, much more legitimate than any political expansion into a 'Germany-over-all.' *Doctor Faustus*, Zeitblom's and Thomas Mann's work, has been composed in spatial and moral distance from the German fall and catastrophe, yet—without composure—in the most intimate proximity of a trembling soul to the German fate. At heart, Thomas Mann has never emigrated from his native country. His return to the German-speaking part of Switzerland is more than a political and even a symbolic gesture; it is the expression of an existential need on the part of the German author. He renounced solidarity with the German people only so far as he denounces the element of the demoniacal in his own German heritage. He has turned away from German provincialism only to immigrate into man's true homeland—humanity.

Even so, Mann's work is a break-through *in actu*, not an accomplished fact. It is not a Beethovenian "Thanksgiving for Recovery"; rather, it shows all the tokens of a developmental crisis and the heavy laboring for a new era of the new and unknown God, the God to be born.

Baring himself, at last, with unsparing frankness, thrusting forward to the last things, recording as it were the last words of the old world, Thomas Mann wrote what, in its report of the daily news, is literally a novel, while cutting the ground from under the novel as such, the novel taken as the artistic form of that age which is consigned to the grave. He himself felt this work to be his *Parsifal*.* [33] In its dialectical unity of perfect construction and boundless expressiveness, it marks a break in the magic circle of proud and hopeless isolation. Yet it conquers by means of the same weapons which it outlaws. Like the aged Faust, Thomas Mann can-

---

* In this sense it is also the last word of Thomas Mann. *The Holy Sinner* and *Felix Krull* do not mark a new epoch in his work. Bravuras of the virtuoso and the humorist in Mann, they are like satiric dramas— the epilogue after the curtain has gone down over the tragedy.

not do without the very magic which he abjures. Nor can he, as Shakespeare did, break his staff and drown his book "deeper than did ever plummet sound." He still enjoys as an artist what as a moralist he condemns to death; and in the moral desolation of the middle forties he found comfort in the morning hours of solitary absorption in his artistry, in an atmosphere akin to that of his principal character.[34]

New Meaning

Of Ambiguity

Breaking down the walls of isolation by breaking through to the sphere of the soul and unobstructed communion—that is what "The Lamentation of Dr. Faustus" signifies in Leverkühn's life and *Doctor Faustus* itself in Thomas Mann's. This correspondence is another token of the consubstantiality Mann feels with his ill-fated hero. And indeed, both works overcome the sphere of play, above all the half-playful, half-melancholy ambiguity of ironical suspension, artistic neutrality. (In "Faust's Lamentation" the prolonged notes and retardations are but rhythmical devices; they have ceased to express a spirit of reserve, the irresponsible dwelling on the not-yet.)[35] Even so, neither work dispenses with ambiguity as such or with any of the factors of musical constructivism characteristic of Thomas Mann's own compositions, such as mythical identity and repetition, number and letter symbolism, and so on. But like the recurrent suspensions, most of these constituents assume a new meaning at their new developmental stage.

Of Repetition

Repetition, for example, takes on the form of quotation, self-quotation of a leitmotif, variation of a fundamental musical figure, but also, and above all, quotations from letters and works of other writers and even slogans of the time (such as "*Durchbruch*").[q] In this way, in the way of an interweaving of myth and reportage, threads are followed out which lead beyond the context of Thomas Mann's story into the historical reality which it symbolizes. The adoption of old forms and motifs assumes a new seriousnesness and is much more than a mere escape from sterility, the witty yet desperate recourse to patterns which, while having ceased to be genuine forms of life (as in Chirico's and Picasso's classicism), are still good as toys, wooden bricks, in a superior, though hopelessly resigned, intellectual play.

As Travesty (the Helena Motif)

The festive mood in which the Joseph saga and the Goethe novel celebrated repetition as mythical imitation is always threatened by a recurrence of the paralyzing feeling of re-presentation as mere substitute for a truly creative life, as a satanic mimicry of a great tradition. It is this suspicion of cynical and even nihilistic travesty that falls upon Leverkühn's and, with a heavier impact than before, upon Thomas Mann's own earlier works. It is overcome only in the supreme effort of the final break-through. The Faust cantata is "without parody." And in Thomas Mann's own novel, travesty itself has not disappeared, but in view of the shameless travesty by Nazism of the genuine motifs in German life, it has lost all of its roguish smile; and even where it appears as an artistic device or as part of a mythical process, it is imbued with the feeling of fathomless grief.

There is for instance the abysmal gloom in the revival of the sublime Helena motif within the life of today's Faust. The lower world from which the royal, fateful hetaera ascends for a propitious wedding with the Nordic mind has now turned into the brothel of Leipzig, and Helena into the whore who infects Leverkühn with the stimulant of deadly disease. What a frightful degradation of a great epical theme! Yet, it is not without example. It is prefigured in the old chap-book on Faust, and its tenor is close to what we find in Joyce's *Ulysses*. It measures as it were the measureless distance not only between the heroic and the modern age, but also between Goethean humanism and the doomsday of our historical world.[r]

As Dehumanization (the Echo Motif)

Imitation is transformation. But it is not necessarily spiritualization, the upward trend which prevailed in *Joseph and His Brothers* and in most of *The Beloved Returns*. It may be depersonalization as well, as in the case of little Nepomuk, or Echo as he calls himself, mispronouncing his name in a childlike yet meaningful way. For he is a Christian elf and thus echoes the loveliness and wisdom of an

earlier and purer age and stage of being. He does it in his heavenly
appearance and near epiphany and in the old German verses which
he so strangely uses for his prayers. And when the little Ariel has
returned "to the elements," Leverkühn's art, in one of the allegorical
contrivances in which it is rich, enrolls him among the gods of the
elements, as the echo, "this giving back of the human voice as a
sound of nature."

The echo as a musical effect derives from Monteverdi's madri-
galism. There it serves as the expression of an experience which in
"Doctor Faustus' Lamentation" reaches a point of climactic emphasis, namely, the lament over the fact that, in the face of all his
spiritual aspirations, man is a part of nature to which he is destined
to return. This musical echo transfigures and preserves Echo's existence, but it also prefigures Leverkühn's fate.

*"Ewig lebendige Natur/ macht auf uns Geister,/ wir auf sie
vollgültigen Anspruch"* ("Eternally living nature lays fully legitimate
claims upon us spirits just as we do upon her").[36] Adrian's last
music is elemental in the outburst of human lamentation and in man's
coming home from his solitary flights. "Icarus! Icarus! Pity and
Pain!" [37] There is no solo in Leverkühn's "Faustus." [38] And whereas
in Beethoven's "Ode to Joy" (of which the "Faustus" cantata is the
recantation) the human voice comes to dominate the instruments,
Adrian lets the "continuo" of the orchestra rise from human lament
and conclude the whole. The human voice is silenced.

The last word is nature's; the last station on one's way is the
native ground of 'Buchel.' The spirit's break-through is not to Nirvana as in Schopenhauer, at least not to Schopenhauer's Nirvana. It
is to life and love. But this means the end, the transgression of the
boundaries of Leverkühn's existence. Hence, it means also the end
of this novel. The process of *The Magic Mountain* repeats itself
in this regard. Just as Naphta is survived by Settembrini, and as in
Hans Castorp's case the break-through to life has to be paid for by
death—so the humanist Zeitblom lives on to relate the break-down
of the absolute spirit. Cruel and mild, mother Leverkühn, mother
Nietzsche, mother Earth, takes man, this "poor, dear child"—"life's
delicate child" as *The Magic Mountain* had it—she takes him back
to her "bosom from which she cannot help feeling he would have
done better never to turn away." [39] In one of her mocking games,
nature who in his childhood showed him semblances of life where

there were only dead crystals, now lends a semblance of the purest spirituality to Adrian's face when the spirit has fled.*

Of Identification

Repetition is variation of an identical motif. And just as, in *Doctor Faustus*, the inner meaning of this process has changed, so has also the meaning of the identity which underlies all the differences and even contrarieties of appearance. The former implications of this reduction of the many to the one are still alive, but they contribute to a new moral and religious end. The category of the "at once," of simultaneity, still serves as a metaphysical stratagem to 'kill time' and deny substantial change in the course of events: but the magic circle of Leverkühn's existence in the stagnant air of Buchel and Kaisersaschern has become an ominous sign of a specific historical constellation.* *

Artistically, the identity of the themes and the recurrence of the leitmotifs in Thomas Mann strengthen the conciseness of his composition and the unity of its mood—a mood which, thanks to the overlapping of individual contours, always had a touch of a

---

* The bittersweet resignation to the sway of Mother Nature, who will take over 'after all,' is a new tone in Thomas Mann's work during the last decade. We hear it again in *The Black Swan*.

** Still, it should be noticed that the magic square, which seems to show how all things may amount to the same, since its numbers always yield the identical result (34) in whatever way one may add them—this square not only belongs to the furnishings of Dürer's 'Melencolia' and Leverkühn's room, but is a permanent implement of Thomas Mann's own world. 34—that had been the number of Hans Castorp's room in the Sanatorium Berghof; and with this numeral, its constituents, and its sum—the holy 7—a half-serious, half-roguish play is performed in *The Magic Mountain*. The same number 34 reappears 3 times over the chapters of *Doctor Faustus* which are centered around the problems of the "affinity between aestheticism and barbarism" and of "calculation raised to the point of mystery." The 47 chapters can thus be grouped in $\underbrace{13+(3\times7)+13}_{34 \qquad 34}$; the ominous import of 13 is 'duly' emphasized in the chapter at the head of which it stands. The humanist in Thomas Mann—Zeitblom—may protest that "mystic numbers are not in his line" (p. 174), but for the whole of Thomas Mann's being this is contradicted by the very composition of *Doctor Faustus* itself—even by the less important fact that its 47 chapters were brought to conclusion in January 1947. Cf. also p. 213 above and "Lebensabriss," *Neue Rundschau* (1930), p. 769. *The Holy Sinner* is full of this 'mathematical' hocus-pocus.

dreamy vision. Now, however, it is not done any longer with the thoughtful confusion of mystic-mythical participation. Not only, as in the story of the patriarchs, the morally positive but, above all, the incriminating ingredients of *imitatio* are brought to light. The *imitatio Nietzsche* appears in its fatal significance; the mythical identification with him has as its moral counterpart the critical recognition of co-responsibility and a confession of common guilt.

Religious Dialectics

The atonement for this guilt may in itself be indicative of a final at-oneness between man and man, and men and God. This leads to the problem of a religious dialectics in which the opposites collide and coincide without the mediation of a Hegelian synthesis. There may be a mediator in whom this antagonism is brought to a head, one who "bears our griefs and carries our sorrows," but there is no mechanism by which the opposites are reconciled in a comforting harmony.

This belongs to the signature of our time. In affixing the claim of absoluteness to dissonance rather than harmony, modern music expresses a universal and radical experience of man today and endorses Kierkegaard's indictment of the "fraud of mediation." [s]

The same inexorability of feeling and insight dictates the refusal to sneak into a sham comfort or to accept a specious happiness which is disowned by the wretchedness of the creature. It is the purest and deepest element in Leverkühn which gives the lie to this world's goodliness and rejects as devilish temptation any offer of salvation in the form of false, flabby, and complacent piety. He is a brother of Ivan Karamazov, who would return the entrance ticket to heaven and superior harmony rather than acquiesce in the tortures of an innocent child,[t] and who despises a hosanna that has not first gone through the melting furnace of doubt.[u]

Thomas Mann himself clings to that strict paradox of "inversion" which makes its appearance in Leverkühn's last work; there artistic construction itself becomes a means of expression, and the unmitigated despair of the reprobate is transfigured into a hope against all hope, beyond all faith, and apart from all speculation on mercy—mercy growing in proportion to the sinfulness that cries out for it. But this paradox is not simply stated for its own sake; in all its irrationality it is made to be experienced and understood. Similarly the *coincidence* of A and Non-A is finally lifted beyond the sphere of confusion and stagnation in which black magic had felt at home. There still remains the dwelling on the twofold sense of the phenomena: but the cutting pain of the ambivalence of being has replaced the pleasures of ironical suspense and ambiguity which Leverkühn—like Thomas Mann—enjoyed in his youth. Transcendence overcomes the motionless state in which two factors countervail one another. The second factor, however, does not annihilate the first. If for instance "The Lamentation of Dr. Faustus" has, after all, "a jubilant, a highly triumphant connotation," [40] it does not cease to be lament emitted in the "cauldron of oil" and in burning pain.[41] Its last dying sound, the dying away of the wailing, does not cease to be the voice of mourning, even though, to use Thomas Mann's verselike sentence, it "changes its sense, abides as a light in the dark." [42] Let us try to understand this metamorphosis within the very heart of identity.

Judas and His Kin

Doctor Faustus is the continuation and woeful deepening of the Judas story, whose sadness is not fully developed in the idyllic, patriarchal atmosphere of the Joseph saga and is even partly drowned out by the noise of an uneasy buffoonery. Judah, the "slave of hell," the victim of Astarte, he who despairs of his own salvation, he who in the "pride of conscience" insists on his pain and penalty and cannot believe in the supreme blessing whose heir he is elected to be—Judah is the somewhat burlesque prefiguration of Leverkühn. Notwithstanding their individual differences, they both are brought to a point of mythical identification with Judas Iscariot, the Antichrist. But the extremes touch. Judah is also the ancestor of Jesus; and Thomas Mann stresses the Jesus-like features in Leverkühn just as well as his satanism.[43] This is not a cynical neutralization of good and evil nor an aestheticistic extolling of the latter. Nothing is taken away from the terror of Adrian's sins and fate. But did not Christ himself descend to Hell? And is not, as the Prelude to *Joseph and His Brothers* has it, each sounding of the soul's depths such a descent? The way through the hell of self-knowledge, says the *Theologia Germanica* (ch. XI), is a secure way for man; in his insecurity he is safe, and God himself will take care of him even though man will feel unworthy of any comfort and seem eternally lost and condemned:

> Decaying, dying,
> I live uncomforted.
> Damned I am
> Without, within.
> No one pray
> That I be redeemed.[44]

This is the spiritual setting from which an ultimate understanding of Leverkühn's life and works must be derived.

Thomas Mann and the God to whom he confesses have always sided with the sinners rather than with the lukewarm, the Pharisees, and even the angels. Like Judah, the slave of Astarte, Leverkühn sins in the flesh against the purity of the spirit—and, yet, impelled by this pure spirit itself. This purity is sterile since this spirit is loveless. In obedience to his calling, Leverkühn needs the fever of lust to make up for his lack of warm and creative devotion. "Sin is a determination of the spirit." [45] The brute does not sin. Only he who is in God, and in whom God is himself, is able to fall from him.[46] While Joseph and his kin, those who are luckily safe from apostasy (though not from compromise), will be subject to the strict verdict of "withholding love," redemption may come through the ennoblement of suffering from, and even perishing by, sin. Pillory and throne may be one. One who is condemned and condemns himself to hell may be, like Dante's Virgil, carrying at night on his back a lamp which does not light the path for him but illumines it for those who follow.[47]

The question on which *Doctor Faustus* concludes (the question as to a ray of hope) is even more desperate than that at the end of *The Magic Mountain;* but, as a question, it is not as hopeless as the notice of Aschenbach's surrender to death. Notwithstanding his aloofness, Leverkühn has, in his works, com-posed the tendencies of his age. Like Aschenbach, he is (in spite of his satanism) " 'a hero of our time,' a man who bears the sufferings of his epoch" [48]—in a way which Thomas Mann feels to be not altogether at variance with his own way. "Not resisting the evil," he has accepted the fate of reprobation, has diagnosed the state and borne the pains and transgressions of his time as his trangressions and pains, without heroic histrionics, but with the conscientiousness of the religious man "who seeks hard things and to whom it is hard," as the apostle says.[49] In his intercourse with the diseased whore whom, a sinner and saint, he restores to the state of a loving human being, he chooses both sin and penalty. He forfeits his own salvation, as it were, to 'work out' that of the others by means of vicarious suffering. "Somebody must always have been sick and crazy so that the others may be better off." [50] Throughout the book "lust-hell" and Gethsemane, *Daemonologia* and *Theologia Deutsch*, are one. "*Die dunkle Hölle und die leuchtende Helle hallet aus e i n e m Herzen*"—an untranslatable observation of Jakob Böhme* and another token of the consanguinity between Thomas Mann and German mysticism.

The personal union of features of Christ and Antichrist in Leverkühn does not mean the sentimental or blasphemous proclamation of Judas the Redeemer. There is no flourish of trumpets over Leverkühn's grave. His "Lamentation" as well as Thomas Mann's novel represent, first of all, a final (and that means also fatal) expiation of the artist. It is the liberation from the frigidity of the spirit to new adventures in the world of human feeling, from frigid isolation to communication with mankind.[51]

Ode to Woe

But how can such real communion come to pass in our time and with artists like Leverkühn and the Leverkühn in Thomas Mann? Not by way of fraternization with the *polloi,* nor as recognition of the artist on the part of a cultural elite, the public, a social category which belongs to the past.[52] Or as national and international fame, a popularity which one enjoys in a glow of gratitude while knowing (as Tonio Kröger already knows) that, to some extent, it is built on a mistake.[53] Nor is it done with the metaphysical dream of a *tat tvam asi*, with the intellectual assimilation of the diverse world views or the half-reverent, half-mocking imitation of mythical prototypes. Mightier, more radical than any of these attempts of almost five decades to break through the walls of individuation is the experience of common destiny, the compassion with suffering mankind. It is

*An approximate translation: "Lucifer's hell and Helios' light hail from the same heart."

this voice which sounds even in the early sketch "The Hungry";[54] Tonio Kröger and Prince Klaus Heinrich are on the point of hearing it, and the grateful audience of Gustav Aschenbach are united by the recognition of the bitter heroism of weakness as the sign under which they can find each other in his work.[55] Later on, the aloofness of the artistic magician in Thomas Mann may prefer to *compassion* and *love* more temperate terms such as Joseph's *sympathy*, in which friendliness to life takes the chill from the veneration for death;[56] not to speak of Leverkühn's strongest feeling, an icy yet poignant *interest*.[57] The ultimate strength and unifying power of compassion reveals itself only in the agony of passion which has gripped mankind since 1933. It is this universal misery which cries out in Thomas Mann's work, both in Zeitblom's threnody, the accompaniment of the German disaster, and in Leverkühn's "Lamentation," which "embraces millions" not in the "Ode to Joy" but in one of lethal grief and despair. It is a crescendo of mourning in which the whole creation joins, and which draws in even the lament of the creator, who (to speak with the young Werfel) blinds himself with weeping while his world burns to ashes. Whereas release *from* despair appears as satanic temptation, there is liberation *in* a despair which finds the voice of lamentation for men to gather in the common confession of their common misery.

Communion of Woe

The break-through to the soul is thus, at once, the breaking through the ice of satanic nihilism, the break-through of love, and the break-through of lament. Compassionate love, that is, love in a community of passion, gives rise to the one thing which is needed now, the only thing which is still permissible in art: not—or ultimately not—the juggling play of the *ioculator Dei*, who gives to human impotence and extremity a specious appearance, but "the undisguised and untransfigured expression of suffering in its actual occurrence." [v] The passionateness of unbearable grief thus finally opens the mouth of one who had long entrenched himself behind the walls of melancholy humor and trenchant irony, but to whom (as to Goethe's Tasso) a god has granted the power to express what he suffers—the sufferings of failing mankind. It is and remains the privilege of the artist, even one of Leverkühn's painful hauteur, that his individual experiences have a symbolic value, a universal bearing. Through this identity of his ultimate concern with theirs he now becomes, with or without his intent, the representative of men's cause, the mouth of their complaint.

Art thus ministers to a compassionate, not an idolatrous, humanism. Ultimately, Thomas Mann is not satisfied with that service which art renders nature by transferring reality from the sphere of temporal flux to that of perennial perfection. His whole work from *Tonio Kröger* to *Doctor Faustus* attests to his suffering from the inhumanness of conceit which gives to existence only one function—"to get into a book," as Mallarmé said. The form is to be a *document humain* in the progressive formation of life, the work one's working on himself, a moral achievement in the self-realization which it works out—at the same time, however, a help for men to find each other, even if only in the form of the wretched We, the chorus which intones the *De Profundis* of distress. (An ethics of self-realization and an ethics of compassion belong together.)

Expiatory Death

Leverkühn's struggle for the soul and its expression is, thus, the struggle for love and its work. It is a fatal, a self-sacrificial struggle because it is against the law of this life, the law written down in the compact with the devil. This pact means the prohibition of love.[w] In obedience to it, Leverkühn contrives the death of Rudi Schwerdtfeger, to whose wooing siege he had surrendered his solitude in a touch of loneliness and a stroke of love. In enforcement of it, little Nepomuk is taken from him, this messenger from a far-off world who cannot stay in one of devil and death. The torment of this thought wrings from Leverkühn the blood of his life and the wine of his "Lamentation." It brings to a head the process of physiological osmosis, the disease which ends in the benighted state of a spirit not made for love. No skies open over his body, no angels fly down to receive his immortal part (as they do to redeem the soul of Goethe's Faust).

But in him, too, "the eternal love" has, after all, "its part," the very part which Nepomuk-Echo represents. (He represents it in an appearance as full of sad sweetness, as incommensurable as

Mignon's in Goethe's *Meister*.)[x] The little angel, like Tadzio a
messenger from another shore, has not come in vain. Adrian's lonely
mind transcends itself in an expression of universal fellowship, even
though, in its present state, it is a fellowship in distress. The last
word of a passing life, the "Lamentation," is a legacy to the future.
While presenting, in a way, Thomas Mann's "German Requiem" as
well as the final judgment in his self-trial, even *Doctor Faustus*
speaks, though in the death pangs of pain,[y] "in the lowest of
whispers," of a "Die and rise."

Ecce Homo

'Symbol' means 'coincidence.' In the symbol of Adrian Leverkühn's sin and expiation there coincide a condemnation of the
German people and a self-condemnation of the German artist, but
also a testimonial for a nation that aimed so high and fell so deep
and Thomas Mann's *apologia pro vita sua*.[z] Just as Leverkühn dies
as a "good and a bad Christian"—this is the general theme of the
variations in that "monster-work of lament"—so are good and bad
inseparable in the German people and its foremost representatives.
At the hour of lowest degradation, Thomas Mann restored German
man to himself in the figure of a Lucifer with his at once sublime
and satanic powers; a monument of wrath and anxiety, warning and
pride, loving and painfully critical solidarity with his people. No
one can do more.

As to himself, the radical wildness of his self-accusation is in
itself his best self-defense. In its heart-searching, heart-rending
manner, it is the resumption of earlier warnings brought out in a
more humorous and even cynical vein[58] (by which short-sighted
critics have been misled to overlook the intense honesty of a true
disciple of Nietzsche). Much as we love the epical naïveté of times
past, we prefer this reckless confession to the paint of health, to
sacerdotal airs and artificial innocence, temptations which Thomas
Mann knew and overcame in his Gustav Aschenbach.[aa] The an-
tistrophe to these confessions and their legitimate restriction is, in
this book, the very existence of the humanist Zeitblom—the Erasmus
in Mann,[bb] that other *Ego* which made him flee from his
country's sin, though not deny his being implicated in its presuppositions. He did not deny them any more than he denounced his

metaphysical patrimony, but he did not acquiesce in them either. He has suffered from them and incessantly sought to transform his chains into ties.

Devoted action, action in a spirit of compassionate love—this is actually the binding link between sinister metaphysical intuition and the postulate of the primacy of practical reason. But this link needs to be forged and strengthened to stand the disruptive forces of which we spoke, a story that can only briefly be recapitulated at this point. It is the story of human alienation and growing nihilism in the world of the machine age which has its measure no longer in either God or man. It is, at the same time, the story of human estrangement, of a disintegrating society under the cheerless sign of the principle of an individuation where the individual is everything and nothing. We have seen how, in Northern Protestantism, this emancipation of the individual was intoned originally on a deep religious note; but it developed there, too, that "demoniacal inwardness with a jammed lock" of which Kierkegaard speaks, and of which Leverkühn is an eminent example. In him, this danger grows into satanism, since here the individual isolation of modern man is coupled with, and intensified by, the homelessness of the modern artist. The detachment, the mental distance which belongs to the nature of aesthetic experience and the freedom of artistic mastery, becomes utter disjunction where it is not balanced by a loyal and loving attachment to men and things.

In the novel the symbol of this total estrangement and lovelessness is that of the icy cold of diabolic nihilism, the coldness as the element of Leverkühn's life, the icy air which breathes upon him from his devil. This is the Nietzschean motif of Zarathustra in his weary hour, Zarathustra in agony as his own victim,

> Cold by dint of every frost . . .
> A sick man now,
> He, sick by snake-poison . . .[59]

The frigid glittering of virtuosity which some people ascribe to Thomas Mann himself is, thus, not his individual fault; it is a painful stigma of the time and its artist. A strong aversion to the world as it is engendered that cold passion of pitiless observation and concise and trenchant expression which has made the arrow a symbol of both Leverkühn's[60] and Thomas Mann's critical art. It is the sad

privilege of this art to show how the formerly holy and still beloved is hollowed out, how much of that which once seemed the
substance of life is either insubstantial now or transsubstantiated into
something ghostlike by which man is both haunted and bewitched.
The artistic analysis proves destructive and confirms destruction in
the very piety and minuteness of its reconstructive effort, in the
thoroughness of its embalming of the dead. The former constituents of solid reality have become mere "materials for *chefs-d'oeuvre*
without faith," toys in a sovereign artistic play. But it is, at the
same time, a bitter play that cannot help exposing the poverty and
sterility of a generation compelled to borrow for its products the
forms and contents of a perhaps venerated, yet actually relinquished,
past. The ironical invalidation of a still officially supported cur-
rency is just as radical as is the open revolt against each and any conventional value. In either case the artist is both the bailiff and the
victim in a bankruptcy which he makes public.

Yet to "clear the ground," to dispose of what is definitely past,
is not necessarily the nihilism of a Bazarov. In Thomas Mann it
goes together with an attempt to follow out the still working
motives, to pour new wine into the bottles of the old forms, and will
thus be put into the service of the "one day" which is at once the
living past and the true promise of the future. The *taedium vitae*
remains the negative expression of his nostaligic longing for atonement and at-oneness, for that ultimate unity of life which, in the
torn conditions of our existence, he can show but in its bifurcations
and prefigurations, in its experimental stages and failures, in the
casting and recasting of types which give the individual a hold, but
leave him also a free hand in the evolution of the whole. We thus
saw a metaphysical longing mature into the earnest search for the
perennial conditions and foundations of communal life—for the
sempiternal, as far as it will emerge from conscientiously fulfilling
the order of the day, from "the daily observance of strict and
earnest services" (*von "schwerer Dienste täglicher Bewahrung"*).[61]

Painfully groping in this crucial hour of human history,
Thomas Mann re-presents his time in a critique which is art and in
an art which is critique—so radical a criticism, indeed, that it goes
to the very bottom, from which a new beginning may be made.
But not by him; not in his world and ours; rather in the messianic
world of a future whose coming we feel as we long and strive for it;

in that third kingdom whose 'martyrs' Thomas Mann's figures are: suffering witnesses, that is, of a faith which pervades their doubts and belies their weakness.

Such is Thomas Mann's work, a soul-searching work—the search for a new soul. In its passionate intensity, in its enduring honesty, in the indefatigable resumption of his efforts lies the greatness of the example which he has set. To be on the way—this is the mark of the presence of the Platonic Eros in his writings, and means his conquest over the desire to have finished and be done with. His restless activities over the years show the spur of the "restless wandering spirit" in one who was not born to be (or ever to become) a "father of faith"; they show the thorn in the spirit as well as in the flesh of a man who was made the epilogist of a past world rather than the apostle of a new covenant. His labor is his reward. In the *Reflections of an Unpolitical Man* he still asks desperately the question of Claudel's Violaine: "Why must my body labor in Christianity's stead?" Now, accepting his part the way his persons do, he resigns himself to his fate in the Dante motto of *Doctor Faustus: "Io sol uno / m'apparecchiava a sostener la guerra"* ("I only, quite alone, made ready to sustain the fight . . .").

Can absolute faithfulness be without some absolute faith? In Thomas Mann's faithfulness to his calling, in his conscientious workmanship faith checks the never silent scepticism, the ever present anguish. In his undiminished, youthful, ever daring productivity, which is, at once, lust and compulsion, duty and grace, he represents the formative will of the ground in always new, unparalleled presentations. And even as a despite, in the face of all inhibitions, he belies the elegiac past tense of the recognition that "God was great in us."

And can a lifelong yearning for the right love be without love altogether? Is there no love in spending oneself in such longing? Having part in creation, has the artist not *eo ipso* part in love too? It is out of love that love is sacrificed for the light of the work to shine.[62] And it is love that makes the artist endure and, to speak with Schopenhauer, "pay the costs" of the repeat performance of that universal spectacle in which the will objectifies itself and persists in lasting pains.[63] In the Nietzschean reading of Schopenhauer's text the representation of the Will thus becomes a will to representation, a productive benediction of suffering, hence a work of contemplative devotion.

While he might endorse this description of the artistic will, Thomas Mann would be as diffident in speaking of his love as he is diffident in speaking of his faith. As an artist—and not only as a critical artist—he feels guilty of that black magic that, "having no charity," condemns living beings to the role of mere artistic subject matter.

Yet, is it not, perhaps, only the *direction* of love which has undergone a change? Insensitive men do not go through a hell of pain for a lack of fellow feeling. And one who has suffered so much from what seems deficient love, who has craved and worked so eagerly for the new word and world of love, as Thomas Mann did—is such a one really so destitute of tender passion as some reviewers believe, and as, at times, he suspected himself to be? To be sure, absorbed as he is by his work, he is surprised, time and again, by the human affection of others for him, the "inhuman." [64] But is he without soul whose whole work is but a work of animating the phenomena? And is he without love whose every book is a new, brave, and desperate struggle for communication, i.e., for a new way of sharing life? There is not only one type of love, that of the face-to-face-relationship with the nearest Thou. There is also the loving community in the spirit with those whom the writer has taught and molded by his language, this "sublime organ of culture, inspired by Eros and a link between man and man." [65]

Thomas Mann's responsible and zealous love for the full growth, the pure form and representation of mankind came into conflict with the glowing love for his own people for which he had labored in the *Reflections*. But this love for man that made him choose the martyrdom of the exile is not foreign to the love which is at the roots of vicarious suffering—this religious aspect of artistic representation, the experience of the writer who spends his life in the Inferno of the human soul.

Finally, is not Mann's humor to a great extent a token of true charity, a bending down and looking, with a sympathetic and comforting smile, into the weaknesses of humankind? It is the counterpart of compassion. "We love man because his life is hard—and because we are a man ourself." [66]

In an inimitable way, to which nothing needs to be added, Thomas Mann has given his own answer to these problems in what appears as Zeitblom's defense of Leverkühn. He has associated it with Andersen's moving, melancholy fairy tale of the little mermaid, Adrian's "sister in affliction," this elemental spirit who seeks so urgently and takes so many painful steps to win, like man, an immortal soul.[67] So is also Leverkühn's music a "fervent prayer for a soul." Is the little mermaid "inhuman"? It is "barbarism, inhumanity" (is it not?) "to speak of soullessness in view of such a pining for the soul—the pining of the little mermaid." [68]

This search for the soul, a religion of self-concern, is the animating power in the concern with and for the soul of man as the center of Thomas Mann's work. It gives the artist's approach to human life legitimacy, vigor, and warmth because the self finds itself and is consummated only as it finds its way into the life of others. Thus is begotten a spirit of infinite sympathy in which the respect for the dignity of man and the compassion for him in his "eminent" exposure are one. In communicating to us this sense for man's great predicament as it is experienced in the elations and agonies of the soul, the artist may contribute his mite to a new ethos in a new covenant.[69]

Ecce homo! Thomas Mann's story is a story of stress and striving in the teeth of death, devil, and temptation. It is the mystery story of the human soul, this enigmatic being whose riddles you cannot try to solve without meeting even deeper ones and, thus, growing richer—with questions, the old and new questions, anxious and loving questions, questions which only action, our action (or will it be not only ours?), may answer in the end.

APPENDICES

Appendix I: NOTES ON THE PROBLEM OF DIALECTIC

The Dialectics of the Naïve and the Sentimental

Schiller's anthropological distinction between the naïve and the sentimental was confirmed by the experiences of Thomas Mann's youth (as, indeed, of any youth), by the painful discrepancy between himself and his environment, between the nostalgia of the spirit and the at-home-ness of life. This rather exacting legacy of Schiller's has long been faithfully preserved as "one of those mythical formulations, those classical patterns of thought, which, being handed down from generation to generation, determine the way a people looks out upon the world." [1]

The artist, to be sure (and none more than Thomas Mann), clings to the unity of being, over and above all the oppositions within it. And the great merit of Schiller's "Letters on the Aesthetic Education of Man" and his essay "On Naïve and Sentimental Poetry" (*the* German essay, in Thomas Mann's eyes) lies precisely in their presenting this unity in the only forms in which it seemed available in the wake of Christian tradition—i.e., in the form of longing and in the form of a task, the task of an "aesthetic education" calculated to build up "humanity by developing most fully and harmoniously the whole of both our sensory and intellectual capacities." [2] Last but not least, there is the form of such promise as held out by the wonderful achievements of a Goethe, in whom culture approached the naïve perfection of nature and nature the ideal heights of spirit and culture.[3]

The Christian dualism, fused with similar ideas of Platonic and Neo-Platonic descent, struggles throughout German history with anti-dualistic trends, both mystic and rationalistic in character—as, e.g., the continuity prevailing throughout the scale of representation in Leibniz's monadology. With Kant and Schiller, however, the transcendental contrast between reason and sensibility once more gains the upper hand.

Schiller's original position had been closer to that of Leibniz: his dissertation as a candidate in medicine at the age of twenty-one emphasizes in its very title "the continuity between the animal and spiritual nature in man." Under the influence of Kant, however, the poet came to assert an infinite, eternal "disparity between matter and form, passivity and activity, sensibility and thought." [4]

Yet even this contrast must fall within the unity of the human personality (*Gemüt*) as such. The two parties cannot be united by finding a common denominator or middle term toward which they both converge; but they can be balanced one against the other in such a way that all our powers are alive and active without tipping the scale in either direction. Though not an ultimate solution of life's problems, this image of poise or balance has become a favorite with Thomas Mann since the period of *The Magic Mountain*. He makes it even clearer than Schiller that the two elements do not, in and of themselves, balance each other; it is *man* who is able to master and hold them in balance just because he harbors both of them within himself, yet is not identical with the mere sum of them. This enables Mann to extend the figure beyond a rare and transient aesthetic equilibrium and apply it to the whole of life as a noble and challenging, though precarious, task.

The affinity between Schiller and Thomas Mann shows up also in a similar use of language. Both tend to distinguish, e.g., between the human "individual" as just this finite animal being and the "person," i.e., man as a member of the intelligible world, playing a certain role as representative of mankind.[5] Likewise Thomas Mann's use (particularly his early use) of the terms "life" and "spirit" has its parallel in Schiller and the German Idealists around 1800. For them too "life" stood for "material being," for "all that has no existence save in the senses";[6] whereas spirit is "free, pure activity," "supreme expansion of being," "the overcoming of all (self-imposed) limitations."[7] To use Schelling's beautiful words, spirit is "the conation of the soul which stretches out into width and freedom."[8] And *vice versa:* matter and life, in the speculations of *The Magic Mountain* as well as in earlier cosmogonies (in Böhme, for example, even in Leibniz, in Lessing and the young Goethe), result from a thickening or "condensation of the spiritual."[9]

From the antagonism between nature and spirit Schiller drew his distinction between naïve and sentimental poetry. While taking over the substance of Schiller's argument, Thomas Mann does not adhere to his terminology, and for two reasons: first, he is more emphatic than Schiller in stressing the fact that "naïve immediacy" may itself be the result of previous development; and secondly, he sees an element of longing even in nature and the so-called naïve artist, a longing for the spirit, corresponding to the spirit's sentimental yearning for naïve unity. Since the latter point is taken care of in the main text of the present book, I restrict myself to some historical comment on the former.

In an influential little article of 1786, "The Probable Beginning of Human History," Kant had pointed the way toward a dialectical synthesis of Leibniz and Rousseau, proclaiming as "the ultimate moral destiny of mankind" a state of life wherein art shall ultimately regain the character of nature.[10] This essay was one of the first of the Kantian writings which Schiller, at the suggestion of the philosopher Reinhold, obtained and studied in August, 1787; and its teaching is reflected in the way Schiller revised the first sketch of his philosophical poem, "Die Künstler." (He did it also to meet Wieland's objections.) Pure naïveté is for him a normative concept and does not designate a state prior in time or crudely primitive in character. Even when in "Naïve and Sentimental Poetry" he attributes to the children of nature the very type of being which once was ours and shall be ours again,[11] this does not mean, any more than it does in Kant, "the fatuous desire to return"[12] to an age of simplicity, innocence, and beatitude. It means the achievement of a state analogous yet superior to that of nature, one in which man finds his fulfillment as both a natural being and a moral agent. To some degree this harmony shines forth from every true work of art, by way of either imitation or anticipation of the ideal; for it is poetry's task, above all, "to give human nature its consummate expression."[13] Just because the poet's mission is considered one with mankind's, Thomas Mann feels justified in viewing the poet as the true representative of man.

The triad *nature* (immediacy)-*culture* (subjective reflection)-*ideal nature* leads up, in its third phase, to what is often called a "mediated immediacy," or, adopting Thomas Mann's terminology, to a "naïveté regained." In *Fiorenza* the Prior claims for himself this miraculous union between the exaltation of the spirit and the integrity of the will.[14] And clearly alluding to this play, Gustav Aschenbach is said to have employed the phrase "naïveté regained" in "one of his dialogues."[15] Thus Thomas Mann identifies himself with the poet of *Death in Venice;* yet it is that kind of critical, ironical identification in which writing means "to go on law with oneself" (an Ibsen motto that stands at the head of one of the early collections of Thomas Mann's short stories). In Aschenbach he follows out another of his own potentialities, the artist's inclination for perfect forms, his propensity for disavowing the second step of the dialectical movement (the antithesis) instead of bringing it into a true synthesis. Aschenbach repudiates critical reflection and sceptical analysis, just because he indulged in them too long and too passionately before. Thomas Mann himself rejects naïveté regained at the expense of the restless spirit. He sides with a vitalized spirit—courageous and compassionate enough to build, as a sublime comfort, ever new phantasmagoric forms over the abyss of suffering.

Once the concept of the naïve and natural has been drawn into the dialectical process, there is no stopping the movement toward relativity. Where a "second nature" comes into being, there is no longer any guarantee that the first one is absolutely first. We may well ask whether there has ever been a totally naïve art, i.e., an art which has all of life's discords ahead of it, and none behind. This is just what, in a previously quoted passage, Nietzsche emphatically denied. "Wherever we meet with the 'naïve' in art, it behooves us to recognize the supreme achievement of the Apollonian culture, whose first task is always to overthrow some dominion of the Titans . . . , and must have triumphed over an appalling depth of insight into the world and a most acute sense of suffering"[16]—a passage that sounds like an echo of Schelling's *Philosophie der Kunst.*[17] Again Nietzsche: "To become Apollonian—this means to break one's will to the titanic, the confused, the monstrous and hazardous, by the will to measure, to simplicity, and to submission to rule and concept." Not even to the Greeks was "beauty simply given—any more than logic or moral poise: it was striven after, struggled for and won;

it was their trophy of victory." [18] The grace and poise of the classical form presupposes the abrogation of "barbaric advantages." This is, as a complement to the phrase "the favorites of nature," a decisive feature in Thomas Mann's picture of Goethe.

The Nature of Thomas Mann's Dialectic

In Thomas Mann as well as in Hegel the *Geist* (mind, spirit) is the principle of negation that needs to be animated, i.e., enlivened, just as much as the soul must be spiritualized, i.e., re-minded of its spiritual mission. But the Hegelian spirit is from the very beginning operative in, yea the actual operator of, the universal process, while the spirit in Thomas Mann is dis-inclined to compromise with soul and nature and liable to abide in the remoteness of its absolute chastity. Hence the dialectic of Thomas Mann is obviously not of the same type as Hegel's. *Aufhebung,* the key term in Hegel's dialectic, lays chief stress on the progressive evolution in which thesis and antithesis are both mediated and mediatized (i.e., dethroned) by a new power called the synthesis. In Thomas Mann, however, we find critical analysis and poetic imagination (the conjuring up of the *soul* of things), natural impulses and spiritual aspirations counterbalancing one another, i.e., standing in a relationship of productive tension, without evolving by themselves into a third and higher entity. The *person,* responsible for their equilibrium and representative of the whole over against their particularities operates on both sides (though more distinctively on the side of the spirit), kindling as it were their longing for unity and bringing about their ultimate metabolism. Exercising this regulative function, and making use even of katabolistic forces for his constructive purpose, the person himself comes to be the principle of active synthesis within the human sphere; whereas in Hegel the person is a mere organ of the absolute Idea. The synthesis brought about by the person is more than a passing phase of an impersonal movement, a kind of higher mechanics, more than a wave thrown up only to be devoured once more in the restless surge of the dialectical process.

In all these respects the structure of Thomas Mann's dialectic is much closer to Schiller and Goethe, Schelling and Schleiermacher, than to the classical triadic schema of Hegel. It is a mistake to treat these other systems as mere approximations to Hegel. They have a character and interest of their own. We have seen that Schiller the aesthetician had a special attraction for Thomas Mann in his youth; and this relationship has never been broken off, but rather heightened and strengthened in accordance with Schiller's own example, by a (never unqualified) devotion to Goethe, who long ago had ceased to be "the other one," becoming instead the "projection of one's own being upon the absolute plane," i.e., its "confirmation in a transfigured, ideal and perfect state." [19]

The aesthetic experience was extolled by Schiller as the state of purest poise, of perfect balance between life and the spirit. Both this dualism and the celebration of the aesthetic state as a "sabbath of our toil" (a state which has the flavor of eternity without lasting in time and without guaranteeing man's true redemption) Thomas Mann came upon once more in Schopenhauer's metaphysic. Schiller and Schopenhauer, in fact, are fused into a paradoxical unity in Thomas Mann's "pessimistic humanism." This phrase itself is a good example of what Jonas Cohn[20] has called "bipolar dialectic," i.e., a twofold scale of values, whereby (in Schopenhauer's case) an increase of consciousness means both an intensification of life and, contrariwise, its decay. Thus (to state this bipolar relation a little more technically) consciousness is at once a higher form of life and not a higher form of life. And natural existence is both prior to spiritual existence and not prior to it.

Clearly, the problem formulated in these terms cannot be solved unless it has gone through a process of clarification, refinement, and differentiation of its component parts. This, indeed, was Thomas Mann's procedure in *The Magic Mountain*, one which may be described as an ingenious attempt to differentiate between life as sensual drift and life as creative energy, between immediate or naïve health and the higher health of the spirit. It exhibits sickness and death in both their noble and their slovenly expressions; and it distinguishes, within the mental realm proper, between spirit *qua* intellect, the instrument of the *homo faber* in his earthly workshop, and spirit as the absolute, transcendental principle of a *homo mysticus* who sneers at the rationalistic distinction between good and evil, and indulges in a *guazzabuglio* between God and devil.

A second consideration is equally important. The very fact that the "spirit of this world" (Settembrini, the advocate of progress and the rational organization of human life) and the absolute, otherworldly spirit in the person of Naphta are represented as competing for the soul of man, the young Hans Castorp—this very fact shows that the whole problem is preeminently a human problem, a problem for man to solve. The human being is not only a battleground, the human soul the scene of action for universal conflicts; man is quite strictly the *objective* of the whole struggle, and in the end he must be counted on as the *subject* who will decide its outcome. The opposites radiate from a center upon which they never cease to depend. It is man's task to find the "golden mean" and hold the balance between the extremes—in the words of another German writer, "to spread forth his own contrarieties from the middle, like wings." [21]

The balance and complementary unity between the two poles never becomes an indiscriminate fusion or a quasi-automatic result. It is always regulated by a superior, responsible agent, usually called "man" in Thomas Mann, "soul" in the later Schelling. It is the soul, according to Schelling, which attends to the interests of the whole. Freely moving toward the Highest, it organically combines the antagonistic principles, holding sway over them like a military commander whose task it is to make an army out of raw unorganized recruits. Oriented toward the whole, the antitheses are transformed into correlations the terms of which complement one another. But the unity thus engendered has existence only in the form of bifurcation (*Gezweitheit*). Man is the lord and master of the various powers just as long as he remains "in the center, in the locus of freedom:" by virtue of this very fact he becomes an *instar Dei*, an image of God, whose divinity consists precisely in his being the Lord. This is just the position assigned by Thomas Mann (through his young friend, Hans Castorp) to man as the *homo Dei*, he who reigns over the opposites. And just as in Thomas Mann the two principles are to be reconciled through man, with spirit given the Platonic role of the guide, nature the Aristotelian one of matter, the fostering soil, so in Schelling we find one of the two powers placed in subjection to the other—the *latter* inferior to the former, but also its necessary substratum.[22]

Wise and skillful though Hegel was in manipulating his dialectical apparatus and forestalling all possible objections, we may still say that the progressive element is all too prominent in his triads. It is against the restlessness and faithlessness of this continual going further and further (leaving behind the original antithetical structures) that Kierkegaard launched his passionate crusade. In Schelling and Thomas Mann, however, the same original tensions and substantially the same contrasting features recur over and over again, though always at different levels. The restless motion of Hegel's dialectic is checked by a static element which holds its own much more firmly than does Hegel's "preservation" (*Aufhebung*). While Hegel subordinates the past to the future, Schelling lays equal stress on the perennial past. "The time past is not '*aufgehoben*' (annulled). To be sure, the past cannot be contemporaneous with the present in the sense of being actually present; but it must be contemporaneous with it in the sense of being its actual past." [23] In Thomas Mann we observe the same sort of endorsement of the perennial past. His theory of repetition contains an element of piety which gives passing history a foundation in the enduring forms of the myth; and even when a new and higher ground is reached, it is usually at the expense of something from which the poet cannot quite tear himself away.

At the same time, Thomas Mann's anxiety for the future of mankind has shown itself more and more strongly in the way he has warded off the demoniacal forces of the *definite* past which threatened to engulf humanity in a chaos euphemistically disguised as a "new order." The merely "obediential" potency of matter (to speak with the Scholastics) would be perverted and completely falsified if permitted to usurp control over the royal youth of the spirit. Nature stands ever in need of "a redeeming power to transfigure it into a higher state." [24] "What is nature," inquires Schelling in a similar context, "what is nature in comparison with living history, whereby man bends open once more the very circle which had been closed in the form of nature?" [25] On this point at least, i.e., in the emphasis on repetition as being intensified and spiritualized in the dialectical process, Hegel, Schelling, and Thomas Mann are in full agreement.

In Part I, Chapter 2 we have pointed out how in Thomas Mann the dialectical principle lays hold of the concept of *representation* (the central concept in our interpretation of Thomas Mann's work), molding and remolding it in such a way that what was first contrasted with actual life as its winsome but unsubstantial shadow—i.e., 'mere' representation —now comes to be the very nature of reality, its fundamental *modus essendi*. The ambiguity of art, both in its essential nature and in its actual functioning, is a fitting expression of the duality, indeed the multifariousness, of being as such, destined always to be what it represents and to represent what it is. In the "performance" of life the discrepancy between being and its representation will at last be *"aufgehoben"*—i.e., preserved, shifted onto a higher level and thus overcome: *esse est repraesentare*.

Dialectical Style

At the same time, the perfection of art is no longer the perfect tense of life, its end and terminus. *Repraesentare est esse*. Story and history are no longer related to each other as shadow and substance; for the re-production of life in art is now viewed as a form of that repetition which is of the nature of life itself. Since history proper as a context of living motives depends upon inner reality and is constituted by personal awareness and an appreciation of the facts, it proves plastic even as regards the past, molded as it is in historical memory as well as in historical perception. By sounding and exhibiting the historical depth of the actual moment, the poet helps to bring about a new phase of history. In his narrative he does not step out of historical life. He adds to life's drama a new act, on the stage of the mind, which is the proper locale of the historical. At the end of his Joseph saga Thomas Mann could well have written the words with which Plato concludes the story of Er in the *Republic*: "Thus the mythical event has been saved and has not perished; and it may likewise save us, if we hearken to its meaning."

The dialectical unity of story and history, ideality and reality, is reflected in Thomas Mann's literary style, for instance through the blending of ironical detachment, the superiority of the author over against his creations, on the one hand, and on the other his attachment to the cause being represented—the cause of man; through the exaggerated emphasis laid upon the narrative's antiquity (be it *The Magic Mountain* or the Joseph saga) over against the living repetition, with the minutest details, of the age-old tale in terms of one who was present; through the repeated assurance that the story "tells itself," and, nevertheless, the continual interruptions and detailed directions of the stage manager Thomas Mann; etc.

He had never made himself a slave to the time-honored dogma of epic "distance," or any ascetic doctrine à la Flaubert, that the *energeia* should vanish completely in the *ergon*, the poet in his work. From the very first, a melancholy, ironical smile lights up the countenance of Thomas Mann's writings, just as it did those of his old mentor, Theodor Fontane. In an essay on Fontane, written in 1910, we read: "That stylistic mimicry which enables an author to fill all the passages of his narrative with the atmosphere of the world he is depicting does not by any means exclude unity of style and personal, idiomatic expression: . . . While the artist does not speak on his own account, but lets the things speak for themselves, he still does it in his own personal way.[26]

This dialectical synthesis of subjectivism and objectivism in artistic representation has been accentuated meanwhile by the growth of other dialectical features—the dialogue technique, playing off contradictory *Weltanschauungen* one against another; an ever deepening insight into the dialectical nature of the situations and phenomena of life, into the ambiguous, symbolic character of a thing, whereby it is "at the same time" the something else which it stands for: e.g., a mountain five thousand feet above sea level, but also (among other things) the crater of the lower world, peopled by idle and empty shades. Thus Thomas Mann's objectivity is identical with that irony which dissolves the immediacy of everything in a way both playful and pensive, the way leading from the melancholy pessimism of his youth to the pain-delivered and serene, yet undeluded, wisdom of the mythopoeist of the Joseph legends.

As a thorough dialectician, Thomas Mann not only observes opposite tendencies in the world at large and exhibits them in a dynamics of action and dialogue, in the distribution and confrontation of the figures on the stage of his works. He sees this polarity at the bottom of every thing and person.

Not only is each particular mood, figure, or motif set off (i.e., accompanied or followed) by its opposite, in order to round out the picture of being, and above all of human being as a whole; but each *character*, in himself, is a union of polar opposites, and is often (perhaps a little too often) introduced to the reader in pairs of antithetical terms.

A good example of this is the description of the shrewd and sleepy, mild and stern Mai-Sachme, the governor of Joseph's prison in Egypt. The same holds true of the two main women figures in *Joseph the Provider*, counterpoised as they are—Asnath, maidenly yet biddable, and Tamar the Canaanite, an Astarte type yet austere and forbidding, the spiritual precursor of Ruth and actually the ancestress of Boaz (and therefore of David and Christ) in point of physical descent. While Tamar thus takes her place in the story and in history with a barbarian resoluteness, the more delicate Asnath remains an outsider in "the beautiful . . . God-invention of *Joseph and his Brothers*"; and in a movement counter to Tamar's, Joseph himself, having become a prince of this world, steps back and does not assume the function of a link and the role of a leader in the holy story.

Another impressive example of complementary movements in the sphere of the plot is Pharaoh's nightly pondering over the bird Phoenix and the mystery of his rebirth by way of unisexual, spiritual generation (a motif which itself repeats the subject of Joseph's first peroration before Potiphar). This discussion of miraculous procreation by the lordly spirit is immediately followed by Pharaoh's famous dream of the seven fat and the seven lean cows, a dream that pays tribute to the bounties of Mother Earth. For it is just because the young king feels himself above all a scion of the spirit that his conscience is burdened by a sense of his royal responsibility for the other side of life, i.e., his people's material well-being.

Appendix II: TYPOLOGY IN DILTHEY, MAX WEBER, AND FRANZ MARC

A brief comparison between Thomas Mann's concept of the "type" and those put forward by Wilhelm Dilthey and Max Weber may not be entirely out of place. In his profound and subtle "Beiträge zum Studium der Individualität" [27] Dilthey shows how in the artistic process the original subject matter (the individual) comes to be transformed into a type. It is characteristic of the genesis of Thomas Mann's works that the individual experience, arresting yet still quasi private, comes first, sometimes long before it yields its true significance and reveals its typical bearing. In the adroit phrasing of F. Scott Fitzgerald: "Begin with an individual and before you know it you find that you have created a type; begin with a type—and you find that you have created nothing."

According to Dilthey it is of the very nature of human understanding and hence characterizes artistic representation only because it characterizes experience as such (1) to see things against the background of a type, i.e., according to the way they fit into or deviate from it, and (2) to throw into high relief that which is regular and normative in a certain group of human traits. "Seeing things according to types thus comes to be the best way of setting forth uniformity, the recurrence of differences, gradations and relationships . . . in persons, states, circumstances and destinies." Finally, Dilthey elaborates upon a third mark of the typical which has also been noted by Thomas Mann ("I do not believe a thing can take shape in the poet without sympathy," etc.).[28] Like the members of a single family, all of a poet's figures are typically alike; for they show the side which is of concern to him and thus reflect the peculiar sensitivity, the total experience and judgment of their author. The whole scheme of *The Magic Mountain*, with the quasi-systematic relations of its characters, reveals (as Dilthey would have it) the life and nature of the poet himself, its various facets and potentialities being as it were "distributed" among the different figures of the story. According to Dilthey, the artist knows how "to represent [!] the totality of life through the relations amongst a number of characters."

But whereas Dilthey viewed the type primarily as a tool for understanding our fellow beings, Thomas Mann stresses its existential significance for interpreting and conducting one's own life. Dilthey's analysis is first and foremost a theory of common, scientific, and artistic *knowledge* (though his type is not as exclusively a mental construct as Max Weber's "*Idealtyp*"). This does for the social sciences precisely what Kant's categories did for the natural sciences; and its implications likewise point in the direction of a critical, transcendental idealism.

Thomas Mann's "type," on the other hand, especially in the time before *Joseph the Provider*, comes closer to Platonic realism, attributing to the ideas the status of metaphysical entities and thus encroaching upon the claims of the individual and particular. The true reality of the individual is not in itself but in the type into which it merges with other kindred beings.

The dreamlike mood of this experience, as it is captured in Thomas Mann's work, has a close parallel in a letter of the German expressionist Franz Marc (died at Verdun, 1916): "The ancient doctrine of reincarnation and Nietzsche's eternal recurrence . . . are far from being idle thoughts. They penetrate into the mysterious depth of artistic creation; and perhaps they are the very key to this mystery. True artistic forms are probably nothing but just such somnambulistic glimpses of the typical, the sighting of certain cogent (and therefore normative) dynamic relationships. What is according to the norm has always been normal, i.e., it has always been present before." [29]

Appendix III: THE LEITMOTIF IN THOMAS MANN

The will to representation, naïve and strong or morbid yet passionate, is the motive power of Thomas Mann's world. Recurrences and repetitions are the means of representing a thematic groundwork in ever new variations. This character of his world is reflected in the style of his composition, an intellectual music[30] in the richness of its texture, in its rising and falling dynamics, in its contrapuntal weaving and inter-weaving of thetic and antithetic features. This profound affinity to music is both the cause and the effect of Thomas Mann's own intimate relationship to it, which makes music also a subject matter to be represented in a long series of stories from "Little Herr Friedemann" and "Tristan" or the painful and almost nefarious "Blood of the Walsungs" down through the years to the musical novel on the composer Leverkühn.

Music and *medicine* have always flanked and supported Thomas Mann's art of writing;[31] music, rising from metaphysical depths, expressing the wine of the *mythos*, which the writer administers together with the bread of *logos;* and medicine, consanguineous to his analytical power, treating what the myth expounds.

Metamorphosis of the Leitmotif

In the score of such an opus the leitmotif will have a preferential status; and its plying and varying will correspond to the intensification of strict, objective recurrence into personal renewal by way of repetition. The old Homeric device of the leitmotif Thomas Mann took over from Wagner* and from members of the realistic and naturalistic schools (Dickens, Zola, Tolstoy, Fontane, Ibsen). In *Buddenbrooks* such motifs are still applied in a somewhat external and almost mechanical way, to distinguish the characters from one another by their features and external habits, a technique which is resumed in *Doctor Faustus*, but mostly in order to paint, as it were, the cheeks of the phantoms in the Munich Walpurgis Night. (Stereotyped life is characterized by stereotyped phrases.) As early as *Tonio Kröger*, the leitmotifs have become vehicles of emotional content;[32] themes that vibrate with music, have their musical variation, draw our sentiments into deeper and darker realms. For example, there is the lyrical refrain in which the narrator

---

*This is the quasi-technical point of view from which Thomas Mann has called himself "merely a disciple of that prodigious artist" ("Richard Wagner and the *Ring*," in *Decision*, Vol. III, no. 1-2, p. 81 = *Essays*, 354).

sums up his young poet—"His heart was alive; deep longing was therein, melancholy envy, a faint contempt and no little innocent bliss." This refrain occurs again at the end of the story, this time to sound Tonio Kröger's self-confession and self-evaluation. Throughout this story repetition is above the plane of the purely factual (e.g., the reappearance of the same things or persons).[33] In kindred circumstances and kindred persons, Tonio Kröger recalls persons and circumstances of his youth; the new figures are thus mysteriously interwoven with the old.

Symbolical Leitmotifs

In *The Magic Mountain*[34] the repetition of situations, forms, and turns of speech fulfills a similar function; and so does the dense web of corresponding figures, actions, and linguistic forms in the Joseph legend. One example among many is the *well motif* with which the whole work commences—the well of memory, the well of the past and therefore of death, but also the well of the future and of life. It thus expresses a dialectical principle, a principle of thesis and antithesis. It is the entrance to the lower world, the pit into which Joseph twice descends, to come forth reborn, purified, and grown in wisdom. (The Hebrew word *bor* stands at once for cistern, prison, and the lower world.) [35]

Or take the example of the veil, which is, at the same time, Rachel's, Leah's, and Joseph's veil and the deceptive veil of Maya, this fatal, image-laden "cloak of confusion." It is the garment rent from Joseph's body by his brother's teeth and by Potiphar's wife and will be Jesus' garment on the day of Crucifixion. It is the veil which pleases man and to which he clings, but which must be torn for him to know the truth of the suffering will. As it functions in both covering and discovering truth, it is spoken of in symmetrical phrases which relate it still further to the lover's cloak in the Song of Solomon (5:3). It is there that appear the words: "I have taken off my garment; shall I put it on again?"— words that are embroidered on the veil, and could be Leah's words at the time she rises from Jacob's bed after their nuptial night. They recur in reverse and in a kind of roguish parody when Joseph asks his father, "I have donned my garment; shall I take it off again?" [36] In the symphonic texture of all these stories, recurrence takes place by way of metamorphosis.

In the same way, *Lotte in Weimar* is full of correspondences and mysterious identities, which Charlotte Kestner senses half-confusedly in the twilight atmosphere of matriarchal symbolism, while they are clearly realized and put to creative use by Goethe. In this work Thomas Mann strikes a masterly variation on a theme of which he has often made use (e.g., in the grave support grandfather and grandson Castorp seek for their not quite steady chins),[37] I mean the slight trembling of Charlotte's head and Dr. Riemer's hand. This theme has the same source and the same meaning in both persons. Its function is not so much to label these two individuals as to indicate the perilously high tension of Goethe's being and the heavily charged atmosphere around him; it makes plain what has happened to these people from their encounter with genius. In *Doctor Faustus* it has its counterpart in the convulsions of stammering of Leverkühn's music teacher, Dr. Kretzschmar, who is charged with putting into words what the human tongue is not made for. Symbolizing the general infirmity and shakiness of human existence, the trembling itself has gotten out of hand in this cataclysmic story. It is no longer checked in the slipping of Zeitblom's pen.

Migration of Leitmotifs

The symbolic weight of certain of these leitmotifs thus gains by their emerging repeatedly in several of the poet's writings. An all-pervasive mood is created which welds the different works of Thomas Mann into a single work of monumental scope.* The same purpose is served by the thorough blending of different spheres in the spirit of a Heraclitean coincidence of the opposites. Thomas Mann's symbolism owes much of its fascinating power to the iridescent light which his symbols emit, to their strictly meaningful ambivalence as vehicles of dialectical thought. By virtue of these dialectics the same symbol can stand for good as well as for evil, for life and for death, cold and heat, holiness and voluptuousness, nobility and prostitution, perfection and frustration, the all and the nil. In the medium of such thought there is very little difference between "perishing" on the magic mountain (which is at the same time the crater of Tartarus),[38] like Hans Castorp, and (on the other hand) sinking in the deep well, the "Earth's womb," the spring of life and death, like young Joseph;[39] little difference between losing oneself in the infinitude of the dunes at the seashore and falling asleep in the perpetual snow of the high mountains; between feeling the dizzy pleasure of letting one's individual being dissolve into the darkness of "holy night" and yielding it up in the glaring sunlight of

---

*This is also done with the help of some other devices and their discreet use. The carrying over of Tonio Kröger's family name from *Buddenbrooks* into "Tonio Kröger" might be mentioned in this connection. Tonio is related to Hanno—e.g., in his descent from a bourgeois father and a non-bourgeois mother. But unlike Hanno, he survives childhood. Thomas Mann's poets grow in age, wisdom, and endurance, along with the poet himself. Similarly, Lisaveta's words in "Tonio Kröger" (*Novellen* II, 39 = *Stories*, 106) on sanctification through literature and redemption through language are qualified, yet not altogether discredited, by recurring as a rhetorical bravura in one of Settembrini's manifestoes (*Zauberberg* II, 306 = *Magic Mountain*, 661). Cf. also the list of Aschenbach's works in *Death in Venice*, which summarizes Thomas Mann's own works and plannings up to that date and places them in the light of a unity of interpretation.

Venice. The general motif of the *abyss* can be adapted to different thematic settings, since it is equally well expressed in the terms of height and depth, day and night.*

"The Red One"

Likewise, the representative of the abyss, the *Devil*, on his way from *Death in Venice* to *Joseph the Provider* acquires a positive value to complement his negative aspect. The figure of "The Red One" first appears in the spectral, diabolically grinning faces of *Death in Venice*—the wanderer at the Munich North Cemetery, the suspicious gondolier "who had no license," the grimacing guitarist on the hotel balustrade. In this context the Red is still "a monstrous progeny of fire and filth," looming up from nowhere, while in the Joseph novels (as well as in Goethe's *Faust*) he belongs to the basic structure of a world that merges with the darkness of prehistoric times. The person condemned to the role of the Red, the Evil One, takes up a primordial and essential function; and as an individual he is entitled to the same sympathy from both author and reader as are the other figures in the play.[40] This sort of respectability, which accrues to the devil in the serene light of the all-comprehensive and all-comprehending myth, is lost again by the adversary in *Doctor Faustus*, the embodiment of that knowing nihilistic coldness which threatens man with sterility and, at the same time, the stirrer-up of unhealthy ecstasies and, thus, the patron of an art which is a bastard of frosty calculations and feverish lust rather than of life and love.

Various other motifs, for instance that of the poet's hermaphroditic nature (a nature he shares with the gods), have their symbolic resonance deepened in a similar way.** Of these, the motif of the "veiled and broken glance" has been worked out with special thoroughness.

*This is so even though a dark foreboding as well as responsible thought insist on "distinction" and warn man against merging in the "unity of the womb of origin," a temptation which may be just as deceptive and perilous as the veil of maya. Cf., e.g., *Geschichten Jaakobs*, 303 = *Joseph and His Brothers*, 201f, and *The Holy Sinner*—the story of a twofold offense against this moral. The profound, but also abysmal, knowledge of a primeval unity of being is increasingly counterbalanced in Thomas Mann by the sense for the demands of an alert moral consciousness and an articulate moral order. The following pages should be read with this qualification in mind.

**In its positive aspect a symbol of the unity of the receptive and productive elements in the artist, the androgyne motif is also dangerously close to sterile homosexual love and to the excessive cult of *l'art pour l'art*, the perfection of death. It stands for the desire of haughty and impotent spirit to create without intercourse with the senses. The idea of this self-begetting spirit loses the mythical charm it has in Joseph's comforting perorations before Potiphar and Pharaoh and shows its abysmal implications in the pitiless trial (which is self-trial too) of *Doctor Faustus*.

"The Broken Glance"

The "broken glance" occurs only parenthetically in *Tonio Kröger* (1903) and in what seems to be a purely negative sense, i.e., in the artist-analyst's critique of the passions whereby "man's gaze is broken, blinded with sentiment." [41] Yet *Tonio Kröger* itself marks a turning away from all such analytical acuteness that lacks the penetrating glance of love. May not sentiment be blind only when confronted by particularities in the blinding light of consciousness? In itself may it not afford a true insight into a realm—incommensurable with space and time?

In *Tristan* (1902) the motif had already taken a positive turn—though here too it was used only in passing: "Now, when deceitful daylight pales, when my eye grows dim [*sich bricht*] with rapture—then all that from which the deceptive light of day would shut away my sight, seeking to blind me with false show, to the greater torment of my longing soul—then, O wonder of fulfilment—then am I, am I myself the world." [42] This is Wagnerian exegesis, Schopenhauer's philosophy interpreted in terms of Wagner's erotic mysticism—a glance into Nirvana, the infinite nought in whose ocean depths the single and particular are drowned. This broken glance, so full of knowing ignorance, is the glance of Hans Castorp, estranged from everyday life and wandering dreamily on eternity's shore, bereft of all sense of space and time.* [43]

The glance that pays homage to the monotony of the ocean was not unknown to Thomas Buddenbrook—a dreamily "veiled, hopeless, and knowing glance that had once looked deep into tragedy and disorder." [44] This "nocturnal veil" of a glance "which did not serve for seeing," but also the veil of the softly tuned voices of Tadzio, Pribislav Hippe, and Clavdia Chauchat, draws Gustav Aschenbach and Hans Castorp into a perilous spell. Maya's daylight veil drapes the unity of being in the manifold of appearances; but the dark foundations of truth unveil themselves only to the glance that nocturnally veils itself against the multifariousness of things.

Love is a form of knowing, deeper than that of consciousness: It achieves a real union with being; it is the light that abides not in its own shining, but shines into the darkness. The "broken glance," therefore, breaks not in the darkness of death but in the light of prior knowledge that does not spring from individual consciousness.

*The symbol of the broken glance affords a passage from the realm of the *logos* to that of the *myth*. This has an interesting parallel in the way in which Wagner himself justifies his turning from the world of history to the world of legends. (It is worth noticing that the following sentence is quoted in Baudelaire's Wagner essay, Part II.) "Through this legendary tone the mind is put forthwith in such a *dreamy* mood as will enable it soon to reach the state of perfect *clairvoyance*. Then it will see—what could not be seen with the eyes of common consciousness—a new context of the world's phenomena." (It was apparently Baudelaire who underlined the two italicized words above.)

What in love remains an ineffable mystery, the same is made "mysteriously manifest" in art. In bringing to light this dark, unconscious knowing, poetry has been really psychoanalysis *ante literam*. Art and psychoanalysis mutually confirm and corroborate each other. Both throw light upon certain connections and dependencies that prevail in the living relationships of man to man and man to thing even without being apprehended in the full and sober light of consciousness. The greatest, deepest hours of life are often those in which the truth of existence reveals itself to man in the passing and passive state of a dreamlike vision such as was granted to Thomas Buddenbrook after his reading of Schopenhauer, to Hans Castorp in his mountain retreat, and to Charlotte Kestner in the final scene of *The Beloved Returns*. From Nietzsche Thomas Mann had learned to "look around the corner" and decipher the signs of what eludes rational analysis but is known and duly acknowledged in the myth.

The motif of the broken, melting glance thus makes appearance in the Joseph legend with an altered meaning and a heightened emphasis that stem from the fertile union of mythical thought with Schopenhauer's metaphysics. No longer is the given multiplicity of sensuous phenomena simply absorbed in the uniformity of the supersensuous. Instead, the single phenomenon grows in significance by assimilating to itself whatever, by reason of its analogous function, may be seen in the same perspective. The glance is broken with contemplation in the face of present appearances, so that the particular has its identity dissolved with other particulars in a specific eternal form of being. This perspective, as Thomas Mann says, is dark from excess of light.[45]

At the same time we see that a change of mood has taken place since *Buddenbrooks*. By recognizing and inaugurating their symbolic meanings, Thomas Mann gives the world of appearances a mysterious depth of its own and rehabilitates sensory experience by lending it a fascination precisely for the meditative mind. No more must a knowing, hopeless glance pass over them and lose itself in the blank identity of no-thingness.*

*To the broken glance a fact is like a text that yields different meanings by virtue of its ambiguous unity. "Is not my word like . . . a hammer that breaketh the rock in pieces?" (Jeremiah 23:29). "As the hammer splits the rock into many splinters, so will a scriptural verse yield many meanings" (*Talmud, Sanhedrin* 34a).

On the other hand, in *The Holy Sinner*, Sibylla's frank and straight look into the Pope's, her son's and husband's, face ends the lovely and sinful confusion in which once her broken glance had both recognized and not recognized her son in the (for this very reason) so attractive young Knight Gregorius. Cf. *Der Erwählte*, 162, 309 = *The Holy Sinner*, 169, 325.

APPENDICES

The Morning Shower

Spiritualization is the most important but not the *only* way a motif grows and changes in Thomas Mann's works. It may also take on a more elemental significance and a more universal bearing. The cold morning shower, for example, was first a stimulant to Thomas Buddenbrook, a means of refreshment after a night's dull slumber; [46] it occurs again in both *Tristan* [47] and *Death in Venice*,[48] symbolizing a somewhat violent form of discipline without which artists such as Herr Spinell and Gustav Aschenbach cannot do. But in the Goethe novel the "pleasantly shocking" effect of pouring cold water over the neck furthers "healthy circulation, the Antaeic contact with the elements and nature" (a motif first touched upon by Peeperkorn in *The Magic Mountain*)[49] and turns into the serene, exalted vision of Galatea in the second Walpurgis Night.[50] This scene, we must not forget, is a celebration of the holy elements and especially of water, out of which everything originated, by which everything is held together, and in which pure spirit (Homunculus) passes away in bliss and love. Thus is elevated into the realm of hymns and festival consecration what the soul with its dark yearning has ever known of the unity of being. Goethe here anticipates (although in a clear and limpid mood) Wagner's Tristan motif of the deep, heaving swell of the ocean of bliss. Supported by the infatuating experience "of being borne and carried away" by the waves of music,[51] this figure of water as the cradle and grave of everything has always had a special appeal for Thomas Mann, born and brought up as he was in a Hanseatic town. Man's union with the All, "the very dissolution of one's own being into the universal whole" rose in him only when, with infinite tenderness, he was absorbed in viewing the water and sensing its primal power.[52] Yet these primitive notions are all equivocal. Dissolution into the whole means also universal expansion of the individual soul. "While poets love the sea for the sake of death—has it not been said that life rose out of the sea?" [53] A disciple of Nietzsche as well as Schopenhauer, Thomas Mann was to find the All in Schopenhauer's nothingness. This ecstatic feeling dawns even in Thomas Buddenbrook's nightly vision, to die away again in the hopelessness of the day. It took four decades for his gloomy gaze over the dreary sea to be transmuted into a fiery phantasmagoria of the ocean seen through the blessed eyes of Thomas Mann's Goethe during his morning shower.

To this, often dialectical, movement of leitmotifs, creating a web of correspondences within each work and between one work and the other, has been added, in *Doctor Faustus* even more than in the Joseph legends, an element analogous to the leitmotif proper: a style of allusions, quotations, and outright reportage, which, exploding the selfcontainedness of the individual work of art and transcending not only the life-work of the artist but the sphere of art as such, reduces past and present, fiction and reality to merely different renditions of the same score.

The procedure resembles, on the one hand, the montage technique of contemporary painting, fusing as it does daily news with imagination and imagination with historical documents. This fits well, of course, into the conception of reality as the enacting of roles. The work moves all the time on different planes. Reality having a part in it, it becomes a part of reality just as much as it becomes a prelude *and* an epilogue to the historical drama. Whatever happens is endowed with the specific power of the leitmotif, the power of both recalling the past and intimating the future. This is the case with Joseph, who gives just one performance of an eternal story. And it applies to Leverkühn, who is, at once, Dr. Faustus, Nietzsche, the German people, the artist as a magician, Thomas Mann himself—all these and none of them exactly—and whose story is, therefore, full of reminiscences and dark premonitions. Similary the episodes within these lives are saturated with allusions. Leverkühn's idea to entrust his friend Schwerdtfeger with his marriage proposal to Marie Godeau has its historical antecedents, e.g., in Nietzsche's life, its literary ones in the Marke-Tristan story, so intimately familiar to Thomas Mann, and in Leverkühn's favorite readings, Shakespeare's sonnets and comedies. Hence, quotations from Shakespeare drift, not quite aimlessly, through Leverkühn's talk, above all in the scene of his sending Schwerdtfeger out on what proves his Uriah mission. They function as leitmotifs in this enlarged literary realm with its cult of repetition and variation.

This second type of montage, viz., by way of quotations, reminds us, on the other hand, of the so-called *mosaic technique* such as is found in the Hebrew poetry of the Middle Ages. It does not serve the purpose of mere adorning and illustrating the actual theme by the *quid pro quo* of classical imagery. Rather, it negates the independence of the modern subject matter, makes it the copy of a great model, but supports also, by the chorus of a strong tradition, an otherwise lonely and dwindling voice. It gives to appearance the significance of a perennial motif in the warp and woof of reality.

Appendix IV: "REPETITION" AND "SIMULTANEITY"

Novel and Midrash

A few notes may be in order regarding the interpretation of the Bible which Thomas Mann has adopted in his Joseph novels.

In the first place, we find him leaning heavily on certain scientific writings, especially those of the astral-mythological school associated (from 1906 on) with the Society for Comparative Mythology and headed by such men as H. Winkler, P. Jensen, E. Stucken, D. Völter, A. and F. Jeremias. This "Pan-Babylonian" school stressed particularly the importance of the moon in the whole cycle of myths originating in the Near East. Whatever the merits and demerits of this theory (it has been subjected to very sharp criticism by such scholars as W. Wundt, F. X. Kugler, F. G. Horowitz, and W. L. Wardle), Thomas Mann is indebted to it only in so far as it provided new support for a mythical attitude toward life, which had sprung up in him spontaneously and was later nourished by contact with Schopenhauer, Bachofen, Nietzsche, and Freud. The various mythological identifications (e.g., those between astral and historical events, between human life and death, and the life and death of the gods, Tammuz, Adonis, and Osiris) are all corroborated by an original experience, both artistic and metaphysical in character. "*Ces grandes rêveries archéologiques, quand il les eut fait entrer dans la poésie, s'epurèrent et devinrent même un ressort de notre vie intellectuelle.*" ("After he had transposed these great archeological dreams into his poetry, they gained in purity and even became a spring of our intellectual life.") These words spoken by Maurice Barrès of Leconte de Lisle may also be applied to at least one side of Thomas Mann.

Still more instructive may be a few hints (it is impossible here to go into details) as to how Thomas Mann's epic fits into a tradition that is still alive—and keeps the meaning of the Bible from growing stale and hackneyed. What is in question is the Joseph *motif*, which may well antedate the Joseph *story* itself (e.g., in the Egyptian tale of the two brothers) and has a more or less independent history of its own in post-Biblical times (e.g., in the Sijawush and Sudabe episode of Firdusi's Shah Namah). The significant thing in Thomas Mann's Joseph novel (as in all art) is not the invention, but rather the development and elaboration of the motif, so that it takes on new life and power. I shall draw attention first to certain material similarities between Thomas Mann's narration and the post-Biblical tradition of the Midrashim, which he knew through M. J. bin Gorion's *Sagen der Juden* (as has been pointed out by Shalom Spiegel), and then turn to several correspondences in structure and general treatment.

In the first category belongs Thomas Mann's emphasis on the enthralling unity which spirit and beauty have attained in Joseph: this unity is celebrated by Flavius Josephus in the second book of *Jewish Antiquities*. The same emphasis occurs in the famous 12th *Sura* of the Koran and subsequently in the Persian-Arabian literature, where Joseph's supernal beauty is praised in the most extravagant terms. There is the anecdote of how the Egyptian women, confounded by Joseph's good looks, cut their fingers while peeling oranges (in the Koran itself only a banquet is spoken of, while the peeling of the fruit is not yet mentioned). This anecdote finds a place both in the Persian epic and in Jewish folklore, etc. (e.g., in *Tanchuma, Vayesheb* 5), whence it passed into the Hebrew "Common Book" of the Middle Ages, the *Sepher Hayashar*.

Again, the Koran draws attention to Potiphar's dilatory attitude and the mild tenor of his judgment (so do *Bereshit Rabbah* 87.19, and *Yalkut* to *Bereshit*, 146). In Philo, the *Book of Jubilees*, and *Bereshit Rabbah* 86.3, Potiphar is a eunuch, according to one meaning of the Hebrew word *saris* (cf. Genesis 37:36 and 39:1). While Flavius Josephus and the Septuagint read his name as Petephres, similar to Thomas Mann's Peterpê, the connection between this name, interpreted as "He who is consecrated to Re" (cf. *Pariser Rechenschaft*, 70), and his fate of being a eunuch seems to be of Thomas Mann's own making—destined to be a salient factor in his composition.

The man in the field who shows Joseph the way to his brothers and later reappears as guide on the journey to Egypt is rather a strange figure, a somewhat grumpy angel partly on the Islamic model (but Jewish sources too, dating from the time of the Tannaim, have it that the angels disapprove of God's concern for men). He is taken to be an angel in the Hebrew commentaries also: for the most part he is Gabriel, the same Gabriel who in Firdusi's *Yusuf and Zuleikha* helps Joseph after he is flung into the pit and also assists him on the trip to Egypt.

To pick out but two interesting features among many others: We find in the Jewish literature many parallels to Thomas Mann's subtle explanation of Joseph's chastity and also a definite prefiguring of his interpretation of Joseph's fateful garment of veils. In the reading accepted by Ginzberg (*The Legends of the Jews* V, 329) the "*Kethoneth Passim*" of Genesis 37:3 is quite literally a coat into which figures are woven. Its relation to the idle dream-world may be seen from the words of *Bereshit Rabbah* 84.14: "Lo! he who comes, wrapped about in his dreams."

As for the structural relationships, it is by no means easy (as we have already seen) to distinguish identifications, repetitions, and correspondences from one another. The main example, of course, is Joseph himself, a figure who in every way transcends the individual and particular. His mystic unity with Adonis, Tammuz, and Osiris has already been pointed out; and we also find in the traditional writings the same allusions to Moses, to Jesus, and the Messiah. According to the Egyptian historian Manetho, Osarsiph, i.e., Osiris of the Reeds (the name adopted by Joseph in Egypt), was the original name of Moses (Josephus, *Contra Apionem*, c. 26 and 28). And the allegorical conception of Joseph as the Messiah is still alive in the seventeenth century, in Manasseh ben Israel's tract, *Mikveh Israel*. The Syrian Joseph stories and Ambrosius are concerned with finding correspondences between Joseph and Jesus.

In analyzing the structure of Thomas Mann's epic it is important to note the way in which the features of Jacob seem to merge into those of Joseph on the one hand and into those of Joseph's lords, Potiphar and God, on the other. The first of these fusions, that between Jacob and Joseph, has many precedents in the commentaries; a detailed discussion of this parallelism may be found in *Bereshit Rabbah* 84.6 and *Midrash Hagadol 554*, and also in Rashi. The second moment, the interpenetration of the faces of Potiphar, Jacob, and God, is anticipated in the Old Testament, above all in the account of Joseph's temptation, when he speaks in answer to Potiphar's wife: "Behold, my lord [Adonai] wotteth not what is with me in the house. . . . How can I do this great wickedness, and sin against God?" (Genesis 39:8,9).* As early as Philo's treatise on Joseph the reference to "the lord" sounds peculiarly ambiguous. In many of the Jewish commentaries, furthermore (cf. *Bereshit Rabbah*, chapters 87 and 98, *Talmud*, *Sotah* 36b, and Rashi), we find that Joseph's speaking of "the lord" applies at one and the same time to Jacob, Potiphar, and God. Moreover, at the very moment when Joseph is in danger of yielding to his temptation, God appears to him in the form of his father Jacob (according to most of the old interpreters as well as Thomas Mann). The ambiguities and various implications of this Biblical passage are also strongly underlined in the Koran, where at the crucial moment there appears to Joseph "a sign of his lord" (Sura 12, 23ff). And the Persian epic makes use of the same personal identifications. In *Sijawush and Sudabe* it is even his real father whom Sijawush is supposed to betray. The repeated phrase, "the Lord who created me," therefore, is necessarily ambiguous. In Firdusi's *Yusuf and Zuleikha* it is the angel Gabriel who appears to Joseph "in the soul-stirring form of Jacob."

"Correspondence" is indeed the fundamental category of Jewish thinking about existence and its problems. This Thomas Mann has

---

*This "simplest, most pertinent" saying of the Bible story has been made the cornerstone of Thomas Mann's interpretation (the words are spaced out on p. 626 of *Joseph in Ägypten*). It is also treated symbolically in the German mysticism so familiar to Thomas Mann. Angelus Silesius, e.g., uses it in the Preface of the *Cherubinische Wandersmann* (i.e., *The Cherubic Wayfarer*) to elucidate the concepts of mystical vision and man's union with God: "In his whole house, that is within himself, God has nothing to hide before such a man."

sensed from the depths of his own very similar attitude toward life. This correspondence has an ethical-religious aspect: "A just weight and balance are the Lord's (Proverbs 16:11)—words that are quoted by the Jewish sages just when pondering the balance between punishments and rewards in Joseph's life (*Bereshit Rabbah* 84.7). But inseparable from this is the metaphysical-cosmological aspect: "Everything that God created He created in correspondence" "as the counterpart of something else," so says, e.g., the book *Bahir* (§§9.555. 129), referring to Rabbi Akiba and Ecclesiastes 7:14. This fact is expressed in the pregnant diction of the Old Testament, with its responsive cadences and repetition of *words* to indicate correspondences between *events*.

An example will show how nearly akin is Thomas Mann's interpretation of history to that of the Jewish tradition. For his Joseph the trip to Egypt is a journey to the underworld, for this is what the Southland signifies, according to Alfred Jeremias and the astral-mythical school—the land of the past and the veneration of the dead. This characteristic of Egypt plays a vital part in Joseph's decisions, since it marks the opposite pole to the embracing of the future in Jewish religion. It is the past and death which in Joseph's temptation rise up against the future of life. This had once been a temptation to Thomas Mann himself, and Joseph's conquest of it is related to Thomas Mann's own conversion to life in the period of *The Magic Mountain*. It is doubly significant, therefore, that the Bible itself confirms this interpretation of Egypt. When Jacob learns of the death of his beloved son, he wants "to go down to his son into the land of graves, mourning." This is at the end of the thirty-seventh chapter of Genesis; and the thirty-ninth chapter, which continues the action, interrupted by the Tamar episode of Chapter 38, begins with the words that have a symbolic meaning over and above their geographical reference: "And Joseph was brought down to Egypt" (in the Hebrew, the verb in this verse is the causative form of the verb used by Jacob in the verse cited above). The repetition of the words "go down" points to the common denominator of the two events: the journey to Egypt *is* in this sense a descent into the tomb.

Identity of meaning serves to bind together happenings widely separated in time; it makes them into repetitions of one and the same happening, which thus loses its "past" character and becomes a perennial possibility. The concordance between Old and New Testaments thus had its analogue in a concordance within the Old Testament itself. Of the many examples of such repetition to which scholars like Alfred Jeremias, Leo Baeck, Martin Buber, and Franz Rosenzweig have recently called attention, I shall mention but two related ones, which give us "repetition" in precisely Thomas Mann's sense—i.e., no mere external duplication, but an intensified, solemnly enhanced repetition of some previous event. In the *Pesikta of Rab Kahana* we find the completion of the Tabernacle and in the *Yalkut Shimeoni* that of the first Temple considered as events in which the creation of the world is repeated and brought to fulfillment. (A similar teaching can be found in the Epistle to the Hebrews 8:2-5.) "Not only did the earlier return, but something new was added to it. God had reconciled Himself with the earth and admitted it to His grace again, and each reconciliation brings with it something new. A parable is used to explain it. When a king takes back a wife whom he had cast forth, she naturally expects that he will grant her something new, now that she is being called back. Just so, when God again took up his abode on earth, He must needs grant something new. Before, He had accepted sacrifices from above; now He accepts them from below" (Leo Baeck, "Zwei Beispiele midraschischer Predigt," *Monatsschrift für die Geschichte und Wissenschaft des Judentums*, 69th Year, 1928, 269f.) Cf. also *Midrash Tanchuma* and *Midrash Aggadah ad Exodum* 38:21, according to which the Tabernacle is built first as an image of the world, while the world is then to be renewed after the image of the Tabernacle.

I have been concerned to show how close are Thomas Mann's views, not only to modern Biblical criticism, but also to that interpretation of events human and divine which is implied in the Bible itself and set forth in the early commentaries.

The methodological principle which I have tried to maintain (viz., that the legitimacy of a poetic motif rests on its poetic verification and not on any scientific one) holds true for Thomas Mann's next creation, the Moses story *The Tables of the Law*. Thomas Mann's idea of making "the man Moses" the inventor of the alphabet may have been suggested by the conclusions drawn by scholars like K. Sethe and H. Grimme from the oldest alphabetic inscriptions, found on the Sinai peninsula; its poetical truth, however, consists in conjuring up the affinity between the idea of a universal religion and that of a universal script. In this way the idea of the human cosmos for which Thomas Mann's Moses stands is given its 'literal' realization.

In conclusion, it should be emphasized that the mythical identifications of the Joseph novel—e.g., the repetition of Abel in Jacob, of Cain in Esau—have their precedent in Christian mysticism as well as in the Jewish tradition. These two lines of thought intersect in the theosophy of Jakob Böhme, to which Thomas Mann's view of the absolute is closely akin. Böhme may well be quoted in connection with these identifications. Using imagery that has its analogue in Thomas Mann's figure of the universe as a whirling sphere, he says (*De Signatura Rerum*, ch. XVI, 36f): "In Jacob the *linea* of Christ has turned up on the whirling wheel, and in Esau the fall of Adam. . . . Jacob means Christ and Esau Adam. . . . Jacob, that is Christ, later took on Adam's soul and flesh. . . ."

Thomas Mann and Kierkegaard

As to later Christian thought, particular interest accrues to the affinity as well as the contrast between Thomas Mann's concepts of "repetition" and "simultaneity" on the one hand and Kierkegaard's "repetition" and "contemporaneousness" on the other. (Thomas Mann studied Kierkegaard while working on *Doctor Faustus.*)

There is no intention of drawing, at this point, a thorough comparison between the two writers—not even with regard to the two categories mentioned above. But I cannot refrain from calling the reader's attention first to the agitating scene in Kierkegaard's *Stages on Life's Way* called "Solomon's Dream," in which the young prince comes to realize that God is not the God of the pious, but the God of the sinners, and that one must be a sinner in order to become one of God's elects. Then there is, in the fourth chapter of the *Concluding Unscientific Postscript* (in the section on "The Pathetic") a passage which could almost serve as a motto to *Doctor Faustus:* "Aesthetically the highest pathos of a poet would be marked by his self-demolition, self-demoralization if that should prove necessary for him to produce poetical works of the highest caliber; aesthetically it is quite proper to sell oneself to the devil (to use a strong word, calling to mind something that may happen more often than people believe) and then have the privilege to produce the most wonderful works."

In Kierkegaard and Mann as well as in Nietzsche, *imitatio* means to conjure up into the present the truth of the past. The appropriation and repetition of a perfect form of life serves as an antidote against the menace and despair of nihilism in their own souls and the dysphoria of their age.

Kierkegaard, of course, turns both this desolation and the remedy for it *in majorem Dei gloriam:* not only is the decisive act of the past the Christian incarnation, the entering of eternity into time, the annihilation, in an act of supreme grace, of the abyss between the actual corrupt and the primeval pure states of man, but even after the divine sacrifice the actual repetition of the state of grace is possible only as a new gift of grace. It is no human achievement. Through grace we become contemporaries of Christ and can shoulder his cross. This advent of Christ happens to the soul in her complete solitude, stripped of all other support. Hence the single one who receives it and responds to it is played off against the irresponsive and irresponsible anonymous individual, the everybody who is nobody, who faces nothingness instead of his God and is utterly lonely in his *en masse* existence.

Thomas Mann, too, knows of the ultimate solitude in which man faces his fate. But he knows also of the element of unity within all life. Instead of risking faith's headlong leap over nineteen centuries, his figures let time's boundary grow misty and indulge in a dreamy identification with the past. Even when they are singled out by the spirit, they seek, or are supposed to seek, almost as intensely as those of Kafka do, their place in common life, driven by a love which is first full of admiration and envy to become increasingly compassionate in the end.

Thus Thomas Mann tries to overcome the loneliness of modern man: he replaces the principle of individuation by that of a new human community—in the spirit of the Highest. The individual person finds himself in this covenant, in the frame of a both given and chosen tradition whose steadiness stabilizes and integrates life in its different appearances and whose heightening means the ennoblement of both man and his God. At the same time, man's destiny depends on his faith in the integrity and integrating power of this tradition and the spirit which rules over it. If this faith is abandoned, if total estrangement supersedes faithful at-oneness then man is utterly forsaken and "no loneliness equals his." The Joseph stories and *Doctor Faustus* bear witness to the passionate struggle between faith and unbelief, yes and no, in Thomas Mann's own soul.

THOMAS MANN'S MAIN WRITINGS

KEY TO THE SOURCES

References to the works of Thomas Mann omit the name of the author. For the works published up to the year 1934 the references follow the titles and pagination of the *Gesammelte Werke*, S. Fischer Verlag, Berlin. For later works the references follow the titles and pagination of the *Stockholmer Gesamtausgabe der Werke von Thomas Mann*. Whenever other editions have been used this fact is indicated in the notes or in the list of "Thomas Mann's Main Writings" on pages 267-268.

As far as possible the notes include parallel references to the standard editions of Mann's works in English, published by A. A. Knopf, New York. *The Magic Mountain* has been used in the one-volume edition of 1939 (of which the page numbering is the same as the earlier two-volume edition). The references to the Joseph stories are to the one-volume edition published in 1948 under the title *Joseph and His Brothers*.

The following abbreviations are used in the notes for titles of Mann's works:

Adel	= *Adel des Geistes*
A.N.	= *Altes und Neues*
Bekenntnisse	= *Bekenntnisse des Hochstaplers Felix Krull*
(= *Confessions*	= *Confessions of Felix Krull, Confidence Man*)
Betrachtungen	= *Betrachtungen eines Unpolitischen*
Betrogene	= *Die Betrogene*
(= *Black Swan*	= *The Black Swan*)
Bu.	= *Buddenbrooks*
(= *Bbr.*	= *Buddenbrooks*)
Entstehung	= *Die Entstehung des Doktor Faustus*
Erwählte	= *Der Erwählte*
(= *Holy Sinner*	= *The Holy Sinner*)
Essays	= *Essays of Three Decades*
Faustus	= *Doktor Faustus*
(= *Faust.*	= *Doctor Faustus*)
Forderung	= *Die Forderung des Tages*
Jaakob	= *Die Geschichten Jaakobs*
J.J.	= *Der junge Joseph*
J.Ä.	= *Joseph in Ägypten*
J.E.	= *Joseph der Ernährer*
(*Jos. Bros.*	= the last four novels = *Joseph and His Brothers*)
K.H.	= *Königliche Hoheit*
(= *Royal*	= *Royal Highness*)
L.G.M.	= *Leiden und Grösse der Meister*
Lotte	= *Lotte in Weimar*
(= *Beloved*	= *The Beloved Returns*)
Order	= *Order of the Day*

R.A.   = *Rede und Antwort*
Schopenhauer   = *The Living Thoughts of Schopenhauer, presented by Thomas Mann*
Stories   = *Stories of Three Decades*
T.V.   = *Der Tod in Venedig = Death in Venice* in *Stories of Three Decades*
V.K.   = *Die vertauschten Köpfe*
(= T.H.   = *The Transposed Heads*)
Zb.   = *Der Zauberberg*
(= *Magic*   = *The Magic Mountain*)

TEXTUAL NOTES

Chapter 1

Spiritual Background

a. For his picture of Moses as a second maker, Thomas Mann is indebted not only to Michelangelo but probably also to Heinrich Heine, one of the great influences of his youth. This applies, above all, to Moses as the builder of his nation: cf. "Geständnisse," *Heines Sämtliche Werke*, ed. E. Elster, IV, 54f.

b. Cf. *Betrachtungen*, 79, where Thomas Mann confesses to his kinship and sympathy with the Swiss poet and novelist Conrad Ferdinand Meyer (1825-1898). Meyer's mingling of the melancholy with the luxuriant is distinctly his own and creates his own sensory-spiritual climate; but common to both writers is the resolute affirmation of life in the shadow of death and the moral as well as artistic conscientiousness which Thomas Mann considered typical of "German workmanship."

c. *Novellen* II, 388 = *Stories*, 401. In this confession of the pull toward nothingness we find Thomas Mann in explicit agreement with the young Flaubert, that fanatic of pure form who for precisely this reason conjures art up against "the deep love of nothingness . . . which the poets of our time have in their inmost souls" (*Bemühungen*, 186 = *Order*, 42f).

Thomas Mann's usually negative attitude toward an author whom he does not cease to reread needs and deserves some explanation. His relation to Flaubert is one of criticism as regards the personal, ethical tenor of the writer, while he is close to Flaubert with regard to specifically artistic problems. With Nietzsche (*Werke* XIV, 160) he shares a respect for Flaubert's artistic Platonism; but, again with Nietzsche (*Werke* XV, 219; VIII, 194f), he objects to Flaubert's asceticism and polyhistorical nihilism, his Pascalian hatred of life and the self—or at least of the bourgeois within himself. Objectification of inner states, though it is the paramount interest of both writers, means escape from the self, *impersonnalité surhumaine* to Flaubert; to Mann it means realizing one's true self. Art is not only for art's sake; it is a means of life. Thomas Mann's concern is with the perfection of the work of art only in so far as it is an organ and expression of man's striving for inner perfection. Additional remarks on Flaubert, e.g., in *Betrachtungen*, XXVIf, 75 (influence of Georg von Lukácz!), 79, 197ff, 202f, 358, 533; *Entstehung*, 70.

It is easy, however, to put together a florilegium of Flaubert passages which might serve to characterize Thomas Mann's writings: "*Rien s'obtient qu'avec effort, tout a son sacrifice. La perle est une maladie de l'huitre et le style peut-être l'écoulement d'une douleur plus profonde.*" "Nothing can be obtained without effort; everything requires a peculiar sacrifice. The pearl is the sickness of the oyster, and style is, perhaps, the effluence of a deeper pain." (Letter of September 14, 1853; *Correspondence* [Bibliothèque Charpentier], II, 318.) "*Les très belles oeuvres . . . sont sereines d'aspect. Par de petites ouvertures on aperçoit des précipices, il y a du noir en bas, du vertige, et cependant quelque chose de singulièrement doux plane sur l'ensemble! c'est l'idéal de la lumière, le sourire du soleil, et c'est calme! c'est calme! et c'est fort. . . . Ce qui me semble la plus haut dans l'art (et le plus difficile) . . . c'est—de faire rêver.*" "Really great works have a serene look. Through small openings one perceives precipices; down at the bottom there is darkness, vertigo; but above the whole soars something singularly sweet. That is the ideal of light, the smiling of the sun; and how calm it is, calm and strong! . . . The highest and hardest thing in art seem to me to create a state of reverie." (Letter of August, 1853; *ibid.,* 304f.)

Thomas Mann read Flaubert's correspondence in 1910. From there, in all probability, comes the learned quotation at the beginning of *Der Tod in Venedig* (1911): "that *'motus animi continuus'* in which, according to Cicero, true eloquence consists" (*Novellen* II, 349 = *Stories,* 378; cf. Flaubert, *op. cit.,* 277: *"ce motus animi continuus—definition de l'éloquence par Cicéron"*).

d. Meister Eckhart, *Predigten,* ed. Franz Pfeiffer, 66; cf. 204. That "life works in order to work" is a reverberation in Thomas Mann of the old mystical tendency of identifying man with God. This attributes to man what originally—in Genesis 2:3, or at least in its traditional interpretation— was said of God himself: "He created in order to build."

e. In his "Letter to Switzerland," the year before, Thomas Mann refers explicitly to Troeltsch's religious progressivism and endorses his attempt to reconcile German and Western thought on the basis of the idea of humanity— that common (if often misused) legacy of classical and Christian origin. Cf. *Bemühungen,* 327f.

f. For his purposes Thomas Mann accepts the interpretation of the name Abram as an abbreviation of Abiram, "which may mean: 'my father is exalted' or again: 'father of the exalted' " (*J.J.,* 52; cf. 63 = *Jos. Bros.,* 285, 291). In this case Abiram is understood as *status constructus. Pater altitudinis,* "father of majesty" is indeed the translation suggested, e.g., by Gesenius. For "in a certain sense," continues Thomas Mann, "Abraham was God's father," inasmuch as he "recognized God's being, . . . spread it abroad and realized it in his own thinking." In the following passages Thomas Mann stresses the power with which Abraham's own soul "embraced" the divine attributes and consciously "coalesced" with them. This way of conceiving God as the son of man (which does not cancel the divine sonship of man on the other hand) can in Thomas Mann as well as in Rilke be traced back to Angelus Silesius (*op. cit.* I, 256):

> *Ich bin Gotts Kind und Sohn, er wieder ist mein Kind:*
> *Wie gehet es doch zu, dass beide beides sind?*

> ("I am God's child and son; my child in turn is He.
> We both are both. And yet—how can that be?")

g. *The Theme of the Joseph Novels* (1942), 19. A similar function accrues to man, as the mediator between God and nature, in Schelling's philosophy: "Because everything depends on man, God cannot possibly do without him, for man is the *vinculum* of divine unity" (*Sämmtliche Werke* I, X, 273).

h. *Lotte,* 303 = *Beloved,* 301f. Cf. *Forderung,* 22. In *Lotte* Goethe develops this thought while theorizing about the formation of clouds. He speaks in accents of the little poem "In Honor of Howard's Memory," which pays tribute to the meteorologist:

> *Was sich nicht halten, nicht erreichen lässt,*
> *Er fasst es an, er hält zuerst es fest;*

Bestimmt das Unbestimmte, schränkt es ein,
Benennt es treffend!—Sei die Ehre Dein!
("What never can be touched nor stopped at will,
He grasps it first and handles it with skill.
The unfixed he does fix and well define
In terms most fitting.—Be the honor thine!")

i. As a personal expression, language is never exclusively form. The perfect purity of form remains to Mann a frightening phantom; it never becomes the idol it was to Flaubert. He distrusts the spell he cannot help weaving. The magic power of artistic transformation reacts upon the magician himself. His own enchanting play alienates the artist from his environment, the normal interplay between man and man and the absorption by human needs and claims. It is moving to see how in Thomas Mann's political activities, etc., the writer atones as it were for the guilt involved in the artist's very calling.

j. This does not exclude a sort of civil war. Just as in *Fiorenza* the main opponents were of different brands of the spirit, Lorenzo Medici who makes art triumph over ugliness and Savonarola whose asceticism makes up for his frustrations, so now *Die Betrogene* (*The Black Swan*) shifts the loving struggle entirely to the realm of naïve and less naïve life. The story shows a woman in her climacteric years, already threatened by death and perhaps, therefore, slightly over-emphasizing her intimacy with nature. It shows her wooing an American boy in his prime, the very paragon of healthy life (though, it is true, Thomas Mann's irony picks a hole in his coat: like another flirt, Rudi Schwerdtfeger in *Doctor Faustus*, young Keaton lacks a kidney). Hence polarization within nature takes the place of the polarity between nature and spirit. The new emphasis on this possibility marks, perhaps, also a new leaning toward nature, a new creaturely consent with her in Thomas Mann himself.

k. This corresponds—in the spirit, though not throughout in the letter—to the Midnight Song in Nietzsche's *Zarathustra* (*Werke* VI, 332f) and to his remarks *Zur Geburt der Tragödie, Nachlass*, ed. Baeumler, I, 390: "The will to *semblance*, to illusion, to deception, to becoming and changing is more profound, more 'metaphysical' than the will to truth, to reality, to being. Joy has deeper roots than pain; the latter is merely an outgrowth of the will to joy (to creation, formation, demolition, destruction); in its highest form it is a mode of joy."

Chapter 2

The Metaphysical Pattern

a. Goethe, "Zahme Xenien" III. Cf. Plotinus, *Enneads* I, 6, 9. I cannot here trace the influence of the Neo-Platonic tradition from Hellenistic and medieval mysticism to Leibniz and Goethe, and through Goethe to Thomas Mann. I shall only indicate the affinity of the following ideas in Plotinus and Thomas Mann: the general notion of universal representation of different degrees of clarity (e.g., *Enneads* VI, 7, 7), the impossibility of assigning to the self any definite limits (*Enneads* VI, 5, 7), the narcissism of the soul bent over its own image (*Enneads* IV, 2, 12; 3, 17; I, 6, 8f).

b. The function of representation comes out very clearly in the following aphorism of the Romantic writer Novalis, one of Thomas Mann's favorite authors: "It is only through representation that a thing becomes plain. There is no easier way of understanding it than by seeing it represented. Thus the Ego is understood only as represented by the Non-Ego. The Non-Ego is the symbol of the Ego and serves only to give the Ego an understanding of itself. . . . *Vice versa*, the Non-Ego cannot be understood except as represented by the Ego and through the Ego as its symbol" (Novalis, *Fragmente*, ed. Ernst Kamnitzer, 178f).

c. I mention Hume in this context partly because his anti-rationalism was of great influence on Hamann's, Herder's, and Schopenhauer's thought.

d. While Schopenhauer, in spite of his philosophical indebtedness to Leibniz, could not but speak antagonistically, and even with contempt, of the great optimist, there is to be found in Nietzsche a high appreciation of Leibniz. For him, Leibniz is "more interesting than Kant," a "dangerous" thinker, full of subterfuges, "audacious and mysterious in the extreme," and above all the very prototype of a German (in both the good and the bad sense). He is the only philosopher Nietzsche deigns to mention among the representatives of the "strong German type," describing it in terms that evoke, even more than that of Nietzsche himself, the image of Thomas Mann in his middle period: men "who live with equanimity in the midst of contrasts; full of that agile strength which cautiously avoids beliefs and doctrines, by playing off one against the other and reserving absolute freedom for themselves."

Nietzsche realized that side of Leibniz's philosophy which is of importance in the present context: the significance of "representation" as a broader category than that of consciousness. *The Will to Power*, on the other hand, has to make up for the decay of vital strength in conscious representation. Hence Nietzsche praised Leibniz for his conception of *petites perceptions*, for his emphasis on the power of the *fundus animae*, for his "incomparable insight . . . that the mode of consciousness [*Bewusstheit*] is only an *accidens* of representation and *not* its necessary and essential form; that consequently what we call consciousness is merely a state of our psychical and spiritual world (perhaps a morbid state) and is *far from being this world in itself*." "The whole of life would be possible without its seeing itself as it were in a mirror; as in fact, even at present, by far the greater part of this life goes on without this kind of mirroring—even our thinking, feeling, volitional life, however shocking this statement may sound to an old-fashioned philosopher." Consciousness is an outgrowth of an ever increasing urgency of communication which reaches its climax in the heirs of this whole development, above all in the artists, *etc.*—"men who come at the end of a long line, 'late-borne' always, in the best sense of this word, and . . . squanderers by their very nature. . . . In its final outcome, the growth of consciousness is a reál danger; and he who lives amongst the most highly conscious Europeans knows even that it is a disease." (Cf. Nietzsche, *Werke* V, 291ff, 299f; XIII, 9; XVI, 297f.)

e. Even during the high tide of optimism in the wake of the Darwinian theory, the antagonism inherent in the process of evolution was emphasized also by English writers such as Thomas Hardy, Thomas Henry Huxley, and the young Bertrand Russell. The following quotation is from Huxley's classical essay "Evolution and Ethics" (1893): "Where the cosmopoietic energy works through sentient beings, there arises, among its other manifestations, that which we call pain or suffering. This baleful product of evolution increases in quantity and in intensity, with advancing grades of animal organization, until it attains its highest level in man . . . and it is a necessary consequence of . . . the full development of his noblest powers."

f. The will shares this fate with "appetite" ("passion" in animals, "will" in intelligent beings) in Leibniz. Appetite is "the tendency in the monads to move from one perception," i.e., "one representation of the manifoldness in the unity," "to another perception" and so on. As animated by this tendency, representation itself has the character of an intention in the voluntaristic sense. Cf., e.g., Leibniz's letter to Remond, July, 1714 (*Gerhardt* III, 622).

g. Cf. Heraclitus, fragment 52 (Diels). Also Goethe, "Der Deutsche Parnass":

> *Nicht die Leier nur hat Saiten,*
> *Saiten hat der Bogen auch.*

> ("Strings are given to the lyre,
> Yet the bow, too, has its strings.")

h. Cf. Thomas Mann's characterization of Nietzsche's style in *Betrachtungen*, 56. An antithesis (that of will and idea) is also illustrated by the drawing on the flyleaf of Thomas Mann's Schopenhauer anthology.

i. Analytical art—art which is both "recreation and verdict"—and productive criticism complement each other in Thomas Mann's output as a writer. The predicament of the *Reflections* is overcome in *The Magic Mountain*, and *Lotte in Weimar* profits from the Goethe-Tolstoy essay. Likewise the mood, the problems and tendencies of the novelist determine the books with which he surrounds himself, with which he entertains a critical dialogue, and to which he pays again and again the tribute of unstinted admiration and glowing love.

j. Schopenhauer, *The World as Will and Idea*, Book IV, ch. 41 (Reclam II, 568 f).

While holding its own ground, Thomas Mann's conception of the myth is indebted not only to Schopenhauer and Nietzsche but also to writers such as Merezhovski, Ludwig Klages, and the Nietzsche-interpreter Ernst Bertram; and it is confirmed and enriched by Freud and his school and the congenial research work of the Classical philologist Karl Kerényi.

k. Biedermann, *Goethes Gespräche* II, 419. For the whole, cf., of course, Schopenhauer's way of contrasting universal history with (auto-)biography, poetry, and philosophy of history—a scale which leads closer and closer to recognizing the eternal truth of being amid all vicissitudes of appearance, and realizing man's perennial nature in the face of different outer circumstances, customs, and costumes: *The World as Will and Idea* I, Book III, §§35, 51; II, ch. 38, "On History."

l. Schopenhauer, *The World as Will and Idea* I, Book IV, §58 (Reclam I, 416). In his Hymn on the Eternal Present (§54; I, 356) Schopenhauer refers to the circular question in *Quid fuit?—Quod est.—Quid erit?—Quod fuit*. It must be said, however, that this word is far from being truly representative of Hebrew wisdom as a whole. It is rather an echo from Greece; for this is the way Aristotle speaks in the *Meteorica* (Bk. I, ch. 3) and in the *Problemata* (XVIII:3). But all of these cyclical theories are incompatible with the Jewish-Christian view of creation and redemption, which gives a meaning and a *direction* to the course of world events, intensifying them into events of history. Augustine (*Civitas Dei*, Book XII, ch. 14) had made bold to reinterpret Solomon's saying to the effect that such recurrence applies only to sinners, being caused by the whole bent of their lives and the whole trend of their thoughts: "*In circuitu impii ambulabunt; non quia per circulos, quos opinantur, eorum vita est recursura, sed quia modo talis est erroris eorum via, id est falsa doctrina."* The circle of being is not a *factum* given apart from ourselves; rather is it the outcome of the way men misconstrue their own lives. Notwithstanding his independence of the doctrines of the Church, Thomas Mann's thinking is too deeply imbued with Christian ideas for him ever to be content with observing the vanity of all things and the sterility of mere recurrence.

m. The hallucinatory scene that concludes *The Beloved Returns* and, in *The Magic Mountain,* the appearance of Joachim Ziemssen in the occultist experiment have their roots also in the formative will that creates what it desires.

n. This elimination of the accidental in its literal sense has its logical expression in Leibniz's *"praedicatum inest subjecto"*—"the predicate inheres in (is a mark of) the subject"—a bold and heretical formula which is tenable only from the viewpoint of voluntarism. (E.g., despite all the unhappy accidents which accelerate it, there is nothing accidental in Romeo and Juliet's death: they are its prompters rather than its victims.)

o. The indeterminate status of these experiences just as well as the diffusion between individually different beings expresses a feeling that has one of its roots in the singular union of spontaneity and receptivity in the artist. Object and product of imagination are inseparably one. This general correlation is greatly intensified in Thomas Mann's own case. Where has the impregnation by the spirit of the great past borne more abundant fruit in artistic achievement than with him? Cf. below, note c. to ch. 5.

p. Such correspondence may also occur in a negative sense—as repetition in reverse, as revocation rather than resumption: "Doktor Fausti Weheklag" ("The Lamentations of Doctor Faustus") is meant as a recanting of Beethoven's "Hymn to Joy."

q. *Zb.* II, 249 = *Magic*, 618. Cf. Storm's poem "Abseits." On Thomas Mann's relation to Theodor Storm cf. the article "Theodor Storm" in *Adel,* 518ff = *Essays,* 270ff. Also *Betrachtungen,* 62, 75, 79. It is particularly the lyricism of *Tonio Kröger* which shows the indebtedness of the young Thomas Mann to Theodor Storm (1817-88), the poet of Husum—a Slesvig town not far from Lübeck, Thomas Mann's birthplace: see, above all, Theodor Storm's story *Immensee* and his poem "Hyazinthen."

r. These lines from Schiller's ode "To the Friends" serves as motto for Louis Ginzberg's *Legends of the Jews.* Certainly it is a matchless expression of the truth contained in the old but ever rejuvenated stories—and exactly the way in which Thomas Mann understands them also. Incidentally, it is symptomatic of the relation in which Thomas Mann stands to his closest contemporary, André Gide, that the latter cites the very same lines in his autobiography, *Si le Grain ne meurt* (261), to indicate (with reference to Schopenhauer) his disapproval of any view of history in which actual events are not treated as the merest transparencies for the "play of characters."

s. *Jaakob,* 160 = *Jos. Bros.,* 123. The ambiguity in our use of the word "course" is intended to render the meaningful ambiguity in Thomas Mann's own speaking of *"Geschichte,"* once in the temporal sense of "story" and "history" and once in the spatialized one of "layer"—an ambiguity originating in his attempt to suspend time and replace it by the figure of simultaneity. Cf. the similar process in R. M. Rilke's poetry, described in my *Sprache als Schöpfung* (1934).

t. The character and function of *imitatio* as reproduction and rejuvenation was clearly recognized by Josiah Royce. The imitator "never merely repeats" the act of his model. Imitation succeeds in bridging the gulf between two different courses of actions by making them "appear as a *diversity of stages* in the same series." It serves here, too, to overcome what, following Schopenhauer, Royce considered the wretchedness of individuation, the feeling of life's being split into isolated entities. "The finite world has hereby won a new consciousness of the unity of its own life" (Josiah Royce, *The World and the Individual* II, 311f). Cf. also the far-reaching analogy between Mann and Royce in the latter's interpretation of sin and atonement with reference to Joseph and his brothers (!). Cf. "The Christian Doctrine of Life," *Hibbert Journal* XI, 3; 495.

u. Schopenhauer, "Transzendentale Spekulation über die anscheinende Absichtlichkeit im Schicksale des Einzelnen," *Parerga und Paralipomena*, Vol. I (Reclam IV, 250). In his speech "Freud und die Zukunft," Thomas Mann emphasized the intimate relationship between this essay of Schopenhauer and the ideas of psychoanalysis. For the origin of Schopenhauer's theory of the fundamental, yet preconscious, productivity of the will cf. Fichte, e.g., *Grundlage der Gesamten Wissenschaftslehre* (*Werke* I, 246ff), and, above all, Schelling, e.g., *System des transzendentalen Idealismus* (*Werke* I, III, 573, 633).

v. "It is in the entelechy," according to Leibniz, "that spontaneity is to be found"—a spontaneity, however, which is not left to the impulse of an isolated moment, but proceeds on the basis of something like "memory and presentiment." (Leibniz, second pamphlet against Bayle [*Gerhardt* IV, 558].) Even death may be considered a spontaneous act of the monad, withdrawing from a certain mode of appearance in order to adopt a new embodiment: cf. Biedermann, *Goethes Gespräche* II, 170ff.

Chapter 3

The Genealogy of the Artist

a. In its universal application to man as such, this problem is indicated in the Gilgamesh epic whose hero is woeful and joyful, plagued and well-favored: *J.Ä.*, 401, 577 = *Jos. Bros.* 655, 748. Cf. *Jaakob*, lviii = *Jos. Bros.*, 30. Thomas Mann speaks of himself this way in the concluding words of his last letter to the author, April 24, 1955.

b. These lines by Stefan George, the great German lyricist (1868-1934), are taken from *Der Teppich des Lebens* (*Werke* IV, 57). While denouncing the haughty aestheticism of George's school—cf., e.g., the poet Daniel zur Höhe in *Doctor Faustus*—Thomas Mann places George, alongside Hofmannsthal, first among the contemporary German lyric poets toward whom he feels a kinship and a certain obligation. No less characteristic of this side of his nature—the disavowed predilection (*absprechende Liebe*) for pure form in its melancholy perfection—is his fondness for other great classicists such as Count August von Platen (1796-1835), who was also a favorite of Nietzsche's, and for the Swiss poet Conrad Ferdinand Meyer.

c. Toni Buddenbrook, so full of life in her chatty way, is particularly reminiscent of one of the great literary loves of Thomas Mann's youth. One cannot overemphasize the influence the Berlin novelist (and poet) Theodor Fontane (1819-98) had, not only on the *causeur* but, above all, on the dialogist in Thomas Mann. In an essay of 1910 (*Rede und Antwort*, 85) the latter confesses that no other writer, past or present, has ever fascinated him as much as Fontane, that no other author arouses in him quite "the same sympathy and gratitude, the same instant instinctive delight, the same warm sentiment and satisfaction he feels at every word, every epistolary line, every little scrap from a dialogue" of Fontane's. Even Thomas Mann's birthday speech of 1925 is still a personal confession in the self-critical attitude of the artist à la Fontane (*Forderung*, 11). Thomas Mann shares with Fontane the union between the bard and the moralist, the epic poet and the critical psychologist, the humorist and the pessimist, the conservative and the revolutionary. Both writers are sceptical of the spirit of the *littérateur* and entertain a somewhat unhappy but artistically rewarding love for the "bright and strong ones," the "smug, handsome, laughing vanquishers of hearts," the favorites of the gods; cf., e.g., *Tonio Kröger* with the Fontane letter quoted by Thomas Mann in *Rede und Antwort*, 79 = *Essays*, 294f. Both writers have also a marked preference for picturing man over against depicting nature; they love man 'passionately,' i.e., in a sort of distrust—and, therefore, man with all his weaknesses rather than with his specious virtues, the publican better than the pharisee. And if Fontane's Crampas (in *Effie Briest*) as well as Thomas Mann's Joseph are credited with "enjoying life" while knowing "that there is not much to boast about it," they can well be said to represent the *Weltanschauung* of their intellectual fathers.

d. For this Schopenhauerian phrase cf. also *Novellen* I, 351f = *Stories*, 154; *Schopenhauer*, 41 = *Adel*, 387 = *Essays*, 403. The formula of the error of human existence appears first, perhaps, in Pierre Charron's famous *De la Sagesse*: "Dullness and blindness dominate the beginning of our lives, the middle is toilsome work, the end is pains, the whole is an error."

e. *Bu.* II, 348 = *Bbr.*, 527. The sentence sounds like an echo from Lucretius. Cf. *Schopenhauer*, 18 = *Adel*, 364 = *Essays*, 389: "Death, according to Schopenhauer, is nothing but the disappearance of an imaginary partition-wall shutting off the self you are encased in from the rest of the world."

f. "One cannot long maintain his ground on the summit of a situation" (Goethe). In the evening, in the light of consciousness, in the "atmosphere of high civilization" Hans Castorp, too, loses the grasp of that dreamy vision by which he was blessed for one afternoon hour in the solitude of the snowy mountains; cf. *Zb.* II, 262 = *Magic*, 628.

g. Cf., as a good example, "the perfectly unequivocal character of love in its very ambiguity" (*Zb.* II, 434 = *Magic*, 755).

Chapter 4

The Dominion of Man

a. It is significant of the persistence of motifs in Thomas Mann's work that the narrator of the Joseph legends compares himself to the wayfarer who stops not at any point of his course. Herewith he comes under the sign of the moon—according to the mythical mode of interpretation which prevails in this work of Thomas Mann's older age. At the same time, mutual representation is established between him and the patriarchs whose only home is the tent. (Cf. *Jaakob*, lxi. = *Jos. Bros.*, 32.) According to Genesis 13:3, Abraham journeys from place to place like the moon. Such at least is the interpretation of this passage which Thomas Mann may have found in the writings of H. Winkler and A. Jeremias. (Cf. Alfred Jeremias, *Das Alte Testament im Lichte des Alten Orients*, 2nd ed., 1906, 341.)

Of the moon as symbol of the poet's mediating between the ideal and sensible worlds, Thomas Mann also speaks in his little book on Schopenhauer, *Schriftenreihe Ausblicke,* 17 = *Adel,* 344f = *Essays,* 377.

With regard to Thomas Mann's intimate relation to Goethe, it may be relevant to point out the significance of the wanderer motif both in Goethe's life and works (e.g., *"Wanderers Sturmlied," "Wanderers Nachtlied," "Der Wanderer," "Pilgers Morgenlied," Meisters Wanderjahre,* etc.). In the beginning of the seventies his friends had given just this epithet of *"Wanderer"* to the young Goethe—"a messenger between mountain and plain"—a characterization that agrees with André Gide's description of Goethe's personality (cf. "Goethe," *Nouvelle Revue Française* XXXVIII, 372) and may have certain symbolic overtones for the author of *The Magic Mountain.*

b. Thomas Mann's interest in such figures appears not only in his creative writings but in his criticism as well. It is the driving force behind such essays as those on Kleist's *Amphitryon* and Chamisso's *Peter Schlemihl.*

c. Concerning the specific German meaning of this symbolic term (i.e., "plain"), cf. Nietzsche's *Twilight of the Idols* ("What the Germans Lack," §4): "Germany is coming more and more to be considered Europe's flatland."

d. *Zb.* II, 295 = *Magic,* 652. "The silent protest of Germany which has not yet succeeded in finding the true expression of its innermost being"—this "tremendous" dictum is taken from Dostoievsky. In the *Betrachtungen,* 3ff, it is played off against the propaganda emanating from "the old Roman formula of universal amalgamation," one of the watchwords of the French Revolution. Even in the *Reflections,* however, Thomas Mann does not intend to forsake this formula and its social implications, but rather to go beyond it and overcome its degeneration in bourgeois liberalism. Even the *Reflections,* for all their allegiance to conservative ideals, point toward a (nonhumanitarian) humanism and a true socialism, though not of the Western type. Even the *Reflections,* finally, hint at the danger of the mute and, therefore, barbarian protest which Germany raises against Western civilization (*Betrachtungen,* 12). Thomas Mann's endorsement of Settembrini's warning proves that it is more than mere Enlightenment rhetoric—the more so as even Settembrini's Eastern antagonist, Madame Chauchat, inveighs against incommunicative German self-concern (*Zb.* II, 425 = *Magic,* 749).

The problem of German muteness ("the visible action failing to be the self-manifestation of inward life") had been discussed as early as 1873-74 in Nietzsche's *The Use and Abuse of History,* §IV—one of the most searching and far-sighted analyses in his work, anticipating Thomas Mann's later postulate of a union between life and the spirit. (Thomas Mann's quotation from Dostoievsky refers to the Russian's essay "Germany, the Protesting Empire," 1877.) Cf. Nietzsche, "Nutzen und Nachteil der Historie" (*Werke* I, 315ff). The problem is resumed in *Doctor Faustus.*

e. Here, too, we are reminded of *Tonio Kröger* and particularly of *Death in Venice*—of the art-fevered atmosphere of Munich and of cholera-stricken Venice. In both cases, fever acts as a stimulant—it heightens life's intensity, but it brings with it the peril of decomposition and the lust for death. Venice is the Tristan-city, *"où la mort projette ses secrètes fusées et nous propose ses vertiges"* ("where Death sends out his secret fumes and invites us to his vertigos"). *"Vertige, ivresse des hauts lieux et des sentiments extrêmes! A la cime des vagues où nous mène Tristan, reconnaissons les fièvres qui, la nuit, montent des lagunes."* ("Vertigo, intoxication of high places and extreme feelings. Let us realize, at the crest of the waves where *Tristan* leads us, the fevers that, during the night, rise up from the lagoons.") These words are from Maurice Barrès' "La Mort de Venise" [!], in *Amori et Dolori Sacrum* (Librairie Plon), 21, 95. *Death in Venice* has, indeed, the burning fiery hues associated equally with fever of the body and fever of the soul, and *The Magic Mountain* literally exemplifies the saying about the vertigo of the "high places." In *Jaakob*, xlviii = *Jos. Bros.*, 25 we still find the spirit's mountain abode contrasted with the lower world of the senses.

f. Thomas Mann does not disown a genuine sympathy with pious attitude altogether. We said that, in one of their aspects, his own works are a representation and transfiguration of a beloved, yet definitely past, era of life. The melancholy of this retrospective view, which makes the artist a historian if not an antiquarian, is particularly eloquent in the years after World War I, in *Disorder and Early Sorrow* and even before, in 1919, in *Gesang vom Kindchen*, e.g., 59:

Nicht gemein, nicht bösen Willens nenn' ich den Mann mir,
Der, wenn vieles versinkt. . . .
. . . dem Abgelebten, dem Tode und der Geschichte
Einige Treue immer bewahrt und still auf der Dinge
Steten Zusammenhang fortpflegenden Sinnes bedacht bleibt.

("Neither vulgar nor ill-willed do I call the man who, seeing
Everything crumble around him. . . .
. . . still keeps faith with the outlived,
Death and historical past and keeps some faith, to tradition,
Mindful of steady coherence for things to live on and prosper.")

g. Just because beauty is perfection, this imperfect life of ours makes it a fateful thing, to which little Herr Friedemann falls victim as well as the master-artist Gustav Aschenbach, and Potiphar's wife, Mut, not less than Shridaman and Nanda in *The Transposed Heads*.

h. *Zb.* I, 201ff, 559ff = *Magic*, 154ff, 419ff. Gustav Aschenbach never dares speak to the boy Tadzio, for whom he feels such consuming love. And Hans Castorp speaks to little Pribislav Hippe and to Clavdia Chauchat only after having laid siege to them for a long time—and then as though in trance.

i. Baudelaire, *"A celle que est trop gaie."* Our repeated allusions to Baudelaire, the greatest among the poets of the French *décadence*, are intended to show the community of intellectual atmosphere between these artists and Thomas Mann, the disciple of Schopenhauer and Wagner. Nietzsche included Baudelaire among "those incredible amphibious beings that are no less German than Parisian"; and without prior knowledge of Baudelaire's articles on Wagner, he sensed "how much Wagner there is in Baudelaire" (Nietzsche, *Werke*, XIV, 181). All this makes Baudelaire akin to Thomas Mann—or, rather, to one side of his being. Is it not—together with the language of Whitman—the French of the *décadence* that comes from Hans Castorp's mouth at the very moment when he plunges into the abyss of lust?

j. *Forderung*, 12. While *ideas* of Bachofen (and Klages) have entered into Thomas Mann's conceptions of life and death, spirit and soul, they are held in check by impulses originating from Nietzsche's conquest over boundless, nocturnal romanticism: cf. particularly *Pariser Rechenschaft*, 58ff.

k. Cf. Hugo von Hofmannsthal, *Der Tor und der Tod* (1893), and, for contrast, *Zb.* II, 260 = *Magic*, 626. In pleading for life against death, Thomas

Mann defies a feeling that is only too familiar too himself. Hofmannsthal is one of the lyric writers whom he has loved—and outlived. Cf. *Forderung*, 317ff (In Memoriam Hugo von Hofmannsthal).

l. "Dualism, antithesis—such is the moving, the passionate, the spiritual principle" (Naphta in *Zb.* II, 58 = *Magic*, 474). It ought to be added that the antagonism of the persons in the dialogues mirrors, too, the *pro* and *contra* in the writer's own soul, his playing with possibilities, his long irresolution and even his taking delight in suspension—though not forever. The antithetic tendencies in Thomas Mann himself, which make the *Reflections of an Unpolitical Man* a painful human document, are in *The Magic Mountain* distributed among different figures as their personal representatives and advocates.

m. Cf. *Zb.* II, 508ff = *Magic*, 809ff. The idea of "logical music" in contrast with the intoxicating music of romanticism first appears in 1911 in a little article on "Richard Wagner's Art" (*Rede und Antwort*, 363), then again in the 1920's, in *Pariser Rechenschaft*, 60f. Touched already by Nietzsche (e.g., *Will to Power*, Book III, §842; *Werke* XVI, 259ff), the problem becomes central in *Doctor Faustus*. There even the logical is an outgrowth of productive intoxication.

n. "Music, no matter how high it soars, remains feeling; it keeps company with moral activity without being such an activity itself; . . . it lacks the ethical will and propulsion." So speaks Richard Wagner himself in the "Art-Work of the Future" (*Gesammelte Schriften* X, 100).

o. "*Je ne souhaite à personne de se soumettre aux influences de cette sublime tragédie, car ce qu'elle met dans notre sang, c'est une irritation mortelle, le besoin d'aller au delà, plus outre que l'humanité.*" ("I would not advise anybody to expose himself to this sublime tragedy, since it instils into our blood a mortal irritation, the need to go beyond, to leave humanity behind.") (Barrès, "La Mort de Venise," in *Amori et Dolori Sacrum*, 95.)

p. *Bemühungen*, 254; *Zb.* I, 190ff = *Magic*, 145ff. According to Schopenhauer, "music could hardly exist apart from death"—any more than could philosophy: *Schopenhauer*, 52 = *Essays*, 394f.

q. *Zb.* II, 425ff = *Magic*, 749ff. The phrase recurs repeatedly in Thomas Mann's works, showing its autobiographical origin.

r. *Zb.* II, 525 = *Magic*, 822. "Humanism. . . . I possessed the thing long before I professed the name, and I may say that for me it is an idea that comes from life, not from reading" (*Bemühungen*, 165 = *Order*, 24f). Cf. also the contrast drawn in the "Letter on Switzerland" between the world of true humanity and the magic mountain of romantic aestheticism (*Bemühungen*, 328).

Chapter 5

The Myth of the Soul: The Period of the Joseph Novels
A. From *The Tales of Jacob* to *Joseph in Egypt*

a. *K.H.*, 216 = *Royal*, 164. With this compare Nietzsche's account of the artist as a sensual being, open to stimuli from near and far—but withal temperate and in many cases even chaste "under the dominion of his task and his will to artistic mastery" (*Will to Power*, no. 815).

b. *J.Ä.*, 453ff = *Jos. Bros.*, 685. In *Death in Venice* the danger of the excessive cult of pure form is symbolized by homosexual love. It is sterile love, the *astre inutile* of which Baudelaire speaks—a love of beauty which serves no purpose and leads to nothing but the intoxication of nothingness. Cf. *Leiden und Grösse der Meister*, 177 = *Essays*, 267.

   c. *Lotte*, 337 = *Beloved*, 338; *J.J.*, 87 = *Jos. Bros.*, 305. "The bi-sexual nature of every deity" has been especially stressed by Alfred Jeremias, e.g., in his *Handbuch der Altorientalischen Geisteskultur*, 231. Thomas Mann was familiar with this thought through his studies in German Romanticism. Both the genius and the god are taken there to be of a male-female character. No one was more enamored of this idea of the "androgyne" than Friedrich Schlegel. Zeus's bisexuality, alleged in an Orphic fragment, was interpreted by him as a symbol for the ultimate unity between the principles of the real and the ideal: *Jugendschriften*, ed. J. Minor, II, 366. "The spirit in its self-formation represents the divine androgyne," says Franz von Baader in his lectures on Jakob Böhme (*Werke* II; III, 89)—echoing the hermetic idea of the νοῦς ὁ πρῶτος ἀρρηνόθηλυς ὤν (W. Scott, *Hermetica* I, 118). The speculations of Thomas Mann's Amenophis move in exactly the same direction.

   Plato's Aristophanes, who in the *Symposium* first introduces the idea of the androgyne into philosophy, takes it to be a third genus, an offspring of the moon, just as the male sex is descended from the sun and the female from the earth—mythical correlations which find their way into the Joseph saga. Here the sun, the masculine, generative principle, and the father-spirit belong together, just as the maternal, female element is represented by the fertile earth. And it is a matter of discussion between Joseph and Potiphar and between Pharaoh and the priests of Aton whether or not there may exist a being who is above sexual distinctions, begetting and bearing fruit at once, as the king should be (and as the artist is)—a being like the fabled bird Bennu, the Phoenix of the Greeks, who was motherless and self-begotten (*se ipsum impraegnans*, as we have it in Arabic-Latin texts). Yes, there is, declares Joseph in his peroration before Peterpê, as with his usual shrewdness and enthusiasm he begins to speak of the divine *pneuma*, the breath of the Spirit, and, in the human realm, of the hermaphroditic character of the arts. "Ptah's sculptors fill the world with beautiful figures, and no one can tell whether their activity is to be called male or female, since it is really both and neither; in other words it is virginal-fruitful" (*J.A.* 203f = *Jos. Bros.*, 599. Cf. also *Lotte*, 377 = *Beloved*, 338.

   d. With this cf. *Zb.* II, 343ff = *Magic*, 689ff. We are reminded of Baudelaire—passages such as this one from "Hymne":

> *Elle se répand dans ma vie*
> *Comme un air impregné de sel*
> *Et dans mon âme inassouvie*
> *Verse le goût de l'éternel*

> ("The very air I breathe she fills
> With a tang of salt from a boundless sea,
> And into my thirsting soul she spills
> The savour of eternity.")
>   —Translated by Conder

Or this from "Le Goût de Néant":

> *Le temps m'engloutit minute par minute,*
> *Comme la neige immense un corps pris de roideur.*

("Time overgrows me every minute more
—A pall of snow that covers stiffened bones.")

We should also think, however, of Walt Whitman, to whom the Thomas Mann of this period is deeply indebted. Walt Whitman, too, has dreamed these "Sea-Shore Fancies," and knows the emptiness and awesome simplicity of sea and shore, with its smell of reeds and its lure to self-abandonment. Thomas Mann says that "the sea, its rhythms and its musical transcendence" are present in mood and sound throughout his books (*Forderung*, 41f = *Order*, 43); and for Walt Whitman likewise, the seashore became "an invisible *influence*, a pervading gauge and tally" for himself and his compositions. Cf. Walt Whitman, *The Complete Poetry and Prose*, ed. Malcolm Cowley (1948), II, 91f.

e. *Jaakob*, xxxvii = *Jos. Bros.*, 18. The formulation shows clearly how deep a debt Thomas Mann still owes to the romantics. Romantic philosophy had shown the underlying kinship between the mythical and the artistic. In §§38f of Schelling's *Lectures on the Philosophy of Art* we find the present idea best expressed. Schelling identifies absolute art with the symbolic type and the latter with the mythological: "Mythology is the soil and sphere wherein alone art can bloom and subsist" (§ 38). "For absolute art demands representation with *complete indifference*, in such a way, that is, that the universal *is* in the fullest sense (and not merely *signifies*) the particular, and *vice versa*"—but this clearly is symbolic representation. "This demand is poetically solved in mythology. . . . Here the meaning is at the same time being itself, having passed over into the object and become identical with it. . . . Reality is thus one with ideality. Their great charm lies just in the fact that, by thus simply *being*, absolute in themselves and without any relation, things still contrive to let the meaning shine through" (§39).

But as early as 1797 we read in Goethe's essay "On the Subjects of the Fine Arts": "Represented in this way—i.e., symbolically—the subject seems to stand for itself alone, and yet is deeply meaningful, because of its ideal nature which always carries with it universality." It is in this sense that Thomas Mann remarks: "Light is that which shines through" (*J.J.*, 61 = *Jos. Bros.*, 290).

f. Since Abraham is "the father of many nations," the Jewish people is not "racially pure" so far as the ancestors and descendants of Jacob are concerned; and he who "sits fast at the fountain head of the holy story," like Laban, does not really participate therein. Cf. *Jaakob*, 88f, 238 = *Jos. Bros.*, 82f, 166.

g. This is an attitude which Thomas Mann adopted long ago. Far from being only the result of recent events, it comes to the fore as early as 1926—in *Pariser Rechenschaft*, where the poet reflects on the problem of the mythical attitude and his new work, the Joseph novel.

h. "*Die* Geschichte" and "*das* Geschichte" had confronted each other in Friedrich Gottl, *Die Grenzen der Geschichte* (1904).

i. The same tendency shows up in the semantic aspect of Thomas Mann's compositions—viz., in the weaving together of leitmotifs. Leading forward and backward, they tend to arrest the very time that seems to be "the condition of life and narration"; they suspend and crystallize it in a present that "presents" everything of the same type at the same time: cf. *Zb.* II, 391 = *Magic*, 724.

j. This way of spiritualization is not the only one in which former states and events are at once repeated and varied. It is the way, however, that particularly interests the poet, since it shows him the origin and growth of his own nature. As a matter of fact, things may also grow coarse in repeating themselves. Thus the rise of the Buddenbrooks is challenged by that of the Hagenströms, which takes place, however, in the new environment of a callous and sterile capitalism—no longer in a patriciate that permits of sublimation into the artistic. (These problems are discussed in the *Betrachtungen*, 115ff.)

k. "Relation is everything. And if you care to give it its proper name—it is 'ambiguity' " (*Faustus*, 74 = *Faust.*, 47). The solemn vagueness of mythical simultaneity with its wealth of cross-relations has its sinister counterpart in a hypermodern magic calculus which makes ambiguity the vehicle of a subtle and tricky system. To enhance the perennial truth and portentous nature of mythical experiences without disgracing it by the machinations of cynical indifference to the here and now—this is the precarious task of a 'com-poser' such as Thomas Mann who needs both the dreamy sense for the timeless at the bottom of time and the acute awareness, the conscientious realization of the timely as the order of the day, the calling for a new embodiment of the timeless.

l. See *J.Ä.*, 297 = *Jos. Bros.*, 601. *Salvator mundi*, "saviour of the world," is Jerome's translation of Joseph's title "Zophnat Paneach."

Chapter 6

The Myth of the Soul: The Period of the Joseph Novels

B. *Joseph the Provider* (The City of God and the City of Man)

a. See the obituary for Franklin Delano Roosevelt: "Macht und Güte," in *Aufbau*, April 20, 1945. Cf. *Altes und Neues*, 655ff. The coupling of greatness and kindness appears first, perhaps, in Schiller's distich "Güte und Grösse." But it is noticeable that this combination of characters is by no means foreign even to Nietzsche: cf., e.g., *Werke* XIV, 286, 294, 302.

b. This may be illustrated by a note of Nietzsche, who has been so influential in the shaping of Thomas Mann's style: "The art of the novelist," he writes, "lies above all in touching upon the theme by way of prelude; in repeatedly anticipating it in a symbolic manner; in laying the foundation of a certain mood in which the outbreak of the coming thunderstorm is foreseen; in having the contour of the main theme exhibited, and thus in every possible way provoking the reader's creative imagination, as it were a riddle he himself had to solve—and, after all this, *solving* it *for* him in such a fashion as to take him by surprise" (Nietzsche, *Werke* XI, 113).

c. Cf., e.g., *Jaakob*, 90 = *Jos. Bros.*, 84; *J.E.*, 538f = *Jos. Bros.*, 1147f. The rise of God (Elohim) from the gods corresponds, however, to the catholicity of a deity comprehensive enough to account for the pagan gods as well.

d. Cf. Thomas Mann's letter of March 24, 1934, in Karl Kerényi, *Romandichtung und Mythologie*, 32. In *Death in Venice* Tadzio's last appearance is in the image of the "pale and lovely psychagogue" Hermes. And Hans Castorp and Joseph are equally susceptible to 'hermetic' magic: cf., e.g., *Zb.* II, 284f; 428 = *Magic*, 644f; 752.

e. *Bemühungen*, 138. The English translation (*Essays*, 173) misses the point. Nietzsche, in a similar way, came to realize "the comfort and encouragement of truth just by taking sides against myself and my preferences" (Nietzsche, *Werke* XI, 121).

f. It is the suffering of mankind which the true poet bears and relates in his works. "Art is intensified life, even in the artist himself. She gives deeper joy, she consumes more swiftly" (*Novellen* II, 365 = *Stories*, 388). Aschenbach's features as well as Mann's are molded by his adventures in the spirit and imagination as thoroughly as they could have been by the most restless or toilsome life.

g. Judah's kiss is invented by Thomas Mann as one of the features through which Joseph's story—the story of the Provider—is to prelude, in a minor key, that of Christ (*J.J.*, 288 = *Jos. Bros.*, 416). This sequence has the approval of Mann's religious socialism. "First comes the bread, the hosannah comes after." The earthly bread must be provided for before we have the right to preach and enjoy the bread of heaven. God is the God of the needy and suffering *soul*, not of the empty stomach (cf. *J.E.*, 487 = *Jos. Bros.*, 1116). But while he protests against the ignoble misery in which men are kept by men, Thomas Mann does not denounce the deepest experiences of his youth—the ennobling power of suffering. His ultimate concern is and remains with the entire soul whose thirst (he knows) will never be stilled by the drinks from the well of prosperity; man thirsts for the catharsis through pains as well as he insists—and rightly so—on his share in the goods of this life: cf. "Dostojewski —mit Maassen," in *Neue Studien*, 109f.

Having suffered most, Judah will be blessed most. ("They that are whole have no need of the physician, but they that are sick; I came not to call the righteous but the sinners"; "where sin abounded, grace did much more abound" [Mark, 2:17; Romans 5:20].) But Thomas Mann has to warn in both *Doctor Faustus* and *The Holy Sinner* against making this Lutheran "*Pecca fortiter*" ("Dare to sin!") the matter of an artful speculation on grace (*Faustus*, 382, 762 = *Faust.*, 246f., 503; *Der Erwählte*, 320 = *Holy Sinner*, 336). Cf. also Novalis, *Fragmente*, ed. Kamnitzer, 560: "The Christian religion is the true religion of voluptuousness. Sin is the great stimulus to the love of Deity. The more sinful one feels, the more of a Christian one is." And even Nietzsche, in a quite similar vein, confesses to the fascination which emanates from the dynamic contrast between divine transcendence and the paltriness and contrition of the sinner: "The *tension* between the God whose purity and distance is more and more emphasized, and man, conceived more and more as a wretched sinner—this is one of the greatest, boldest ventures of mankind. God's love for the sinner is a wonderful feat" (*Werke* XI, 313, 320).

h. The relationship between Joseph and Amenophis is occasionally pictured in colors reminiscent of the friendship between Goethe and the Duke Karl August. Cf. *J.E.*, 309 = *Jos. Bros.*, 1013. Thomas Mann sees, indeed, in this friendship a not entirely unconscious revival of a type of alliance which once united Pharaoh and Joseph, his viceroy. Cf. "Phantasie über Goethe," *Neue Studien*, 50f.

i. The consciousness of and conscientiousness in acting a classical part in a new performance of life distinguishes the spectacle of Thomas Mann's world from that against which Kant inveighs in his criticism of Mendelssohn's "Abderitic" philosophy of history as an oscillation around the ever same state of human affairs: "To watch this tragedy for a while may be, perhaps, quite instructive and moving; but some time the curtain ought to drop. For on the longer run the whole becomes a farce; and even if the actors do not grow tired, since they are fools, the spectator certainly will; one act will do for him if from it he can reasonably conclude that the unending play is but the same thing in perennial monotonous repetition" (Kant, *Werke*, ed. Cassirer, VI, 393; cf. VII, 393ff).

In his introduction to the Dial Press edition of Dostoievsky's Short Stories, now a part of *Neue Studien*, Thomas Mann observes (p. 100) that eternal recurrence is mentioned also in Dostoievsky. The · devil in *The Brothers Karamazov* calls it "the most indecent boredom." And Nietzsche, its ardent proclaimer, admits it to be "the most frightful" demand of the will upon itself. In Thomas Mann these misgivings can disappear: to him eternal recurrence is not only—just as to Nietzsche—willed repetition but above all, an ever new and often fresh variation of perennial classical themes.

Chapter 7

Imitatio Goethe

a. A reference in "Schwere Stunde" (*Novellen* I, 253) to Schiller's "Philosophische Briefe"—a correspondence between Julius and Raphael—has been misunderstood by the English translator: cf. *Stories*, 295.

b. Letter to the author of February 3, 1943. It is characteristic that Thomas Mann (in *Leiden und Grösse der Meister*, 11 = *Essays*, 67) renders a passage in Carlyle's necrology on Goethe (which counts Goethe among the men "whose impulses . . . might perhaps be seen still individually subsistent after two thousand years") in a translation which grants these two thousand years of subsistence to the great men themselves. Indeed, so he adds, "nobody can say into which dimensions his figure may still grow as time goes on."

c. *Lotte*, 477 = *Beloved*, 449. That all his beloved ones are one in his love is true of Goethe as well as his Faust, who in his own metamorphoses experiences also the metamorphoses of his one love, whose name is now Gretchen, now Helena, now "*una poenitentium, sonst Gretchen genannt.*" Cf. esp. *Faust* II, vv. 10039ff.

d. *West-östlicher Divan, Buch Suleika.* Cf. also Hölderlin's words:

Es gilt als Ziel, es ist das wahre Leben,
Von dem Sichgeistigen des Lebens Jahre zählen.

("It is man's aim and measures life's true size
to count life's years in terms of spirit's rise.")
—Hölderlin, "Höhere Menschheit"

e. The irony in which the unconscious is played off against the conscious and *vice versa* comes out in Charlotte's priding herself on the opposite maxim "that one ought resolutely consort with the real while leaving the possible alone" (*Lotte*, 252 = *Beloved*, 248). She embraces it theoretically at the very moment when she is about to act against it. As regards the transfer of essentially the same love from one individual to another, cf. Hans Castorp's love for Pribislav Hippe and Mme. Chauchat, and Mai-Sachme's story of "his first love which was, at the same time, his second" in *J.E.*, 51ff = *Jos. Bros.*, 867ff.

f. *Lotte*, 311 = *Beloved*, 310. The sensuous counterpart to this occurs in *The Magic Mountain*. Just as Goethe shudders at life's refusal to fulfill the demands of the *spirit*, so is Peeperkorn horrified as emotion fails to meet those of *life*.

g. Points of comparison with the writing of Franz Kafka occur particularly in Thomas Mann's allegedly "naturalistic" early period—e.g., in such short stories as "The Wardrobe" and "The Way to the Churchyard." His sketches of this period have a touch of surrealism *ante literam*. Kafka, on his part, gives us a religious version of the "Tonio Kröger" problem in his story *The Castle*—depicting the man of the spirit who yearns to find his true place in the human community. See Thomas Mann's introduction to the second English edition of *The Castle*, viii.

h. From Goethe's *Kunst und Altertum* (Art and Antiquity) (1826). Compare the famous saying from the *Wanderjahre* (1829). "What is the universal? The single instance."

i. *Lotte*, 353 = *Beloved*, 355—a saying of Mephistopheles (v. 4928) whose original meaning is here changed with a willfulness that is only apparent. For is not the poet just such a wizard as Mephistopheles proves himself in the scene at the Imperial Court?

j. *Lotte*, 286 = *Beloved*, 282. Compare in the notes to the *West-Eastern Divan* "Eingeschaltetes" ("Interpolation"): "The discerning power of the poet has its proper point of application in the form; his material is given him by the world—all too freely."

k. *Lotte*, 442 = *Beloved*, 444; cf. *J.Ä.*, 296 = *Jos. Bros.*, 601. "The man of spirit will not be content with what is externally presented to him, but will regard everything that strikes his senses as a mummery, behind which a loftier, spiritual life is wilfully, roguishly concealing itself" (Goethe). For spirit as "the predominance of the higher, guiding power" see the note "Allgemeinstes" ("Most General") in the *West-Eastern Divan*.

l. Matthew 4:17; *Faust*, v. 5629. To the same general category belongs Goethe's placing alongside another trinity (that of God, Goodness, and Immortality) the three corresponding demands of "the higher sensibility"—"Wealth, Health, and Long Life."

m. *Vide supra*. Cf. Joseph's saying, "I and my mother are one" (*J.J.*, 88, 139 = *Jos. Bros.*, 306, 334f) and "This is my blood" (*J.Ä.*, 14 = *Jos. Bros.*, 450).

n. Goethes *Werke* (Weimar ed.), 42:I, 91. Cf. the following passage from a fragmentary preface to *Poetry and Truth*: "Biography should present life as it is in and for itself and *for its own sake*. The writer of history cannot be blamed for trying to draw a definite outcome from the historical process; but in this way the individual deed and the individual person are left behind. Should one try to appraise the springtide in all the glory of its blossoming by the mere handful of fruits that are finally taken from the trees, one would certainly gain a very inadequate notion of that lovely season of the year." Cf. *Meister Eckhart*, ed. Franz Pfeiffer, 66.

o. It is characteristic that, in *Faust*, the tongues of flame which shoot from the charioteer's hands are not the eternal gift of the Holy Spirit; at best, they have a short, meteoric bloom. And in *Zahme Xenien* Goethe impresses on the reading youth that the Muse knows how to accompany, but not how to guide, life, i.e.:

> *Dass die Muse zu begleiten,*
> *Doch zu leiten nicht versteht.*

p. Cf. *Lotte*, 56, 86f, 92f, 294, 409f, 413 = *Beloved*, 52f, 81f, 86f, 291f, 411f, 415f. *Bemühungen*, 80 = *Essays*, 137. The remark cited in *Bemühungen* has been made by Ernest von Pfuel. Goethe "is tolerant without being benign. . . . None the less, he has made a wonderfully pleasant impression on me—

not as to inspire secret adoration, but as to give the understanding of some truth that had long been dimly felt . . . the impression of a task gracefully solved—a solution that I myself long sought in vain." (Biedermann, *Goethes Gespräche* II, 87.) Here, inspiration is not denied to Goethe himself, as Riemer denies it in Thomas Mann's novel; it is his own impression of Goethe which Herr von Pfuel calls elucidation rather than inspiration.

q. Cf. *Lotte*, 55, 93, 448 = *Beloved*, 51, 88, 450. The paradox involved in this state of being—the oxymoron of the "graceful spirit" (*Lotte*, 72 = *Beloved*, 68)—is developed by Thomas Mann in terms of Nietzsche's philosophical anthropology (which itself would have been impossible without the example set by Goethe). Compare Nietzsche's *Joyous Science*, § 382, "The Great Health": here is presented "the ideal of a spirit who in all naturalness—i.e. unintentionally, by virtue of a stream of powers that simply well up and overflow—*plays* with everything hitherto considered good, holy, inviolable, and divine . . . the ideal of a human-superhuman welfare and benevolence that may frequently appear *in*human—e.g., when set beside all former seriousness on earth, and compared with all former solemnities of bearing, tone, word, look, moral habit and obligation, as their truest, involuntary parody." The unpretentiousness of Goethe's style is repeatedly emphasized in *Lotte*, e.g., 85, 353 = *Beloved*, 80, 355.

r. Cf. Goethe, "Diderots Versuche über die Malerei" ("Diderot's Essays on Painting"): "Grateful to nature that produced him together with all other beings, the artist gives in return a second nature, which is now a product of thought and feeling, a humanly consummate nature."

s. *Lotte*, 89f, 344 = *Beloved*, 85f, 335. See K. Ph. Moritz, *Über die bildende Nachahmung des Schönen* (*On the Creative Imitation of the Beautiful*), ed. Auerbach, 25: "Man . . . apprehends . . . all that is organically subordinate to him. He assimilates it to the whole of his existence by *mirroring* it on what is the most highly polished plane of his being, and represents it externally in a figure of more intense beauty—whensoever his organ of representation has perfected itself by means of its inner, formative power."

t. *Lotte*, 325 = *Beloved*, 325. This is taken from Goethe's notes to the dialogue of Diderot entitled "Rameau's Nephew." Here it stands in the section on Voltaire. It is deserving of notice that reflections of Goethe on the continuity of life through the generations have also entered into the thinking of Maurice Barrès and the whole school of French traditionalism. Two passages in Thomas Mann's novel that go back to Goethe himself (*Lotte*, 324, 325 = *Beloved*, 324, 325) are found in *L'Appel au Soldat* (260) and in *Mes Cahiers* VI, 249f. (Like Thomas Mann (328f) Barrès emphasizes the significance of the Romantic element in Goethe's racial and cultural heritage.)

u. The change of Thomas Mann's position toward Nietzsche was expressed in a letter of August 27, 1944, written in reply to an essay, "Thomas Mann und Nietzsche," by the present author. It found its artistic realization in *Doctor Faustus* and was explained in the lecture on "Nietzsche's Philosophy in the Light of Contemporary Events" (1947).

v. *Achtung, Europa!* 129 = *Order*, 93. The last words of the quotation are Goethe's (Goethe to Eckermann, October 23, 1828). Even in *Betrachtungen*, 314, the proclamation of the "true profit of the people" as the highest standard of value is branded as ultimately destructive to any spiritual life. In *Zb.* II, 92f = *Magic*, 500f, a corresponding problem is discussed with regard to truth, in a politely far-sighted way.

w. Goethe, letter to Lavater, May 7, 1781; cf. another letter to the same person, April 9, 1781. See also the strange passage in the conversations with J. D. Falk, Biedermann, *Goethes Gespräche* IV, 473f (the subject of discussion is Goethe's well hidden "Walpurgis-bag," full of "stygian" rancor): "Deep down within, there burns an inextinguishable flame which, when it is on the loose, spares neither friend nor foe. At any rate I'd not advise anyone to get too close to it. I myself am filled with terror. . . ." Cf. finally the following, from the notebooks on natural science (1823): "Our condition we ascribe now to God, now to the Devil, and are as wrong in the one ascription as in the other: being the outgrowth of two different worlds, we set the riddle for ourselves."

x. *Lotte*, 87 = *Beloved*, 82f. A positive version of the same idea, plus an existential justification of irony, may be found in a Strindberg dictum, taken over by Thomas Mann in the *Reflections of an Unpolitical Man*, 202f: in contrast to the flat view of the party man, that of the artist is stereoscopic; it embraces a phenomenon from more than one single point of view.

y. From the Princeton lecture on *Faust, Mass und Wert* (1939), 601, *Adel*, 685 = *Essays*, 21. The "irony-enthusiasm" combination goes back to Friedrich Schlegel: see *Jugendschriften* II, 362. In its negative features Thomas Mann's portrayal of Goethe and his world is doubtless influenced by the Goethe pages in Heine's *Die Romantische Schule* (*Werke*, ed. Elster, V, 250ff). Cf., e.g., *Adel*, 319 = *Essays*, 178f. Heine finds fault with the perfect, yet frozen and sterile, beauty of Goethe's works: words without children; statues as from Egypt, land of the dead(!); a pantheism which makes for indifferentism and knows of inspiration and enthusiasm only as subject matters for artistic manipulations. In his extraordinary essay "On the Nature of Human Freedom" (*Werke* I, VII, 336ff), Schelling has some sentences, not meant for Goethe and not applicable to him without qualification, yet sounding the depths of the same problems which bewilder Goethe's contemporaries both in life and in *Lotte*: "Knowledge may have something analogous to propriety and bashfulness, just as, on the other hand, it may be bent on dissolution and libertinism, a sort of faunlike lust which nibbles at everything without being in earnest and in love (with anything). . . . The unifying power of our personality is the spirit . . . Hence inspiration, enthusiasm are at work in every creative and integrating effort of art and science" (*op. cit.*, 414).

z. *J.J.*, 54 = *Jos. Bros.*, 286. Let it be emphasized once more how Nietzsche has worked his way into this whole conception of the "divinely great" as transcending the opposition of good and evil. It was Nietzsche, again, who taught Thomas Mann to think of the great and the fearful together (the *mysterium tremendum* contained within the holy): see, for example, *The Will to Power*, 1035: "God, conceived as emancipation from morality, concentrating within himself the whole array of life's contrasts . . . God as the 'beyond good and evil' "; 1037: "God as supreme power—that is quite enough"; 1038: "God conceived after the type of creative spirits, of great men." Cf. 1051f. "The highest evil is one with the highest good: this, however, is the creative" (*Thus Spoke Zarathustra*; also in "Ecce Homo," *Werke* XV, 117).

aa. Cf. Augustine, *Enarr. in Ps.* 146:20: "God's 'wrath' means the righteousness of his punishments," and Jakob Böhme: "All that of which this world is an earthly mirror and parable has its consummate form in the spirituality of its divine sphere; not only spirit in the sense of thought or intention, but actual existence, corporeal being, flesh and blood. . . . This [visible world] is not constituted out of the eternal being, but out of the exhalation of the eternal being, out of love and wrath, the evil and the good" (*De Signatura Rerum*, ch. 16, §§ 20f).

bb. The affinities between Mann and André Gide have often been mentioned. They include also their peculiar relationship to Goethe and, as one of its points, the intertwining of good and evil. In *Les Faux-monnayeurs* (*Nouvelle Revue Française*), 498, the good Lord and the Devil are suspected of conspiring with one another; and in *Incidences* (*Nouvelle Revue Française*), 169, Gide confesses that he can read only with a shudder of recognition and dread "such passages in Baudelaire's Diary as this: 'In every man, at every hour, there are two simultaneous urges—one toward God, the other toward Satan.'" And he found a confirmation of this experience not only in Dostoievsky, who speaks of man as cherishing Sodom and the Madonna at one and the same time, but also in Goethe and his concept of the Demonic (cf. end of the *Journal des Faux-monnayeurs*).

cc. *Faust*, v. 7134ff. Regarding the secrets of his "Walpurgis-bag," Goethe imagines his "dear Germans" when, in *Faust*, "they eventually arrive at the passage where the Devil himself finds grace and pity before God . . ." (to Falk, June 21, 1816). Thomas Mann's metaphysics, colored as it is by artistic experience, is anticipated by such sayings as Augustine's: "as an artist . . . and a great artist—God makes use even of the Devil. If He could not use him, He would not let him exist at all" (*Tract.* XXVII, 10, in ev. Joh.). Cf. also the 15th Sura of the Koran, and for the whole, see Thomas Mann's lecture on *Faust*, loc. cit.

dd. Goethe to Eckermann, December 16, 1828. Greatness as such (*Format*), even if not qualifiable at all, has a positive value and casts a mysterious spell which the impressionable artist cannot but recognize—witness the monumental figure of Peeperkorn with his profuse though rather inarticulate emotions. In admiring the pristine power of Tolstoy's nature, Thomas Mann confesses: "The European instinct was and is ready to give its aesthetic placet to the phenomenon of human greatness" (*Forderung*, 282). In Peeperkorn (who is, of course, much more than a portrait of Gerhart Hauptmann) we see an embodiment (albeit in its final stages) of Tolstoyan grandeur, the epic majesty of nature with its demonic forces: the intoxication in which he feels akin to the wondrous, mighty bird of prey as it swoops down upon its victim (*Zb.* II, 421 = *Magic*, 746)—this scene in *The Magic Mountain* is modeled after an anecdote in Gorki's account of Tolstoy's life (cf. *Bemühungen*, 69 = *Essays*, 130f).

ee. For the dialectical conception of the good, in which he precedes Nietzsche and Mann, cf. Schelling, "On the Nature of Human Freedom" (*Werke* I, VII, 400): "Dialectically it is quite correct to say that Good and Evil are one and the same, only seen under different aspects. Or, in other words, that—viewed in itself, i.e. in the root of its identity—the Evil is actually the Good, just as—seen in its disunion or non-identity—the Good is the Evil. Therefore also this other statement holds true that he who does not possesss the stuff and strength of the Evil, is equally unfit for the Good."

With regard to Schelling, just as in the case of Leibniz, Thomas Mann speaks of a "very indirect influence" (letter to the author, February 3, 1943). The mediation took place through Nietzsche (*Birth of Tragedy*) and Russian writers such as Merezhkovsky.

ff. Cf. Nietzsche, *Also sprach Zarathustra* (*Werke* VI, 59): "It is with man as with a tree. The more either one reaches upward toward the light, the stronger do their roots strike earthward, downward, into the darkest depths—the depths of Evil." Cf. *Lotte*, 438 = *Beloved*, 440.

gg. Nietzsche, *Schopenhauer als Erzieher* (*Werke* I, 428). It is interesting to note that Nietzsche is not alone in converting this saying to the praise of a "heroic career"; the Frenchman Maurice Barrès (in many ways an ideological parallel to Thomas Mann) also uses it to give a meaning to the heroic endurance of the French soldiers during the First World War. Cf. *Les Diverses Familles Spirituelles de la France* (1917), 5.

hh. *Jaakob*, 338; cf. lv = *Jos. Bros.*, 222, 28. For the history of philosophy behind this declaration cf. Kant's *Idea of a Universal History with a Cosmopolitan View*, particularly Propositions IV-VI: "The means which Nature employs to secure the development of all her gifts is their *antagonism* in human society" (Kant, *Werke*, ed. Ernst Cassirer, IV, 155ff). Similarly the justification of the "ruse of reason" in Hegel's *Lectures on the Philosophy of History*, ed. Lasson, I, 83: "The particularity of passion is necessary to activate the universal; for it is only from what is particular and determined, plus its negation, that universality results."

ii. Goethe's "Legende" is analyzed in *Lotte*, 356ff = *Beloved*, 358ff, and transformed in *The Transposed Heads*.

Chapter 8
Last Judgment: *Doctor Faustus*

a. The irony with which the classical humanist Zeitblom is treated and treats himself mirrors, of course, Thomas Mann's scepticism as to the future of this type of life, preserved in its pure culture, without an ingredient of the demonic. On the other hand, spirit grows satanic if it is not drawn down to earth by love and charity, humanism and even humanitarianism. Certainly, the humanist proves less fascinating than his demoniacal antipode; yet, he represents in Thomas Mann's life and world the necessary complement and balance to the genius. The way of the genius has not ceased to be what it was in Z*b*. II, 429 = *Magic*, 752: the "evil way." On the other hand, his fascination by his great friend and his devotion to him save Zeitblom from mere erudite philistinism. Like Settembrini, he survives his antagonist. The fullness of human being and the richness and dramatic quality of Thomas Mann's novel consist in the tension and alliance between the trends which the musician and the classical scholar embody (and which had found a sort of personal union in the musical philologist Friedrich Nietzsche). It is only in Thomas Mann's political harangues—and quite rightly so—that the dialectics and dialogue between the civilized and the satanic powers yield to the sober, but thinner, voice of moral reason, and "predilection" is silenced by "obedience" (to use Jacob's language). Cf. the little article "Dürer" of 1928 (now in *A.N.*, 715ff).

b. Is it not legitimate to see in Nietzsche a *Faustus redivivus*, and in their tragedies a prefiguration of the burlesque tragedy of the German people after 1933? That Thomas Mann's Faustus (like his Devil) has assumed the demoniacal features of our time is equally justified. His Leverkühn is the representative of the German genius—the perilous and imperiled genius of the German [nati]on in the twentieth century; he is this rather than merely a symbol of [Thom]as Mann himself. It is true that, as an artist, Thomas Mann could not help considering himself a representative of the people in whose language he wrote. His nature and theirs are not foreign to one another. He is called to represent them just as they are represented in him. The poet does not generalize his own exceptional character and position to attribute them to the German people. Leverkühn's loneliness is not a pathological feature of the "born emigrant" Thomas Mann: it is a German, Protestant heritage besides being the fate of the artist in modern society. Thomas Mann simply endows Leverkühn with the greatness and the misery of a spirit which he himself had received from his people. But, in contradistinction to Leverkühn as well as the German followers of Hitler, he has worked hard to overcome the dangers of his past by carefully and precariously balancing them through the counterweights in the human mind. Without dissociating himself from the Leverkühn in his soul, he put him in his proper place—instead of going with him 'to hell.' "Where arrogance of the intellect is joined with an archaic and illiberal attitude of the mind, there is the devil," so he has said in disavowing the German stand. It is heroic to accept one's fate as Leverkühn does; it is greater to fight death and devil in one's own and one's people's soul.

c. As to the elimination of the soul as a factor which mediates between spirit and flesh, it is relevant to note that in his pamphlet against Erasmus Luther ridicules as mere fancy Origen's idea of the soul as an in-between, able to turn toward the spirit as well as the flesh (*Vom unfreien Willen*, ed. Friedrich Gogarten, 318).

d. It will be remembered that the motif of homosexuality which we met repeatedly in Thomas Mann's works, and which casts its shadows also upon Leverkühn's life, is (in one of its meanings) symbolic of the obstinate attempt of the spirit to remain within its own sphere, avoid pollution by the flesh, and become productive without intercourse with female matter. The failure of this effort, coupled with the insistence on productivity, results here in a wretched, sexual intercourse in which the purity of the spirit will be lost, though there may be an element of redeeming love even in the deadly lust which Leverkühn experiences in his dealings with an anonymous prostitute.

e. This is the dark side of Thomas Mann's experience that in all his loneliness the artist is the representative of his people, the voice of their muteness. The materials of the musician, his tones, are as pregnant with destiny as is the language of the poet. Even and just as he seems free to obey only the dictate of musical logic, the composer expresses, in a sort of "preestablished harmony," the peculiar possibilities—and impossibilities—of his time, the prerogatives and the taboos of the historical situation whose meaning or meaninglessness is exhibited in the meaning or meaninglessness of his expressive or merely constructive phrasing. Cf. *Faustus*, 567ff, 369ff = *Faust.*, 371ff, 238ff (one of the passages which reproduce—in Thomas Mann's way, and yet often verbally—ideas taken from Theodor W. Adorno's *Philosophie der Neuen Musik*, e.g. 21f, 28, 29, 69ff. This use to which Thomas Mann gratefully confesses in *Entstehung*, 42ff, bears in itself witness to today's artistic constellation; it, too, shows, in the very technique of mere montage, the writer's sovereign handling of his materials; it fits in with the style of quotations which is characteristic of this novel as well as of *Lotte in Weimar* and *The Holy Sinner*. A similar statement applies to the working in of the motif of Schönberg's twelve-tone technique to characterize the reckless constructiveness of Leverkühn's music.

f. In this fictitious Kaisersaschern the same medieval St. Vitus dances be imagined in which the young Nietzsche recognized a reincarnation of the Dionysian spirit: cf. *Faustus*, 58 = *Faust.*, 36, with Nietzsche's *The Birth of Tragedy*, §1.

g. *Faustus*, 382 = *Faust.*, 247; cf. 762 = *Faust.*, 502. Cf. Luther's *Facilius in peccatis* . . . (*est*) *sperare in Deum et tutius, quam in meritis et bonis* ("it is easier and more secure to hope in God in a state of sin than in one of merits and well-being"): quoted after Jacques Maritain, *Trois Reformateurs* (*nouvelle édition*), 253.

h. In Thomas Mann himself and his main figures egocentrism in the sense of ultimate self-concern has different ways of religious justification: in his Schiller as a rebound to suffering; in Jacob as the knowledge and heeding of his mission, the universal significance of his doing; in his Goethe as the feeling of a teleology which makes him, in the sequence of generations, the quintessence of their gifts, and of an entelechy, an inner law, which he is called upon to fulfill. The following out of his entelechy, the obedience to his "angel," is even Leverkühn's distinction. Cf. *Novellen* I, 252 = *Stories*, 244; *J.E.*, 523ff = *Jos. Bros.*, 1139; *Lotte*, 325 = *Beloved*, 325; *Faustus*, 149f = *Faust.*, 94.

i. Cf. *Faustus*, e.g., 463f, 472 = *Faust.*, 300f, 306. Quite similar ideas occur in Jacques Maritain, *The Rights of Man and Natural Law*, 40: "The German notion of community is built on a nostalgic longing to be together. . . . Fusion within the community thus becomes a compensation for an abnormal feeling of loneliness and distress . . . the trend of a dream, an undefined march towards nobody-knows-what conquests."

j. "Schopenhauer," quoted from *Essays*, 406 = *Adel*, 391. To Thomas Mann the productive intercourse between the spirit and the senses has lost the stigma it has to both Aschenbach (in *Death in Venice*) and Leverkühn.

k. The entering of the spirit into the realm of the soul is, perhaps, the secret of its mission, according to Thomas Mann as well as Hegel. But the masculine spirit (*animus*) tries again and again in Mann's writings, by way of homo-erotic production, to do without promiscuity with the feminine principle of the soul (*anima*).

l. Cf. *Faustus*, 204 = *Faust.*, 131, with a statement in the Preface to *Anna Karenina*, where Thomas Mann credits the science of the nineteenth century with having "lived for God in spite of denying him": *Adel*, 335 = *Essays*, 188.

m. See *Faustus*, 83 = *Faust.*, 53; "Goethe als Repräsentant des bürgerlichen Zeitalters" (*Adel*, 142ff = *Essays*, 91f). Cf., e.g., the Preface to *Anna Karenina* (also in *Adel*, 319 = *Essays*, 178f). It is interesting to see how in this point so vastly different lines of influence as those from Heine and Merezhkovsky can meet.

n. As an individual (and a Protestant), Leverkühn is tempted to speculate on the supreme challenge divine grace may find in the most wicked sin; but there is no such leering in the person of the artist, no such self-comfort in the ultimate surrender of his last work. It leaves hope—infinite hope—*for* the sinner in man, without holding it out *to* him as a means of relief in the boundlessness of his despair.

o. The representative nature of the artist accounts for the fact that all the perversions of the time are, in a way, mirrored in Leverkühn's work even though he seems hardly to notice what happens around him. "I have to listen only to my inner voice in order to hear the voice of the time," says Thomas Mann in *Betrachtungen*, xxxii. Cf. above, note e.

p. The dilemma in which life and art appear in Thomas Mann is not exclusively an expression of their actual situation in the twentieth century. It is aggravated by his Schopenhauerian metaphysics, which makes art both a crowning finale and the finis of life, life's last transformation, its transfiguration. This idea is strong in Thomas Mann and is not always balanced by that of resurrection, the "Die and rise." And in the shocks and spasms of Leverkühn's music, life is denied even the benefit of its euthanasia in art.

q. *Entstehung*, 34. Cf. also the method of quotation in T. S. Eliot and Joyce, in which analogy serves to show the sordid degradation of formerly sublime motifs.

r. The shocking (even though discreetly handled) parallelism between the Greek heroine and the prostitute is not entirely of Thomas Mann's own making. In his Faust lecture of 1938 he had already described the mythical presuppositions which prevail in the coupling of Faust and Helena with the appearance of a prostitute in the role and under the name of Helena. This motif was allegedly created in the time of declining antiquity by that Simon Magus who is mentioned in the Acts of the Apostles. In accordance with the principle of mythical identity and reincarnation, it was resumed in the sixteenth century, another "time of fanaticism and mental confusion." There it has its place in the mythical charlatanry of a Georg Helmstätter, *alias* Johannes Faustus—the very name that (according to an old Christian novel) had been adopted by Simon on his flight with Helena. Finally in Thomas Mann's *Faustus* the same motif is taken out of the atmosphere of humbuggery and endowed with the weight of an excruciating symbolism. To create is to intensify. Cf. "Über Goethes Faust" (*Adel*, 676ff = *Essays*, 13f).

s. It is this insistence that made Kierkegaard a spiritual power between and after the World Wars. Leverkühn reads just before the scene with the devil the reflections on Mozart's *Don Juan* in *Either-Or*. This is in 1912. Thomas Mann's own Kierkegaard studies, however, are as late as 1944 when that scene was written.

t. This may well be compared with Leverkühn's "recantation" of Beethoven's Ninth Symphony after little Echo's painful and revolting death.

u. Adrian's Devil is a replica of that gentleman in reduced circumstances who visits Ivan during his headaches—such headaches as are also characteristic of Adrian and his kin. The German Devil is distinguished, however, first of all, by his chameleonic appearance: "we shall always look like thy own thoughts," says the Devil in Heine's *Doctor Faust*. In addition, Leverkühn's Shemmael plumes himself on his knowledge from the witches' kitchen of syphilology and from the modern musical laboratory with its refined but not prolific output. He is as different from Dostoievsky's Devil as Leverkühn's spiritual and artistic pride differs from the intellectual pride in which Ivan dreams of the scientific and technical progress of mankind and the era of a Man-God.

v. *Faustus*, 372 = *Faust.*, 240; cf. *Faustus*, 281 = *Faust.*, 181. The collage technique in *Doctor Faustus* is, of course, one of the ways to overcome the fictional character of self-contained beauty: the mounting of historical raw material and the passionate reaction to the news mediatize, i.e., practically depose, art in favor of actuality and contribute to giving the artistic expression the wild immediacy of a direct discharge of emotions. The *concordia discors*, the unity of discord in *Doctor Faustus*, consists precisely in this encounter between uninhibited passion on the one hand and icy constructivism on the other.

While the extremist formulation of the passage quoted above is taken over from Wiesengrund-Adorno, it is entirely in tune with the eschatological mood of *Doctor Faustus*, Thomas Mann's own mood at the end of the Third Reich. Part of the truth of the novel consists in the truthful documentation of a desperate time.

w. In his Faust lecture, Thomas Mann emphasizes a corresponding prohibition—that of marriage—in the German folk tale of *Doctor Faustus* as being the motif by which allegedly the young Goethe, Friederike's unfaithful lover, was first attracted to the Faust theme: cf. *Adel*, 674 = *Essays*, 12.

x. The comparison of the Echo story with that of Mignon has been approved by Thomas Mann himself (letter to the author of August 17, 1948).

y. *Entstehung* mentions again and again the "atmosphere of sacrifice" (27) around the work; that it is "throughout a confession and sacrifice of life" (80), bearing the "stigmata of the 'utmost'" (140).

z. Throughout Thomas Mann's life, we find him confessing what he formulated in his "first letter to Bonn"—that "as a dreamer and sceptic, I am forced to save and justify my own life" (*Rede und Antwort*, 1).

aa. In *Betrachtungen*, 542, Thomas Mann stresses the fact that Aschenbach's defeat is a *moral* necessity.

bb. Passages such as *Faustus*, 764f = *Faust.*, 504f, show under a thin disguise the far-reaching identity between Thomas Mann and the *emeritus professor et praeceptor Germaniae* Serenus Zeitblom.

REFERENTIAL NOTES

Introduction

1. Goethe, *West-östlicher Divan*, "Vermächtnis altpersischen Glaubens."
2. Henri Bergson, *Les Deux Sources de la Morale et de la Réligion* (Alcan), 304.
3. Cf. *Adel*, 472ff = *Essays*, 353f.

Chapter 1
Spiritual Background

1. Max Weber, *Religionssoziologie* I, 93.
2. *Ibid.*, 95.
3. *Bu.* II, 341. = *Bbr.* 523f.
4. Letter to the author, February 23, 1944. Cf. *Betrachtungen*, 535ff. Thomas Mann's attitude toward Luther is part of his *imitatio* Nietzsche: cf., e.g., Nietzsche's letter to Peter Gast, October 5, 1879.
5. *Novellen* II, 86 = *Stories*, 132.
6. Cf. *Zb.* I, 44 = *Magic*, 30.
7. *Novellen* II, 191 = *Stories*, 251.
8. *Betrachtungen*, 127. For a criticism of these ideas cf. H. M. Robertson, *Aspects of the Rise of Economic Individualism*, 1935.
9. *Zb.* I, 58f = *Magic*, 42f.
10. *Zb.* I, 61 = *Magic*, 44.
11. Cf. *Zb.* II, 481ff; 573ff; 622 = *Magic*, 789ff; 857ff; 894.
12. Thomas Mann, *Schopenhauer*, (*The Living Thoughts of Schopenhauer, presented by Thomas Mann*, 1939), 8 = *Adel*, 338 = *Essays*, 372.
13. Cf., e.g., *Die Betrogene*, 71f = *Black Swan*, 77f; *Der Erwählte*, 184 = *Holy Sinner*, 192; *A.N.*, 433ff, cf. "The Artist and Society" in *The Listener*, June 5, 1952.
14. *Novellen* I, 359 = *Stories*, 158.
15. Cf. the similar statements in *Novellen* II, 359 = *Stories*, 384, and, twenty-two years later, in *L.G.M.*, 117f.
16. *L.G.M.*, 61 = *Essays*, 49.
17. *Zb.* II, 425 = *Magic*, 749.
18. Cf. "Goethe's *Werther*," in *Corona* (In Honor of Samuel Singer, 1941), 195.
19. *J.E.*, 524 = *Jos. Bros.*, 1139.
20. *Betrachtungen*, xvi; cf., e.g., 74ff and *Lotte*, 351 = *Beloved* 352.
21. *R.A.*, 274.
22. *The Theme of the Joseph Novels* (Washington, 1942), 19; cf. "The Coming Humanism," in *Patterns for Living*, ed. O. J. Campbell, J. van Gundy, C. Shrodes (1940), 1193; cf. also letter to Karl Kerényi, October 7, 1936: Kerényi, *Romandichtung und Mythologie*, 56f.
23. Ernst Troeltsch, *Christian Thought*, 165f.
24. Ernst Troeltsch, *Gesammelte Schriften* III (*Der Historismus und seine Probleme*), 210; 187. This may be compared with the concluding words of Mann's "Lob der Vergänglichkeit" in *A.N.*, 268.

25. Max Scheler, *Die Stellung des Menschen im Kosmos*, 76-83. Cf. also, e.g., *Faustus*, 185ff = *Faust.*, 118ff, with Scheler, *Der Genius des Krieges und der deutsche Krieg*, 17, 56f, 61, etc.
26. "The Coming Humanism" (*op. cit.*), 1193. Here Thomas Mann makes use of statements in Karl Kerényi's article "Eulabeia," *Byzantinisch-neugriechische Jahrbücher* (1931): cf. Thomas Mann/Kerényi, *Romandichtung und Mythologie*, 56f.
27. *Order*, viii.
28. *Betrachtungen*, 88.
29. *Jaakob*, lviii, 14 = *Jos. Bros.*, 30, 40; *J.Ä.*, 243, 733 = *Jos. Bros.*, 573, 830.
30. Romans 8:19. Cf. *Schopenhauer*, 22, 24, 29.
31. *Lotte*, 189 = *Beloved*, 183.
32. See Leviticus 22:32; Deuteronomy 32:51; Isaiah 8:13. For Midrashic and Hasidic comments see Martin Buber, *Tales of the Hasidim* I, 149. Cf. *J.J.*, "Wie Abraham Gott entdeckte."
33. "Das Gesetz," in *Ausgewählte Erzählungen*, 860 (English in *The Ten Commandments*, ed. Armin L. Robinson, 1943), 69.
34. Pascal, *Pensées* (Léon Brunschvicg), no. 485.
35. Cf., e.g., *J.J.*, 52, 56; *J.E.*, 22, 129, 230f, 340f = *Jos. Bros.*, 285, 287; 850, 911, 968f, 1032.
36 *Sonnets to Orpheus* II, 24.
37. *J.J.*, 32 = *Jos. Bros.*, 274.
38. *Ibid.*
39. *J.E.*, 22 = *Jos. Bros.*, 850.
40. Angelus Silesius, *The Cherubic Wayfarer* I, no. 105.
41. Cf. *J.J.*, 61 = *Jos. Bros.*, 290.
42. Psalms 22:4.
43. Zechariah 14:9. Cf. *J.J.*, 59 = *Jos. Bros.*, 288f.
44. Cf., e.g., J. Gasquet, *Cézanne*, 93.
45. Schelling, *Über das Wesen der menschlichen Freiheit*, *Werke* I, VII, 411.
46. *Achtung, Europa!*, 103 = *Order*, 109.
47. *Novellen* II, 42 = *Stories*, 107.
48. *Novellen* II, 27 = *Stories*, 99; *Lotte*, 350 = *Beloved*, 351.
49. Letter to the author, February 17, 1941.
50. Nietzsche, *Götzendämmerung*, (*Twilight of the Idols*), "Streifzüge," no. 24. Cf. *Betrachtungen*, 606.
51. Cf. *Faustus*, e.g., 294 = *Faust.*, 189f.
52. Cf. *J.E.*, 129ff = *Jos. Bros.*, 911ff.
53. *Novellen* II, 447 = *Stories*, 434.
54. *Lotte*, 356 = *Beloved*, 357f.
55. *J.E.*, 552f = *Jos. Bros.*, 1155.
56. Cf. *The World as Will and Idea*, §34; Thomas Mann, *Adel*, 396f.
57. *Novellen* I, 231 = *Stories*, 282.
58. *Zb.* II, 258 = *Magic*, 625.
59. *J.E.*, 277 = *Jos. Bros.*, 996.
60. *Jaakob*, lvii = *Jos. Bros.* 32f.
61. *Lotte*, 89f. (The English translation, *Beloved*, 84, is misleading.)
62. Nietzsche, *The Will to Power*, Book IV, no. 1038.
63. *R.A.*, 352.
64. *Forderung*, 209.
65. *J.E.*, *pass.* Karl Kerényi, *op. cit.*, 32, 83.

66. *Adel*, 391 = *Essays*, 406.
67. *Forderung*, 24.
68. Schelling, *System des transzendentalen Idealismus, Werke* I, III, 628.
69. Cf. *J.E.*, 621 = *Jos. Bros.*, 1195.
70. Letter to the author (February 17, 1941), with reference to the last paragraph of Mann's Preface to *Anna Karenina*.
71. "Versuch über Tschechow." *Neue Rundschau* (1956), 35.
72. Letter to the author, February 17, 1941.
73. *Ibid.*
74. Cf. "Goethe und Tolstoy," *Adel*, 313; cf. also the Preface to *Anna Karenina*, 320 = *Essays*, 175, 179.
75. *Novellen* I, 227 = *Stories*, 282. Cf. also *Fiorenza* of the same year (1904).
76. Thomas Mann's idea of mutual longing comes close to Schelling's position in "Über das Wesen der menschlichen Freiheit" (*Werke* I, VII, 359ff; 447). He himself discussed the theme first in the *Betrachtungen* (e.g., 61) and developed it further in "Goethe und Tolstoy."
77. Nietzsche, *Geburt der Tragödie = Birth of Tragedy* (*Werke* I, 33); cf. *Werke* XVI, 387f.
78. *Novellen* II, 440f = *Stories*, 430f. As to the motif, cf. Goethe's poem "Deutscher Parnass."
79. *J.Ä.*, 519 = *Jos. Bros.*, 718.
80. Goethe, "Weimarische Kunstausstellung vom Jahre 1801 und Preisaufgaben vom Jahre 1802," concluding sentence.
81. Nietzsche, *Götzendämmerung = Twilight of the Idols*, "Skirmishes in a War with the Age," no. 49.

Chapter 2

The Metaphysical Pattern

1. Cf., e.g., *Lotte*, 323f = *Beloved*, 323f.
2. *Stories*, vif.
3. *R.A.*, 10.
4. *Forderung*, 32.
5. Goethe, *Wilhelm Meisters Wanderjahre*, "Betrachtungen im Sinne der Wanderer."
6. *R.A.*, 16f.
7. *Zb.* II, 521f = *Magic*, 819.
8. A saying of Campanella (from *De Sensu Rerum et Magia*) in the modified form given it by Goethe in the *Morphologische Hefte*, "Zwischenrede."
9. Goethe to Eckermann, March 30, 1831 (Biedermann, *Goethes Gespräche*, IV, 359).
10. Cf. Spinoza, *Ethica* III, 3.
11. Cf. particularly Herder's "Journal meiner Reise im Jahre 1769," *pass.*
12. Cf. Herder, *Auch eine Philosophie der Geschichte zur Bildung der Menschheit* (1774), *Dritter Abschnitt*, "Zusätze." Thomas Mann describes the ambivalence of the development very often; one of the many instances is *A.N.*, 394.
13. Cf. *Adel*, 387 = *Essays*, 403.
14. *Novellen* II, 407 = *Stories*, 411f.
15. *Jaakob*, xlv = *Jos. Bros.*, 23.

16. Cf. *Zb.* II, 407 = *Magic*, 735f.
17. *Jaakob*, xlvii = *Jos. Bros.*, 24; *Bekenntnisse*, 18 = *Confessions*, 11.
18. Schopenhauer, *The World as Will and Idea* II, Book IV, ch. 41; Reclam II, 587f.
19. *Zb.* II, 527 = *Magic*, 823f.
20. *R.A.*, 392.
21. Cf. William James, *The Varieties of Religious Experience*, Lecture 20, with, e.g., "Freud und die Zukunft" (= "Freud and the Future" in *Essays*, 411ff); also *Zb.* II, 257 = *Magic*, 624.
22. *Zb.* I, 62; cf. 59ff; II, 321, 527 = *Magic*, 44; 42ff; 671; 823f.
23. *Novellen* II, 407 = *Stories*, 412.
24. *Lotte*, 354 = *Beloved*, 356.
25. *Zb.* I, 62 = *Magic*, 44; *Bekenntnisse*, 103f = *Confessions*, 84ff.
26. *Zb.* II, 265 = *Magic*, 230.
27. *Zb.* II, 135 = *Magic*, 533.
28. *Zb.* II, 585; cf. II, 117, 208 = *Magic*, 866; cf. 520; 588.
29. *Zb.* I, 575; II, 428 = *Magic*, 431; 751.
30. *J.Ä.*, 608ff = *Jos. Bros.*, 765ff.
31. Cf. *V.K.*, 192ff = *Transposed*, 161f. Resuming several ideas from *Fiorenza*, *Novellen* II, 191, 218f = *Stories*, 251, 267.
32. *Bekenntnisse*, 81; 20 *et pass.* = *Confessions*, 65; 13 *et pass.*
33. Cf., e.g., *Novellen* I, 166 = *Stories*, 172.
34. Bazarov in Turgenev's *Fathers and Sons*, ch. 10.
35. Cf. Bakunin's article "Die Reaktion in Deutschland" (quoted after Th. G. Masaryk, *The Spirit of Russia* I, 444f) with Friedrich Schlegel, *Jugendschriften*, ed. Minor, II, 303 (Fragment 131).
36. Thomas Mann to Karl Kerényi (*Romandichtung und Mythologie*, 66).
37. Cf. *Zb.* I, 59 = *Magic*, 42, with *Faustus*, 760 = *Faust.*, 597. Cf. "Versuch über Tschechow," *Neue Rundschau* (1956), 34f.
38. *Betrachtungen*, 606. Cf. Preface to *Anna Karenina* (*Adel*, 319ff = *Essays*, 178ff).
39. Cf. *A.N.*, 31ff.
40. Cf., e.g., *J.E.*, 374 = *Jos. Bros.*, 1052; *Adel*, 597f = *Essays*, 426.
41. Cf. *A.N.*, 458.
42. *Bekenntnisse*, 222ff = *Confessions*, 191ff.
43. *Bekenntnisse*, 210f = *Confessions*, 179ff.
44. Cf., e.g., *Adel*, 340 = *Essays*, 374.
45. Cf. *Bekenntnisse*, 12, 66 = *Confessions*, 6, 51.
46. Cf. *Bekenntnisse*, 24 ff = *Confessions*, 17ff.
47. *J.E.*, 382 = *Jos. Bros.*, 1056.
48. Ecclesiastes 1:18.
49. *Inferno* VI, 106, transl. Binyon.
50. Cf. Schopenhauer, *World as Will and Idea* (Reclam I, 213, 253, 259, 352, 402, 685; II, 442ff).
51. Nietzsche, *Jenseits von Gut und Böse* (*Beyond Good and Evil*), §270.
52. Aeschylus, *Agamemnon*, vv. 173ff, 249ff, 1133f, 1426, 1619f; cf. Heraclitus, fragment B11 (Diels); Sophocles, *Antigone*, v. 927.
53. Romans 8:17. Cf. Hebrews, 5:8.
54. Cf. Goethe's poem "Das Göttliche" with Thomas Mann's "Lob der Vergänglichkeit" (1952; *A.N.* 265ff); and Goethe's(?) prose poem "*Natur*" with *Betrogene*, 126f = *Black Swan*, 140f.

55. *Betrachtungen*, 541.
56. Schopenhauer, *The World as Will and Idea*, Book 4, §61 (Reclam I, 430f).
57. *Erzählungen*, 860 = "The Law" (in *The Ten Commandments*, 70).
58. *Forderung*, 206.
59. Spinoza, *Ethica* III, 27, schol. 2. Cf. Schopenhauer, *World as Will and Idea* I, Book IV, §67 (Reclam I, 483); Thomas Mann, *Schopenhauer*, 46.
60. For a detailed appraisal, see H. J. Weigand, "Der symbolisch-autobiographische Gehalt von Thomas Manns Romandichtung Königliche Hoheit," *P.M.L.A.*, (1931), 867-879. Cf. *R.A.*, 46; *K.H.*, 453.
61. Cf. *A.N.*, 262.
62. *Jaakob*, lxii = *Jos. Bros.*, 29.
63. Cf. Schopenhauer, *The World as Will and Idea* II, Book 4, ch. 41 (Reclam II, 563).
64. *L.G.M.*, 16 = *Essays*, 70f. Cf. Goethe, *Aus meinem Leben, Dichtung und Wahrheit*, Part III, Book XIII. Cf. also *Zb.* II, 124 = *Magic*, 525.
65. Goethe, *West-östlicher Divan*, "Vermächtnis altpersischen Glaubens."
66. "Lebensabriss," *Neue Rudschau*, (1930), 762.
67. Gregory of Nyssa according to Hans Urs von Balthasar, *Der Versiegelte Quell*, 14.
68. Cf. *Adel*, 588f = *Essays*, 420.
69. Nietzsche, *Also sprach Zarathustra* (*Werke* VI, 322); *Werke* XIV, 301.
70. Cf. *Adel*, 586f = *Essays*, 418.
71. Cf. *Versuch über Schiller*, 27.
72. *J.E.*, 248 = *Jos. Bros.*, 980.
73. *The Theme of the Joseph Novels* (Washington, 1942), 22.
74. Nietzsche, *Werke* I, 511.
75. Cf., e.g., letter to Karl Kerényi, March 24, 1934 (*Romandichtung und Mythologie*, 30); *The Theme of the Joseph Novels*, 7.
76. *Zb.* II, 250 = *Magic*, 619.
77. *J.E.*, 193 = *Jos. Bros.*, 947.
78. Cf., e.g., *J.E.*, 314 = *Jos. Bros.*, 1017.
79. Friedrich Schlegel, "Rede über die Mythologie," *Jugendschriften*, ed. Minor, II, 363.
80. Goethe, "Dauer im Wechsel."
81. Goethe, "Vermächtnis."
82. *Jaakob*, 161 = *Jos. Bros.*, 124. Cf. Appendix II: "Typology in Dilthey, Max Weber, and Franz Marc."
83. *J.E.*, 332 = *Jos. Bros.*, 1027.
84. Goethe to Eckermann, October 29, 1823.
85. Goethe, *Die natürliche Tochter*, vv. 1066f.
86. *Lotte*, 324 = *Beloved*, 324.
87. *Adel*, 592 = *Essays*, 423.
88. *J.E.*, 235 = *Jos. Bros.*, 971.
89. Letter to the author, August 27, 1944.
90. *Betrachtungen*, 53.
91. "Ansprache bei der Eröffnung des Goethe-Museums in Frankfurt am Main" (*Goethe-Kalender auf das Jahr 1933*), 35.
92. Goethe, "Vermächtnis."
93. Goethe, "Urworte. Orphisch."
94. A. J. Toynbee, *A Study of History* (abridgment), 49.
95. *Lotte*, 354 = *Beloved*, 356.

96. Cf. *Faustus*, 150 = *Faust.*, 94.
97. Letter to the author, August 27, 1944.
98. Schopenhauer, *Grundlage der Moral* §10, *Anmerkung* (*Werke*, Reclam III, 560).
99. Schopenhauer, *World as Will and Idea* II, Book II, ch. 25 (*Werke*, Reclam II, 376).
100. Plato, *Republic*, 617E.
101. *Betrachtungen*, 112; Schopenhauer, 16 = *Essays*, 387f.
102. *V.K.*, 50 = *Transposed*, 39.
103. Cf. Schopenhauer, *World as Will and Idea* II, Book II, ch. 25 (*Werke* II, 376); *Grundlage der Moral*, §§10, 20 (*Werke* III, 560, 634). Thomas Mann refers to these passages in *Betrachtungen*, 111f.
104. *Lotte*, 327 = *Beloved*, 327f.
105. *V.K.*, 102 = *Transposed*, 83f.
106. *Novellen* II, 402 = *Stories*, 409.
107. Cf. e.g., *J.Ä.*, 593 = *Jos. Bros.*, 757.
108. *V.K.*, 221f = *Transposed*, 187.
109. R. M. Rilke, *Sonnets to Orpheus*, II, XXIX, transl. Leishman.
110. As to Aschenbach, cf. *Novellen* II, 361 = *Stories*, 385; to the similar position of Leverkühn Thomas Mann attests, e.g., in a letter to the author, August 14, 1948.
111. Cf. *Bemühungen*, 58 = *Essays*, 124; *Adel*, 362 = *Essays*, 388; also Schopenhauer, *Grundlage der Moral*, §20 (*Werke* III, 637ff).
112. Romans 9:22f.
113. Cf. *Jaakob*, 33, 174f, 352f = *Jos. Bros.*, 51, 130f, 231; *J.E.*, 15ff = *Jos. Bros.*, 846f; *Novellen* II, 382 = *Stories*, 397; *Gesang vom Kindchen* (1928), 14, *Unordnung und frühes Leid* (1926), 33ff = "Early Sorrow," in *Stories*, 505ff.
114. Goethe, *Faust* II, v. 7135.
115. Nietzsche, e.g., "Zur Genealogie der Moral," 2 *Abhandlung*, no. 7 (*Werke* VII, 358).
116. Bertrand Russell, "A Free Man's Worship," in *Philosophical Essays*, 59ff.
117. *The Cherubic Wayfarer* II, 198.
118. Friedrich Schlegel, *Jugendschriften*, ed. Minor, II, 364. Cf. Schelling, *Philosophie der Kunst*, *Werke* I, V, 368.
119. Cf., e.g., Schopenhauer, *Werke*, I, 249f; II, 521; IV, 357.
120. Nietzsche, *Also sprach Zarathustra*, "Das Lied der Schwermut" (*Werke* VI, 434); cf. *Werke* V, 296ff, 311ff.
121. Nietzsche, *Die fröhliche Wissenschaft* (Joyous Wisdom), no. 356 (*Werke* V, 296f).
122. *Jaakob*, 8 = *Jos. Bros.*, 37.
123. *V.K.*, 53 = *Transposed*, 42.
124. Baudelaire, *Eloge du Maquillage*.
125. *Jaakob*, 175 = *Jos. Bros.*, 131.
126. *Forderung*, 317.

Chapter 3

The Genealogy of the Artist

1. From Baudelaire, "Semper Eadem."
2. *Novellen* II, 38 = *Stories*, 105.

3. *Lotte*, 423f = *Beloved*, 426.
4. *Lotte*, 324 = *Beloved*, 325.
5. *L.G.M.*, 137.
6. *Novellen* II, 6ff, 35ff = *Stories*, 87ff, 103ff.
7. Nietzsche, *Also sprach Zarathustra*, *"Vom Wege des Schaffenden"* (*Werke* VI, 92ff). Cf. *Betrachtungen*, 39ff.
8. *Bemühungen*, 21ff = *Essays*, 100f. Cf. *J.J.*, 121f = *Jos. Bros.*, 324.
9. Cf., e.g., Storm's poem "Hyazinthen."
10. *Novellen* II, 28 = *Stories*, 99.
11. *Novellen* II, 40 = *Stories*, 106. Cf., e.g., *J.J.*, 239f, *J.E.*, 25ff, 641 = *Jos. Bros*, 389, 852ff, 1207. Cf. *Erwählte*, 309 = *Holy Sinner*, 324.
12. *Betrachtungen*, 126; cf. 120.
13. A frank admission of this artistic license in *Schopenhauer*, 56. The idea is foreshadowed, however, in Schopenhauer passages such as *Werke* (Reclam) III, 654.
14. For the whole, see *Bu.* II, 342 = *Bbr.*, 524ff.
15. *Zb.* II, 231f = *Magic*, 605f; *Lotte*, 360ff = *Beloved*, 362ff.
16. "Lob der Vergänglichkeit," (*A.N.*, 266); *Bekenntnisse*, 312ff = *Confessions*, 271ff.
17. Cf., e.g., *Forderung*, 52; *Novellen* I, 337 = *Stories*, 146.
18. Goethe, *Faust* II, v. 6287f.
19. The same motif is to be found, e.g., in Rilke's *Sonnets to Orpheus* I, 16.
20. *Bu.* II, 463ff = *Bbr.*, 595. Compare the effect of the little theme from Vinteuil's sonata in Marcel Proust's *Remembrance of Things Past*.
21. *Bu.* II, 466 = *Bbr.*, 597.
22. The same motif appears in "Tristan," *Novellen* I, 337, 360f = *Stories*, 146, 159.
23. *Zb.* II, 434 = *Magic*, 755f.
24. "Tod in Venedig," *Novellen* II, 388 = *Stories*, 401.
25. Cf., e.g., "*Schwere Stunde*," *Novellen* I, 255 = *Stories*, 296; "*Das Gesetz*" *Erzählungen*, 783 = *Tables of the Law* (1947), 5.
26. Cf. Hölderlin's hymn "Wie wenn am Feiertage. . . ."
27. Cf. Schopenhauer, *The World as Will and Idea* I, Book II, §29 (*Werke* I, 229).
28. *Bu.* II, 471 = *Bbr.*, 599f.
29. *Lotte*, 311 = *Beloved*, 309f. Cf. *Entstehung*, 11f.

Chapter 4

The Dominion of Man

1. From Paul Valéry, "Le Cimetière Marin."
2. *Novellen* II, 87 = *Stories*, 132.
3. Cf. *Bekenntnisse*, 127 = *Confessions*, 105, with *Betrachtungen*, 77.
4. *K.H.*, 98 = *Royal*, 73.
5. Cf. *Zb.* II, 78 = *Magic*, 489. See also *Novellen* II, 389, 404, 424f = *Stories*, 401, 410, 422.
6. *Novellen* II, 35 = *Stories*, 103.
7. Leconte de Lisle, "Midi."
8. II Corinthians, 12:9.
9. Novalis, *Fragmente*, ed. Kamnitzer, no. 984.

10. *Faustus*, 361 = *Faust.*, 233. Cf. Aristotle, *De Anima*, Book II, 2; 414a 11f.
11. *"L'humanité se confirme par l'infirmité"* (*Freud und die Zukunft*, 8 = *Essays*, 414), a quotation from Victor Hugo. "Man is born to suffer" (Novalis, *Fragmente*, no. 984). "Man is a sick animal" (Nietzsche, *Genealogie der Moral* III, no. 13). And so on.
12. Nietzsche, *Der Wille zur Macht* I, no. 109.
13. Novalis, Fragmente, no. 987.
14. *Wilhelm Meisters Lehrjahre*, Book VIII, ch. 1.
15. *Zb.* I, 58ff = *Magic*, 41ff.
16. Barrès, *Tout Licence sauf contre l'Amour* (Perrin), 60f. Cf. Fritz Kaufmann, "*Imitatio* Goethe: Thomas Mann and his French Confrères," *Monatshefte*, October 1956.
17. Walt Whitman, Preface to first edition of *Leaves of Grass*.
18. *Zb.* I, 57 = *Magic*, 40-41.
19. *Zb.* II, 613 = *Magic*, 887.
20. *Wilhelm Meisters Lehrjahre*, Book VIII, ch. 5.
21. H. A. Korff, *Geist der Goethezeit* III, 344.
22. Schiller in a letter to Goethe, July 5, 1796.
23. Goethe to Lavater, September 20, 1780.
24. *Zb.* I, 43 = *Magic*, 30.
25. *Zb.* I, 247; II, 362, 429 (and often)= *Magic*, 187, 703, 752.
26. Cf. *Zb.* II, 401 = *Magic*, 731f.
27. Cf. *Zb.* II, 429 = *Magic*, 752.
28. Cf. *Forderung*, 381.
29. From Baudelaire's "La Beauté."
30. Cf. *Zb.* II, 231f = *Magic*, 605f; *Lotte*, 362 = *Beloved*, 364; also the essay "August von Platen," *Adel*, 506 = *Essays*, 260f.
31. Baudelaire, "L'homme et la mer."
32. *Novellen* II, 409 = *Stories*, 412f.
33. See Stefan George, *Der Siebente Ring* (1907—four years before *Death in Venice*).
34. *Zb.* II, 283, 429 = *Magic*, 644, 752.
35. *Bemühungen*, 187 = *Order*, 43.
36. *Zb.* II, 259 = *Magic*, 625f.
37. Cf., e.g., Thomas Mann's declaration in Havenstein, *Thomas Mann*, 284. The degree to which Thomas Mann feels entitled to call himself a German is discussed in *Betrachtungen*, 35f, 76f.
38. Cf. "Tonio Kröger," *Novellen* II, 29 = *Stories*, 100, a passage still couched approximately in the terms of Ibsen's *When We Dead Awaken*. This "romanticist" idea is disavowed, however, in *Betrachtungen*, 77.
39. Cf., e.g., Nietzsche, *Werke* VI, 480.
40. "Death in Venice" (*Novellen* II, 360 = *Stories*, 384).
41. *Novellen* II, 27 = *Stories*, 99. Cf. R.A., 386f.
42. *Novellen* I, 255 = *Stories*, 296.
43. Nietzsche, *Also sprach Zarathustra*, Part I, Preface, §5 (*Werke* VI, 19).
44. *Zb.* I, 576 = *Magic*, 432f.
45. *Zb.* I, 566 = *Magic*, 425.
46. *R.A.*, 117.
47. *Zb.* II, 429 = *Magic*, 752.
48. *Zb.* II, 257ff = *Magic*, 624ff.
49. *Zb.* I, 572f = *Magic*, 430f.

50. *Zb.* II, 363 = *Magic,* 704.
51. *Novellen* II, 191 = *Stories,* 251.
52. *Zb.* II, 383 = *Magic,* 718.
53. Cf. Schopenhauer, *The World as Will and Idea,* Book III, §52 (*Werke* I, 343, 348f). In *Novellen* I, 254 = *Stories,* 295, Thomas Mann adopts Schopenhauer's doctrine of music as the "pure prototype of Being," as the direct expression of will itself, the in-itself of all phenomena.
54. *Zb.* II, 520ff = *Magic,* 818ff.
55. *Zb.* II, 622 = *Magic,* 894.
56. *Zb.* II, 345 = *Magic,* 691.
57. *Zb.* II, 629 = *Magic,* 900.

Chapter 5
The Myth of the Soul
A. From *The Tales of Jacob* to *Joseph in Egypt*

1. *Bemühungen,* 84 = *Essays,* 140.
2. *Novellen* II, 46 (cf. 27) = *Stories,* 109 (cf. 99).
3. *Bu.* II, 404 = *Bbr.,* 563.
4. *Novellen* II, 29 = *Stories,* 100.
5. *Novellen* II, 360 = *Stories,* 384.
6. Cf., e.g., *Betrachtungen,* 78; *Bemühungen,* 115 = *Essays,* 160; "Lebensabriss," *Neue Rundschau* (1930), 752.
7. *Bemühungen,* 84 = *Essays,* 140.
8. *Novellen* I, 324 = *Stories,* 138.
9. *Novellen* II, 35 = *Stories,* 104.
10. *K.H.,* 63 = *Royal,* 46.
11. "*The Magic Mountain* aspires to be a European book" (*Bemühungen,* 272).
12. Goethe to E. Ortlepp, autumn, 1825. "Charioteer" scene in *Faust* II; cf. *Lotte,* 366f = *Beloved,* 368.
13. Cf. *J.J.,* 72f = *Jos. Bros.,* 296; *J.Ä.,* 582ff = *Jos. Bros.,* 748ff.
14. The artist's need of external support is emphasized by the poet Mattini, as early as *K.H.,* 215 = *Royal,* 163. Cf. also Goethe's "noble indigence" (*Lotte,* 363 = *Beloved,* 365).
15. *J.Ä.,* 296 = *Jos. Bros.,* 601.
16. *J.Ä.,* 280 = *Jos. Bros.,* 593.
17. *J.Ä.,* 302 = *Jos. Bros.,* 604.
18. *J.Ä.,* 304 = *Jos. Bros.,* 605.
19. *J.Ä.,* 733 = *Jos. Bros.,* 830.
20. Cf. *J.Ä.,* 747 with 291f = *Jos. Bros.,* 837f with 598f.
21. *J.Ä.,* 747 = *Jos. Bros.,* 837f.
22. *Jaakob,* 80f = *Jos. Bros.,* 78. For the psychological parallel to Mann's fundamentally metaphysical tenet cf., e.g., William James, *Principles of Psychology* I, ch. X ("The Self").
23. *Jaakob,* 80f = *Jos. Bros.,* 78.
24. *Lotte,* 316 = *Beloved,* 315.
25. *Neue Studien,* 162 = "*The Theme of the Joseph Novels*" (Washington, 1942), 8.
26. Cf. Appendix IV, "Novel and Midrash."
27. *Jaakob,* 44 = *Jos. Bros.,* 57.

28. Novalis, *Fragmente* ed. Kamnitzer, no. 671.
29. *Ibid.*, from fragment 1112.
30. Cf. "Freud und die Zukunft" (*Adel*, 593ff = *Essays*, 423ff).
31. Schopenhauer, *Die Welt als Wille und Vorstellung*, Reclam-Ausgabe I, 416.
32. *Novellen* I, 171 = *Stories*, 72.
33. *Zb.* II, 617 = *Magic*, 890.
34. *Zb.* II, 336 = *Magic*, 684.
35. *Zb.* I, 175f = *Magic*, 134f.
36. *Zb.* II, 121 = *Magic*, 523.
37. *Zb.* II, 129, 150 = *Magic*, 528f, 544.
38. *Zb.* II, 617 = *Magic*, 890.
39. Goethe, "Prooemion."
40. *Zb.* II, 256ff = *Magic*, 623ff.
41. *Zb.* II, 618 = *Magic*, 891.
42. *Zb.* I, 9 = *Magic*, 1.
43. *Ibid.*
44. *Novellen* II, 414; cf. 392, 403 = *Stories*, 416; cf. 403, 409.
45. *Zb.* II, 342 = *Magic*, 689.
46. *Zb.* I, 409f = *Magic*, 309f.
47. *J.Ä.*, 296 = *Jos. Bros.*, 601.
48. Cf. *L.G.M.*, 100 = *Essays*, 314.
49. Cf. *Jaakob*, 160ff = *Jos. Bros.*, 123ff. Cf. Appendix III, p. 255.
50. *Bu.* I, 29 = *Bbr.*, 15.
51. *Bu.* II, 475 = *Bbr.*, 602.
52. Augustine, *Confessiones* XI, 20.
53. *Bu.* II, 348 = *Bbr.*, 527.
54. *Lotte*, 362 = *Beloved*, 364.
55. *J.E.*, 176f; cf. 196 = *Jos. Bros.*, 937f; cf. 948.
56. *J.E.*, 125, 170ff = *Jos. Bros.*, 909, 934.
57. *J.E.*, 176 = *Jos. Bros.*, 937.
58. *J.Ä.*, 593f = *Jos. Bros.*, 756f.
59. *Jaakob*, xxxv = *Jos. Bros.*, 17.
60. *Jaakob*, 175f = *Jos. Bros.*, 131f. For the whole cf. also 28ff = 48ff.
61. *J.Ä.*, 272 (and elsewhere) = *Jos. Bros.*, 589.
62. *Jaakob*, 318 = *Jos. Bros.*, 210.
63. Cf. *J.Ä.*, 621f = *Jos. Bros.*, 771f.
64. Heraclitus, fragment B45 (Diels).
65. Cf. *J.Ä.*, 346, 630 = *Jos. Bros.*, 627, 776.
66. *J.Ä.*, 723 = *Jos. Bros.*, 825.
67. The contrasting of black and white magic appears in Thomas Mann's essay "The Coming Humanism," *Patterns for Living*, 1196.
68. *Neue Studien*, 167 = *The Theme of the Joseph Novels* (Washington, 1942), 12.
69. *Neue Studien*, 172ff = *The Theme of the Joseph Novels*, 16ff.
70. Goethe, "Hegire," introductory poem to the *West-Eastern Divan*.
71. Goethe, "Bei der Betrachtung von Schillers Schädel."
72. *Neue Studien*, 173 = *The Theme of the Joseph Novels*, 17.
73. *Jaakob*, 165 = *Jos. Bros.*, 126.
74. *Zb.* II, 627 = *Magic*, 898. For the whole conception see also *V.K.*, 10 = *Transposed*, 4.

75. *V.K. = Transposed, loc. cit.*
76. Cf., e.g., *J.Ä.*, 342ff, 711, 737 = *Jos. Bros.*, 624ff, 813, 832.
77. Cf. *Pariser Rechenschaft*, 59ff.
78. *J.Ä.*, 386 = *Jos. Bros.*, 647.
79. Cf. *J.J.*, 238f = *Jos. Bros.*, 388f.
80. *Jaakob*, 156 = *Jos. Bros.*, 121.
81. *Jaakob*, ix = *Jos. Bros.*, 3.
82. Cf., e.g., *J.J.*, 76ff, 281ff; *J.Ä.*, 240, 577 = *Jos. Bros.*, 298ff, 412ff, 572, 748.
83. *J.Ä.*, 211 = *Jos. Bros.*, 557.
84. Hegel, *Philosophie der Weltgeschichte*, ed. Lasson, "Die Vernunft in der Geschichte," 11.
85. Cf. Appendix IV.
86. *Jaakob*, 58f = *Jos. Bros.*, 65—a passage that reminds us of Kierkegaard's interpretation of the story of Abraham in his *Fear and Trembling*.
87. *J.J.*, 242 = *Jos. Bros.*, 391.
88. *J.J.*, 169 = *Jos. Bros.*, 352.
89. *J.J.*, 236f = *Jos. Bros.*, 388f.
90. *J.J.*, 240 = *Jos. Bros.*, 390.
91. *J.J.*, 206-208 = *Jos. Bros.*, 372-374.
92. *J.J.*, 241 = *Jos. Bros.*, 390.
93. See *J.Ä.*, 50, 164 = *Jos. Bros.*, 470, 521. Cf. M. Güldemann, *Religionsgeschichtliche Studien*, 26ff.
94. *J.J.*, 78 = *Jos. Bros.*, 299.
95. *Jaakob*, 157 = *Jos. Bros.*, 121f.
96. Cf. especially *Jaakob*, 160ff = *Jos. Bros.*, 123ff.
97. *J.J.*, 288 = *Jos. Bros.*, 415.
98. *Freud und die Zukunft*, 30 = *Adel*, 592 = *Essays*, 422.
99. From Schiller's letters to Goethe, July 2 and 8, 1796.
100. Letter of Schiller to Goethe, July 8, 1796.
101. Cf., e.g., *Forderung*, 286. Kierkegaard's dictum that "there is no such thing as immediate [!] health of the spirit" (*The Sickness unto Death*, 37) also expresses Thomas Mann's lasting conviction.

Chapter 6

The Myth of the Soul

B. *Joseph the Provider* (The City of God and the City of Man)

1. For intimations of the final outcome cf., however, e.g., *Jaakob*, 62ff, 76, 318f; *J.J.*, 288f = *Jos. Bros.*, 67ff, 75, 210f; 416.
2. *J.E.*, 492 = *Jos. Bros.*, 1119.
3. *J.E.*, 413f = *Jos. Bros.*, 1074.
4. Merezhkovsky, *Akhnaton*, 181f.
5. Cf. *J.E.*, 356f and *J.J.*, 288 = *Jos. Bros.*, 1041; 415.
6. *J.E.*, 553, 566, 588 = *Jos. Bros.*, 1156, 1163, 1175f.
7. *J.E.*, 273 = *Jos. Bros.*, 993.
8. Genesis 22:18.
9. *J.E.*, 235 = *Jos. Bros.*, 971.
10. *J.E.*, 184 = *Jos. Bros.*, 941. Cf. *J.J.*, 135 = *Jos. Bros.*, 332, and Thomas Mann's letter of February 18, 1941, in Karl Kerényi, *Romandichtung und Mythologie*, 83.

11. Cf. *J.E.,* 278f = *Jos. Bros.,* 996.
12. Richard Wagner, "Eine Mitteilung an meine Freunde" (1851) (*Sämtliche Schriften und Dichtungen, Volksausgabe* IV, 297).
13. Letter to the author, August, 27, 1944.
14. *J.E.,* 552 = *Jos. Bros.,* 1155.
15. *J.E.,* 547, 594 = *Jos. Bros.,* 1152, 1179.
16. *Lotte,* 90 = *Beloved,* 84f.
17. Cf. *Bemühungen,* 140, in "Goethe und Tolstoy"; also *Adel,* particularly 314 = *Essays,* 175.
18. Richard Wagner in the concluding sentence of "Die Kunst und die Revolution," *op. cit.* III, 41.
19. *Bemühungen,* 140 = *Essays,* 175.
20. *Betrachtungen,* 609.
21. *Bemühungen,* 333.
22. Cf. *Jaakob,* 91ff = *Jos. Bros.,* 84ff.
23. Isaiah 53:7f.
24. *Jaakob,* 282 = *Jos. Bros.,* 190.
25. Cf. Thomas Mann's letter of February 20, 1934, in Kerényi, *op. cit.,* 19.
26. *J.E.,* 620 = *Jos. Bros.,* 1194.
27. Cf. *J.J.,* 100 = *Jos. Bros.,* 312.
28. *J.E.,* 552, 566, 621 = *Jos. Bros.,* 1154, 1158, 1194.
29. *J.E.,* 551f = *Jos. Bros.,* 1155.
30. *J.E.,* 308 = *Jos. Bros.,* 1012f.
31. *J.E.,* 614 = *Jos. Bros.,* 1191.
32. *J.E.,* 29 = *Jos. Bros.,* 854.
33. *J.E.,* 27 = *Jos. Bros.,* 853.
34. *J.E.,* 29 = *Jos. Bros.,* 854.
35. *J.E.,* 614 = *Jos. Bros.,* 1191.
36. *J.E.,* 327 = *Jos. Bros.,* 1024.
37. *J.E.,* 340 = *Jos. Bros.,* 1031. Cf. Ruth 1:16.
38. Cf. Matthew 1:3ff
39. Cf. *J.E.,* 14, 356 = *Jos. Bros.,* 846, 1041f.
40. Cf. the little article "The Bible," in *Good Housekeeping,* August, 1944.
41. Cf. *J.E.,* 539 = *Jos. Bros.,* 1032.
42. *Betrachtungen,* 607.
43. Richard Wagner, *Die Meistersinger von Nürnberg,* Act III.
44. *Betrachtungen,* 610. Cf. *Death in Venice* (*Novellen* II, 447 = *Stories,* 434f).
45. "Schopenhauer" in *Adel,* 344 = *Essays,* 376.
46. *J.E.,* 548 = *Jos. Bros.,* 1153.
47. *J.E.,* 620 = *Jos. Bros.,* 1194.
48. *J.E.,* 324 = *Jos. Bros.,* 1022.
49. *J.E.,* 453 = *Jos. Bros.,* 1097.
50. *J.E.,* 515 = *Jos. Bros.,* 1133 (in Mrs. Lowe-Porter's ingenious paraphrase).
51. *Loc. cit.*
52. *J.J.,* 57 = *Jos. Bros.,* 288.
53. *J.E.,* 13 = *Jos. Bros.,* 845.
54. *J.E.,* 230 = *Jos. Bros.,* 968.
55. *J.E.,* 196 = *Jos. Bros.,* 948.
56. *J.E.,* 230f = *Jos. Bros.,* 968f.
57. *Bu.* II, 477 = *Bbr.,* 604.

58. *J.E.*, 113, 231 = *Jos. Bros.*, 902, 969.
59. Cf. "The Bible," *Good Housekeeping* (August, 1944), 17, 141.
60. Cf. *J.E.*, 382 = *Jos. Bros.*, 1056.
61. Cf. *J.E*, 124f = *Jos Bros.*, 908.
62. Nietzsche, letter to Peter Gast, November 19, 1886.
63. See *Entstehung*, 78; and Kierkegaard's *Werke* (Diederichs), VII, 191.
64. *J.E.*, 382 = *Jos. Bros.*, 1056.
65. *Betrachtungen*, 610.
66. *J.E.*, 170 = *Jos. Bros.*, 934.
67. Dante, letter to Can Grande. This motif is very strong and moving in the posthumous essay on Chekhov (*Neue Rundschau*, 1956).

Chapter 7

Imitatio Goethe

1. "Schach Sedschan und Seinesgleichen," in Goethe's *West-östlicher Divan;* motto of *Lotte in Weimar* = *The Beloved Returns*.

> *Durch allen Schall und Klang*
> *Der Transoxanen*
> *Erkühnt sich unser Sang*
> *Auf Deine Bahnen!*
> *Uns ist für gar nichts bang*
> *In Dir Lebendig;*
> *Dein Leben daure lang,*
> *Dein Reich beständig!*

2. "Lebensabriss," *Neue Rundschau* (1930), 738.
3. *Novellen* I, 253f = *Stories*, 294; cf. *Lotte*, 286ff, 290f, 298, 310, 354 = *Beloved*, 282ff, 287f, 296, 308f, 356.
4. *Versuch über Schiller*, 78f.
5. This list is taken from Thomas Mann's letter to the author, February 3, 1943.
6. Cf. *Faust* II, vv. 8204f. Cf. *Lotte*, 89, 352 = *Beloved*, 84, 353.
7. *Novellen* II, 358 = *Stories*, 383.
8. *Ibid.*
9. *Lotte*, 294ff = *Beloved*, 292ff.
10. *Lotte*, 320 = *Beloved*, 319.
11. *Lotte*, 310 = *Beloved*, 308.
12. "Lebensabriss," *Neue Rundschau* (1930), 753.
13. *Freud und die Zukunft*, 4; 37; cf. *Adel*, 595ff = *Essays*, 424ff.
14. *Lotte*, 319f = *Beloved*, 319.
15. *Lotte*, 311 = *Beloved*, 310.
16. Goethe, according to Councillor von Müller, November 4, 1823 (Biedermann, *Gespräche* III, 37).
17. *Lotte*, 315; similarly 310 = *Beloved*, 314; 308.
18. *Lotte*, 324ff = *Beloved*, 324ff.
19. *Lotte*, 214, 228 = *Beloved*, 208, 223.
20. *Lotte*, 212, 224, 227, 252, 277, 282, 326, 327 = *Beloved*, 206, 218, 221, 248, 273, 278, 326, 327.
21. Goethe, *Aus meinem Leben, Dichtung und Wahrheit*, Part IV, Book XVI.
22. Plato, *Phaedo*, 64 Af.

23. Shakespeare, *Measure for Measure*, Act III, Scene I.
24. *Lotte*, 315 = *Beloved*, 314; cf. the entry in Riemer's diary of May 24, 1811.
25. *Lotte*, 311f = *Beloved*, 310.
26. *Literatur*, XXXII, 129ff.
27. *L.G.M.*, 60f = *Essays*, 48.
28. *Faust* II, vv. 12069-75 (the first four lines being a variation of *Faust* I, vv. 3587-89). The translation is Priest's.
29. *Lotte*, 449 = *Beloved*, 451. Cf. Goethe, *Tasso*, vv. 3432f.
30. From "Hegire," in *West-östlicher Divan*. See also the poem "Dauer im Wechsel" ("Permanence in Change").
31. Goethe, "Zur Logenfeier des 3. September 1825" ("For the Celebration of the Lodge, September 3, 1825").
32. Cf., e.g., *L.G.M.*, 125ff = *Essays*, 329f; "The Bible," *Good Housekeeping*, August, 1944; see also Nietzsche's criticism of the artist's "predilection for the brilliant and profound interpretations of life" in *Menschliches, Allzumenschliches*, §146.
33. *Lotte*, 310 = *Beloved*, 309.
34. For this ascription cf. Friederike Brun in Biedermann, *Goethes Gespräche* I, 233f.
35. Goethe to Eckermann (cf. also Eckermann's entry of March 11, 1828) and in *Werther*, letter of July 20, 1771. Cf. *Lotte*, 292 = *Beloved*, 289f.
36. Goethe, *West-östlicher Divan*, "Allgemeinstes" ("Most General").
37. *Aus meinem Leben, Dichtung und Wahrheit*, Part II, Book X.
38. Goethe on Mérimée to Eckermann: entry of March 10, 1830.
39. Cf. *Lotte*, 350, 355 = *Beloved*, 351, 356.
40. *Lotte*, 355 = *Beloved*, 356. "Spirit," "survey of worldly affairs, irony, and the freest employment of one's talents"—these "belong conspicuously to old age or to an aging period of world-history"—annotation to "Allgemeinstes" ("Most General") in *West-östlicher Divan*.
41. Nietzsche, *Werke* XI, 78.
42. *A.N.*, 678 = *Jos. Bros.*, vi; *Forderung*, 47.
43. "Lebensabriss," *Neue Rundschau* (1930), 751f. Cf. *Betrachtungen*, 72f.
44. *R.A.*, 359.
45. *Lotte*, 355 = *Beloved*, 356.
46. *Lotte*, 367 = *Beloved*, 368f.
47. "Form and immediacy—don't you realize that they are mutually exclusive?" (*K.H.*, 98 = *Royal*, 73.)
48. Cf. *Lotte*, 81, 353 = *Beloved*, 76, 355.
49. *Lotte*, 292 = *Beloved*, 289f.
50. *West-östlicher Divan*, "Gingo Biloba." Cf. Goethe, *Weimarische Kunstausstellung vom Jahre 1801 und Preisaufgaben vom Jahre 1802*, concluding sentence.
51. These Goethean words, intended to be a refutation of Schiller's ambition, are noted by Eckermann, November 13, 1823. For Thomas Mann, cf. *Faustus*, 236 = *Faust.*, 152.
52. *Lotte*, 86 = *Beloved*, 81.
53. Cf. Biedermann, *Goethes Gespräche* I, 176, 287; V, 49. Cf. *Bemühungen*, 50f = *Essays*, 119; *Lotte*, 93ff = *Beloved*, 88ff.
54. Biedermann, *op. cit.* I, 231.
55. *Lotte*, 92 = *Beloved*, 87; Biedermann, *op. cit.* I, 176, 287.
56. *Lotte*, 415 = *Beloved*, 418.

57. *Lotte*, 448f = *Beloved*, 451. Cf. Goethe's "Selige Sehnsucht" ("Holy Yearning").
58. *Lotte*, 255 = *Beloved*, 251.
59. Riemer, *Mitteilungen über Goethe*, ed. Arthur Pollmer, 339.
60. *Lotte*, 325 = *Beloved*, 325.
61. Schopenhauer, *The World as Will and Idea* II, Book IV, ch. 46 (Reclam II, 687): "This world is ordered and arranged exactly as it must be in order barely to subsist" (*"um mit genauer Not bestehen zu können"*). In *Schopenhauer*, 30 = *Essays*, 383 = *Adel*, 354f, Thomas Mann himself cites this passage.
62. *Zb*, I, 464 = *Magic*, 350.
63. *Novellen* II, 84 = *Stories*, 130.
64. *Lotte*, 325 = *Beloved*, 325; also *L.G.M.*, 39 = *Essays*, 85 (from Goethe's *Zahme* Xenien VII).
65. Goethe, "Auf den Kauf." Quoted in "Europe Beware," *Order*, 71.
66. *Lotte*, 327f = *Beloved*, 327.
67. Goethe, letter to Sophie La Roche, September 15, 1774.
68. *Novellen* II, 360 = *Stories*, 384.
69. Karl Philipp Moritz, *Über die bildende Nachahmung des Schönen*, the closing sentences.
70. Letter to the author, February 17, 1941.
71. Cf. *Tonio Kröger* (*Novellen* II, 43 = *Stories*, 105). And later on, *Achtung, Europa!* 129 = *Order*, 93; *Faustus*, 555ff = *Faust.*, 368f; *Leiden an Deutschland* (1946), 11.
72. *Achtung, Europa!* 135f = *Order*, 98.
73. Cf. *Nietzsche's Philosophy in the Light of Contemporary Events* (Washington, 1947), 21f = *Neue Studien*, 137.
74. Cf. *Lotte*, 89f, 353 = *Beloved*, 84f, 354.
75. Letter to Sophie La Roche, June 1774. In this connection cf. *Lotte*, 448f = *Beloved*, 451f.
76. From Goethe's review of J. G. Sulzer's *Die schönen Künste in ihrem Ursprung* in the *Frankfurter gelehrten Anzeigen*, December 18, 1772.
77. *Rede zum Shakespearetag*. Cf. *Lotte*, 92, 438 = *Beloved*, 87, 440. *Bemühungen*, 78f, = *Essays*, 137; *R.A.;* 397.
78. Cf. *Bemühungen*, 79 = *Essays*, 137. Biedermann, *op. cit.* II, 86; cf. also I, 233f and elsewhere.
79. Motto to Part IV of Goethe's *Aus meinem Leben, Dichtung und Wahrheit*. Cf. Riemer, *Mitteilungen über Goethe*, ed. A. Pollmer, 319.
80. *Lotte*, 87 = *Beloved*, 82.
81. *Bereshit Rabbah* 12.15.
82. *Lotte*, 87; cf. 438 = *Beloved*, 82; cf. 440. Cf. *J.E.*, 12f = *Jos. Bros.*, 844f.
83. *Faust* I, vv. 3988f.
84. Cf., above all, Schelling's essay "On the Nature of Human Freedom," *pass.*
85. *Achtung, Europa!* 158 = *Order*, 123. Cf. also *Betrachtungen*, 402-405; "The Coming Humanism," in *Patterns for Living*, 1194f.
86. Cf., e.g., *J.E.*, 324 = *Jos. Bros.*, 1022f.
87. *Novellen* II, 29, 360 = *Stories*, 100, 384.
88. *Meister Eckhart*, ed. Pfeiffer, 338.
89. *Betrachtungen*, 402, 405.
90. *Novellen* I, 250 = *Stories*, 293.

91. *Zb.* I, 573 = *Magic*, 430.
92. Nietzsche, *Werke* VIII, 261; cf. 253, 258; XV, 260f, 264f, 296.
93. *R.A.*, 397; cf. *Betrachtungen*, 402, 406.
94. *J.E.*, 620 = *Jos. Bros.*, 1194.
95. Letter to Karl Kerényi, February 20, 1934.
96. *Bemühungen*, 156 = *Order*, 15.
97. See note "O" in textual notes to this chapter.
98. Letter to the author, February 17, 1941. Also Preface to *Anna Karenina* (*Adel*, 336 = *Essays*, 188).
99. Cf. *Lotte*, 352 = *Beloved*, 353f.
100. Cf. Goethe to Charlotte von Stein, October 9, 1781; to Plessing, May 14, 1779, July 26, 1782; Biedermann, *op. cit.* II, 42f, III, 316; *Zahme Xenien* III, 82; *Faust* II, v. 12088.
101. Goethe, *Wilhelm Meisters Wanderjahre*, Book II, ch. 1.

Chapter 8
Last Judgment: *Doctor Faustus*

1. Nietzsche, *Also sprach Zarathustra*, *Werke* VI, 444.
2. Gide, *Interviews Imaginaires*, 165: "the loveliest example, smiling and grave at once, of what, without any support by Grace, man can obtain through his own efforts."
3. *Novellen* II, 439ff = *Stories*, 430f.
4. *Faustus*, 739 = *Faust.*, 487.
5. *Entstehung*, 81f.
6. *Faustus*, 444 = *Faust.*, 289.
7. Cf., e.g., *Faustus*, 147, 278, 296, 299, 740 = *Faust.*, 92, 179, 191, 192, 488; also *Entstehung*, 44, and Th. W. Adorno, *Philosophie der neuen Musik*, 37, 42, 67.
8. *Faustus*, 83 = *Faust.*, 53.
9. Cf. *Faustus*, 419 = *Faust.*, 272.
10. *Faustus*, 211 = *Faust.*, 135: an Angelus Silesius verse in Mrs. Lowe-Porter's translation. The thought has its orgin in Eckhart; cf. *Meister Eckhart*, ed. Pfeiffer, 43.
11. Cf., e.g., Rilke's "Der Goldschmied": the problem of love is just as urgent with Rilke as it is with Thomas Mann.
12. Cf. also Heine, *Die romantische Schule* (*Werke*, ed. Elster, V, 261).
13. From Hölderlin, "Lebenslauf."
14. Much of the Lutheran idiom is audible in Nietzsche's language.
15. Cf. *Faustus*, 119, 296ff, 738 = *Faust.*, 73f, 190ff, 486; and Adorno, *op. cit.*, 25, 54, 77.
16. Cf. *Faustus*, 204 = *Faust.*, 131.
17. From Luther's letter to Melanchthon, August 1, 1521.
18. *Faustus*, 382 = *Faust.*, 247.
19. Cf. Franz Kafka, *Tagebücher und Briefe*, 216 (= *The Great Wall of China*, 306).
20. From Nietzsche's *Antichrist*, quoted in *Betrachtungen*, 538. For Thomas Mann's complementation of this thought see *J.E.*, 523f = *Jos. Bros.*, 1139.
21. Cf. *Faustus*, 290, 372 = *Faust.*, 186f, 241.
22. *Faustus*, 404 = *Faust.*, 262.

23. *Faustus*, 280 = *Faust.*, 180.
24. *Faustus*, 204, 206 = *Faust.*, 131, 132.
25. Cf. *Faustus*, 130ff to 204 = *Faust.*, 81ff; 131.
26. *Faustus*, 240f, 297, 738, 742 = *Faust.*, 155f, 191 (not clearly rendered), 486, 489.
27. Cf. *Faustus*, 346f = *Faust.*, 223f.
28. Cf. *Faustus*, 345, 386 = *Faust.*, 222, 249.
29. *Zb.* II, 259 = *Magic*, 625.
30. *Faustus*, 757 = *Faust.*, 500.
31. *Novellen* II, 87 = *Stories*, 132.
32. *Faustus*, 472ff = *Faust.*, 306ff.
33. *Entstehung*, 23, 193.
34. "I worry only in the afternoon": Letter to the author, October 28, 1950.
35. Cf. *Faustus*, 741 = *Faust.*, 489, in contrast with *Bemühungen*, 137 ("Goethe and Tolstoy," in *Essays*, 173.)
36. Goethe, *Faust* II, vv. 9989-9991.
37. Goethe, *Faust* II, vv. 9901f.
38. *Faustus*, 739 = *Faust.*, 487.
39. *Faustus*, 767 = *Faust.*, 506.
40. *Faustus*, 736 = *Faust.*, 485.
41. *Faustus*, 542 = *Faust.*, 354.
42. *Faustus*, 745 = *Faust.*, 491.
43. Cf., e.g., *Faustus*, 733, 736, 743, 744 = *Faust.*, 483, 485, 490, 490; also the "Judas" chapter in *Nietzsche* (particularly 153) by Ernst Bertram, once Thomas Mann's brother in the spirit.
44. Cf. *Meister Eckhart*, "Von dem Zorne der Seele," ed. Pfeiffer, 542.
45. Kierkegaard, *Die Krankheit zum Tode*, *Werke* (Diederichs) VIII, 78.
46. Cf. *Faustus*, 204 = *Faust.*, 131. Cf. *J.E.*, 324 = *Jos. Bros.*, 1022: "*Die Hölle ist für die Reinen*" ("Hell is for those who are pure").
47. Cf. *Faustus*, 251 = *Faust.*, 163.
48. Letter to the author, August 14, 1948. Cf. the Dante motto to *Faustus* and *Novellen* II, 361 = *Stories*, 385.
49. Cf. *Faustus*, 336, 760 = *Faust.*,—, 501 (the paragraph in which the first passage occurs has been left out by the translator).
50. *Faustus*, 365, 376 = *Faust.*, 235, 243.
51. Cf. *Faustus*, 494f = *Faust.*, 322f.
52. *Faustus*, 494 = *Faust.*, 322.
53. Cf. *Faustus*, 350 = *Faust.*, 225; *Novellen* II, 38ff = *Stories*, 106ff; *R.A.*, 386f. This feeling is very strong in the Chekhov essay and in Thomas Mann's last letter to the author, April 24, 1955.
54. *Novellen* I, 157ff = *Stories*, 167ff.
55. *Novellen* II, 361 = *Stories*, 385.
56. Cf. *J.E.*, 277 = *Jos. Bros.*, 996.
57. *Faustus*, 113 = *Faust.*, 69.
58. Cf., e.g., *Novellen* II, 447f = *Stories*, 434f.
59. From Nietzsche's *Dionysos-Dithyramben*, "Zwischen Raubvögeln." The icy cold of satanism had also been stressed in Heinrich Heine's "Doctor Faust" (*Werke*, ed. E. Elster, VI, 515; cf. IV, 411). In our context, it is worth mentioning that Nietzsche considered the iciness of solitude a "preserving element." Cf., e.g., his letter of May 12, 1887, to Malvida von Meysenbug. Thomas Mann stresses the same element in Goethe: cf., e.g., *Lotte*, 327 = *Beloved*, 327f.

60. Cf. *Faustus*, 239, 599 = *Faust.*, 154, 393.
61. Goethe, *West-östlicher Divan*, "Vermächtnis altpersischen Glaubens." Cf. *Faustus*, 346ff, 383, 385f, *et pass.* = *Faust.*, 223ff, 247f, 249f, *et pass.*
62. Cf. *Lotte*, 448f = *Beloved*, 451; *Faustus*, 384f = *Faust.*, 248f.
63. Cf. Schopenhauer, *The World as Will and Idea*, Book III, §52 (*Werke*, Reclam I, 352.)
64. *Entstehung*, 158f. Cf. *A.N.*, 298f; *Adel*, 288 = *Essays*, 160.
65. *Adel*, 288 = *Essays*, 160.
66. *Adel*, 207 = *Essays*, 110.
67. *Faustus*, 385, 526ff, 539, 758 = *Faust.*, 249, 343ff, 352, 500.
68. *Faustus*, 576 = *Faust.*, 377.
69. Cf. *Neue Studien*, 156 = *Nietzsche's Philosophy in the Light of Contemporary Events* (Washington, 1947) 37; also *J.E.*, 170 = *Jos. Bros.*, 934.

Appendices

1. *Forderung*, 400; cf. *Order*, vii.
2. Schiller, *Werke, Säkularausgabe* XII, 188.
3. Schiller, *Werke* XII, 189, 213f.
4. Schiller, *Werke* XII, 67f.
5. Cf. Schiller, *Werke* XI, 193; XII, 39-45.
6. Schiller, *Werke* XII, 55.
7. Schiller, *Werke* XII, 45.
8. Schelling, *Werke* II, I, 461f.
9. *Zb.* I, 481 = *Magic*, 362f.
10. I. Kant, *Werke*, ed. E. Cassirer, IV, 336.
11. Schiller, *Werke* XII, 163.
12. Kant, *Werke* IV, 341.
13. Schiller, *Werke* XII, 230 *et pass.*
14. *Novellen* II, 221 = *Stories*, 269.
15. *Novellen* II, 363; cf. 448 = *Stories*, 386; cf. 435.
16. Nietzsche, *Geburt der Tragödie*, §3 (*Werke* I, 33).
17. Cf. Schelling, *Werke* I, V, 394f.
18. Nietzsche, *Wille zur Macht* IV, §1050 (*Werke* XVI, 387f).
19. *Goethe-Kalender 1933*, 34f.
20. Jonas Cohn, *Theorie der Dialektik* (1923), 259ff.
21. S. Friedländer, *Schöpferische Indifferenz* (1918), 28f.
22. Cf. Schelling, *Werke* II, I, 411, 422; I, X, 268, 274, 276; II, III, 356; I, X, 261ff, 241—in this sequence.
23. Schelling, *Werke* I, VIII, 302.
24. Schelling, *Werke* I, VIII, 261.
25. Schelling, *Werke* II, II, 144.
26. *R.A.*, 84 = *Essays*, 298.
27. W. Dilthey, *Schriften* V, 280ff.
28. *Betrachtungen*, 126.
29. Franz Marc, *Briefe* I, 41.
30. *Bemühungen*, 253; cf. *Betrachtungen*, 47, 306; *Bemühungen*, 332; *R.A.*, 363.
31. *Bemühungen*, 274.
32. "Lebensabriss," *Neue Rundschau* (1930), 746.
33. *Novellen* II, e.g., 16; 88 = *Stories*, 92; 132.
34. Cf., e.g., *Zb.* I, 203 and 247; I, 572; and II, 363, etc. = *Magic*, 155 and 187f;

429f and 704. Even the words with which the curtain is playfully rung
down between the first and second part of *The Magic Mountain*—
"N'oubliez pas de me rendre mon crayon"—are opportunely anticipated in
Pribislav Hippe's enjoinder to Hans Castorp.

35. *J.J.*, 241 = *Jos. Bros.*, 390. Cf. Alfred Jeremias, *Das Alte Testament und der Orient* (2nd ed.), 384.
36. *Jaakob*, 292 = *Jos. Bros.*, 195; *J.J.*, 118f = *Jos. Bros.*, 322f.
37. *Zb.* I, 39, 45f, 561 *et aliis locis* = *Magic*, 27, 31f, 421 *et aliis locis*.
38. *Zb.* I, 99f = *Magic*, 75.
39. The two events, as depicted, certainly coincide in a great many features: cf. *Zb.* II, 215ff = *Magic*, 593ff, with *J.J.*, 228ff = *Jos. Bros.*, 384ff. For other variations of the motif cf., e.g., *Zb.* II, 283ff = *Magic*, 643ff., *J.E.*, 29ff, 457f = *Jos. Bros.*, 854, 1100.
40. Cf. *Jaakob*, 160ff = *Jos. Bros.*, 140ff.
41. *Novellen* II, 41 = *Stories*, 106f.
42. *Novellen* I, 352 = *Stories*, 154. Cf. *Betrachtungen*, 83.
43. *Zb.* II, 344 = *Magic*, 690.
44. *Bu.* II, 365 = *Bbr.* 537f.
45. E.g., *Jaakob*, 44 = *Jos. Bros.*, 58; *J.J.*, 45ff, 239 = *Jos. Bros.*, 281ff, 389; *J.Ä.*, 296, 733 = *Jos. Bros.*, 601, 830.
46. *Bu.* II, 290 = *Bbr.*, 495.
47. *Novellen* I, 331 = *Stories*, 142.
48. *Novellen* II, 359 = *Stories*, 383.
49. *Zb.* II, 387 = *Magic*, 721.
50. *Lotte*, 309ff = *Beloved*, 307ff.
51. *Novellen* I, 285f = *Stories*, 174. Cf. *Adel*, 315f.
52. *Novellen* II, 291 = *Stories*, 470.
53. *Bemühungen*, 188 = *Order*, 43.

INDEX

Abraham, 132, 136, 218
Absolutism, artistic, 8-9
Action, devoted, 234
Active representation, 145
Aeschylus, 19; *Eumenides*, 72
Ages, the truth of, 66-68
Akhmaton. *See* Amenophis IV, King
Ambiguity, new meaning of, 223
Amenhotep, trust in artist's work, 26-27
Amenophis IV, King, 23, 70, 149, 150, 151
Amor fati, 74-77, 214
Analytical art, 43-45
Angelus Silesius, 18, 79, 262 fn.; quoted, 21
Antichrist, 228, 230
Anticlimax, climax as, 148
"Apocalipsis," 220
Apollonian illusion, Dionysian delight in, 49
Apollonian trend, 27-29
Aristotelian-Scholastic tradition, challenged by Mann, 19
Aristotle, 15, 50, 72, 246
Art, spirit and nature in, 23-27; analytical, 43-45; repetition in, 173; as prostitution, 213-214; the black magic of, 215-218
Artist, vocation of the, 16-17; relation to the whole, 33-34; the problem of the, 85-86; does not belong, 95
Artistic irony, 178-183
Artistic reproduction, and tradition, 134-135
Artistic symbolism, 177-178
Aschenbach, Gustav, 11, 23, 29, 30, 36, 39, 44, 74, 95-96, 107, 109, 120, 136, 162, 171, 203, 221, 229, 231, 233, 243
Astarte, 228
"At the Prophet's," 24
Autobiographical elements, in the Joseph novels, 137
Autobiography, as research into the origins, 88-89

Baader, F. X. von, Deity in God, 25

Baeck, Leo, 263, 264
Bahnsen, Julius, 52 fn.
Bakunin, Mikhail A., nihilism, 44
Barrès, Maurice, 100, 260
Baudelaire, Pierre C., 81, 207, 256 fn.; quoted, 85; "Beauté," 107
Baxter, Richard, *The Saint's Everlasting Rest*, 7
Bazarov, nihilism of, 235
Beauty, messenger of death, 107-108
Beer-Hofmann, Richard, *Jaakob's Dream*, 14
Beethoven, Ludwig van, 206, 219, 222, 225
Being, and representation, 36-38, 86-88
"Being of being, the," 163, 164
Beloved Returns, The, 81, 91, 107, 224, 257
Beyond good and evil, 185-190
Bible, "the withholding love" in, 149; Mann's interpretation of, in Joseph novels, 260-264
Black magic of art, 215-218
Black Swan, The, 226 fn.
Böhme, Jakob, 15, 16, 40, 242; Deity in God, 25; quoted, 230; theosophy of, 264
Boundless representation, 90-93
Bourgeois, metamorphosis into an artist, 92
Brahmanist teaching, in Schopenhauer, 73
Break through, 222-223
"Broken glance, the," 256-257
Buber, Martin, 263
Buddenbrook, —— (old "radical"), 89
Buddenbrook, Christian, 80, 89
Buddenbrook, Gerda, 130
Buddenbrook, Hanno, 44, 45, 89, 91, 92, 94, 120
Buddenbrook, Consul John, 11, 89
Buddenbrook, Senator Thomas, 5, 74, 88, 89-90, 91, 92, 164
Buddenbrook, Toni, 89
Buddenbrooks, four generations as symbols, 89

315